D1806935

The Slow Philosophy of J. M. Coetzee

Also Available from Bloomsbury

J. M. Coetzee in Context and Theory
Edited by Elleke Boehmer

J. M. Coetzee's Disgrace
Andrew van der Vlies

States of Exception in the Contemporary Novel: Martel, Eugenides, Coetzee, Sebald
Arne De Boever

Strong Opinions: J. M. Coetzee and the Authority of Contemporary Fiction
Edited by Chris Danta

The Slow Philosophy of
J. M. Coetzee

Jan Wilm

Bloomsbury Academic
An imprint of Bloomsbury Publishing Plc

B L O O M S B U R Y
LONDON · OXFORD · NEW YORK · NEW DELHI · SYDNEY

Bloomsbury Academic

An imprint of Bloomsbury Publishing Plc

50 Bedford Square	1385 Broadway
London	New York
WC1B 3DP	NY 10018
UK	USA

www.bloomsbury.com

BLOOMSBURY and the Diana logo are trademarks of Bloomsbury Publishing Plc

First published 2016

An earlier version of Chapter 9 of this volume has been published previously as
"It Takes All Kinds to Make a World: The Worlds of J. M. Coetzee's The Childhood of Jesus"
in J. M. Coetzee: Dead Ends and Beyond, edited by Ludmiła Gruszewska Blaim and
Tomasz Wiśniewski. BETWEEN.POMIĘDZY series volume 8. Gdańsk: Wydawnictwo
Gdańskie, 2015, 145–169.

All archival material from the J. M. Coetzee Papers is held at the Harry Ransom Center
at the University of Texas at Austin and is reprinted here by permission. © J. M. Coetzee

British Library Cataloguing-in-Publication Data
A catalogue record for this book is available from the British Library.

ISBN: HB: 978-1-4742-5645-2
ePDF: 978-1-4742-5647-6
ePub: 978-1-4742-5646-9

Library of Congress Cataloging-in-Publication Data
A catalog record for this book is available from the Library of Congress.

Cover design: Eleanor Rose
Cover image © Santu Mofokeng

Typeset by Integra Software Services Pvt. Ltd.

for A.

Contents

Acknowledgments

My warmest thanks are to Julika Griem, whose intelligence, appreciation, and good spirits were always most treasured sources of encouragement during the writing of this book. My warm thanks are also to Frank Schulze-Engler and Ingo Berensmeyer, to Troy Blacklaws, Malte Kleinjung, Ruth Knepel, Franziska Pölt, and Maren Scheurer, as well as my students over the years. My sincere gratitude is to Dagmar Westberg and the Deutsch-Britische Gesellschaft Rhein-Main e.V. Frankfurt am Main for the Dagmar Westberg-Preis 2013, which funded a research stint at the Harry Ransom Center, The University of Texas at Austin, USA. Special thanks to the helpful and friendly staff at the HRC, especially to Richard Watson. I also thank Carrol Clarkson and the staff and students at the University of Cape Town and Stellenbosch University, South Africa, who provided me with valuable feedback. Thanks for the intellectual sparks to the organizers and participants of the conference *Travelling Texts: Encounters of Literatures* at Jagiellonian University, Kraków, Poland in March 2014. My warm thanks are extended to Rita Barnard and the students in her graduate seminar on J. M. Coetzee at the University of Pennsylvania in Philadelphia, USA, where I presented part of this study in March 2014. I also wish to thank the German Association for the Study of English for awarding this work its dissertation prize in 2015. My deepest thanks are to my family and friends.

W.

Frankfurt, January 2016

Abbreviations of Works by J. M. Coetzee

AoI   Coetzee, J. M. (1990), *Age of Iron*, London: Penguin.

Barbaren   Coetzee, J. M. (1984), *Warten auf die Barbaren*, trans. Brigitte Weidmann, Berlin: Karl H. Henssel Verlag.

CoJ   Coetzee, J. M. (2013), *The Childhood of Jesus*, London: Harvill Secker.

Dis   Coetzee, J. M. (1999), *Disgrace*, London: Vintage.

DoB   Coetzee, J. M. (2007), *Diary of a Bad Year*, London: Harvill Secker.

DtP   Coetzee, J. M. (1992), *Doubling the Point: Essays and Interviews*, ed. David Attwell, Cambridge, MA/London: Harvard University Press.

Dusk   Coetzee, J. M. ([1974] 1998), *Dusklands*, London: Vintage.

EC   Coetzee, J. M. ([2003] 2004), *Elizabeth Costello: Eight Lessons*, London: Vintage.

EW   Coetzee, J. M. (2008), "Eight Ways of Looking at Samuel Beckett," in Minako Okamuro, et al. (eds), *Borderless Beckett/ Beckett Sans Frontières*, 19–31, Amsterdam/New York, NY: Rodopi.

F   Coetzee, J. M. (1986), *Foe*, London: Penguin.

GO   Coetzee, J. M. (1996), *Giving Offense*, Chicago, IL/London: The University of Chicago Press.

GS   Kurtz, Arabella and J. M. Coetzee (2015), *The Good Story: Exchanges on Truth, Fiction and Psychoanalytic Psychotherapy*, London: Harvill Secker.

H   Coetzee, J. M. (1993), "Homage," *The Threepenny Review*, 53: 5–7.

H&N   Auster, Paul and J. M. Coetzee (2013), *Here and Now*, New York: Viking Penguin.

HR   Coetzee, J. M. (2006), *L'homme ralenti*, trans. Catherine Lauga du Plessis, Paris: Éditions du Seuil.

InW   Coetzee, J. M. (2007), *Inner Workings: Literary Essays 2000–2005*, New York: Viking Penguin.

ItH   Coetzee, J. M. ([1977] 1999), *In the Heart of the Country*, London: Vintage.

K   Coetzee, J. M. ([1983] 1985), *Life & Times of Michael K*, London: Penguin.

MoP   Coetzee, J. M. ([1994] 2004), *The Master of Petersburg*, London: Vintage.

NT   Coetzee, J. M. (1988), "The Novel Today," *Upstream*, 6 (1): 2–5.

S   Coetzee, J. M. ([2005] 2006), *Slow Man*, London: Vintage.

SPL   Coetzee, J. M. (2011), *Scenes from Provincial Life: Boyhood, Youth, Summertime*, London: Penguin.

StS   Coetzee, J. M. (2001), *Stranger Shores: Literary Essays*, London: Penguin.

T   Coetzee, J. M. (1993), "Thematizing," in Werner Sollors (ed.), *The Return of Thematic Criticism*, 289, Cambridge, MA/London: Harvard University Press.

UCT   Coetzee, J. M. (2013), "JM Coetzee visits UCT to read from his new work" [Online video clip], *University of Cape Town South Africa*, *YouTube*, 5 February. Available online: https://www.youtube.com/watch?v=yXufoko-HgM (accessed September 1, 2015).

Warten   Coetzee, J. M. (2002), *Warten auf die Barbaren*, trans. Reinhild Böhnke, Frankfurt am Main: Fischer Verlag.

WfB   Coetzee, J. M. ([1980] 2004), *Waiting for the Barbarians*, London: Vintage.

WW   Coetzee, J. M. (1988), *White Writing: On the Culture of Letters in South Africa*, New Haven/London: Yale University Press.

I Saw Coetzee Today. He Wants a Philosophical Introduction. A Philosophical Introduction

"If I hadn't begun to write by the age of thirty, I would never write." Words spoken by J. M. Coetzee in an interview with Peter Sacks in 2001, as the author commented on the genesis of what would become his first published fiction, *Dusklands* (1974). Coetzee refers to the writing as "tortuous" and informs his interviewer that he "set thirty as a deadline," and so "on the first of January 1970 [he] sat down and started to write *Dusklands*" (Coetzee and Sacks 2001).[1] In the critical biography *J. M. Coetzee and the Life of Writing: Face to Face with Time* (2015), David Attwell writes, "[t]he point of the date is that it was a moment of real crisis and self-confrontation, the origin of a resolve that has stood firm" (2015, 49). What interests me in the date is the compulsory impetus behind such a deadline, which might move one to infer a certain hastiness behind Coetzee's writing, a speedy dash at *des belles lettres* at the eleventh hour. Yet, the notes and drafts of his foray into what would become *Dusklands* tell a different story: how the author searched slowly for a fictional footing, groping and grasping for content and form. Much of what is extant in the J. M. Coetzee Papers at the Harry Ransom Center, the University of Texas at Austin—notebooks, early drafts and abandoned ones—exhibit Coetzee's customary composure, the stillness that characterize his works, and the early drafts are frequently infused with a quivering ardor rather than a hasty overcompensation, a characteristic perhaps more common in a mature writer.

One such early draft of the first story[2] of *Dusklands*, "The Vietnam Project," was originally entitled "Lies." While beginning *in medias res* with a short dialogue, "Lies" delves right into a moment of stasis. The first lines

---

[1] In the *Salmagundi* interview with Joanna Scott in 1997, Coetzee says about the origin of *Dusklands*: "It was a New Year's resolution: to stop thinking and planning and actually start writing" (Coetzee and Scott 1997, 85). David Attwell notes: "'1 January 1970' is a myth of origin. Asked when he started writing, more than once Coetzee has offered this date. It is not true, of course. Long before then, he had written and published poetry, and well into his twenties, in the mid-1960s, he still sought a poetic career, while briefly experimenting with prose" (2015, 49).

[2] Scholarship is undecided about the generic classification of *Dusklands* as a whole and the two texts it consists of. When asked by Scott about the genre of his first fiction, Coetzee had this to offer: "The

are perplexingly terse: "I saw Coetzee today. He wants a philosophical introduction."[3] This demand presses urgently toward the future: the narrator has been ordered to carry out a task. And yet, in these two short main clauses, one also feels a hint of stagnation experienced by the narrator, as if he had arrived at an impasse, a sentiment strengthened by the following exchange between the narrator and Coetzee:

> He: How do you place yourself philosophically?
> I: Post-Marx.
> He: Meaning?
> I: I show why Marx is superseded.[4]

Without back-story, the reader is flung into a world she must struggle to find a footing in as well, in a moment that is at once an impasse and a thrust forward. One may wish to stand still and linger over these words, to reflect on the mysterious world and characters, to think them through. Why is the first question addressed to the narrator? What are these two characters talking about? And who is the elusive Coetzee? The reader is essentially transported into the same mode of thinking as the narrator of "Lies" is. The narrator is asked: *How do you place yourself philosophically?* The reader might as well be asked: *How do you, reader, place yourself in this fictional world, where an author asks for an introduction written by one of his characters?*

This early draft already broaches some of the complex matters of focalization and authorship explored in Coetzee's later works, as the questions regarding who speaks and sees are supplemented by the question: Who is addressed? On one level, it is the protagonist; on another, it is the reader. And, if the reader's mind is successfully provoked to remain with these questions, to linger on them for a moment, then the reader is already, perhaps unknowingly, on the go, moving along in a mode of reflection, moving along with the reflexive flow of the narrative.

One of the most striking aspects of Coetzee's work, on both a formal and a topical level, is its aesthetics of slowness, a complex oscillation between momentum and stasis, a system of deferring and tarrying, which can be

---

two narratives have a relation at the level of ideas, but otherwise the relation is loose. Is it so loose that the two parts might as well be separate publications? I don't know. I don't want to dodge your question, but a novel is ultimately nothing but a prose fiction of a certain length" (Coetzee and Scott 1997, 87).

[3]   Harry Ransom Center (hereafter "HRC"), container 1, folder 1, p. 1.

[4]   Ibid.

illuminated by Joseph Vogl's paradoxical conception of tarrying as "an energetic inactivity, [...] a resolute deactivation" (2011, 17). Like Beckett's characters, who cannot go on but will go on, Coetzee's characters and Coetzee's form are ceaselessly driven forward while simultaneously being slowed down.[5] This creates what Mary Bryden has termed, with regard to Beckett's fiction, a sense of *dynamic stillness*:

> I find the ambiguity of [the phrase "dynamic still"] useful. It draws into collocation two tendencies which, though *potentially* mutually exclusive, are in fact part of an uncomfortable continuum in Beckett's scenic world. (2004, 182; original emphasis)

Similar to Beckett's slowing his characters down while keeping them in motion—two key images in Beckett are the rocking chair and the bicycle—Coetzee animates his narratives with interminable deferrals, continued retardations: From Mrs. Curren's seemingly static existence of dwelling in *Age of Iron* (1990), which is, at the very least, shunted toward death; to Michael K burrowed in the earth as if it were a grave only to resemble a womb from which he moves on; to Susan Barton in *Foe* (1986) stranded on her island with Cruso, ever scanning the horizon hoping for a departure, then taking to the road in England and to the quest toward Friday's language; to Paul Rayment in *Slow Man* (2005), who seems the epitome of the *dynamic still* in Coetzee's work, having had his leg amputated and moving on crutches, having to jumpstart his locomotor system while Elizabeth Costello is trying to stir his narrative to life, his life to narrative.

What Bryden claims about Beckett may also be true of Coetzee: "Beckett's people can neither rest easy nor move easy" (2004, 180). Like Beckett's characters, the Coetzee people are never finally immobile, as long as the synapses are still firing in their brains and their minds are still producing words and thoughts. One of the chief characteristics of this ceaseless textual reflection is the narratives' essentially inquiring nature. The works are overflowing with questions. These are negotiated at the level of the plot, and both the plots' and questions' trajectories are detoured, deferred, shuffled forward in a probing nature less toward resolutions and answers than toward moments of reflection. From the Magistrate in *Waiting for the*

---

[5]   For various comparative readings of Beckett's and Coetzee's work, see Yeoh (2000), Tajiri (2008), Attridge (2009), Ackerley (2011), Meihuizen (2011), and Tajiri (2013). Especially Yeoh's essay is of note here, as the author explores the status of Coetzee's Michael K as a character with an "[i]ndeterminate [i]dentity" (2000, 15).

Barbarians (1980) to the fictional Dostoevsky in *The Master of Petersburg* (1994), to the eponymous *Elizabeth Costello* (2003), to the author's fictional selves in the autobiographical *Scenes from Provincial Life* (1992–2009)— Coetzee's characters remain searchers, doubters, or contrarians to stock beliefs, frequently even to their own fossilized views. Through inquiry and reflection they keep their own positions in check, interminably reworking and evaluating them, analyzing and deconstructing their own lives and times. Having escaped the civil war that ravaged the land, Michael K rests in his burrow and has metaphysical ruminations about the earth, his ancestors, and his life. Having escaped a shipwreck and a painful time on the desert island with Cruso and Friday, Barton ruminates on aesthetics, language, and ethical questions of story ownership. Having been invited to a public lecture tour, Costello finds herself trapped in a community where her ethical opinions are deemed radical, convoluted, or even unimportant, and this moves her to pursue her own ideas even more doggedly. Having been slowed down by the loss of his leg, Rayment begins to reevaluate his life; he ruminates on fatherhood, on care, love, being, and narrative with his discussion partner (or enemy) Elizabeth Costello.

Are such responses not the natural reactions to being slowed down: to rethink, to ruminate, to reevaluate, before being drawn forward and onward by the constant suction of time? This study explores, at the levels of both content and form, how Coetzee's oeuvre probes the functions and effects of slowness, and how these bear on the characters' and more substantially on the readers' reflections; it analyzes how the reader's response to Coetzee's unique aesthetics of slowness may be one that rethinks, ruminates, reevaluates, and perhaps even philosophizes.

It is perhaps because of the inquiring and reflexive character of Coetzee's writing that his work has been placed in the realm of philosophical literature. In their introduction to the collection of essays *J. M. Coetzee and Ethics: Philosophical Perspectives on Literature* (2010), Anton Leist and Peter Singer highlight the "unusual degree of *reflexivity* [of Coetzee's work], meaning thereby a reflective distance to the conventional understanding of everything" (2010, 6f.; original emphasis). They argue that this *unusual degree of reflexivity* "expresses itself, strangely, through a normally rather sparse, sober, precise, restrained selection of words and descriptions" (2010, 7). While a somewhat too narrow assessment of Coetzee's style, which also includes lyrical, tender, and humorous modes, the authors' argument concerning *a reflective distance to the conventional understanding of everything* is of importance to the exploration of Coetzee's work undertaken in this study, to the exploration of the slow philosophy of J. M. Coetzee.

The last decade has seen a spate of excellent studies on Coetzee's philosophical dimensions, even if many have paid too little attention to the oeuvre's aesthetic concerns over a specific engagement with topical explorations of philosophical— particularly ethical—ideas in his works. While a moral quandary staged in a work of fiction may likely provoke ethical thinking by the reader, aesthetic phenomena unrelated to philosophical problems and ideas may encourage thoughts thereof nonetheless.

Perhaps what is needed is a much more basic exploration of Coetzee's work to make sense of the philosophical character of his writing. In order to eschew the trap of narrowing the focus on Coetzee's open and receptive oeuvre, this study does not read Coetzee's work against individual philosophers', nor does it view his oeuvre as a quarry for philosophical ideas. Instead, it views this singular body of work as sharing with the reader moments of dialectic meaning-making which are realized by the complex interplay of form, content, and context. This gives Coetzee's oeuvre a number of philosophical qualities, which go beyond the mere provision of philosophical topics or the permission to saddle the texts with philosophical theories. As will be seen, the main concern of this study is to illuminate the connections between philosophical and literary qualities of Coetzee's oeuvre by focusing on the works' reflexive dimensions crystallized around *slowness*. Why, one might ask, slowness?

To date, no study has tried to describe in an extensive and phenomenologically detailed way which qualities of Coetzee's works give them a character that might be called philosophical. It is the overall argument of this study that the philosophical character is not merely inherent in Coetzee's work in an explicit sense, but that it emerges in the reading, in a reading that is receptive and reflexive to the complexity of various ambiguity increasing techniques which slow down the act of reading and thereby provoke a reflection on the works which might be termed philosophical.

To illuminate the philosophical character of Coetzee's works in relation to the reflection given rise to in reading, it is necessary first to address that complex term *philosophical*. Needless to say, such a reflection cannot be exhaustive; in fact, it should not be. My understanding of philosophy (and philosophizing) sees it as a complex and slow project of thinking, as a potentially endless process of inquiring and searching, as meaning-making through exploration, as an engagement with phenomena in a dialogic and tarrying way, and, above all, as asking and provoking questions in a meditative fashion.

At the most basic level, philosophy is inquiry, and by the definition of the late Martin Heidegger one might even let go of the term *philosophy* entirely and prefer the term *thinking* instead.[6] Some of the basic qualities of philosophical thinking and inquiring are connected to the qualities of Coetzee's literature. His work continually induces one to think intensely and deeply, *slowly*, about the matters dealt with in the works, and one is provoked to immerse oneself in the complexity staged, so that a gain of philosophical knowledge in reading becomes possible. It would all be that simple were it not for the ancient but no less vigorous quarrel between literature and philosophy. It may be useful to reconsider the links and breaks between literature and philosophy in a move toward a description of Coetzee's philosophical literature. The ancient quarrel notwithstanding, one may reiterate that the philosopher and the novelist have a lot in common, perhaps not unlike the way Coetzee and Arabella Kurtz reiterate that "the psychotherapist and the novelist have much in common" (*GS* vii) in *The Good Story* (2015).

Whether one evokes Pre-Socratic thinkers at the dawn of Western philosophy, when the mother of the sciences and natural science were still thought together,[7] or whether one considers more recent attempts at defining philosophy,[8] the two basic aspects that seem to characterize all of philosophy are the asking and formulating of questions as well as deep reflection. These observations seem so trivial that they hardly need mentioning. This is, however, precisely why they should be mentioned, since it is necessary to avoid the perils of undervaluing the basic importance of inquiring and thinking to philosophy—and to Coetzee's literature. However, philosophy inquires into phenomena such as being or the world through analysis in an argumentative way, whereas literature explores them through style and narrative in an imaginative way.

The distinction between the argumentative and the imaginative is Richard Rorty's who separates argumentative and imaginative writing very distinctly, the former roughly consisting of philosophical texts, the latter comprising "[p]oems, novels, literary criticism" (2010, 391). Rorty being Rorty, he claims that the superior of the two is the imaginative, since argumentative writing

---

[6] For a view by which thinking is regarded as philosophy, see also Maurice Merleau-Ponty's idea that "*phenomenology can be practised and identified as a manner or style of thinking, that it existed as a movement before arriving at a complete awareness of itself as a philosophy*" (2002, viii; original emphasis).

[7] Bertrand Russell dates the dawn of philosophy as follows: "Philosophy begins with Thales, who, fortunately, can be dated by the fact that he predicted an eclipse which, according to the astronomers, occurred in the year 585 B.C. Philosophy and science—which were not originally separate—were therefore born together at the beginning of the sixth century" (1946, 25).

[8] See, for example, Craig (2002) and Blackburn (1999).

aims at essences through "maximal clarity and maximal coherence" as well as "easy accessibility and intelligibility" (2010, 390). This endangers argumentative writing of being distilled to ideology, to a few conclusive phrases, a few "truths," to what Rorty dismissively calls "what we would normally say" (2010, 390).[9] To Rorty, literature is more untouchable, as it is suggestive, allusive, and relies on the unstated to engender reflexion and signification. While I agree with the general drive of Rorty's argument, it is too narrow a view to help describe Coetzee's fiction in any meaningful way, as there is an argumentative as well as an imaginative character to all of Coetzee's works.

Rorty's binarism, which seems more of a distinction between literature and *analytic* philosophy rather than philosophy as such, is no more helpful than Plato's banishing artists and dramatists from his Republic as falsifiers of the truth, as being not of the nobler order of the philosopher kings. If one examines a few examples of both literature and philosophy, one comes to appreciate that Plato's division was less maieutic than it was myopic. Are the epigrams of Heraclitus or the dialogues of Plato himself really *only* philosophy? Kierkegaard's first part of *Either/Or* (1843), Nietzsche's *Thus Spoke Zarathustra* (1883–91)—are their philosophical qualities fundamentally different from those of Shakespeare's tragedies, Borges's stories, Camus's novels? Where are the dividing lines? Does a literary text become philosophical when it mentions a philosopher's name explicitly, when a character reads Marx, like Augie March of Saul Bellow's novel; when a character has discussions about philosophy, like Jake Donaghue in Iris Murdoch's *Under the Net* (1954)? Is an author a philosophical writer provided her work flaunts philosophical argot and exhibits an explicit awareness of philosophical theories at the level of the content? Conversely, is a philosopher's work literary if philosophical ideas are embedded in a narrative, or if the writing has an aesthetically pleasing sound that likens it to the cadences of poetry, or if it makes use of a vocabulary that one deems literary? What is, to use Coleridge's terms, the kinship between the "philosophic poet" and the "poetic philosopher"? (1818, 176).[10]

Notoriously "difficult" philosophers, whose style is thick with relative clauses like Schopenhauer's, whose syntax is twisting and writhing like Kant's, whose language is labyrinthine like Hegel's or Heidegger's—have

---

[9] The best essay on these matters is perhaps Rorty's bridging of seemingly exclusive assumptions by Jacques Derrida and Jürgen Habermas, "Habermas, Derrida, and the Functions of Philosophy."

[10] In "Essay VI" of his essay collection *The Friend*, Coleridge speaks chiefly of the Socratic method apparent in Plato's dialogues with reference to writing and education. The aforementioned definitions have analogies in Coleridge's understanding: by "philosophic poet" he refers to the prime example of Shakespeare; by "poetic philosopher" he refers to Plato.

such philosophers perhaps earned a place in the pantheon of great minds not only for their ideas but also precisely because of their puzzling styles? A. J. Ayer notes that "[i]t is by its method rather than its subject-matter that philosophy is to be distinguished from other arts or sciences" (1999, 9). If literature is included in what Ayer calls *the other arts* here, his argument is just as reductive as Rorty's. Ayer claims that philosophy argues in a different way than literature does. Surely, this view may be defended through argument, but it may also be suspect as a form of argumentative sophistry. The arguments presented in literature are frequently of a highly philosophical nature as well, often precisely for their formal qualities, if only because both literature and philosophy argue (and imagine) ideas through language, dramatize them (though in different ways and both not always in narrative form), and *both* arts are distinctly exempt from having to present "formal demonstration," even if Ayer wishes this to be an exclusively philosophical privilege (1999, 9). Ayer seems to discount the fact that both philosophy and literature may use argument and reflection to explore phenomena, and that both may do so in imaginative ways.

Coetzee's oeuvre is an example to contradict such sharp binarisms, as he is a writer of that Janus-faced sensibility which signals toward the argumentative as well as the imaginative, the literary as well as the philosophical. Elizabeth Costello, for example, is "well versed in moral philosophy" (Head 2009, 82); she stylizes herself as a philosopher in her lectures on animal ethics, when she claims her ability to ventriloquize

> Aristotle and Porphyry, [...] Augustine and Aquinas, [...] Descartes and Bentham, [...] [and] in our day, Mary Midgley and Tom Regan [...] to discuss and debate what kind of souls animals have. (*EC* 66)

But does she not here intimate a novelist's rather than a philosopher's quality, does she not argue that a writer never speaks exclusively in her own voice, but rather imagines a chorus of voices for her fictional fugue, where voices harmonize, quarrel, and contradict one another? As David Lodge puts it, by echoing Charles Dickens, it is the "[n]ovelists [who] do the Police in different voices" (1992, 128). Costello says she speaks in the language of philosophy, as if this were her authentic voice, but her statement also highlights her command of "the full armament of poetic tricks and devices" (*GS* 8), since she claims her talent lies in doing the Police in different voices—curiously by summoning a brigade of philosophers. Costello's son, John, detects this Janus-faced sensibility in his mother when he muses about her:

A writer, not a thinker. Writers and thinkers: chalk and cheese. No, not chalk and cheese: fish and fowl. But which is she, the fish or the fowl? Which is her medium: water or air? (*EC* 10)[11]

While John's question seems also to imply the binarism of the ancient quarrel, the fact that he does not argue a case but asks a question works toward blurring this binary. One may continue asking questions: How far do sharp binaries get one? Is it really necessary to categorize? Could it not be argued that philosophy and literature are banded together because they are not easily divided, and that a cross-fertilization between the two enables philosophy to make use of literary techniques and literature to deal with a wide range of philosophical questions? Could one not speak more productively of a continuum, along the lines of which literary texts exhibit philosophical qualities and philosophical tracts exhibit literary techniques, both of which engender imaginative *and* argumentative thinking? It might be useful to think along the lines of Cornel West, who has argued that "philosophy must go to school with poetry" (2011, 96).

Which techniques, then, are employed that permit poetry to go to school with philosophy, what pushes literature toward philosophical reflection? Many writers are called philosophical not only for the themes dealt with in their books, but also for their styles, their formal devices, and for the effects produced by their works' aesthetic choices. For instance, the novels of Henry James or Marcel Proust could be regarded as epistemological analyses for their forms alone, their slow, meandering, minutely detailed descriptions and mappings of inner landscapes, a probing of characters' and readers' minds alike, through a deceleration of time by the means of syntax, vocabulary, and grammar. Their works engender both imaginative *and* argumentative thinking through techniques such as ambiguity, allusion, suggestion, narrative devices, and the ostensible complication of an immediate interpretation, that is to say devices which are often thought of as exclusively "literary." What gives these works their philosophical character is their literary form, the rich interplay of aesthetic and topical complexity. The epistemic depth of such works may stimulate readings which respond not by reducing such complexity but by thinking it in an intense way, by thinking complexly in the first place, especially if the texts themselves

---

[11] The text also opens up an associative realm through the animal metaphors. Costello is made equal with these animals. The text's form is subtler and more successful at creating a non-speciesist equality between humans and animals than Costello is. Curiously, it is one of Costello's doubters, John, who makes a very clear argument in her favor.

do not offer simple ways out of complexity. Costello underlines this argument, when saying: "We understand by immersing ourselves and our intelligence in complexity" (*EC* 108).

The very confrontation with the aesthetic complexity of Coetzee's works touches on my understanding of what constitutes the philosophical character of literature which emerges in reading, as it is in the encounter with complexity that a process of inquiring and deep thinking may be provoked, a dialogic and tarrying response to the text, and, above all, an asking of questions to the text in a meditative and slow fashion.[12] The quality of the meditative is closely linked to slowness in such an understanding, and both are relevant to my understanding of the philosophical character of literature emerging in reading. A complex oeuvre such as Coetzee's provokes a form of slow, meditative thinking by the reader which may be illuminated by Heidegger's understanding of the meditative in his late work *Gelassenheit* (*Discourse on Thinking*). Heidegger distinguishes meditative thinking from calculative thinking:

> Calculative thinking races from one prospect to the next. Calculative thinking never stops, never collects itself. Calculative thinking is not meditative thinking, not thinking which contemplates the meaning which reigns in everything that is. ([1959] 1966, 46)

While calculative thinking is linked to problem-solving and directed toward an end, meditative thinking is a more contemplative form of reflection, disengaged from a goal, but focused on the here and now, on being in the present moment, waiting, tarrying, remaining open to the mystery ([1959] 1966, 55f.). Such openness to mystery may be stimulated in reading if the reader allows herself slowly to pursue the reflections provoked by estranging aspects of topical but especially formal slowness; if she is open to the potential for meditative reflection provoked by Coetzee's elusive oeuvre; if she allows herself to refrain from finding conclusive answers or final interpretations. Rather than aiming at ironing out complexities, dilemmas, or questions, the reading experience I am trying to describe aims at embracing complexity through rigorous, meditative thinking, continued dialectic activity, and close reflexive examination, the very

---

[12] While reflection seems unthinkable in a fast way, slowness seems tied to philosophy even in a general understanding of the signifiers involved. In the French, for example, the word "philosophe" has come to mean calm and composed. The English word "philosophical" carries a similar connotation: "Befitting or characteristic of a philosopher; *esp.* characterized by uncomplaining acceptance of adverse circumstances; wise, calm, stoical" (OED). Needless to say, philosophers are not generally uncomplaining of adverse circumstances.

basis, as it were, of Plato's *examined life*.[13] In this study, then, Coetzee's oeuvre is read with regard to formal devices effecting meditative reflection, those literary tactics which stimulate inquiry, argument, and meaning-making in a slow way.

It is prudent briefly to reflect on how slowness is linked to the philosophical as I understand it. Slowness has a long tradition as a concept in philosophy, from Zen Buddhism to otium in Greek philosophy to Jean-Jacques Rousseau's celebration of meditative reverie and Bertrand Russell's praise of idleness.[14] But a more general case could be made that philosophy is itself in part a method of slowing down in order to generate deep reflection, that philosophy as an art of inquiry is related to slowness: slow contemplation, contemplative thinking, thoughtful argumentation. In the essay "On Slowness in Philosophy" Joseph Sen writes of the long tradition of slowness in philosophical inquiry; he claims that "genuine philosophizing cannot be rushed" (2000, 607), that

> [p]hilosophy [...] is concerned with healing the human mind, its task is therapeutic and philosophical teachings are in this respect like medicines. They do little good unless they stay a length of time in the mind. (2000, 607)

Sen's thoughts on the links between philosophy and slowness also specifically include reading:

> [I]n reading philosophy we are not merely entertaining the *thoughts* found in the text but also trying to trace the *thinking* which gives rise to them. This takes time. It is all very well *that* she thinks like this but *why* does she think like this? The way is as important as the destination. (2000, 613; original emphases)

Sen's argument is one for the relevance of considering the formal complexities of texts during the reading, an implied argument for aesthetics. The epistemic

---

[13] In the *Apology*, Plato's Socrates says:

> If [...] I tell you that to let no day pass without discussing goodness and all the other subjects about which you hear me talking and examining both myself and others is really the very best thing that a man can do, and that life without this sort of examination is not worth living, you will be even less inclined to believe me. Nevertheless that is how it is, gentlemen, as I maintain; though it is not easy to convince you of it. (38*a*)

This example, of course, also illuminates how Socrates's fundamentally slow form of dialectic is the very opposite of solipsistic navel-gazing and rather a form of reflexive activism.

[14] The potentiality of idle, tarrying states of being with regard to meditative reflexivity inform the aforementioned work by Joseph Vogl *On Tarrying* as well as Peter Sloterdijk's *Stress and Freedom*, which describes a form of liberty (and liberality) that is developed precisely from the idle reverie of Rousseau's drifting along the Lake of Bienne. For Rousseau's tranquil epiphany, see *Reveries of the Solitary Walker*, especially the fifth walk, which defines an *ur*-middle-moment of tarrying between idleness and action, of being in the here and now, "where the present runs on indefinitely" ([1782] 2004, 88). Rousseau's ideas also pervade many arguments on idleness, from Russell to Robert Louis Stevenson's "An Apology for Idlers."

value of complexity to the kind of philosophical thinking while reading Coetzee's works may also be illuminated by Thomas Nagel,[15] who notes that

> [t]he center of philosophy lies in certain questions which the reflective human mind finds naturally puzzling, and the best way to begin the study of philosophy is to think about them directly. (1987, 4)

This is apparent in all of Coetzee's work, as it employs the method of inquiry in such a way that the reader is always invited to share in the characters' and the texts' "thinking." And yet, it is not only Coetzee's characters which question and reflect, but it is Coetzee's very unique aesthetics of slowness which provokes a formal deceleration that prompts the reader to ask questions of her own, questions which may or may not correlate with those asked in the worlds of the texts.

In Coetzee's works there exists a parallel of philosophical dimensions at the level of the content and the level of the form; these dimensions develop in a gradual way through a discursive estrangement of the reader and a reflexive involvement by the reader. So, a ceaselessness of reflection is produced; the works reveal a quality which makes them seem ever in development, continually provisional in the way the reader is invited to reflect and reconsider her thinking about the texts. The works seem always open to being constructed and deconstructed by the reader. And they seem ever engaged in constructing and unworking themselves. Coetzee's prose explores ideas rather than positing them, it suggests them rather than professing them, it hovers over ideas, opinions, theories and illuminates them from various perspectives and in that way keeps questions raised. Coetzee's complex formal choices are as important as their topical concerns to give the works a philosophical character, and perhaps more important. About *Life & Times of Michael K* Derek Attridge argues that it is not

---

[15] Nagel's famous paper "What Is It Like to Be a Bat" (1974) is discussed (and criticized) by Elizabeth Costello in her lecture "The Philosophers and the Animals" (*EC* 75–80), where she argues that Nagel takes a limiting view on the impossibility to imagine the other that is a non-human animal, since, to Costello, Nagel sees a bat as "a fundamentally alien creature" (*EC* 76), as fundamentally other. Costello's criticism might be limiting on its own, as she disfavors Nagel's use of the bat in a metaphorical way "to pose questions [...] about the nature of consciousness" (*EC* 76). Costello's daughter-in-law, Norma, seems to regard her mother-in-law's views as flawed in this way, which she expresses through her exasperated sighing from the audience (*EC* 76). What is relevant to this study, however, is Costello's rejection of the authority of a purely rationalist view of phenomena. Elisa Aaltola argues:

> Costello states that we ought to try and see the animal's world via its bodily, living experiences. She criticizes the claim "*cogito ergo sum*" and maintains that existence is not based on "a ghostly reasoning machine" but rather on experience. Experience consists of "fullness, embodiedness, the sensation ... of being alive to the world" [...]. Thus, Coetzee pays attention to the element that Nagel highlights in his paper: *consciousness in the phenomenal sense*. It is "qualia" that matters, the stuff of "what it is like." (2010, 125; second emphasis added)

an ethically relevant text for the philosophical criteria which can be applied to it, but for the reader's coming to appreciate "the contingent, the processual, the provisional that keeps moral questions alive" (2004a, 54).[16] I argue that the philosophical qualities of Coetzee's literature arise in the reading which Coetzee's writing effects, since the slow consideration of the texts allows the reader to reflect upon the works in a meditative way. It may be said that the mode of reading which Coetzee's works give rise to in turn gives rise to a philosophical mode of thinking, which often occurs through a sense of estrangement (or defamiliarization)[17] that the works create in numerous ways.

This sense of defamiliarizing occurs through topical but especially formal slowness, and it motivates the reader to assume a similarly estranged and estranging comportment toward the texts in her reading, which may then give rise to philosophical questions and reflections. Before illuminating these aspects, it is prudent to reflect on the estranging qualities of Coetzee's writing as giving rise to the "philosophical" through Attridge's view of "the text as irreducibly other" (1992, 20). Writing about Derrida's readings, he notes:

> Like all valuable readings of literature, they seek to make the text strange (or perhaps strangely familiar), offering not a reduced and simplified version of the text but one which operates at the level of its own difficulty. (1992, 17)

As will be seen, my readings of Coetzee constitute a similar way of analyzing the estrangement that Coetzee's prose creates as well as keeping the strangeness of his works alive, rather than simplifying or reducing estrangement or strangeness by imposing philosophical ideas on Coetzee's works or trying to shoehorn his oeuvre into reading methods unsuited for it. This way, it will be seen that Coetzee's work has a philosophical dimension not of positing or explaining ideas, but being itself the generator of philosophical thinking, and this is incubated in the kind of slow, processual, immersive comportment to the texts that the narratives provoke in reading.

---

[16] Conversely, Attridge also emphasizes that we cannot "derive [...] ethical lesson[s] from K's condition, but we can return from living through it in a reading to the world of obligation, to that 'other time' which is ours, with a changed sense of its status" (2004a, 56).

[17] *Estrangement* is to be understood in Viktor Shklovsky's definition as a productive obstacle or disruption ([1925] 1991, 13f.). In Benjamin Sher's translation, Shklovsky's *ostranenie* is rendered as *enstrangement*. This coinage is used because, to him, "'estrangement' is good but negative and limited" and "[d]efamiliarization is dead wrong" (Sher 1991, xix). I disagree with Sher's negative view of *defamiliarization*, if only because of the important pair *familiarize* and *defamiliarize*, which is lost by the use of the rather clumsy *enstrangement*. As will become clear later, the pair and the sense of oscillation inherent in the word *defamiliarization* are important for a high sense of reflexivity. I shall use both *estrange* and *defamiliarize* in the following, but will not correct Sher's use of *enstrangement*.

When reading Coetzee's works the reader is continually asked to weigh conflicting ideas, to qualify, to backtrack, and to reconsider formed opinions about the text once they have been made, since for each thought and each opinion there seems to be a counter-thought, another (an other) opinion, a different way of seeing a phenomenon, a statement, or even a word. Since these often conflicting ways of reading are not hierarchized, the reader has to think on her own, much like the various interlocutors that Socrates teaches to lead examined lives.

Coetzee's aesthetics obstruct a quick or superficial reading that ends in an unequivocal interpretation. Formal devices and ways of presentation and arrangement of the texts are used to inhibit fast reading and shortcutting around the ideas dramatized by the works. As will be seen, various narrative techniques continually slow down a quick inattentive reading and instead call for stillness, meditativeness, and reflection. The resulting effect is an instigation of a deeper thought process in the reading and interpreting of these texts. This, in turn, puts the readers on the same level with the characters, whose searching, ruminating, doubting makes them thinkers, philosophers, in their own right, and makes Coetzee's works thinking texts or, as it were, philosophical fiction.

As this study will revolve around slowness in reading literature, one may continue by steering some of the aforementioned ideas about slowness and meditativeness in philosophical thinking toward thinking about reading slowly more concretely, and perhaps even philosophically. Many philosophers and theorists have long addressed the value of slow reading. It is in *Daybreak: Thoughts on the Prejudices of Morality* (1881) that Friedrich Nietzsche coins the expression: "It is not for nothing that one has been a philologist, perhaps one is a philologist still, that is to say, *a teacher of slow reading*" ([1881] 1997, 5; added emphasis). Ludwig Wittgenstein similarly perceives himself as such an unhurried pedagogue when he writes in *Culture and Value*: "Sometimes a sentence can be understood only if it is read at the *right tempo*. My sentences are all supposed to be read *slowly*" ([1977] 1980, 57e; original emphases). Literary theorists of the deconstructivist and reader-response traditions, such as J. Hillis Miller, Wolfgang Iser, and Stanley Fish,[18] have likewise espoused the value of

---

[18] See, for example, Miller's *On Literature*, where he refers specifically to Nietzsche's reading *lento*, as well as the selection from his wide-ranging oeuvre, *The J. Hillis Miller Reader*; see Iser's *The Act of Reading* or his essay "The Reading Process"; and Fish describes his reception aesthetics as follows: "Essentially what the method does is *slow down* the reading experience so that 'events' one does not notice in normal time, but which do occur, are brought before our analytical attentions" (1980, 28; original emphasis). Reader-response theories have been important for analyses of Coetzee's work, with Attridge's deconstructivist slant being the most cogent. Jarad Zimbler's recent study *J. M. Coetzee and the Politics of Style* takes a different path, situating itself as closer to "sociolinguistics,

Nietzsche's reading *lento*, while Terry Eagleton has recently gone so far as to say that "'slow reading' [is] in danger of sinking without trace" (2013, ix).

In a lecture delivered at the University of California at Berkeley in 1991, titled "Homage," Coetzee speaks about his influences, his "teachers"—about Beckett, Faulkner, Ford, Joyce, Musil, Rilke, but above all Ezra Pound. He reflects:

> What was it about the Cantos that held me? Something to do with the way in which time slowed and stopped as one sense-datum after another was impeccably and unforgettably registered. (*H* 6)

Coetzee says that to him "Pound is, as Nietzsche said of himself, a teacher of slow reading" (*H* 6). Years before, during the writing of *Life & Times of Michael K*, Coetzee had reflected in his notebook on the values of the Nietzschean reading *lento*. In the notebook he kept during the writing of the novel, dated "25.viii.82," Coetzee makes a number of notes on ideas from Nietzsche and concludes: "(4) 'Teacher of slow reading' (Nietzsche)."[19]

Judging from the various philological works he has written—a dissertation on Samuel Beckett's aesthetics, a book of essays on literature and censorship, his many essays on classical and contemporary literature—one does well to call Coetzee a philologist also, a teacher of slow reading. What Coetzee had found and experienced in Pound, this study will find in Coetzee and describe the experience of reading and thinking his work in a very particular way, meditatively, slowly, philosophically. From this singular reading experience, there will be developed the method of *slow reading* particularly suited to the analysis of his singular oeuvre, but whose productiveness may extend well beyond Coetzee. And while the expression is not my own, the method is, taking its cue from Coetzee as a teacher of slow reading to read Coetzee slowly. As will be seen, my slow reading is first a technique of reading, of actually lengthening the clock-time spent with a literary work, the time spent in that little world embraced by book covers. More substantially, however, it entails an attitude toward a literary artifact, an openness to the text, embracing of elusiveness and ambiguity, of the text's strangeness and otherness, as Attridge puts it, welcoming the contemplative impetus that lies in formal complexity. My slow reading aims at being at all times perceptive of the

---

pragmatics and narrative rhetoric" (2014, 6). One point which Zimbler raises against Iser's reception aesthetic seems unfounded, however. He writes that "it is difficult to agree that the reading of a literary work is ever so cool, rational and attentive as that proposed by Iser" (2014, 6). The willing submission to the strangeness of a text which Iser's implied reader would advocate stands in contrast to the rational and cool disposition which Zimbler attests such a reader. Iser's readers are not wholly rational and cool, and their attentiveness may, in fact, be a drifting one, one of reverie, as is implied in his concept of the "wandering viewpoint" (I return to this in Chapter 7).

[19] HRC, container 33, folder 5, pp. 82–83.

subtle music of the words on the page, and receptive to the signifying potential of the ambiguity increasing techniques in an elusive oeuvre. My slow reading is a method of reading that is not a flashy way of re-describing close reading or other hermeneutic models. Slow reading does not, first and foremost, ask what a text *means*, it asks how a text can be *reflected* upon, how it can be *responded* to, what its *effects* are, and how these effects, reflections, and responses can be *described* in a phenomenological way. Slow reading rests on the assumption that a certain kind of literature actually engenders a slow, detailed, deeply reflexive response by the reader.

Slow reading and meditative thinking are effected by the formal presentation of Coetzee's novels and memoirs, the continued sense of having to pass through the narrative world with the characters, of having to endure[20] being immersed deeply in the slow procession of the work. The philosophical facet of Coetzee's works, then, lies not so much in the illumination of philosophical ideas but in the sense in which his works are themselves generators of philosophical modes of thinking, incubated in the kind of slow, processual, and immersive reading provoked by the narratives. Such a way of reading is not only stimulated by the questions which the texts evoke in the reader, but also by the works' protean gaps, their subtle complexity in style, by the questions of authorship many of his works raise, and by the general sense of ambiguity with which one may come away after a reading of his works. Works such as *Life & Times of Michael K* or *Elizabeth Costello* confront the reader with ethical dilemmas and arguments in ways that one's life does as well, that is phenomenologically and without explication or guidance on how to proceed; the reader is faced with ethical questions and conundrums, but these are never puzzled out for her. Rather, ethical matters are reported, staged, or explored in conflicting ways, so that the reader "alone is left to do the thinking" (*SPL* 140), as young John at the end of *Boyhood* (1997) realizes about his place in the world.

---

[20] Enduring the text should be understood in an entirely positive way here as a way of reading the text phenomenologically and ethically—slowly—and thus hardening it against the one theological meaning (as Roland Barthes would say), hardening it against an instrumental reading (as Derek Attridge would say). The idea of hardening the text needs explanation. I arrive at this understanding etymologically, since *to endure* descends from Old French *endurer* to make hard, to endure; Provençal *endurar*; Italian *indurare* from the Latin *indūrāre*; to harden, to endure, from the Latin *dūrus*, hard (OED). While I perceive the text as an open entity that is receptive to signification and that stimulates a wide range of responses of a possibly unlimited variety, the slow reading of a text as based on an ethical and phenomenological encounter with the text means that each reading of a text must be an altered one, an alternative one. As an ideal, during every slow reading the reader also reflects this phenomenon and thus hardens the text against a conclusive hermeneutic. So, when slow reading understands a text as a fluid event, it understands this fluidity as a hardening against finality. See Chapter 9 of this study for further explorations of the idea of endurance in and regarding Coetzee's fiction.

Surely, slowness in reading (and the willingness to do the thinking) is dependent on the reader's disposition and deportment. She who does not care to read slowly may not be able to philosophize with the writing, to trace the meandering flow of argumentation, and there is little a text can do about that. Or is there?

A take it or leave it attitude is not often adopted by any "serious" text: neither by those philosophical texts which have earned the highly diffuse term "literary," nor by those literary texts which are described by the equally wanting term "philosophical." A certain density of allusion and ambiguity might be deemed both highly literary and highly philosophical, even though many philosophical thinkers (arguably more the analytic than the continental ones) pride themselves on the eradication of ambiguity in the pursuit of the higher goal of Truth, while many fictional works (especially in the realist tradition) try to eradicate suggestions for the doubtful possibility of absolute clarity through mimesis.

Applying these ideas to Coetzee's fiction, the first thing that comes to mind is the objection that his style does not seem complicated or vague at all, but rather characterized by what Dominic Head calls "the gap between the surface lucidity and the underlying complexity of Coetzee's work" (2009: xi).[21] The syntax seems uncomplicated, the language is limpid, possessing what John in *Youth* (2002) finds in Flaubert's language, "the hard, jeweller's craft of poetry" (*SPL* 163). The reference to poetry is not made lightly here, since poetry possesses a density of allusion also found in Coetzee's work.[22] For all its clarity, its straightforwardness, the hasty skimming of a page of a Coetzee novel can hardly yield a deeply reflexive response to the literary and philosophical richness of his writing. From his first published fiction, Coetzee's work seems at once to welcome and to vex the reader. Beginning with the Nabokovian impersonation of an editor and a character named Coetzee in *Dusklands*, the author's work seems to play a post-modern game, albeit a different one from the feverish post-modernisms of Pynchon, Barth, and Barthelme. The clarity of the language seems to suggest a clear invitation to the reader. Yet, immediately after having read a few pages of a work by Coetzee, whose stance is similar to the matter-of-fact and finely tuned lucidity of Kafka's prose, one is struck by the sense that everything seems brimming with meaning, as if the text called to the reader to help free its

---

[21] As will become clear in the following, the seemingly innocent surface/depth-metaphors can be instrumental in steering the reading very distinctly in the direction of an instrumental reading.

[22] Peter Childs supports the argument concerning the slow reading of poetry and writing such as Coetzee's when arguing that "[m]odernist prose is enormously compressed, which means that it should be read with the attention normally reserved for poetry or philosophy" (2000, 6).

signification. Coetzee's fiction does a lot of the work for the reader: she does not have to run to the dictionary every other paragraph and does not have to grapple with experimental language games of the sort that are in danger of estranging the reader from the text in a final way. But for all their clarity and readability, the texts never do the reader's thinking.

To provoke thinking Coetzee's works favor ambiguity in a program of opening up room for the reader's interpretations, ideas, thoughts, and reflections that are a direct result of a slow, careful engagement with the text, an engagement that can be called philosophical. In Coetzee's notes of his reading Jonathan Culler's *Flaubert: The Uses of Uncertainty* (1974),[23] he writes: "JC discusses the close description of objects in Flaubert, passages which block the progress of the text while having a high degree of organization."[24] The note directly below reads:

> The most beautiful works are "of serene aspect and incomprehensible." They are "immobile like cliffs, stormy like the sea,... blue like the sky." They are "unfathomable, infinite, multifarious. Through little gaps one glimpses precipices; there is darkness below, dizziness."[25]

And, then, two notes later Coetzee writes: "If the highest goal of art is to create reverie, then to Flaubert a masterpiece must be incomprehensible."[26] In Coetzee's fiction, too, one finds a strong motion toward the incomprehensible, the elusive, the complex. While Coetzee's texts are never perversely obscure, their density and allusive stimuli for reflection ensure diverse analyses and readings. Their uses of literary techniques explored in the following study engender slowness and careful analysis, and so illuminate the philosophical dimensions of this elusive oeuvre.

It was not for nothing, then, that Coetzee has been a philologist, perhaps he is a philologist still. As will be seen in the following chapters, it is certainly not for nothing that Coetzee is a *teacher of slow reading*, and neither was it for nothing that the writing process of *Dusklands* was as tortuous as Coetzee described it. In his characters' lives, in the style and arrangements of his narratives one encounters a twisting, winding ingenuity, which seems simultaneously unhurried and resolute and yet urgent and explorative. Paradoxically, the urgency is a result of

---

[23] In *Youth* John describes himself as a reader of Flaubert, having read "first *Madame Bovary*, then *Salammbô*" (*SPL* 163), and that to Ezra Pound "[Ford Madox] Ford [was] the sole heir in England of Henry James and Flaubert" (*SPL* 257).

[24] HRC, container 94, folder 10.

[25] Ibid.

[26] Ibid.

the seeming control of language, preparing for moments of rupture to stand out like stark shocks or improvisations in a strictly arranged suite. Reading Coetzee's work one is reminded of the abstract as well as the transformative qualities it shares with philosophy: the trembling aspects of an unceasing hovering between absolute clarity, sentences chiseled as into stone, like axioms, and total ambiguity, a positive openness through which allusion, poetry, and signification seep into the readers' minds.

A *supreme fiction* is J. M. Coetzee's, and to use Wallace Stevens's triad for organizing his poem "Notes toward a Supreme Fiction," one might say: "It must be abstract," "[i]t must change," "[i]t must give pleasure" (1997, 329; 336; 344).[27] This study will show how these three instructions could have been an imaginary manifesto pinned above Coetzee's writing desk. Stevens's triad holds as true of the work of the American poet as it does of the oeuvre of the South African-Australian writer, though it is particularly the first of these orders, which will be looked at in the following, even if under *abstract* one might understand one of its synonyms: *philosophical*.

Coetzee, who seems less inclined toward explication than to allusion, at a reading from his then unpublished novel *The Childhood of Jesus* (2013) at the University of Cape Town in 2012, summed up some of these ideas in customarily crisp fashion:

> The extract I'll be reading is taken from the middle of the book, and therefore it refers to events here and there which have taken place before. I'm not going to waste time explaining each single internal reference. A little obscurity never did anyone any harm. (*UCT*)

This study explores how right he is.

---

[27] In Coetzee's *Slow Man*, Elizabeth Costello tries to remember a quote from Stevens's poem when she says to Paul Rayment: "I urge you. don't cut short these thought-trains of yours. Follow them through to their end. Your thoughts and your feelings. Follow them through and you will grow with them. What was it that the American poet fellow said? There weaves always a fictive covering from something to something" (*S* 158). Of course, the sense of carefully *thinking through the thought-trains* might bring with it its own sense of a slow discursive movement from *something to something*. In the essay "Achterberg's 'Ballade van de gasfitter': The Mystery of You and I" (collected in *Doubling the Point*), Coetzee quotes from "Notes Toward a Supreme Fiction" and engages with the poem's Nanzia Nunzio. See also Pellow (2009, 546–548).

1

Very Much the Tortoise—Slowness
and J. M. Coetzee

In *Summertime* the late John Coetzee is described as "very cautious, very much the tortoise" (*SPL* 464). This chapter explores various forms of being *very much the tortoise* in Coetzee's oeuvre, as it considers slowness in its topical representations as waiting and tarrying; slowness as a dimension of Coetzee's characters, both physically and philosophically, since their thinking may be deemed meditative; and finally slowness as an aspect of writing before it will be considered as informing the act of reading in the following chapters.

Throughout Coetzee's oeuvre one encounters a number of slow characters who are held up, hanging in the air, momentarily drifting and floating; characters in the midst of slow journeys, in waiting, in limbo. Whether in a hole in the ground or in his own mind, like Michael K; on an island or in her own mind, like Susan Barton; trapped in a house and in a slow body, like Magda, Mrs. Curren, or Paul Rayment—Coetzee's characters find themselves hovering. Circumstance, setting, history, mortality, at times existence itself slows them down—and because of this, all of them seem engaged in a very singular kind of slow thinking. I propose, then, a singular kind of thinking slowness to consider the works of J. M. Coetzee.

The second part of *Dusklands*, "The Narrative of Jacobus Coetzee," relates two journeys, and the text itself constitutes a journey as well, the way every narrative may be thought metaphorically as a way of getting, in the words of Elizabeth Costello, from a point of nowhere "to the far bank" (*EC* 1). But whereas "The Narrative of Jacobus Coetzee" narrates slow and arduous journeys, the text itself may only be called arduous and slow if these terms are not invested with negative connotations of final obfuscation or boredom. The oscillation between the vital slowness and the pivotal dynamism of *Dusklands*, maybe of Coetzee's oeuvre as a whole, contributes to the keen reader's fascination with the work. "The Narrative of Jacobus Coetzee" is absorbing precisely because it swiftly draws one into the world of the text by narrating tersely and concisely dramatic and painful slowness. The discursive tension in this text between *what* is narrated and *how* it is narrated is a key to my understanding of Coetzee's work as an oeuvre of dynamic stillness, or as a former mistress of John's recalls one of his phrases, "[*m*]*ovement in stillness, stillness in movement*" (*SPL* 418; original emphasis). This expression highlights a sense of dynamic slowness at the heart of one of Coetzee's characters, but the expression is itself formally tarrying through its chiastic structure. As will be seen, Coetzee's works employ a number of such structures and techniques to slow down reading and thinking.

In the beginning of "The Narrative of Jacobus Coetzee" slowness has a narrative function:

> The narrative. We set out on July 16 and made a steady twelve [English] miles a day for six days. We stopped short of the Oliphants River at a place people call the Gentlemen's Lodgings, a cave in the mountains, to allow the oxen to rest. Having crossed the river we made slow progress, travelling a day and resting a day, until we reached [Koekenaap], where there was grazing. (*Dusk* 63; original square brackets)

The text draws attention to itself as a text and highlights the slowness and the hardships involved in the narrated journey. By exposing itself as a narrative, the text alludes to a possible dramatization and fictionalization of the reported journey, a feeling that is increased through the information that the text was edited by one S. J. Coetzee and then translated into English by one J. M. Coetzee.[1] So, the text presents itself as being at least twice removed from the "real" journey of Jacobus Coetzee. His narrative begins by recounting slowness, but it immediately speeds up our thinking about the text. It does so paradoxically by deautomatizing the reading, by slowing down through estrangement (or defamiliarization). The text is presented as having a slow journey behind it as a text as well, a slow compositional and translational process,[2] and this "accelerates" our interpretive approach by prompting us to reflect on these. What is at work in the text is a palimpsest of slowness; various levels of slowness are superimposed over one another: Jacobus narrates his experience of the physical slowness involved in the

---

[1] For an account of the historical Jacobus Coetsé, how Coetzee found Coetsé's *Relaas*, a travel account, at the university archive in Austin, TX, and how he "used it as a source, adapted and skilfully transmuted [it] into a pseudo-documentary for 'The Narrative of Jacobus Coetzee'" (Kannemeyer 2012, 21), see Kannemeyer's account, pp. 19–21. Kannemeyer is on track calling Coetzee's text a *pseudo-documentary*; in the Lannan Interview in 2001, Coetzee describes his first work as a "spoof." Coetsé's *Relaas* itself seems to have been germinated through a complicated process of authorship, probably involving a ghost writer, since Coetsé was most likely illiterate (Kannemeyer 2012, 21).

[2] This aspect of a putative translational process behind the text is an aspect which informs part of my reading of Coetzee's latest novel *The Childhood of Jesus* in Chapter 9 of this study.

trek; the editor's additions (in square brackets) give us pause; we are provoked to believe we are reading a translated work—all this gives the text a dense, tarrying quality that mirrors Jacobus's journeys and provokes us to read carefully and contemplatively.

The form is tethered to the content, and both defamiliarize. We are estranged by Jacobus's violent acts, which produce objection in the reader, a sense of ethical estrangement from Jacobus, and to a certain degree, from the text. The narrative presentation of the work, however, challenges a straightforward ethical estrangement from the text and, to a certain degree, from Jacobus. The homodiegetic focalization through Jacobus slowly pulls us into his mind, and envelops us in the arduous trek of his "exploration" journey. To a degree, this pushes us to become complicit with him.[3] This sense of complicity is emphasized by the formal arrangement of the text, by the slowness generated through the work's dramatic structure. The frequent stops and delays in the journeys function as dramatic devices to increase tension and to heighten suspense through the formal arrangement of delaying certainty and dramatic payoff. These basic devices of narrative structure are deployed in a self-aware and complex way of using dramatic plotting as if against the reader. The text uses the basic principle of generating suspense through "interruption and delay" (MacKay 2011, 84).[4] Through a frequent slowing down of the forward-motion of the trekkers and of the narrative as a whole, through the obstacles placed in Jacobus's way, the reader may be tempted momentarily to root for the colonist trekker to succeed, until this is kept in check when the reader's ethical estrangement from Jacobus has kicked in.

The topical estrangement from Jacobus's actions occurs straightforwardly and makes the reader retreat. But the formal estrangements from the text function as ways of pulling in the reader, so she can make sense of the more complex structural and stylistic qualities of the text as juxtaposed against the content

---

[3] Poyner makes a similar argument:

> The act of reading these two 'confessions' [the texts comprising *Dusklands*] necessarily encourages the reader to empathize with Dawn and Jacobus, and thus on a symbolic level the reader is made complicit in their abuse even though, paradoxically, the gratuitous nature of their violence marks a radical hiatus that refuses to allow the reader to enter fully the life of the text, or, in fact, to empathize with its protagonists. (2009, 24)

See also Poyner (2009, 30).

[4] While I refer to suspense here in its function for narrative, it is helpful to remember its etymology as signaling standstill, waiting, deferral, tarrying, and essentially "in-betweenness." The OED specifies: "Anglo-Norman, Old French *suspens* […], in phrase *en suspens* […] in abeyance, or Old French *suspense* < deferring, delay, repr. medieval Latin *suspensum* (in phrase *in suspenso*)." The narrative that makes us wait, provokes us to respond, to react.

and the character. This wavering of familiarizing and defamiliarizing produces slowness in the reading. It takes time to read and to think through the text in a responsive way. By taking one's time to read responsively, one may already be reflecting, contemplating, deconstructing the text deeply and philosophically; one may already be reading not merely *responsively* but also *responsibly*.[5] The slowness wrought in *Dusklands* suspends the reader in a precarious situation by forcing her to position herself ethically and politically in and toward Jacobus, in and toward the text, without any moral guidance from either.

A further level of discursive "familiarizing-defamiliarizing" occurs through the implicit comparison and contrast of Jacobus's narrative with the preceding novella (or novelette), "The Vietnam Project," whose character Eugene Dawn and his megalomaniacal acts and thoughts have already estranged us by the time we meet Jacobus Coetzee. The reader is thus continually provoked to go back and forth in the text, to reevaluate any kind of complicity with and estrangement from Jacobus that she may experience. In consequence, the reader's (physical or reflexive) moving about in the text replicates the hobbling dramatic structure of the work she is reading. This produces a temporal and a spatial dislocation and prompts the reader to analogize, compare, and contrast the two narratives and the two characters. The juxtaposition between Dawn and Jacobus generates, as Rosemarie Jane Jolly argues, a feeling of atrocious historical self-repetition. Jolly asserts that Dawn and Jacobus seem "reciprocally mimetic," that they are "colonizers in a history that repeats itself in the rise and fall of successive empires" (1996, 111).[6] Because the two characters are paradoxically linked by the gap between the two narratives, the reader is much less likely to infer any positive development from Jacobus's more lyrical and carefully regretful remarks at the end of his narrative, since a future of violence and atrocity has already dawned on the reader via "The Vietnam Project," whose dramatization of imperial and megalomaniacal forces are now retrospectively qualified as springing not merely from one man's madness, but from a colonist current running through the history of civilization.

---

[5]   The notion that *responsive reading* is twinned with *responsible reading* is argued by Attridge's outlining of an ethical reading both in *The Singularity of Literature* (2004b, 89–93; 128–131) and *J. M. Coetzee and the Ethics of Reading: Literature in the Event*, especially the idea that "it is through *responsive reading*, an immersion in the text, that we participate in, and perhaps are changed by, [a] complex understanding of hope and fear, illusion and disillusionment" (2004a, 48; added emphasis). Attridge's example for this responsive and responsible reading refers to *Waiting for the Barbarians* with regard to the Magistrate's dreams as a locus for enacting a deep immersion in the text.

[6]   Rosemary Gary makes a similar argument about the text when she draws attention to "the ideas that history repeats itself and that 'civilized' man is naturally pernicious" (1986, 32).

In the linking of Dawn and Coetzee one may see mirrored a discursive quality of getting close to the two while being estranged from them, or being estranged from the one while being close to the other, and vice versa. The gap between the two texts implicitly forces the readers to think the two characters together, to characterize the other through the one, and vice versa. The reader's pleasure in finding similarities between two characters is exploited as a way of drawing the reader close to the text and the characters (through a sense of *recognition*), and then sharply estranging the reader from the text through the character's imperialist stances and violent actions (through a sense of *repulsion*). This thought process of going back and forth between two ways of responding to the text takes a certain amount of reflection and so a certain amount of time. By lengthening reflection through the textual characteristics and devices described earlier, a wide realm of philosophical signification is opened up because of the connections that the reader draws.

A similar effect is achieved through another repetition in "The Narrative of Jacobus Coetzee." The text firmly lifts the reader out of a realist reception of the text when Jacobus's slave, Klawer, dies the second time. Through the repetition of the character's death the reader is further jarred out of any receptive stupor and advised to reflect in detail on the events described in the text. One is tempted to leaf back through the book and check if one is guilty of a lapse in reading when Klawer has died the first time. This can be illuminated by drawing on Coetzee's correspondence with his publishers upon the release of the book. Coetzee's publisher Peter Randall assumed Klawer's twofold death must have been a lapse by the author, while early critics saw in it a negligence on the part of the publishing house. To an inquiry by Randall whether Klawer's reappearance is an oversight, Coetzee replies tersely: "No, there is no oversight on my part on p.93" (letter from November 5, 1973).[7] To repeated inquiries by Randall, Coetzee answers:

> Regarding the alternative deaths of Klawer: I don't believe in the principal of authorial explication, so what I have done is to ask [Jonathan] Crewe—who gave the work a reading which was in my eyes amazingly responsive—what he made of the pages in question. He referred me to the passage on p.2 of his review where he discusses "the disclosure of the stage-machinery," and suggested (a)

---

[7]   Hermann Wittenberg meticulously charted the correspondence between author and publisher, drawing on archival material when Coetzee's papers were still in the National English Literary Museum in Grahamstown, SA. See Wittenberg (2011). Today the correspondence is held by the HRC (Container 69, folders 1–4).

that Jacobus Coetzee is telling stories to cover up the "facts" of Klawer's death, and (b) that someone (who?) is writing a document called "The Narrative of Jacobus Coetzee" and has been caught with the edges of his revision showing. I don't know how you feel about this interpretation. I find it quite plausible. (letter from February 22, 1974).[8]

The event of Klawer's death, his immediate return, and his second death have the effect of holding the reader still in the text, first stimulating a fundamental reflection on the act of reading and subsequently raising fundamental epistemological questions.[9]

Different effects on the reader are achieved through the topical and formal forms of slowness in *Waiting for the Barbarians*. The novel also uses topical delays and interruptions for dramatic purposes, for example in the central waiting for the "barbarians" or when the locust swarm of Biblical proportions interrupts the journey back to the "barbarian" girl's people. Yet, here the represented slowness serves different and perhaps more complex functions than in *Dusklands*. Here, the reader's sympathies are much more readily with the two characters around whom the narrative is built. Even though the Magistrate is employed by the Empire and shares in the colonist project, his acts of generosity, his ultimate abandoning of his bad faith, and his renunciation of his imperial alliances all allow us to be more comfortably his ally. We feel a more direct injustice about the obstacles that the Magistrate and the girl have to overcome during their journey, while their suffering under its slow progress conversely increases our sympathies for them.

In *Waiting for the Barbarians*, the experienced slowness is, first of all, conveyed to the reader through the phenomenon of *waiting*. The novel's title suggests what Harold Schweizer calls "instrumental waiting, waiting with a purpose, waiting for a denouement" (2008, 11). The kind of waiting suggested by the title is a Kafkaesque waiting, ostensibly end-oriented, but unjustly delayed and detoured.[10]

---

[8] Ibid.
[9] Robert Pippin illuminates this: "Coetzee narrates incidents, the death of Klawer, that are then contradicted by others, such as Klawer's reappearance in the narrative only to die again, all of which makes us wonder what, if anything, 'really' did happen to Klawer" (2010, 29).
[10] The analogues to waiting in Kafka are found at the level of the plot in Josef K.'s (*The Trial*, 1925) and K.'s (*The Castle*, 1926) being continually denied the reaching of their goals, crystallized most distinctly in "At the Gate" (part of *The Trial*). This kind of waiting is, of course, also echoed in Gregor Samsa's existence in *The Metamorphosis*, 1915. Samsa's waiting is related to the Beckettian and Coetzeean *dynamic still*, to which I have referred before, as regards distinct stasis (Samsa is confined to his room and his "new" body) combined with high agility (as an insect he can scrabble up the walls and ceiling).

While Coetzee's *Waiting for the Barbarians* seems structured along the lines of a *waiting for*, an end-oriented waiting, a change transpires when the Magistrate takes into his home and his care the "barbarian" girl (*WfB* 29). Slowly, his teleological mindset, influenced by an imperial rationale and the fear of a coming "barbarian" attack spread by "the empire of pain" (*WfB* 24), is altered; he begins a new way of being through a new way of waiting. At first, the Magistrate's existence is strongly marked by imperial and institutional associations,[11] and so his waiting is directed in an unreflected way toward the future, the end of waiting. Slowly, however, he comes to re-privilege the present and implicitly to question teleology. The moments when he cares for the girl, the ritual washing of her body, are moments of slowness, which gradually detach the Magistrate's mind from the teleological thinking associated with the Empire. His acts of care both transform his associations with the Empire and make him reject the frenzied end-oriented thinking introduced by Joll and his men, make him reject an instrumental *waiting for*, an instrumental, end-oriented thinking.

As the Magistrate begins to care for the girl, he initially thinks himself no better than her oppressors: "She is as much a prisoner now as ever before," he says (*WfB* 60; see also 29; 41). And yet, the Magistrate's exaggeration signals a change in his thinking. When he compares himself to the servants of the Empire, he has come to an impasse, but by comparing himself *to* them he paradoxically also already distances himself *from* them. The words of lament *I am just like them* signal an awareness that undercuts the literal comparison that they state. The implication represents an insight, which the Magistrate has about himself, about his role in the Empire, maybe his role in the world. His insight develops in part because of those moments of slow time he spends with the girl, when the present moment of being with another person is privileged over the future-oriented mode of waiting propagated by the Empire. This is not achieved suddenly. In fact, the Magistrate's teleological thinking is broken down subtly and gradually. When he decides to take the girl back to her people, he feels an unfamiliar sense of happiness at the prospect of an outcome, an achievement, "[n]ow that [he] ha[s] committed [him]self to a course" (*WfB* 63). But this course is very different from the teleology of the Empire, which is structured around hierarchies and directed

---

[11] Note how at first the binary of *I* and *they* is clearly erected by the Magistrate regarding the "barbarians." Slowly, the novel shifts away from this binary logic, and, in the course, the Magistrate begins a new way of thinking that deconstructs imperial structures, and effectively, teleological thinking, of which the binary is but the most flagrant example. The Magistrate's language has long been influenced by hierarchical imperial structures of a master–slave logic: a demeaning *they*, the use of the word *barbarians* and *vagrants*, and a binary view of leader–follower. See, for example, *WfB* 16; 20; 29; 64.

toward power. The Magistrate's course is a more ethical commitment whose repercussions will prove to be detrimental to his position in the structures of the Empire, and his course is essentially an undermining of teleology: he is granted no distinct satisfaction from his journey, not even an altruistic gratification, and after his return his life spins, or drifts, out of control—and so he slips, or drifts, out of the Empire's grasp. He gives up his attachment to the Empire and his impulse toward an end; he gives himself over toward another person, maybe even toward another life.

The novel explores a privileging of the present that has an ethical and an ontological dimension. Early in the composition stage of the novel Coetzee moves very slowly toward the present tense and the first person for his narrative, the *I am*. The creation of the novel's voice is connected to Coetzee's creation of its ambiguous setting. In the early stages of the conception, the novel was originally set on Robben Island, revolving around a guard named Manos Milis and a developing relationship with a refugee woman. Coetzee's manuscripts show that he slowly finds the present tense and the first person while writing, as he discovers the uncertain landscape.[12] The setting and the narrative situation simultaneously familiarize and defamiliarize, drawing one in through the unusual, dream-like narrative situation, and estranging one through an unrecognizable place in which orientation happens only gradually, like groping through a darkened room. The first person combined with the present tense give the impression of an unfolding tale, making the reader pass through the events with and through the narrator in a slow and precarious way. The reader has to wait with the Magistrate, reading, to simplify crudely, phenomenologically rather than teleologically.

As the narrative unfolds, the present moment gains centrality to the Magistrate, and so to the reader. By *present* I do not mean what Coetzee in "The Novel Today" has termed "the so-called historical present" (*NT* 2). Neither do I refer to the time of the moment of writing, nor to the present of a *specific* time and place. By *present* I mean not the hegemony of one time over another, but rather the *present moment* as an ideal, that fleeting container in which every living thing seems to float along the time bar of being. By *present* I wish to invoke a phenomenological present, the feeling of the present as an event, a present that is omnitemporally present, as a moment in the here and now lived through in

---

[12] In the Salmagundi interview, Coetzee notes: "In *Waiting for the Barbarians* the challenge was not to describe or represent an unfamiliar landscape. It was to construct a landscape. A landscape that I've never seen and that probably doesn't exist" (Coetzee and Scott 1997, 95).

all its transience. The Magistrate's world has shrunken down to moments of this kind in the presence of the girl, and through his attentiveness in these moments a new thinking transpires in the Magistrate.

The effect of his caring for the girl is a slowing down of his existence and of the narrative. After each administration of the washing ritual, he falls into deep sleeping spells, which "are like death to [him], or enchantment" (*WfB* 33); likewise, his dreams explode stable notions of linearity, both in his life and in the narrative. The political time of history, of the Empire, is slowly undermined, while the present moment, the caring moment, is emphasized and foregrounded. Even if at the beginning the Magistrate confesses to "us[ing] her body" (*WfB* 32) for his own mysterious gratification, he ultimately comes to favor a more responsible, less egotistical attachment to her, which is the precondition for a more ethical detachment from her. Thereby, he chooses (perhaps subconsciously) a form of deep engagement with another person that paradoxically expresses itself in separation, the way love can sometimes only let go.

Through the privileging of the present moment, the Magistrate is attentive to another person's being. Ultimately, this makes him deprivilege his plans for a future and allows the overcoming of his own desire to hold on to the girl. His initial holding on to her prepares him to let her go.[13] The privileging of the present moment occurs through the slow development of what waiting signifies in the text. The aforementioned form of waiting suggested by the title, the *waiting for*, becomes a slower form of waiting, but a more ethically and ontologically engaged waiting. It becomes a waiting which ultimately grants the Magistrate a stepping beyond the temporal and spatial boundaries of the Empire and finally the confines of his narrow instrumental thinking, a thinking that may have rationalized his holding on to the girl.

The waiting in the novel slowly assumes what Schweizer suggests about Beckett's *Waiting for Godot*; it may be said that Coetzee's novel does not show "how we *pass through* waiting but how we *are in it*, not [...] the expectation of the end of waiting, but [...] the *quality* of waiting as such" (2008, 11; original emphases). Through the ritual of washing the girl the Magistrate tries symbolically to cleanse her of part of the taint the Empire has inflicted, and he is also cleansing himself, as if through the almost religious care he administers

---

[13] At the same time, there remains a problematic relationship with the "barbarian" girl, staged around the question whether the Magistrate does not continue to *use* her even when he leaves her with her people, whether he does not only *use* her to bring about a change within himself, but also an even more problematic possibility one should at least entertain in thought: whether he does not simply want to get rid of her.

he baptized into being a new kind of waiting, less a *waiting for* and more a *waiting with*.

As an alternative to instrumental waiting, it is useful to conceive of the idea of *meditative waiting* to show a wide range of potentiality in idle lingering, in instances of hovering time, as Mrs. Curren calls this in *Age of Iron*.[14] These moments of meditative waiting are present in a number of Coetzee's works, particularly in *Life & Times of Michael K* and *Age of Iron*, and they are usually disconnected from specific goals that an instrumental waiting posits. In *Age of Iron* the time of waiting Mrs. Curren finds herself in assumes an existential urgency. Her waiting cannot be a *waiting for* in the sense of "looking forward to," since the only thing awaiting her is the confrontation with eternity's void, death. So, while Coetzee's characters are often waiting, their waiting stalls in the experienced phenomenon of waiting and allows the characters to hover for a moment, to reflect, and to unfold phenomenologically before themselves and before the readers, intra- and extra-textually.

My idea of *meditative waiting* is closely connected to the idea of *meditative thinking*, which many characters in Coetzee's oeuvre privilege over *calculative*, or *instrumental thinking*. As mentioned in the introduction, my language here borrows liberally from Heidegger's *Gelassenheit* (*Discourse on Thinking*) and like his concept of meditative thinking my idea of meditative waiting is to be understood as related to contemplative reflection, being focused on the here and now, and on being *open to the mystery* ([1959] 1966, 55f.).[15]

---

[14] In *Age of Iron* the time of waiting also has both a philosophical and a political dimension, though in a different way, since here Mrs. Curren is waiting *for* (or rather, *helplessly against*) her own death, but also finds herself in a strange political middle period, an interregnum in the history of South Africa, which might have its parallels to the State of Emergency from 1985 to 1986, when the power of apartheid was waning, while its brutality increased. About this time Leonard Thompson notes: "To re-establish control of the black population, the government resorted to bannings, arrests, detentions, and treason trials. Police interrogators tortured victims, and unidentified persons who were widely believed to be members of the security police assassinated antiapartheid activists inside and outside South Africa" (2001, 235). Michael Neill writes:

> *Age of Iron* is self-consciously a document of the "interregnum"—that time of uneasy "waiting" which is mirrored in the disturbingly arrested moment at the end of Part 3 when the narrator waits for the police to gun down the armed schoolboy-revolutionary hiding in her house: "[a] hovering time, but not eternity. *A time being*, a suspension, before the return of the time in which the door bursts open and we face the great white glare." (2010, 87; quoting *AoI* 176)

[15] "That which shows itself and at the same time withdraws is the essential trait of what we call the mystery. I call the comportment which enables us to keep open to the meaning hidden in technology, *openness to the mystery*" (Heidegger [1959] 1966, 55; original emphasis). Heidegger speaks more broadly—and normatively—about the increased influence of technology on human beings and how it inhibits meditative thinking. He sees this technological influence as having a detrimental effect on meditative thinking, although he sees value in technology and in calculative thinking as well (Heidegger [1959] 1966, 44f.; 54). He thus proposes an ethical application of calculative thinking

Heidegger's pathos-laden language is a far cry from Coetzee's lean prose, but the connection between the calculative and the meditative is integral to a consideration of the types of thinking at work in Coetzee's characters. As with so much in Coetzee's complex oeuvre, it is rarely a case of Either–Or,[16] *not only but also*. His characters are usually deeply rational, which in Coetzee's work is never specific to being well educated or even to what is ordinarily understood as being intelligent.[17] Their extreme rationality—in characters like Dostoevsky in *The Master of Petersburg* or the John Coetzee of *Youth*—is often dramatized as a *status quo* that is challenged through an event, or an opening, in their lives, when their calculative thinking cracks and becomes meditative. This change frequently occurs during a period marked by slowness, some moment during which the clasp of reason is momentarily loosened and the characters come to perceive the world's phenomena in an altered way. In his erudite essay on "Coetzee's Critique of Reason," Martin Woessner writes about this change with regard to the Magistrate:

> The Magistrate's moral awakening in *Waiting for the Barbarians* does not come quickly, but it would be incorrect to say that it is the product of slow and careful deliberation. There is no moral balance sheet to be drawn up, discussed, and debated. Instead, what finally convinces him of the evils of empire is an immediate and visceral reaction to bodily harm. (2010, 233)

This *reaction to bodily harm* includes a variety of physical pains that the Magistrate witnesses and experiences himself. Woessner continues to argue that it is through the move away from a deliberating and calculating hegemony of reason that "the Cartesian cogito breaks down" (2010, 234). I would accentuate Woessner's significant arguments here about the Magistrate's encounter with

for its own purposes and without superseding meditative thinking. My own understanding of the meditative with reference to Coetzee is simply a more wholesome awareness, attentiveness, and engagement with whatever that mystery might entail, whether in the natural world, in objects, or in other human beings. Coetzee's use of lists of seemingly mundane objects (foodstuffs, tools, plants, sights) in *Life & Times of Michael K*, for example, is evidence of K's growing awareness and attentiveness to the world after having immersed himself in his burrow and so in his own mind. At the same time—and this is one further similarity between a Coetzee character and Robinson Crusoe—the profusion of lists in the narrative also show the shrinking of K's world. Is it easier to be attentive to the world and think meditatively about it, if one's focus is concentrated? For a fascinating reflection on the political dimensions of Heidegger's concept of *Gelassenheit* and its links to Coetzee's work, see Hayes (2010, 23–24).

[16] In an interview with *World Literature Today* after the publication of *Giving Offense*, Coetzee says: "I am not enamored of the Either-Or. I hope that I don't simply evade the Either-Or whenever confronted with it. I hope that I at least try to work out what 'underlies' it in each case (if I can use that foundationalist metaphor); and that this response of working-out on the Either-Or isn't read simply as evasion" (Coetzee and World Literature Today 1996, 107).

[17] Michael K is the clearest example of a deeply thoughtful character, despite the fact that he has virtually no education. I will return to this aspect in subsequent chapters.

pain both in others and in himself (2010, 234), but focus more directly on the Magistrate's encounters with the girl's body. This way, the argument is less in peril of privileging pain and his own body as being conducive to change, but seeing behind the outcome of change the Magistrate's complex emotions and responses involved when caring for another person's body, the girl's. It is during the washing of the girl's body that the Magistrate becomes most *gelassen*: "I am abstracted, lost in the rhythm of rubbing and kneading the swollen ankle" (*WfB* 59). When with her, the Magistrate falls into sleep that is "blank, *outside time*" (*WfB* 33; added emphasis). The strange feelings of blankness, of inertia, when he is with the girl are related to the hovering moments described earlier and may likewise be illuminated by Heidegger's *Gelassenheit*, a word whose complex German etymology suggests leaving, letting go, letting be, as well as composure.[18] In English *Gelassenheit* is usually translated as *releasement*, since through *Gelassenheit* being comes to an understanding about things (or people) by way of a *releasement toward* them (Heidegger [1959] 1966, 54). As mentioned before, *Gelassenheit* may be brought to bear on my notion of meditative waiting: slow, contemplative, *awaiting*[19] something in a moment of hovering time rather than *waiting for* something. Hubert L. Dreyfus glosses *Gelassenheit*: "Releasement […] is only a stage, a kind of holding pattern we can enter into while we are awaiting a new understanding of being that would give a shared content to our openness […]" (1993, 365). In the course of his waiting the Magistrate finds a certain sense of *releasement toward*, an openness toward an other, toward himself, maybe toward being in general.[20] His slowness when

---

[18] In the McNeill and Walker translation of Heidegger's *The Fundamental Concepts of Metaphysics: World, Finitude, Solitude*, the word *Gelassenheit* is translated as *composure* ([1938] 1994, 137).

[19] My idea of *awaiting* is influenced by Attridge's comments on the complex forms of waiting in Coetzee. Attridge relates waiting to Jacques Derrida's concept of the *arrivant* developed in *Aporias*. What Attridge notes about *The Master of Petersburg* is equally pertinent regarding *Waiting for the Barbarians*:

> It's a novel of waiting, then, and waiting without any clear sense of what would constitute the longed-for-arrival. A Beckettian situation, but not lightened by any Beckettian humour. Thanks to Derrida we can propose a name for what Dostoevsky is waiting for: the *arrivant*, which might be translated into English as "the one who arrives" or "arrival" […]. (It is also worth bearing in mind that the word *arriver* can mean "happen".) […] The *arrivant* is closely tied, therefore, to the *event*, understood, as a happening that could not have been predicted […]. (2004a, 120f.; original emphases)

[20] Note how his reflection changes and he, like the medical officer in *Life & Times of Michael K*, seems to try and turn his hardest gaze on himself, and then engages with this sense of letting go, of *releasement*: "I have achieved nothing by letting myself go" (*WfB* 59). In this instance, the idea of letting go that the Magistrate refers to is his sense of not keeping "a cunning tongue" (*WfB* 57) and of speaking out for the "barbarians." The dual meaning of the phrase "letting go" is subtly used here to suggest both a careless letting oneself go in the sense of being idle, as well as a letting oneself go toward an other, in this instance in the sense of releasing oneself toward the "barbarians." The moment when this takes

he is with the girl stands in sharp contrast to the fastness and industriousness of the Empire—and what else is an empire but an industry? His slower way of being gradually assumes a moral quality, becoming, in John Gray's Heideggerian terms, more of "an openness to beings, to the things of the earth, in all their contingency and mortality" (1992, 182). We may draw analogies to other characters in Coetzee who experience this, most obviously Michael K, but also Mrs. Curren, and to a lesser degree, Paul Rayment.

In *Waiting for the Barbarians* this altered openness toward the world shows in the Magistrate's gradual revolt against haste in favor of slow being, in the renouncing of imperial teleology and instrumentality. The novel shows the dangerous privileging of teleology at the hands of Joll and offers the Magistrate as a reluctant, though ultimately no less recalcitrant contrarian to instrumental waiting and thinking, in defiance, first and foremost, of the instrumentality of torture. In the novel, torture as the cruel exemplar of a means toward an end is defined as the epitome of instrumentality, when Joll speaks of his instruments of pain for burning out the truth.[21] The Magistrate's care for the girl, then, appears as a first alternative to instrumentality, since the motivations behind it are far less teleological and offer a far more elusive stimulus. By caring for the girl even without the orientation toward an end (the Magistrate does not even care for her with the prospect of sex, which is, after all, another form of teleology), the Magistrate slowly proposes a challenge to instrumental living and instrumental being.

Ultimately, he breaks out of the teleological structures of the Empire by offering his own slowness, in caring, in waiting, and even in acting.[22] Without wanting to glorify indecision, or, indeed, the character of the Magistrate, his dithering hesitancy may be regarded as, at the very least, a counter-version to the industrious teleology of the Empire, even if his indecisiveness is paradoxically influenced by the residue of imperial thinking within him. Head argues that the Magistrate wishes to escape "the history that Empire has imposed"

---

place is crucial, since the Magistrate is more and more dissatisfied with himself and his care for the girl, as if he needed a grander gesture of "washing" himself of his alliance with the Empire, a stronger letting go. This begins to materialize shortly afterwards, as he decides to take the girl back to her people, and so ultimately releases (and "frees") her (and himself) to the "barbarians."

[21] This is expressed most clearly in Joll's explanation of his "method" to move toward truth, as un-Socratic as they come: "First I get lies, you see—this is what happens—first lies, then pressure, then more lies, then more pressure, then the break, then more pressure, then the truth. That is how you get the truth" (*WfB* 5).

[22] It should not be forgotten that the Empire is presented as an inept one. As I have noted elsewhere, the novel "shows a bumbling army that seems less effective even than a militia and more like a grotesque carnival attraction" (2015, 190). However, the Empire's brutality is not diminished by its ineptitude; if anything, it makes the Empire *more* dangerous and capricious, empowered "with a reckless brutality manifest in those who have nothing left to lose, or in the insane. Like a cornered animal, [the Empire] snarl[s] and bite[s] with violent ferocity" (2015, 190).

(1997, 89),[23] but that his change remains "an *incomplete* reaction to Empire, to its end-oriented, teleological version of history" (1997, 89; added emphasis). By viewing the Magistrate as being under the sway of meditative waiting, one comes to appreciate the change in his comportment as a form of potentiality, rather than one of accomplishment, even if the force of this potentiality is no less philosophically and politically significant.[24]

It is important to stress these points by highlighting that the slowness, the meditativeness, the idleness of many of Coetzee's characters are never solipsistic rejections of but rather direct engagements with the world and with others. Paradoxically, their intensified comportment toward the world is actualized by a detour via extreme inwardness and meditative reflection. Only the inwardness that is enabled in and by a meditative moment of slow time prepares the characters to gaze outward, at the world and others in a way that Heidegger calls being *open to the mystery*.

When Mrs. Curren in *Age of Iron* says "[m]y eyes are shut in order to see" (*AoI* 175), she intimates this immersion in inwardness and in the present moment, which only subsequently becomes a reaching out to the world.[25] In *Slow Man* Paul Rayment laments that his accident has "shrunk his world" (*S* 54), has "trapped [him] in a stuffy flat" (*S* 100), has "turned him into a prisoner" (*S* 54), that he is "trapped with the same old self as before" (*S* 54), in short that his accident was not a lesson that made him a different person. But despite his insistence to the contrary, his being trapped with the same old self has, in fact, forced him to consider himself (his self) in a very different way. Being literally trapped in his stuffy flat has indeed shrunk his world down to the present moment, to the time being, the hovering time, and has made him think differently of himself and others.

---

[23] Coetzee's novel goes back and forth between the expressions *Empire* and *the Empire*. Elsewhere, Head comments: "The omission of the definite article is one of the features that help cultivate the air of a universal allegory: 'Empire' seems to represent imperialism *per se*" (2009, 49). However, Head is a bit too sweeping here, it seems, since the novel refers to *the Empire* just as much as it does to *Empire*, so that the air of a *universal* allegory Head attests the novel seems too enthusiastic.

[24] To remain significant as potentiality, his change has to remain incomplete within the diegetic frame. It is, therefore, not unimportant that the novel ends ambiguously, further emphasizing the sense of drifting and floating that has characterized the text. The novel's final word *nowhere* may be regarded as signifying a potential counter-version to the *somewhere* of history. Head notes about the novel's last dream sequence:

> In losing his way in the linear scheme of things (the road metaphor is pointed) [the Magistrate] has advanced to a level where his subconscious works its own mythology. [...] The dream sequence amounts to an accreted narrative of sublimation and human advancement which belies the negativity of the final 'nowhere' of the novel, and which is validated by an appeal to a mimetic moment in which the lessons drawn from the dream-vision can be "actualized" for the character: the magistrate awakes into a new present in which the traces of Empire are eradicated from his identity. (1997, 92)

[25] In *Age of Iron* this is reflected in the previously mentioned moment when Mrs. Curren speaks of *a hovering time* (*AoI* 176).

The self-involved loner Paul Rayment of before,[26] who claims he used to lead "an active life" (*S* 69), is, in another sense, leading a much more active life now that he is slowed down, a more engaged, a less self-contained life (not least because of Costello's ploy to jumpstart his life, his life story). Only a few pages after his insistence that nothing has changed, we find him responding purely and ethically to Marijana's youngest child Ljuba. After the child has eaten a snack prepared, at first hesitantly, by Paul, he wipes a bit of jam off of the girl's wrist, and upon touching her arm he cannot think anything but "[p]*erfect*" (*S* 56; original emphasis), as if he were in the company of a miracle, as if he were *open to the mystery*.

The strongest example in Coetzee's oeuvre of this openness preconditioned by a slow meditative moment is the epiphanic event in *Youth* when John, living an austere life in London, "retreats to Hampstead Heath" (*SPL* 242). At a low point in his life, a period of utter loneliness and despair, after a time of drifting, "sauntering around a foreign city" (*SPL* 241),[27] there occurs a moment that warrants the term Augustinian, not least because of its mood of equanimity and its setting in a garden of a kind, the heath:

> Tired out, one Sunday afternoon, he folds his jacket into a pillow, stretches out on the greensward, and sinks into a sleep or half-sleep in which consciousness does not vanish but continues to hover. It is a state he has not known before: in his very blood he seems to feel the steady wheeling of the earth. The faraway cries of children, the birdsong, the whirr of insects gather force and come together in a paean of joy. His heart swells. *At last!* he thinks. At last it has come, the moment of ecstatic unity with the All! Fearful that the moment will slip away, he tries to put a halt to the clatter of thought, tries simply to be a conduit for the great universal force that has no name.
>
> It lasts no more than seconds in clock time, this signal event. But when he gets up and dusts off his jacket, he is refreshed, renewed. He journeyed to the great dark city to be tested and transformed, and here, on this patch of green under the mild spring sun, word of his progress has, surprisingly, come. If he has not utterly been transformed, then at least he has been blessed with a hint that he belongs on this earth. (*SPL* 242; original emphasis)

---

[26] "He might have been solitary, but only as certain male animals are solitary. There was always more than enough to keep him occupied. He took out books from the library, he went to the cinema; he cooked for himself, he even baked bread; he did not own a car but rode a bicycle or walked" (*S* 25). While one need not doubt that Paul is relating the truth about his past life of simple pleasures, it cannot be denied that he was a solitary man (he claims so himself) and that there is reason to believe it was not a responsible life, not responsive to others.

[27] The use of the word *sauntering* seems pointed here when reflected in light of Henry David Thoreau's essay "Walking," which explores the advantages of sauntering, of slow walking and aimless drifting, which, of course, also influences the style of Thoreau's text.

This moment functions as the *signal event* it claims to be in the narrative, but it also functions as a *signal event* in Coetzee's work as a whole, with relevance to the texts and to the reader. It is the primary example of the kind of meditative, slow moment of openness and the effects of such a phenomenon on consciousness; the effects of this moment on John in the work are paralleled, as will be seen, in the effects on the reader. This Augustinian moment is located in a work which Coetzee calls "autrebiography" (*DtP* 394), a work which oscillates elusively between autobiography and fiction. In *Youth* this moment is presented as a kind of founding myth in the life of John Coetzee, allowing him to become the artist J. M. Coetzee. On the level of the plot, John will soon give up thinking along the lines of binaries, along a teleology of calculative thinking. The moment of *hovering time*, then, ushers in a new way of being in the life of John Coetzee, a new way of thinking, which is linked to a specific kind of writing.

In one of Attwell's interviews in *Doubling the Point* Coetzee comments on the act of writing, which allows the connection between a slow compositional method and meditative thinking:

> I feel a greater freedom to follow where my thinking takes me when I am writing fiction than when I am writing criticism. [...] Not only that: I tend to be rather slow and painstaking and myopic in my thinking (in fact, in most things I do). (*DtP* 246)[28]

It would be too pat to claim that Coetzee's description of his own *slow* and *painstaking* thinking are in a simplistic way behind his works' slow character. What interests me about his statement is that it allows a fascinating parallelization of the engagement of his work with slowness and a slow writing process that seems to lie at the heart of Coetzee's oeuvre, and the way this opens up an engagement with formal deceleration in his work that will be at the center of my slow readings in the following chapters.

In an earlier interview in *Doubling the Point*, a comment by the author sheds light on his slow composition of interest here:

> It is naïve to think that writing is a simple two-stage process: first you decide what you want to say, then you say it. On the contrary, as all of us know, you write because you do not know what you want to say. Writing reveals to you what you wanted to say in the first place. [...] That is the sense in which one

---

[28] Carrol Clarkson also mentions this statement as the starting point of her ethical and aesthetic analysis of Coetzee's work. She points out how even the "cursory perusal of the titles of some of Coetzee's critical essays bears testimony to the measure of this statement" (Clarkson 2009, 1). The essays on which Clarkson bases this argument are collected in *Doubling the Point*.

can say that writing writes us. [...] Writing, then, involves an interplay between the push into the future that takes you to the blank page in the first place, and a resistance. (*DtP* 18)

The kind of writing Coetzee describes here is a meditative writing, especially when further taking into account his aforementioned comment that he "feel[s] a greater freedom to follow where [his] mind takes [him] when [he] is writing fiction than when [he is] writing criticism" (*DtP* 246).

The hovering, meditative phenomena treated in Coetzee's work described earlier can be analogized with his writing process as a searching, probing, exploratory, and fundamentally slow endeavor, while further parallels may be drawn concerning the aesthetic features of his texts. Writing as a slow process seems integral to the condensed, highly allusive, often elusive, and subtle complexities of Coetzee's style. His slow composition may be gleaned from a consideration of his archival material. The many drafts of Coetzee's works extant in the holdings of the Harry Ransom Center show his distinct, finely calibrated prose right from the beginning of his writing life as well as from the beginning of each individual work.[29] And yet, one witnesses how from draft to draft the form becomes simultaneously thicker and freer, richer with signification and so more conducive to meditative reflection. From revision to revision Coetzee's prose becomes more congealed, the putative effect that John in *Youth* calls the "hard, jeweller's craft of poetry" (*SPL* 163), and which he sees in the exquisitely molded and (often tortuously slowly written) prose of Flaubert.[30] The choice of words is not unimportant here; a closer look at this phrase discloses the formal density to which I refer. The *hard jeweller's craft of poetry* is a metaphor for the meticulous, myopic work, rigorously attentive to detail, which goes into the writing of a poem, but the phrasing itself is dense with allusions that comment on the kind of work referred to. A *jeweller's* craft includes the handling and

---

[29] The most comprehensive work published so far on Coetzee's creative process by drawing on the archival work is David Attwell's excellent critical biography *J. M. Coetzee & the Life of Writing: Face to Face with Time*. In a similar vein and with an extremely detailed view on style, though largely without available archival material, Jarad Zimbler's *J. M. Coetzee and the Politics of Style* closely analyzes Coetzee's aesthetic development by reading his South African works against the culture and politics of South Africa during the time of their composition.

[30] Shklovsky's ideas in "Art as Device" are very helpful regarding Coetzee's highly poetic style when Shklovsky writes that "the language of poetry may be said to be difficult, 'laborious,' impeding language" (1991, 13). Unfortunately, Shklovsky's strict distinction between poetry and prose is far too essentialist: "Poetic speech is *structured* speech. Prose, on the other hand, is ordinary speech: economical, easy, correct speech" (1991; original emphasis). Coetzee is a good example of how limiting Shklovsky's binarism is, which, of course, does not mean that Shklovsky's ideas are off limits for an analysis of prose.

shaping of diamonds, that highest crystalline condensation of carbon; it is an allusion which mirrors the crystallization and shaping of word, sound, and image that is poetry.[31]

The archival material illuminates Coetzee's writing process as precisely such a *hard jeweller's craft of poetry* in prose. Each work reveals itself to be finely wrought as if in a palimpsestic way, by which large chunks of text—protean ideas, meanings, and allusions—are consistently subsumed into smaller passages, or even sentences of the narratives. This may give an insight into the clear concision of Coetzee's writing. All of his works are brief, not one of them exceeds 300 pages—the longest is *The Childhood of Jesus* at 277 pages—and many remain under 200 pages (*Dusklands, In the Heart of the Country, Waiting for the Barbarians, Life & Times of Michael K, Foe, Age of Iron, Boyhood, Youth*). Paradoxically, the brevity of the texts makes them anything but slight. The condensation that has gone into the works during the composition gives them their crystalline character, a characteristic that provokes a slow consideration of the richness and density of the works.

Coetzee's personal archive reveals how the published texts assume their density and richness slowly, and how during the writing he imposes little restrictions on where the text might lead.[32] Frequently, he pursues vastly disparate ideas, even until very late into the writing, until gradually a formally and topically cogent work coagulates. The archival holdings of composition diaries, notebooks, and multiple drafts of the novels and memoirs characterize his writing process as a form of textual meditativeness during which the author hovers at length over ideas, probing them from various different angles. For example, the composition notebook and drafts[33] of *Life & Times of Michael K* reveal the novel's gestation under the sway of the initial plan to rewrite Heinrich von Kleist's novella *Michael*

---

[31] While the English etymology brings *poetry* close to *creating* and *making*, the German and the Dutch word for composing poetry is *dichten*. Coetzee is very aware of this when he comments on a translation by a poem from the Dutch, Gerrit Achterberg's "Ballade van de gasfitter": "English lacks a homonym to parallel Dutch *dichten*: (1) to seal (a hole), (2) to compose poetry (though, on the other hand, it possesses the notorious homophonic sequence *whole-hole-holy*)" (*DtP* 73; original emphases). When arguing that the poem revolves around this pun, Coetzee creates a nice analogy: "[T]he gasfitter sealing leaks is also the poet at work" (*DtP* 73). And he adds: "The craft of the gasfitter is the craft of *dichten*" (*DtP* 73). So is, as will be seen later, the act of reflecting on the manifold gaps in Coetzee's work. Coetzee's translation of Achterberg's poem is collected in Coetzee's collection of translations *Landscape with Rowers: Poetry from the Netherlands* (2004).

[32] In the composition diary kept during the writing of *Foe*, he notes: "17.iii.84 [...] With regard to the present book—which it appears I cannot stop working at—it would seem best to let it take the direction I am really interested in" (HRC, container 33, folder 6, p. 47f.).

[33] The collection holds seven handwritten drafts (including extensive revisions), dating from May 31, 1980 to July 28, 1982, plus two typed drafts with revisions from 1982 and 1983, respectively. The notebook consists of entries dated from "17.x.79" through "9.x.82" (HRC, container 33, folder 5).

Kohlhaas—the published novel retains the protagonist's initials—and to include an act of rebellion against the state of South Africa, an act of vengeance which, contrary to Kleist's text, is planned to occur at the end of the novel.[34] Initially, the protagonist was to be working on a translation of Kleist's novella:

> 4.ii.80 A man ("he") returns home one evening to find his home robbed and devastated. The devastation described at great length (say 10 pages). In his study the robber has shat, and then wiped himself with the typescript of a translation of Michael Kohlhaas.
>
> Hereafter he is possessed with a desire for justice or reparation.[35]

In the writing process the author pursues various strands of this idea: a protagonist writing a translation of Kleist's novella and seeking revenge for an attack on his home; the protagonist as a colored man called Albert who is, like Beckett's Malone, confined to a sickbed, from where he works on a verse translation of Kleist's novella,[36] while he is cared for by a woman (possibly his sister)[37] named Annie, whose monologue forms the narrative;[38] the story is narrated by a nine-year-old boy whose mother reads from Kleist's novella to him each night;[39] the novella is to be written in epistolary form and including letters written to Kleist himself.[40] Slowly, the initial idea of a violent act of resistance inherent in the

---

[34] "31.iii.81. [...] He goes into the mountains to declare his own republic. 'Citizen of the universe'" (HRC, container 33, folder 5, p. 24).

> 26.iv.81 There is an act of violence on K–'s part; the soldiers set about hunting him down; he retreats farther + deeper into the country, toward the Southern Mountains. He lives in caves, suffers terribly from hunger, has visions. One of his visions is of a Michael Kohlhaas revenge: gathering the outlaws of the mountains together and raiding the towns. (HRC, container 33, folder 5, p. 29)

Coetzee's interest in Kleist may also be gleaned from an exchange in the correspondence with Paul Auster, *Here and Now* (2013), where Coetzee answers Auster's admiration for Kleist in a letter from April 17, 2010:

> As for Kleist, I agree with every word you say. To open a page by Kleist is to have it brought home to you that there exists an A league of writers, which has very few members and in which the game being played is very different from the game in the more comfortable B league to which one is accustomed: much harder, much quicker, much smarter, for much bigger stakes. (*H&N* 147)

[35] HRC, container 33, folder 5, p. 2.

[36] Ibid., p. 3. See also the draft "Version 1" (Container 7, folder 1).

[37] HRC, container 7, folder 1, p. 1f. (entry dated "31.v.80").

[38] Ibid.; titled "Monologue of Annie."

[39] "21.x.80. The narrator is a nine-year-old boy whose mother has a bad leg and has kept him out of school to look after her. He is a thief, a prostitute, etc., but also of angelic directness and intelligence. He has dragged him in his box-car from the embattled township to Sea Point to win peace and quiet. His mother reads to him from the story of Michael (Kohlhaas) every night; he spends the day wondering what will happen next. [? He also tries to teach himself to read, but cannot, because he does not realize that the text is in German.]" (HRC, container 33, folder 5, p. 9; original square brackets).

[40] "13.x.80 It is all written in the form of letters, including letters to Kleist" (HRC, container 33, folder 5, p. 9).

Kohlhaas idea and the repose inherent in the character of Albert are fused into the character of Michael K who resists through slowness.[41]

The composition stages of *Waiting for the Barbarians* undergo similar explorations and erasures. I have already indicated the steps on the way to the published novel, as the drafts slowly find the present tense and the uncertain landscape. The Harry Ransom Center houses ten handwritten drafts of the novel (though not all of equal length), lettered from A to J. The first four drafts are all written predominately in the past tense, with occasional swerves into the present in moments of character reflection or through free indirect discourse. Draft A consists of one examination book from the University of Cape Town—Coetzee's chief material for composition until the 1990s (and possibly a preference which the proto-K, Albert, shares with his author while writing his Kohlhaas poem)[42]—comprising merely a few days of writing (20/9/77 to 24/9/77). The very first notes toward the novel, on a piece of printer paper, dated "20/9/77," are pasted into the notebook and reveal the setting of the novel as Robben Island during a state of emergency (A1–2):[43] "From the open window of the guardroom Manos Milis watched the refugees trudge up the road ~~from the jetty to the~~ that led from the jetty to the ~~prison~~ gate" (A1–1).[44] The first sentence sets the draft's beginning inside a guardroom which affords a view outside—a point of view that resurfaces in the published novel when the Magistrate sees the "barbarian" girl left behind in the town. And the first sentence already hints at the topical slowness involved (the refugees' *trudging*). But the setting is entirely different and represents the reverse of the final novel. Where the published work is set in the desert, this first draft is set by the water, in the harbor area of the prison island in Table Bay.

The following pages of the first draft are centered on the protagonist Manos Milis, who has come from Port Elizabeth (A1–3) to Robben Island and is

---

[41] Attwell also analyzes Coetzee's engagement with Kleist via the archival material, and notes that "it was the picaresque quality of Kleist's novel that interested Coetzee as much as its theme. He sought to replicate Kleist's *swift pacing* as he began drafting *Michael K*" (2015, 131; added emphasis). The way Coetzee, in fact, inverts the Kohlhaas theme of violent resistance, so he also seems to invert Kleist's swift style—both inversions fuse into the meditative form and content of the published novel. Peter Horn's fascinating essay "Michael K: Pastiche, Parody or the Inversion of Michael Kohlhaas" makes a similar argument, while limiting his analyses mostly to thematic and philosophical similarities and dissimilarities between the two texts.

[42] "1.vi.80 [...] I saw you huddled over your board with your pencil and paper, with the little exercise books you love to write ~~it~~ in [...]" (HRC, container 7, folder 1, p. 2).

[43] HRC, container 5, folder 1. Note: Given the large number of quotations from various different drafts, the following citation convention will be used in-text for the sake of convenience: upper case letter and number of notebook (A1) followed by a number after the hyphen to indicate a page. If a notebook is numbered A1, as is the case here, this need not mean that there are more than one; it is used simply for consistency.

[44] All deletions will be reproduced exactly as they are in the archival materials.

engaged in work on a book (A1–3). The island in this first draft is only a transit space for refugees, a middle space, a "halfway station" (A1–2). The refugees are shipped to the island and wait to be taken away again; even the officials wait to be taken away on a ship initially called the *Leonardo Da Vinci* (A1–1). In this sketch the topical emphases on waiting and slowness are present already, though more in the form of an instrumental sense of waiting, a teleological waiting, since everyone on the island has but one goal: to get off the island.

Through the autodiegetic focalization of Manos Milis's reflections on the slowness and emptiness of his life, the novel shades into the philosophical in its evocation of basic existential questions, as in this example:

> [...] It is important to me to fill the days. I do not want to think, when I go to sleep, "Today I only died, today there was no living for me." These people think their one life has ended, in South Africa, and they are hoping for another life to begin in Europe. In between these lives, then, they are only dying. I want to know I am living, all the time. (A1–4)[45]

Milis's reflection—possibly in a diary or a letter, though this is unverifiable—picks up on a generality of the transitoriness of life, but does so during a moment of inertia. Through the juxtaposition of two lives, one in South Africa, in the past, and one in Europe, in the future, the time on Robben Island is turned into a time of slow presence, a moment split between what is no more and what is not yet, a moment in the interstice of the present, to which the expression *in between these lives* alerts very clearly. This passage in the present tense in an otherwise past tense narrative further emphasizes this moment as a time of slow waiting through the formal choice of tense. But while in the published narrative the present is used in a different, more meditative way as a gradual *waiting with* (as I have argued before), here, the present moment is clearly constructed as a *waiting for*—a *hoping for another life*—and is thus stirred toward an instrumental sense of waiting. Hence, this present moment could be regarded as the form of death that Milis describes, a form of enforced stasis that has political connotations of suppression and entrapment. This is a form of deprivation from the meditative realm of thinking, which the setting of Robben Island, as the colonial island of imprisonment and isolation that it used to be, powerfully emphasizes. Even though the topical emphasis is on the island, at the center in the present of the people's lives, the present moment as lived experience is neither emphasized nor

---

[45] HRC, container 5, folder 1. This is the first paragraph of two pages of composition dated "24/9/77". The passage does not clarify when and under which circumstances they are stated; the quotation marks represent them as direct speech, though immediately after this passage the text returns to Manos Milis's interior monologue, in past tense.

privileged, as perhaps it cannot be to prisoners, since a prison is a place which chains convicts to the present moment while simultaneously robbing them of it. The present as lived experience, which potentially has the power to be freed from the lure of the past and the future, will only be foregrounded with the meditative resonance in the later stages of the novel.

During Milis's time of waiting, in draft B,[46] a young girl arrives on Robben Island (B1–6), we find out that Manos is a Greek citizen (B1–5), and the book he is writing is possibly a translation of or a tract on the Greek author Kritoboulos ("Often he spent whole days there [in the vacated cab of a crane], working on Kritoboulos" [B1–5]). As in many of his works, Coetzee here foregrounds the *act*, the *presence* of writing: Susan Barton is engaged in and reflecting on the process of writing; Lurie shaping and reshaping his opera; Costello frantically rewriting her speech; and even the Magistrate in the final *Waiting* reflects on the writing process and its ethical implications, so that writing—a form of communication slower than speech—is dealt with through a slow form of thinking, reflection.[47] And Milis's writing of the book is likewise slow, which is implied by the reference to a long time spent on it (*whole days*) and through the progressive tense, foregrounding the idea that working on the book is a gradual activity of exploration, searching, maybe

---

[46] Three notebooks: B1 (24/9/77–2/10/77); B2 (4/10/77–11/10/77); B3 (12/10/77–17/10/77) (HRC, container 5, folder 1).

[47] Before the Magistrate sets out to travel to the so-called "barbarians," he reflects that "there are two documents to compose" (*WfB* 62), the first is a letter, and:

> What the second document is to be I do not yet know. A testament? A memoir? A confession? A history of thirty years on the frontier? All that day I sit in a trance at my desk staring at the empty white paper, waiting for words to come. A second day passes in the same way. On the third day I surrender, put the paper back in the drawer, and make preparations to leave. It seems appropriate that a man who does not know what to do with the woman in his bed should not know what to write. (*WfB* 62f.)

Later, after having returned from the "barbarians," having endured torture, and after he is returned to an altered state of life, we read:

> It seems right that, as a gesture to the people who inhabited the ruins in the desert, we too ought to set down a record of settlement to be left for posterity buried under the walls of our town; and to write such a history no one would seem to be better fitted than our last magistrate. But when I sit down at my writing-table, wrapped against the cold in my great old bearskin, with a single candle (for tallow too is rationed) and a pile of yellowed documents at my elbow, what I find myself beginning to write is not the annals of an imperial outpost or an account of how the people of that outpost spent their last year composing their souls as they waited for the "barbarians". "No one who paid a visit to this oasis," I write, "failed to be struck by the charm of life here. We lived in the time of the seasons, of the harvests, of the migrations of the waterbirds. We lived with nothing between us and the stars. We would have made any concession, had we only known what, to go on living here. This was paradise on earth." For a long while I stare at the plea I have written. It would be disappointing to know that the poplar slips I have spent so much time on contain a message as devious, as equivocal, as reprehensible as this. (*WfB* 168f.)

of transforming (regardless whether it is a translation or an essay).[48] At the same time, real transformation with political resonance occurs, if it occurs at all, only internally, in Milis's mind, through reflection. This is contrasted by the emphasis on external stasis, which is further highlighted topically, since the ship (now called the *ANACONDA*), which could take the islanders to freedom, is stuck in the harbor (B1-4f.) for a Kafkaesque bureaucratic reason, a "refuellery dispute" (B1-5).

In draft B the topical stasis is not mirrored at the level of the narrative tense. The past tense somewhat assuages the sense of being stuck, since the past implies the closure of an event, and one could infer that the time of stasis has now passed. Drafts C[49] and D[50] are also told generally in the past tense, though draft D occasionally shifts into the present.[51] The first three examination books of draft E[52] are told in a mixture of past tense and present tense. However, from notebook E4[53] onward the novel is told exclusively in the present tense. In notebook E4 one comes across the telling expression "the ache of time" (E4-36). This little expression is missing from the published novel, as if the literal reference to the slow passage of time that marks life on the frontier had slowly been subsumed into the form of the work itself. This is suggested by the use of the present tense and its bringing the reader closer to the character's present moment, which effects the above-mentioned sense of *waiting with* that the characters and readers experience. The experience of *the ache of time* is assimilated into the form of the work rather than being represented at the level of the content.

The act of fictionalization is criticized here against an implied Lukácsian ethics of bearing witness, although a further implication is that writing as a form of epistemological objectivity might be a fiction in itself, since the Magistrate seems almost automatically to idealize the town, the time, the people. A synthesis, an ethical judgment of which action, which way of writing, is the "right" one, is withheld, while readers are invited to follow either reading as their own moral criteria allow. The Magistrate implicitly describes the act of writing as a slow process in so far as it is always up to counter-versions, reversals, and erasures. In such ways, the works often subsume (or anticipate) at the topical level the act of reading as a process of co-producing a *writerly* text.

[48] It is not irrelevant that the book Milis is writing is on a thinker engaged with political transformation.

[49] One notebook (18/10/77) (HRC, container 5, folder 1).

[50] One notebook (23/10/77–30/10/77). The notebook seems to consist of a different ensemble of characters, and a different setting, which could however still take place on the island under the same conditions (HRC, container 5, folder 1).

[51] The draft consists of a scene between two women sitting at a desk facing each other. The narrative is told almost exclusively in long passages of dialogue, though one of the women seems to be the girl who arrived on the island in the previous drafts and who had sex with Manos Milis in B1 (B1-22), where the massage motif of the final novel is already registered, even if here the girl massages the man (HRC, container 5, folder 1).

[52] E1 (4/12/77–11/12/77); E2 (12/12/77–18/12/77); E3 (19/12/77–27/12/77) (HRC, container 5, folder 1).

[53] E4 (28/12/77–5/1/78) (HRC, container 5, folder 1).

Of the three further drafts[54] extant in the archive, none will ever return to the past tense after December 28, 1977, which marks the first passage of notebook E4. One day earlier, in his composition diary kept while writing the novel, Coetzee's extraordinary self-reflexivity and self-doubt about his writing process give way to a note of optimism and achievement. In an entry dated "27/12/77," he writes: "Going OK. Hard to believe I have at last found the form I wanted."[55]

What will have become apparent from these examples is the gradual arriving at a form suitable to relate the experience of the slowness of a *waiting with* outlined earlier, as well as the laborious work that has gone into the working out of this novel. The various ways of testing, of trying, of beginning again and anew reveal a search for something desired, but something which is yet unknown and has therefore to be pursued through tarrying reflection, and a form of inquiring writing. Writing also becomes an act of waiting, an act of active waiting, during which something may arrive. The art and craft visible from the archival material suggest what Coetzee has once called "imagining th[e] unimaginable, imagining a form of address that permits the play or *writing* to start taking place" (*DtP* 68; original emphasis).

After the writing has started to take place and begun to imagine the unimaginable, what I have called a meditative writing has come to a desired goal in the form which the author has sought and at last found. It is time, then, to allow a different form of meditative thinking to take place, and to formulate how the topical engagements with slowness in Coetzee's works are merely one aspect of a slow oeuvre, and how a wide range of slowing devices at the level of the form contribute to what may be called the slow philosophy of J. M. Coetzee. This philosophy, however, is not the author's alone, it emerges in the reader's mind by being, as Éamonn Dunne has called it, "open[…] to something to come, waiting with a nonpassive endurance for something to happen" (2013, 48)—it emerges in slow reading.

---

[54] These are F (F1 and F2); G (G1); H (HRC, container 5, folder 1; container 5, folder 2; container 5, folder 3; container 6, folder 1). I and J are typed drafts.
[55] HRC, container 33, folder 3, n.p.

2

A Slow Method for a Slow Man—Reading Coetzee, Slowly

Slow reading is a philosophical and phenomenological way of reading that tries to be as receptive as possible to a literary work and deeply responsive to its devices and effects. Its philosophical character does not aim at identifying philosophical questions and topics in the text, let alone answering or resolving them. Slow reading as philosophical reading is, first of all, to read phenomenologically in an ethical way, to approach a text as one may approach a stranger, appreciating the infinite aspects that will remain forever occluded about this stranger, but to appreciate also that approaching this person carefully, with the greatest possible attention and time, remaining with that stranger in a slow and patient way— that such an encounter may permit an intense and meaningful experience of who is actually before one, what is actually there, who this stranger is—and what this text is. While a text is not a person, this image helps to recall one thing: When approaching a person, one rarely asks what a person *means*. Slow reading does not ask what a text means, as the search for meaning implies arrival, whereas slow reading does not wish to arrive, it does not primarily wish to get reading over with, but it wants to remain in reading. It follows an ideal of reading thoughtfully and attentively at all times, in a potentially unending way. It therefore does not primarily ask how a text can be *interpreted*, but rather how it can be *reflected* upon, how it can be *responded* to, what its *effects* are, and how these effects, reflections, and responses can be *described*.

To describe slow reading and to perform a slow reading of Coetzee's work, it may be ideal to begin with a novel which encompasses many of the implied and inferred figurations and functions of slowness explored earlier: *Slow Man*. The topical emphasis on slowness is implied by the title and the amputation of the slow man's—Paul Rayment's—right leg. The topical manifestations of slowness are underscored by a staging of slowness at the level of the form. The most relevant of these aspects will be explored in the following by applying the method of slow reading outlined earlier to the 2005 novel, while this chapter's passing through the individual aspects of the slowing nature of Coetzee's form prefigures the structure of the following chapters; these aspects are: questions, sentences, literalness, gaps, dialogue, endings, worlds.

Slow Man marks a shift in Coetzee's writing life toward what may be called a *late style*,[1] a more literal style, more minimalist, slower, and at the same time more meditative regarding matters both philosophical and literary. My understanding of late style may be framed by two comments Coetzee makes in the Auster correspondence:

> It is not uncommon for writers, as they age, to get impatient with the so-called poetry of language and go for a more stripped-down style ("late style"). (*H&N* 88)

> In the case of literature, late style, to me, starts with an ideal of a simple, subdued, unornamented language and a concentration on questions of real import, even questions of life and death. (*H&N* 97)

By this yardstick, Coetzee's style has been late from the first work on. And yet, a certain flatness in the language may be perceived in the later works, a flatness which paradoxically provokes a deeper involvement in the literary text and makes those few passages of florid, ornamented prose stand out only more forcefully. A shift toward a more literal use of language is by no means a limitation of signification, the way minimalism is not a curtailing of but an intensifying of signification; and because minimalism proceeds in broadly slow and quiet strokes, it creates a sense of expectation in the reader, possibly along the lines of Miller's aforementioned paradoxical *expectation of the unexpected*.

Late style unlimited to temporal lateness, as being situated at the end of an author's oeuvre, but as an aesthetic may be illuminated by Edward Said's—and in extension Theodor W. Adorno's—notions of "artistic lateness not as harmony and resolution but as intransigence, difficulty, and unresolved contradiction" ([1963] 1992, 7). To Said's enumeration I would add slowness and propound that this style has been present in Coetzee from the beginning formally, but that in his later works, it shades back into the topical aspects of his texts. Beginning with *Slow Man* this topical slowness (and lateness) expresses itself in a subtle paring

---

[1]   For an exploration of Coetzee's late style, see Julian Murphet's article "Coetzee and Late Style: Exile within the Form" (2011). Unfortunately, the article ultimately tries to justify a re-allegorizing of Coetzee's works via Adorno's. With reference to *Elizabeth Costello*, Murphet even goes so far as to claim that the "intensity of vision" in the Lady Chandos Letter "is one of *unabating allegory*, where everything means something else" (2011, 95; added emphasis). This view is pertinent in one respect, if one acknowledges the arbitrariness of the signifier and that everything, be it signifier or text, may be read in a variety of ways. The problem is the exclusivity of Murphet's claim, when allegory in Coetzee is never a case of exclusivity but one of simultaneity. See Chapter 6 of this work.

down of the plot to a seemingly bare scaffold of incident, an increased slowing down of his characters, and a topical tarrying in plot development.

Though the topical catalyst in *Slow Man* is Paul's accident and the resulting amputation of his leg, the plot is slowed down parallel to Paul's slowness after the amputation, and it is only Elizabeth Costello who attempts to accelerate his life and the narrative. Paradoxically—and humorously—Costello herself has lost her magic; she is herself slow and tarrying in finding out where to go with Paul's narrative, and so with his life. At the same time, Costello's advent heightens the ruminative quality of the novel through the metafictional meditations by herself and by the text. So, the novel becomes an oscillatory work of dynamic stillness that exists as if in between the bookends of the Beckettian paradox "I can't go on, I'll go on."

Formally, the novel is marked by frequent jumps in time and setting, beginning with a hole in the narrated time through Paul's loss of consciousness after his accident; the dialogue is bare and frequently lacks speech tags; the arbitrary relationship of signifier and signified is foregrounded, while a free play between the literal and figural meanings of words is brought to the fore; and a profusion of unanswered questions gives the novel its ultimately inquiring quality. All of these are well-worn paths in Coetzee country up to this novel, but they seem more deeply trodden here, in an even more self-conscious and explicit fashion, than in his previous work. This is most apparent in the text's engagement with the genre and form of the novel itself via Costello's writing of the narrative (or of Paul's life) as the story is unfolding.[2] This way, the novel keeps the reader twice removed from the real author, J. M. Coetzee, and productively estranged from the text itself. The text's metafictionality is highlighted more fundamentally than in the now familiar ploy of an author's apparent self-insertion into the narrative, such as in Paul Auster's *City of Glass* (1985), for the reason that, quite literally, Costello could not have inserted herself into the narrative of *Slow Man*, since she is not the novel's real author. In fact, the apparent author of the novel, Elizabeth Costello, is presented to the reader as the novel's implied author and so she surreptitiously replaces the implied author J. M. Coetzee with the effect that the *real* author J. M. Coetzee is further distanced from his work.[3] So, the novel realizes one further level of mystification than even the metafictionally complex *Elizabeth Costello* does, and this is further increased through the complication that both Paul and Costello are apparently involved in writing and being written (Wicomb 2010, 216).

---

[2] "Elizabeth Costello reappears as a character, but also, apparently, as the author of the fiction" (Head 2009, 85).

[3] See also Hayes (2010, 224).

This has a seemingly solipsistic significance when thinking about the real author, but it also designates the literary realms of Coetzee's later works as ever more self-referential and related to the real world in ever more complicated ways than his earlier novels are.[4] Fiction becomes a stage where aspects of reality are played out, and so fiction transcends fiction as a mirror of reality or as a normative lectern from which guidance in the real world is proclaimed.

The implied project of viewing the novel as "a rival to history" (*NT* 3), that is very much related to Coetzee's early works, is developed and even surmounted from *Slow Man* onwards by a significant step, in the sense that the novel situates itself as an exploration of the unimaginable, rather than the engagement with reality and history, that is with the (mimetically) imaginable.[5] *Slow Man*, for the first time in Coetzee's *fiction*, explicitly addresses this project of imagining the unimaginable that is central to Coetzee's work: "Unimaginable perhaps; but the unimaginable is there to be imagined" (*S* 44). While, on the one hand, the setting of the novel is Adelaide, Australia, on the other hand, the setting of the novel is literature, a space where language, fiction, and metafiction engage in a play of signification. Although Coetzee's works have always carried the subtext of exploring of the significance of writing (both as the act of writing and in Barthes's sense of *écriture*), the late works foreground writing through a self-conscious exploration of authorship that depends on the differences between the implied fictional author, the implied real author, and the real author of the text.[6]

---

[4] This becomes more accentuated, and likewise more playful, in the self-referentiality of the house of mirrors of *Summertime*, where historical facts are altered, where characters are named Denoël and Nascimento, while there is constant talk of Christmas and the Coetzee family always gathers at the idealized farm of Voëlfontein for Christmas, where the vegetarian Coetzee is a passionate carnivore, and where J. M. Coetzee's colleague in Stellenbosch is named Martin J.

[5] In the *Salmagundi* interview Coetzee, echoing Shelley, states: "I have never been entirely persuaded that writers are the unacknowledged legislators of mankind" (Coetzee and Scott 1997, 102). See also Coetzee in conversation with Jane Poyner: "It is hard for fiction to be good fiction while it is in the service of something else" (Coetzee and Poyner 2006, 21). For a deeper engagement with the problems of straightforward historical readings of Coetzee, see, for example, Macaskill:

> Do Coetzee's ('materialist') critics not make a […] mistake by thinking of his novels as works from which 'history' (as conceived of by materialist historiography) has been 'omitted,' instead of recognizing here an entirely 'rival,' alternately derived form of expression? And does not even Attwell's more recent reading—an alternative to the orthodoxy of materialist critique—abnegate the possibilities of seriously considering Coetzee's expressive practice as a rival to the discourse of history, favoring instead an analysis determined to uncover a deep-structure discourse of history from which Coetzee's narrative expression is supposed transformationally to derive? (1994, 451)

Attwell's essay to which Macaskill refers is "The Problem of History in the Fiction of J. M. Coetzee" (1991). For a consideration of Coetzee's idea of the novel as a rival to history, see Hayes (2010, esp. 77–80) and Attridge (2004a, 14). See also Bradshaw (2010, 13).

[6] *The Childhood of Jesus* is a good example of the gap that yawns between ideas attributed to the public intellectual J. M. Coetzee and a narrative world that seems, at a first glance, an ideal state befitting his attested beliefs, but implicitly exposes how faulty such author-intentional thinking actually is.

Slow Man consistently unworks authorship by a paradoxical highlighting of authorship, which is further emphasized by the auto-intertextual reference to *Elizabeth Costello*. The novel thus dissolves authority in a politically resonant way, since the novel's engagement with the real world is at best tenuous—its topical exploration of copies is a comment on the purported mimetic quality of art. At the same time, the novel's ties to the real world, of which the novel is a part and from which it is apart—the way a copy is a part of as well as apart from the original—are never fully severed. This aspect, a literary text's relationship to real "questions of real import, even questions of life and death" (*H&N* 97), has already been explored explicitly through *Elizabeth Costello*, since the work speaks about real ethical problems in a normative way, but does so through the estranging and not unproblematic character and voice of Costello. What critics of *Slow Man* have seen as no more than a "pointless exercise in cerebral metafiction" (Gurr 2007, 95), is, in fact, a play with ways of estrangement that develop the idea of the novel as a rival to history by an engagement, possibly above all else, with the form and genre of the novel.[7]

Coetzee's tenth novel heralds a late style that seems both customarily controlled and highly provisional: sparse, flat, finely nuanced, and yet subject to multiple enigmas and erasures. The novel's interplay of form and content creates a style that revolves around the various functions and figurations of slowness in Coetzee's oeuvre. The content is overcast with finitude and effacement, yet the inquiring character is as strong as it has been from Coetzee's first published fiction, in the text's mode of reflexivity developed along *questions*.

---

[7] Gurr's essay "aims to show that such an assessment is most likely the result of having overlooked a number of complex and telling intertextual games, which virtually make this novel a key exponent in the genre I would like to term 'unobtrusive metafiction'. The novel [...] virtually normalizes metafictional elements and makes them part and parcel of the repertoire of novelistic devices" (2007, 95). Gurr's argument goes in the same direction I am going with regard to a dissolution of authorship through an attention drawn to authorship, which has the effect of making metafiction seem more natural. While Gurr's essay is also important with regard to the political dimensions of the novel, part of the reading is also concerned with intentionalist and allegorical readings, which assume a character of the instrumental that I avoid. Gurr sees the novel as "a continuation of Coetzee's long-standing engagement with South Africa and with his own position as—inescapably— also a South African writer" (2007, 95f.). While there is some pragmatic use to Gurr's statements—a person's country of origin cannot be escaped any more than a person's certainty of death can— such an argument, when referring to the real author as opposed to the characters, is, ultimately, not productive, since it presses a novel that is set in Australia and has no immediate connections with South Africa whatsoever back into a South African context. Gurr is detrimental to his own argument here, since he foregrounds the real author J. M. Coetzee, when the author who is really foregrounded is Elizabeth Costello—incidentally, another Australian, not a South African. A connection to South Africa could, in my view, only be supported *ex negativo*. Patrick Hayes argues that in the:

> "Australian fiction—*Elizabeth Costello, Slow Man*, and *Diary of a Bad Year*—Coetzee has moved away from an overt concern with the politics of difference and the problem of inhabiting a radically intercultural society such as South Africa, to focus on the different, though related, moral debate over what it means to live in a cultural space dominated by the sceptical, rational, and egalitarian side of post-Enlightenment political culture" (2010, 223).

Each of Coetzee's texts is woven through with different questions posed by the various focalizers in such a way that the question evinces a reflexive disposition by the characters, by the text, and by the readers toward both of these. The questions asked by and of the focalizers are rarely answered in the text, and so they effect a mode of questioning in the reader as well, since the reader plays these questions back to the text both as if she had asked them and as if they were asked of her. The questions posed explicitly by the text without answers create gaps in the narrative, which function as defamiliarizing devices to draw the reader into a reflexive mode. Since any question is by nature reflexive and any reflection is by nature slow, the questions that seem to puncture the narratives in fact punctuate them, and do so by halting the reader to a fleeting stillness. This ruminative structure is responsive to slow reading, since the staged intra-textual reflexion activates an inquiring way of reading. In Coetzee's work the hermeneutic question *what does X mean?* is frequently frustrated, while the questions *what is the function of X?* and *what is the effect of X?* lead to more productive encounters between reader and text. These encounters are meditative encounters rather than instrumental ones, as they effect inquiry in a ruminative rather than a teleological way.

During one of the many moments when Paul is irritated by "the Costello woman," as he calls her, he asks himself a question: "*Why, why?* Why does she ask a question and then not give the answer?'" (*S* 119; original emphasis). Paul's annoyance with Costello's questions is expressed paradoxically as a question, as what Gottfried Benn termed "the children's query" (1987, 255), the question *why*, notoriously difficult to answer, or entirely unanswerable. *Why are there birds, why is there pain?* These questions do not lead to satisfactory answers, they lead to further questions and reflections. This is probably why, in *The Childhood of Jesus* Simón—who has no patience for philosophizing (*CoJ* 122)—is so irritated by young David's inquisitive nature: "*Why? Why? Why?* That is not how we carry on a proper conversation" (*CoJ* 172; original emphasis). As we consider Paul's why-question in *Slow Man* we must accept that it remains unanswered. It is worth noting that Paul asks this question while he is reading. Browsing through Costello's books, he thumbs through her novel *The Fiery Furnace* and comes across a child forming little animal figurines from plasticine and wondering why the colors of the various plasticines have "*bled into each other,*" wondering "*why does the bright grow dull and the dull never bright?*" (*S* 119; original emphases). In the first instance, this question is asked by Costello's text, which Paul is reading; it leads to a further question that Paul is asking himself or, nonplussed as he is by Costello's style as much as by the woman, that he is asking the text he is reading: "Why does she ask a question and then not give the answer?" (*S* 119).

Paul, in turn, does give an answer, though curiously not to *his* question (*why does Costello ask a question and withhold the answer?*) but to the question in the text (*why does the bright grow dull and the dull never bright?*):

> The answer is simple: the red and the blue and the green will never return because of entropy, which is irreversible and irrevocable and rules the universe. Even a literary person ought to know that, even a lady novelist. (*S* 119)

Slow Man pretends to give an answer to the why-question posed by Costello's text, *The Fiery Furnace*, while subtly sidestepping the why-question posed by Paul. The novel feigns to give an answer to a question by answering another question and thus keeping the more important question untouched, left to linger in the reader's mind: why does Costello always ask questions without giving answers to them? It might be added that this question may likewise be read as a self-referential asking of Coetzee's *Slow Man* and his oeuvre as a whole. One might entertain an answer, though it is not as simple as Paul deems his, and one might say that, first and foremost, the mode and the situation of the query are foregrounded, while the supplication of an exegesis is withheld. Even when Coetzee's works seem to give answers, they frequently subvert the questions, or pose further questions. The reader is asked to ask a question: Am I satisfied with the answer given by the text, or do I remain in an inquiring mode?

Costello is a postmodern novelist, implicitly concerned with entropy—even if Paul does not believe her capable of it—and explicitly more concerned with asking questions than positing statements. By supplying an answer that is not an answer and only a restructuring of the question in the reader's mind, Coetzee's text has its metafictional cake and eats it too: it answers the why-question concerning entropy posed in Costello's text, but leaves unanswered the why-question concerning why-questions, namely *Why does she ask a question and then not give the answer?* By answering as complicated a question as *what is entropy?* the text (*Slow Man*) distracts the reader's attention, leads it away from the question Paul has really asked but not answered: why the profusion of questions in a literary text? Because of Costello's metafictional position in the novel, Paul's question may be transformed in the reader's mind and asked about the text she is reading, not least because at this point in the narrative, the reader is in the same position as Paul, as if glancing over Paul's shoulders during the act of reading, while reading herself.

The questioning awakened in the reader's mind occurs in a ruminative and meditative way, as it demands for a philosophical mode of reflecting on the text. The method of slow reading that is a reflexive inquiry into the text as well as the reader's own processes of perception is to be understood in light of a comment by Coetzee in his article "Farm Novel and Plaasroman," in *White Writing*: "Our craft is all in reading *the other*: gaps, inverses, undersides, the veiled, the dark, the buried, the feminine; alterities" (*WW* 81; original emphasis). Coetzee's statement here is still informed by a hermeneutics of suspicion, the kind of criticism that he will later abandon (*DtP* 196). Nevertheless, the idea of *reading the other* should not be understood as a binary-breaking teleological project that would eventually be concluded, but rather as a lasting project of deconstructing shifting binaries, subverting or inverting them and exploring them in meditative ways, so that discourse is stimulated ever anew. In my understanding, *reading the other* indicates not only the topical stagings of alterity in the novels, but also the receptiveness to a text's otherness, as well as a reading that continually unworks its own presumptions and deductions, a reading that always questions itself, that takes into account other responses to the text as well, that takes into account *the other reading*. A slow reading of Coetzee's work questions the text in a phenomenological way, without trying suspiciously to resolve the text's ambiguities, and it permits being questioned by the text in an ethical way, by keeping ambiguity alive and submitting oneself, to borrow an expression from Hillis Miller, to "the power of the words of the text over the mind and words of the reader" (2005, 58). Reading of this kind is explored topically in *The Childhood of Jesus* when Simón explains reading to young David: "For real reading you have to submit to what is written on the page" (*CoJ* 165). While the metaphorical language of submitting may signal toward a rhetoric of deep reading or toward the Ricœurian hermeneutics of suspicion, which burrows beneath the text to mine its meanings, reading of the slow ilk instead wishes to avoid digging beneath a text's surface and so to avoid "overcoming" a text. Slow reading instead wishes to "stay inside a text," as Stephen Best's and Sharon Marcus's "surface reading" intends as well (2009, 6). The animus in what Best and Marcus call "symptomatic reading" (2009, 2), a reformulation of various suspicious and instrumental forms of reading, implies an "overcoming" of the text and, in extension, an overcoming of reading. The method of slow reading prefers to over-read a text rather than to overcome it, to consider slowly and intensely what is actually there rather than to infer latent meanings. This reading is a method by which "the work can be," in the words of Susan Sontag, "just what it is" ([1961] 2009, 11).[8]

---

[8] Recent arguments against symptomatic reading are also found in Rita Felski's "Suspicious Minds" (2011) and her impassioned manifesto *Uses of Literature* (2008), as well as Heather Love's "Close but not Deep: Literary Ethics and the Descriptive Turn" (2010). What Best and Marcus refer to as symptomatic reading "encompasses an interpretive method that argues the most interesting aspect of a text is what it represses" (2009, 1). The problems with such readings is their shifting the significance of a work away from text-intrinsic considerations and outside to extrinsic meanings

Permitting a work to be just what it is implies a curious and inquiring comportment to a literary text, toward even the smallest aspects of its form.

In Coetzee's work, one of the smallest of such aspects which slows down the reading process and gives rise to philosophical reflection is present in his *sentences*.

> The blow catches him from the right, sharp and surprising and painful, like a bolt of electricity, lifting him up off the bicycle. *Relax!* He tells himself as he flies through the air (*flies through the air with the greatest of ease!*), and indeed he can feel his limbs go obediently slack. *Like a cat* he tells himself: *roll, then spring to your feet, ready for what comes next.* The unusual word *limber* or *limbre* is on the horizon too. (*S* 1; original emphases)

The first paragraph of *Slow Man* lays out the central topical concerns of the novel in such a way that a later rereading reveals a gradual bodying forth of these topics as if from the first sentence onwards, a bodying forth that curiously springs from a moment of a body breaking down. The effects of the accident have their origins in this first sentence, this first chapter, to which Paul literally refers again later (*S* 1; 14), as will be discussed in more detail later. The suggestion to *Relax!* heralds a slowing down, which is here positively linked with a sense of freedom; but because this freedom later takes the shape of a concrete constraint, his amputation, the suggestion to relax also becomes a command—Paul is *forced* to relax. At the same time, *Relax!* may also be read as a request, an invitation to the reader to remain with and inside the text, as in Italo Calvino's metafictional novel *If on a winter's night a traveller* (1979), which begins: "You are about to

---

and shows how arbitrary readings may become once a text's significance is suspected in what a text does *not* say. In the process the serious study of literature and, potentially all reading, may become diluted, capricious, and instrumental. In *Doubling the Point* Coetzee has already inveighed against a critical (and, indeed an existential) impetus whose goal is conclusive demystification and would constitute the end of inquiry, the end of reflection. He notes: "I no longer see opening up the mystifications in which ordinary life is wrapped as a necessary aim, or indeed an obligation of criticism" (*DtP* 106). Coetzee challenges a critical attitude whose goal is to uncover the *deeper truths* beneath writing and propounds a deep *suspicion of suspiciousness* (*DtP* 106), a suspicion of suspicious reading "whose climactic gesture is always a triumphant tearing-off" (*DtP* 106). Rather than a teleological searching with a *tearing-off* as its *climactic gesture*, Best and Marcus's similar proposition emphasizes a phenomenological attention to what is there by offering a rejoinder to traditional views that "the surface is associated with the superficial and deceptive, with what can be perceived without close examination and, implicitly, would turn out to be false upon closer scrutiny" (2009, 4). Consequently, the authors hold that "[a] surface is what insists on being looked *at* rather than what we must train ourselves to see *through*" (2009, 9; original emphasis). The very simple alternative to a seeing through or the aforementioned grafting on of a theoretical surcharge of possibly arbitrary ideas, an alternative to imposing onto or excavating from the text is simply *description*. Through a detailed and rigorous description of the singularity of a literary event, reading can become more receptive to the text *as such* rather than whatever may or may not be latent in the text. And because anything *as such* is very difficult to trace and describe, a reading that attends to the surface needs to proceed slowly.

begin reading Italo Calvino's new novel, *If on a winter's night a traveler*. Relax. Concentrate. Dispel every other thought. Let the world around you fade" (1998, 3).

In *Slow Man's* first sentence the hard jeweler's craft of poetry is at work, as its extreme condensation has resonance throughout the text, not least because Costello repeats it later on (*S* 81). While the first paragraph suggests and estranges in productive ways, the structure of the sentences is particularly slowing of our reading and, conversely, receptive to slow reading: "The blow catches him from the right, sharp and surprising and painful, like a bolt of electricity, lifting him up off the bicycle." The syntax is quite typical of Coetzee's works in the sense that it decelerates the reading speed. What is being described is a jarring, violent, and destructive impact on Paul's body: a car crashing into him from the right. However, the form of the sentence does nothing to suggest the harsh rapidity involved in such a moment. In fact, it does the opposite. It forces the novel's action into slow motion, and the reader's attention as well. In the very first sentence, story and discourse are quite at odds, the difference between them estranges.

A very direct deceleration of the sentence occurs through its syntactic organization. A swifter paraphrase of the sentence might go like this: *The blow catches him from the right and lifts him off the bicycle.* In my paraphrase the rhythm is modulated in a different way, the sentence *The blow catches him from the right* is connected simply and swiftly through the conjunction with the clause *lifts him off the bicycle.* The omission of the slower, bisyllabic progressive *lifting* and inclusion of the quicker monosyllabic *lifts* would accelerate the rhythm of the clause considerably, thus neatly and quickly bringing off the setup of Paul's being caught from the right, and his resulting fall. Through the progressive *lifting*, however, Paul seems not to fall so much as to hover in the air for a while, the effect of which only increases the detrimental outcome of the fall that is relegated to the reader's imagination. The quicker pace of the second paragraph may, then, imply that the fall has occurred. "That is not quite as it turns out, however" (*S* 1)—here the monosyllabic words suggest swiftness, while the adverb *however* seems like a dip at the end, a disappointing shrug of the shoulders, a final drop onto the tarmac of Magill Road.

The first sentence's slowing structure is carefully orchestrated to bring the reader into the mental and emotional experience of the character. The reader's distance to him is decreased, precisely because the reader's distance to the form, the syntax, is increased through the sentence's defamiliarizing qualities. "The blow catches him from the right, sharp and surprising and painful, like

a bolt of electricity, lifting him up off the bicycle." Through the insertion of
the qualifying clause, *sharp and surprising and painful*, the plodding rhythm
is underscored formally. The slowing here is twofold: The polysyndeton of the
repeated *and* causes the clause to lag a bit, while the insertion of the qualifying
clause effects a rhythmic deceleration of the sentence as a whole. (A mere
list, either an enumeration or an articulus—so frequent in Coetzee's work as
well—would create a staccato rhythm rather than this slow modulation.) The
insertion of the simile *like a bolt of electricity* functions in a related way and also
comprises two levels of deceleration. Again, the simile clause is inserted into
the sentence as a whole and has a slowing effect in the sentence's arrangement.
But the simile has larger philosophical functions of slowing down through
deferral, since the simile is a subtle form of digression that enforces reflection: it
steps away, it moves aside from the topic at hand (Latin: *digradi*, "walk aside").[9]
While Coetzee's work is not Shandyan in its digressive reflexivity, the language
performs subtle crabwalks around topics and ideas, bringing words and figures
into close association through their a vast suggestive potential. Let me digress
for a moment on a word, since at the beginning of the novel "[t]he unusual word
limber or *limbre* is on the horizon too" (*S* 1; original emphasis). Paul Rayment is
a French expatriate living in Australia, and the first paragraph already engages
with his sense of displacement that resonates later in the novel on the level of the
word. *Limbre* suggests the French language for the morpheme *re*, as in *timbre*
or *prendre*. It is, of course, ironic that the word is *limber* (agile, nimble), when
what is happening to Rayment is the breaking down of agility, of limberness;
but what demands a limber mind is the estrangement caused by the fact that
the word is spelled in two different ways and yet referred to in the singular. This
subtle repetition cum alteration may be classified rhetorically as an antistasis or
paronomasia, a case of word play that creates a word with the same sound but a
different spelling. The repetition's subtlety has the effect of introducing a little bit
of indeterminacy with that second word, *limbre*.

What looks like a French word is not, in fact, French. It does not exist in the
French lexicon; nor does an alternate spelling of *limber* exist in English.[10] On a

---

9 In *Daybreak* Nietzsche draws a larger analogy between this crabwalk-like movement, inherent in
   digression, and the philologist: "For philology is that venerable art which demands of its votaries
   one thing above all: to go aside, to take time, to become still, to become slow—it is a goldsmith's art
   and connoisseurship of the *word* which has nothing but delicate, cautious work to do and achieves
   nothing if it does not achieve it *lento*" (Nietzsche [1881] 1997, 5; original emphases).

10 In the French translation of the novel, *L'homme ralenti*, by Catherine Lauga du Plessis, the curious
   doubling cum altering of the word is not reproduced by a French equivalent. There the sentence
   merely uses one word: "Dans le lointain se profile aussi un mot plutôt rare comme *ingambe*" (*HR* 7;
   original emphasis) [In the distance also looms a very rare word like nimble.].

small scale, this word is metonymic for the entire formal aesthetics of the novel, an aesthetics of openings and blanks in the text by which signification is provoked in the reader's mind. Very simply, these two spellings, in what are the focalizer's thoughts, foreground language, written language, and so reading. Even on these smallest linguistic levels, one can see how digressions, added information, and associations continually intrude into a straightforward grammar, to facilitate a slow reading of the text at a microscopic level.

The way the syntactic arrangement can slow down the reading process, the complex phenomenon of *literalness* in Coetzee's works also contributes to a slowing down of the reading, and to an entailed heightening of reflexivity. Coetzee's texts oscillate between literal and figural realms and meanings, even between the literal and metaphorical semantics of individual words. When Paul is still under the influence of the trauma that has occurred in his life, he is lying in bed ruminating on his state and his situation:

> From the opening of the chapter, from the incident on Magill Road to the present, he has not behaved well, has not risen to the occasion: that much is clear to him. A golden opportunity was presented to him to set an example of how one accepts with good cheer one of the bitterer blows of fate, and he has spurned it. (*S* 14f.)

At first glance, the fast reader might miss the significance of the words *from the opening of the chapter* that begin the paragraph. The most likely interpretation, then, would be to read these words metaphorically: *from the opening of this new chapter in the life of the focalizer Paul*. However, once Elizabeth Costello has arrived and implied that she is the author of the novel, the text begs a rereading and a reconsideration of what has occurred before her arrival. The metaphorical realm of such a small expression is slowly eroded or at least qualified, and one is now able to read the phrase *from the opening of the chapter* quite literally, since the opening of the novel's first chapter takes place on Magill Road with Paul's bicycle accident. It is in this way that I perceive the normalization of metafictional devices of which Gurr speaks (2007, 95). The metafictional realm is introduced unobtrusively (2007, 95), through the metaphorical reading of the above-noted expression; the fact that Costello appears as the author of the text thus engages in a play of familiarizing and defamiliarizing once more. Now, both the metaphorical and the literal ways of reading are available and can be explored; both readings are held in a balance, and one oscillates between them in a meditative way, thus producing signification from the gap between these readings.

Continually, Coetzee's texts evoke the literal realm while simultaneously connoting the figural realm. *Slow Man* repeatedly highlights signifiers for their literal meanings while playing on their multiple associated signifieds as well. For example, this novel about a man slowed down tells—in an ironic and self-conscious way—of a doctor who is there to "*bring* [Paul] *up to speed*" (*S* 6; original emphasis) about his condition; Paul, blighted by the accident, recalls the young man responsible as being called "Wayne something-or-other, Bright or Blight" (*S* 20);[11] one signifier is shown to have multiple meanings as when Paul notes that "the left leg, the leg left to him, is as weak as putty" (*S* 23); the French émigré Paul considers his nurses (temps, temporary employees) as "nurses who call themselves *temps* and come for a day or two at a time" (*S* 24; original emphasis). The latter example opens up the associative realms of the French language and Paul's history as an immigrant, which the novel explores topically, as well as the realm of time and history (French: *temps*, "time" and "epoch") in a symbolic way.

It may seem paradoxical that works which continually activate both the literal and the figural realms in reading should be read, first and foremost, in a literal way. Yet, as Attridge's arguments for a *literal reading* in *J. M. Coetzee and the Ethics of Reading* have shown, a premature allegorical reading, for example, is susceptible to taking the reader out of the work and never seeing her return. Swift readings of Coetzee's works might miss the productivity of reading, first, in a literal way, and instead moving too hastily toward reading Coetzee's novels as allegorical of political and historical phenomena. However, a literal reading may also become problematic when the literal may be understood as signifying historical specifics, in a realist understanding. Coetzee seems reticent to situate his works in historical realities for fear of falling prey to turning works of art into nothing more than historical reportage, and he seems equally reticent to engage in wholly allegorical modes because the allegorical (and more broadly the figural) is in danger of flattening out in a calculative way. Instead, Coetzee's

---

[11] See also *S* 81f., where it is Costello who refers to the literal meaning of the beginning words when she repeats the opening phrases of the novel, although, in mystifying fashion, she changes the words slightly ("tumbles" instead of "flies"). She says:

> Do you know what I asked myself when I heard those words for the first time, Mr Rayment? I asked myself, *Why do I need this man?* Why not let him be, coasting along peacefully on his bicycle, oblivious to Wayne Bright or Blight, let us call him Blight, roaring up from behind him to blight his life and land him first in hospital and then back in this flat with its inconvenient stairs? (*S* 7; original emphasis)

By repeating the words, with one word changed, the novel provokes the reader to turn back and reread the beginning. Also, at this point Costello's statements are still regarded by Paul as the statements of a "*madwoman*" (*S* 7; original emphasis). So, the reader who wishes to continue reading metaphorically has the *authority* of the focalizer Paul on his side, even if he may not be the *author* of his life.

works explore the literal and the figural in an oscillatory way, going back and forth between literal and figural dimensions of literature, language, and place. This way, the reader is discouraged from hastily localizing the works in time and place and instead encouraged to reflect more deeply on their contexts.[12]

Because of the distinct allegorical dimensions of Coetzee's oeuvre, however, many readings of his work are in danger of becoming too instrumental and too conclusive. To respond with a wholesome allegorical reading to the allegorizing aspects of Coetzee's works is to respond with an unproductive filling of *gaps*, since the vibrant oscillation between literalness and allegory is unproductively closed when an argument veers exclusively toward the allegorical. An allegorical reading may be resorted to as the clutching at a first or last straw when a literary work is bereft of historical or spatial specifics and the reader is simply lost on how to make sense of a text, as may very well be the case with many of Coetzee's works. This becomes apparent in his most recent work, *The Childhood of Jesus*, situated as it is in a place which does not exist in reality. It is, however, in slow reading that many different kinds of gaps may be addressed in a phenomenological way and without filling them finally.

In *Slow Man* as in the other works the reader encounters a variety of gaps on a variety of levels. While *Slow Man* is not an allegorical novel, it is important to consider how to treat the different gaps in reading so as not to fill them too quickly and work with them in a slower and more productive way. Because of its phenomenological focus on the concrete phenomena of the text, the method of slow reading allows a consideration of the many different kinds of gaps encountered when perusing, that is gaps in the narrative, such as in the chronology between scenes or chapters, gaps in meaning, and even the visual gaps, which will be discussed later.

One gap in *Slow Man* is mentioned quite literally, when Paul refers to his lost leg as "*a hole in* [his] *life*" (S 183; original emphasis). Directly after the accident Paul drifts in and out of consciousness, leaving further gaps in the novel's chronology. While in the ambulance on the way to hospital, Paul notices the letter sequences "E-R-T-Y," "F-R-I-V-O-L," "Q-W-E-R-T-Y" being spelled out on "his inner eyelid" (S 3), as he later says, by "the celestial typewriter" (S 123). These incomplete sequences constitute gaps themselves, both because of their fragmentary nature and because of their estranging quality in the narrative; and they foreground, as Zoë Wicomb notes, "the physical aspect of writing, the letters arranged on a keyboard from which the writer taps out words" (2010,

---

[12] For an excellent, comprehensive consideration of these two poles *between* which Coetzee's oeuvre is to be thought, see Head (2009, 29–31).

216). Wicomb notes that these sequences are "arbitrary in terms of meaning," thus highlighting the novel's preoccupation with the signifier/signified relation from the beginning (2010, 216). Wicomb observes that the letter sequences

> speak[…] of beginnings, of the raw material of writing, the real thing in the world from which meaning is made, and from Paul's point of view of the difficulty of coming into being as a character through writing. (2010, 216)

Wicomb highlights the tenuous relationship between literature and the real world as a relationship defined by a gap which is fundamental to language. Nevertheless, the reader's mind will naturally race toward meaning, even starting from nonsensical sequences.[13] The method of slow reading is aware of this constant urge to find interpretations, but slows down this process to test the signification of phenomena in a reflexive way. So, the method is wholly inclusive of the possibility to cluster signification around an initially nonsensical gap by considering it phenomenologically and weighing it against various different meanings, allusions, and associations. Wicomb suggests that the deep reflexivity about the letter sequences in *Slow Man* is due to the text's provocation of a rereading or multiple readings. Regarding the letter sequence's origin she notes: "The question of whose writing only arises once Costello arrives, and that is when the text demands a re-reading" (2010, 216).

Wicomb suggests that the letter sequences may initially be attributed to Paul's loss of consciousness and that the reader might interpret them in a more realist way, as mere remnants of memories or shapes half registered on Paul's retina before drifting out of consciousness. Likewise, the reader might invest them with meaning that is conjectural on a first reading, or see them as symbolic. Only later does the novel play up the discursive quality of Coetzee's works which I have referred to as enigmas and erasures, when the text refers back to an earlier moment and erases an enigma by creating further enigma about it. One enigma (*What* could these letters mean?) is erased, but through this erasure of the enigma new ones are installed (*Who* has written these letters? *How* have they been written?).

Thus, a slow reading is essential to an appreciation of Coetzee's texts, in the sense that a fundamental hermeneutics toward the one final interpretation is played down, while a more epistemologically functional inquiry is signaled. In

---

[13] Paul may not be the author of his life, but he seems to become, more and more, the reader of his life, and he shows how reading does not exist in a vacuum, how reading always tries to make meaning, since when he later interprets his life before the accident as "frivolous" (*S* 83), he may not, in fact, be speaking from the heart, but he may be remembering those letters from the celestial typewriter. Wicomb asks if this moment in the book—Costello quizzes Paul about the feelings surrounding his near-death experience—does not reveal "Paul's identity as an already-written character" (2010, 217).

this way, one gap in Coetzee's oeuvre is reconfigured as the novel progresses and as the reader's experience and knowledge about the novel accumulate, and so a rereading is indicated by these fluctuating gaps. At the same time, even a rereading does not *fill* gaps in any final way, but rather resituates or reconfigures them in an endlessly signifying play that keeps inquiry alive. The text purports to fill a gap for the reader in one way—here the arrival of Costello seems intended to explain the letter sequences on Paul's inner eyelid—but what actually occurs is a widening or deepening of the gap as a realm of indeterminacy.

As Coetzee's later fiction becomes more self-referential, one might conclude that fewer gaps puncture the oeuvre, that the oeuvre is solipsistically at home in and among itself, when, in fact, the opposite is true, since an upshot of self-referentiality is a sense of control, a sense in which a text seems to signal complete self-awareness of what it is doing. This creates many more gaps than might be imagined. Wolfgang Iser elucidates this complex phenomenon when he writes that "the more a text tries to be precise [...], the greater will be the number of gaps between [the different interpretations]" (1989, 9). This also resonates regarding Coetzee's language, since the aforementioned late style, the reduction of the language's ornamentation, give a feeling of concreteness and directness, while the minimalist character of language actually creates further gaps. The close consideration of these gaps, then, further slows down the reading process in a productive way.

Likewise, the reading process is productively slowed down through the complex dimensions of *dialogue*. While reading, it *feels* as though a text answered the reader's call: its linguistic construction *speaks* to the reader. At the same time, of course, it is the reader's mental monologue that speaks the multiple voices of a text.[14] It is helpful to recall Georges Poulet again, as he speaks about reading:

> I am thinking the thought of another. Of course, there would be no cause for astonishment if I were thinking it as the thought of another. But I think it as my very own. (1980, 44)

In a pragmatic way, of course, one senses otherness—the singular strangeness of a text as otherness that Attridge refers to (2004a, 40)—seeping into the reader's consciousness, or as Maurice Blanchot writes once, "in the presence of something other, I become other" ([1949] 1995, 314). In reading, the other's and the other thoughts are like guests in one's mental cosmos. In slow reading this otherness that mixes with the self's consciousness is never assimilated, never mastered. Rather, the method of slow reading is a method of holding on, persisting, waiting

---

[14] For this idea of *speaking* a literary text, slowly, in the reading mind, see William H. Gass's fascinating essay "On Reading to Oneself."

with the otherness of the text in a dialogic way, flickering between the multiple dimensions of voices performed (echoing Attridge's terms) or spoken (echoing Poulet's) in the reader's mind, appreciating "an otherness brought into being by language" (Attridge 2004a, 29).

Coetzee's metafictional techniques in *Slow Man* create multiple layers of dialogic estrangement, meaning that the text already engages in a web of dialogues before the reader enters the picture. *Slow Man*'s techniques are related to devices of Jamesian narrative framing. In general, framing devices have the same effect as a game of telephone, mixing and mingling voices and blurring the narrating referent to complicate communication at the level of the plot or between the text and the reader. Such complications of communication, however, very productively accentuate the polyphonic character of literary texts; on yet another level, by blotting out referents, the philosophical significance of voices is foregrounded, while a complex tissue of distances and estrangements is nurtured in the reader's mind. Coetzee's *Slow Man* inverts the frame narrative by playing with the possibilities (or impossibilities) of metafiction—is Costello the author of Paul Rayment, of *Slow Man*? In what way can a fictional character be the author of anything? By keeping such questions raised the novel engages with metafictional devices not only by using them, but also by interrogating them; the latter not by deconstructing them explicitly in the text, but by inviting the reader to explore and reflect on them in dialogue with the text.

The device of the frame narrative is further deconstructed in so far as it is this device itself which intrudes into the novel in a dialogic way. Note how in a moment of slow time, when Paul is "dithering," "the doorbell rings" (*S* 79). Over the "entryphone" (*S* 79)—like a telephone, a dialogue device—a conversation seems to commence as Paul answers the intercom: "Mr Rayment?" says the voice on the entryphone. "Elizabeth Costello here. May I speak with you?" (*S* 79). At the beginning, it is, indeed, only Costello who speaks, until Paul asks a question: "You are not from the Library?" (*S* 79). Sadly, she is not. Poor Paul has no idea—from now on, it is no longer his voice that embodies the narrative, it is no longer clear if there even is such a thing as *his* voice or whether it is merely Costello's voice doing all the speaking: speaking his life, uttering his narrative, perhaps thinking his thoughts, not unlike Descartes's evil demon.[15]

---

[15] If a novel had a mind, one might say that various Cartesian ideas and motifs are on that of *Slow Man*, from the way in which Costello seemingly activates Paul's *cogito* through deceptions and triggers of doubt, as if she were a version of an evil demon in metafictional clothing; to the topical references to the "mechanical duck" which Marijana's husband was working on at the Art Institute of Dubrovnik and which resembles Descartes's automatons; it even "quacks like a regular duck, it waddles, it lays eggs" (*S* 86).

The significant change of the frame narrative is that it only appears to be a frame narrative after nearly 80 pages of the novel, so that the device is not explicated from the beginning, and may, in fact, not even be a *frame*. Rather, it intrudes, the way Costello intrudes into Paul's life, from the side, like "a blow that catches him from the right."

Costello's question, *May I speak with you?*, should be understood quite literally, as the novel, scene after scene, explores the dialogue between the two characters as a locus for philosophical signification. Because of the metafictional frame, Paul can ask a fundamental ontological question in such a way that the novel both exhibits it as a literal question in the diegetic world and as a near metaphysical question:

> ["]Now let me ask you straight out, Mrs Costello: Are you real?"
>
> "Am I real? I eat, I sleep, I suffer, I go to the bathroom. I catch cold. Of course I am real. As real as you."
>
> "Please be serious for once. Please answer me: Am I alive or am I dead? Did something happen to me on Magill Road that I have failed to grasp?" (*S* 233)

This short dialogue—subtly estranging for the omission of speech tags—shows how the text hovers between the literal and the symbolical at all times, how truly *double-voiced* Coetzee's writings are, as they scuttle back and forth between meanings. The reader engages in a precarious and multilayered dialogue with the text, since the text continually forces the reader to reflect on a much more fundamental question entirely unrelated to semantics: *How do I read this text?* Patrick Hayes's statements concerning *Waiting for the Barbarians* are relevant here as well:

> Coetzee's text brings about a crisis in [...] the reading experience, its aim being to bring about in the reader a disorienting spell of "waiting," through which he or she becomes open to other ways of perceiving [...]. (2010, 70)

The openness to which Hayes refers is crucial to an appreciation of Coetzee's oeuvre, since the texts engender a sense of openness in both text and recipient through a play of involving and estranging the reader, and the resulting slow reading requires an openness to the otherness of the textual event.

As with many aspects of Coetzee's concentrated prose, there is yet a different kind of openness which is part of the texts and is then transported to the reader's mind. The openness of the *endings*. Coetzee's endings offer ways out of an instrumental hermeneutic, in that they offer alternatives to the common understanding that a narrative has to end, that meaning-making, that reading has to stop. The endings resonate back into the reader's life or they involve the reader more deeply in the narrative worlds, such as *Slow Man* does. A circular movement: A deep involvement in the novel enables the perception of those techniques which further *stimulate* our deep involvement in the novel. Only a slow reading enables us to perceive a subtle loop at the end of the text, and this in turn allows us to reflect deeply about the work's political and philosophical implications.

The ending of the novel subtly impels the reader to go back to its beginning. It ends with a dialogue between Paul and Elizabeth Costello, who after her lengthy sojourn in Paul's life, is finally set for departure.

> "But what am I going to do without you?"
> She seems to be smiling, but her lips are trembling too.
> "That is up to you, Elizabeth. There are plenty of fish in the ocean, so I hear. But as for me, as for now: goodbye." And he leans forward and kisses her thrice in the formal manner he was taught as a child, left right left. (*S* 263)

The novel's ending is highly disorienting and decelerating, not least because it subtly invokes contrasting semantic dimensions. Marijana's family have built a new vehicle for Paul, a tricycle as opposed to the bicycle from the novel's beginning. This way, the novel's ending recurs to its opening and suggests a second reading or, at the very least, a return to the novel's opening passages. In the end, the novel is explicitly past-bound, since the time invoked here returns us to Paul's childhood. The word *limbre* in the first sentence of the novel might be said to have evoked Paul's past by alluding to his mother tongue, but in a way which has blurred English and French, and so simultaneously problematized the return to the past. The three last words of the novel, *left right left* are explicitly related to the social gesture of polite cheek kissing, which in France consists of three kisses, left, right, and left. Yet, there is another semantic dimension that these words refer to: *left right left* are to do with right-hand and left-hand traffic, the rules (or manners) of which are taught to children when they are very young. Whereas France, Paul's country of origin, has always driven on the right, Australia, Paul's country of residence, has always driven on the left. This is where the novel very subtly refers the reading back to the beginning, to that blow which "catches him from the *right*." Thus, the ending of the novel reinterprets the beginning's mysterious cause of Paul's affliction. A cyclist crossing an intersection in France would first look to the left for traffic approaching from the cyclist's left but driving on the driver's right side of the road, and so nearer to the cyclist than a car driving on the driver's left side of the road. Following the look to the left, the cyclist would look *right* for traffic potentially perilous, but perilous later than traffic coming from the cyclist's *left*: this is why the intermediate look to the right is concluded by a look to the left directly before crossing, in case traffic had approached from the cyclist's left since the intermediate look to the right. *Left right left*. In Australia, of course, this procedure has to be inverted, *right left right*. Crossing an intersection in Australia and looking first to the left means being exposed to *blows from the right*. Magill Road in Adelaide, where the novel's beginning is set, is a long straight road, spliced by intersections, which allows the argument that Paul, on his bicycle, has crossed one of these intersections and has looked not first to his right, but first to his left, *in the manner he was taught as a child*.

Paul is not merely past-bound, then, but *home*-bound in an altogether different way, as a man exiled is, a man nostalgic, in old age, for that time where his childhood remains cloistered off in memory. Reading the ending in this way, one sees that, on a more pragmatic level, the ending circles (cycles!) back to the beginning, suggesting a loop that encloses the textual domain and invites the reader to remain within it. The ending returns the reader to the beginning of the novel, that metaphorical "birth" of the literary character Paul Rayment, and the ending also returns Paul to his time of birth, his childhood. The novel's form may be said to mirror the character's mind.

While this has the positive function of holding the reader still in the world of the text, allowing her to think through it more deeply, the ending makes Paul an exiled man who is stuck with the old ideas of a past embodied within him, manacling him to manners or traditions which might be "out-dated" in this present environment, remnants of a past lost. Paul's returning to his past in this way is less tragic, but no less forceful than the moment in *Disgrace*, when Lurie, trapped in the lavatory and listening to the atrocious silence of the house and the attack, admits to himself: "He speaks Italian, he speaks French, but Italian and French will not save him in darkest Africa" (*Dis* 95). *Left right left* will not help Paul when crossing a road in Adelaide. *Left right left* ties the cord to his past, shackles him to his own life's history, and with this come both consolation and complication.

The only hopefulness left to him at the end of the novel, nearing the end of a life, is to recur to childhood and mine some kind of solace from the store of memory, even if that solace means outlawing himself from the new life he is groping through in the present. His only hope, as it were, is to return to the beginning, and the reader may follow him, since the novel's ending performs this return in as subtle a way as a memory that bubbles, waywardly but unwittingly, to the surface of consciousness.

The customary ending in Coetzee's works is entirely open, ending on a mystifying note, on a gap, or like looking out into a vacuum. But whereas *Foe*, for example, ends with metafictional and near magic realist fireworks, the later texts seem simply to drift out in a calmer, a more valedictory way, but also in a way that is defiant of the idea of valediction, of having to end. The quiet valediction at the end of especially Coetzee's later works is decidedly not the valediction of death, but an entirely literary and philosophical valediction, one in which the text takes a step back and comes to represent its own gap in the reader's experience, a gap on which the reader meditates after the book is closed, carrying the multiple enigmas of the text back into reality.

The farewell these books enact in their relationship with the reader should not be understood in a negative way, but should be seen as full of a positive potential for philosophical reflection through the slow reading they indicate. The works' forms of farewell may be illuminated by an image Coetzee evokes in a conversation with Peter Sacks at the Lannan Foundation in 2001. He imagines himself as a child sitting at a keyboard next to Johann Sebastian Bach, who is teaching the child to improvise musical composition. Coetzee describes how Bach suggests various ways of improvising and then shows the child the way in which to proceed alone. Coetzee says about Bach:

> The thing that makes him special is that every time he does it [improvizes], there is a mysterious moment in the improvization that he produces, there is a mysterious moment at which he leaves you. He leaves you behind. He leaves your powers to follow him, to imitate him, to do what he is doing, behind. (Coetzee and Sacks 2001).

Coetzee contrasts this image with the Romantic genius epitomized by Beethoven, who he imagines sitting at the keyboard on his own with perfectly composed music flowing into him as if from the heavens. Coetzee says he likes to think of himself as the person who sits beside Bach at the keyboard, working, playing, improvising, revising, trying, maybe failing but certainly trying again.

The ceaseless reflection in which Coetzee's characters are engaged and the ceaseless reflection which the works stimulate mirror very aptly this mode of Bach's guidance. And one could extend this image with a proposition: Coetzee's works represent Bach in Coetzee's image, sitting at the keyboard next to the reader, suggesting, proposing, seemingly improvising. The reader is represented by the child in the image, sitting, listening intently, waiting until she may begin to perform the text herself. And then it comes, the mysterious moment when the text leaves the reader behind. And the text *leaves your powers to follow it, to imitate it, to do what the text is doing, behind.* The text does not leave the reader alone, all the reader needs is there in the text, and the reader has merely to remain inside it, or to return to it. In this way, it is the reader, as much as the text, who makes Coetzee's *worlds*.

His works seem always to straddle two different realms. On the one hand, their socio-historical contexts and associations are always felt to be indebted to a real world perceptible in the text. On the other, this contextual reality seems rather to be running parallel to and not in unison with the textual worlds. Coetzee's works are not the unacknowledged legislators of history and rather aim to explore the genre of the novel as a counter-version to history through fiction. It may seem paradoxical that Coetzee's works create a literary counter-version to history while simultaneously relating to history in oblique ways; but through such paradoxical tenets his works become a complex and dynamic melange of purported opposites, a blending of discourses and realms of experience. It is precisely such qualities which go to the foundation of the kind of literature whose sensibilities I wish to call philosophical.

Through the metafictional technique of introducing Costello as the author of *Slow Man* while the story is progressing, the novel is able to explore the phenomena of "literature" and "the world" in a deeply philosophical way. After Costello has occupied part of Paul's flat, he finds her notebook and reads part of the narrative of his life; the effect of this is the following reflection:

> Is this what it is like to be translated to what at present he can only call *the other side*? Is that what has happened to him; is that what happens to everyone? [...] If this does not amount to a big moment, a Copernican moment, then what does? The greatest of all secrets may just have been revealed to him. There is a second world that exists side by side with the first, unsuspected. One chugs along in the first for a certain length of time; then the angel of death arrives in the person of Wayne Blight or someone like him. For an instant, for an aeon, time stops; one tumbles down a dark hole. Then, hey presto, one emerges into a second world *identical with the first*, where time resumes and the action proceeds— flying through the air like a cat, the throng of curious onlookers, the ambulance, the hospital, Dr Hansen, et cetera—except that one now has Elizabeth Costello around one's neck, or someone like her. (*S* 122; original emphases)

The initial reaction to this passage is bafflement; one is nonplussed reading these words, a feeling which mirrors Paul's feelings upon reading Costello's notebook, and which is brought about by the formal choices of narrating the fictional world(s) Paul inhabits. Paul draws an analogy between Costello's (Coetzee's?) fiction and his own death, and so he undermines the notion of literature as representative of the world in the mimetic way that he actually alludes to (*identical with the first*). It seems to Paul that he has died and has been "reborn" in fiction. However, fictional characters have, in a way, always been dead. (And yet, while fictional characters may be able to "live" if the reader brings them to life within herself, can a fictional character ever really die?) Paul tries to remain positive: If dying turns out to be nothing but a trick that might as well be a trick with words, if death is a mere hiccup in time after which life goes on as before, why all the fuss? (*S* 123). While Paul, as a literary character, can be light-hearted about this, the reader is provoked to reflect on "the big thing," as Henry James is supposed to have called his passing on the deathbed. And the reader is provoked to think about the possibly eschatological dimensions of a literature saturated with mortality.

Slow Man is a curio in Coetzee's oeuvre in the way it takes the real world (there is a real Magill Road in the real city of Adelaide) and interrogates it fundamentally through fiction, developing the project of presenting the novel as a counter-version to history. However, the history that is countered here is no longer a specific socio-historical present, but the world in general, the world which is challenged by an alternative world *that exists side by side with the first*. This is the world of fiction, it follows different rules, it is not a copy of the real world. Rather, it may be thought of as a reading of the world, and reading is never replicating but always rewriting, remaking. At the same time, the relation of this fictional world to the real world is not as flimsy as it seems. Coetzee's work is of this world and responds to this world in an essentially philosophical way; Coetzee's work makes worlds that are recognizable but disorienting, worlds that are defamiliarized and made somewhat uncanny through various estranging devices.

In this way, Coetzee's work, even if at times very subtly, urges to rethink worlds, and thus to remake worlds. Coetzee's oeuvre is far from explaining the real world to the reader (whatever it may be). Rather, the oeuvre imagines an unimagined world, makes it new, makes it strange and probes forth to its philosophical significations and implications. This idea is not as grandiose as it might sound, but is a fundamental aspect of a literature that is as phenomenologically attentive and reflexive as Coetzee's is. It is for the phenomenological and ethical approach to literature through slow reading that the reader is able to match the attentiveness, responsiveness, and reflexivity of Coetzee's texts when reading them. It is as if the reader were sitting next to their "teacher" at the keyboard, waiting with the texts and learning from them to read in a slow way, to activate cognitive processes of responding, of thinking texts, of improvising worlds. One may turn to Maurice Merleau-Ponty for an illumination of the dimensions of reading and thinking regarding what I have called the slow and the meditative way. In *Sense and Nonsense* (1948) Merleau-Ponty argues that philosophy and literature are engaged in the same project, the project

> not of explaining the world or discovering its "conditions of possibility," but rather of formulating an experience of the world, a contact with the world which precedes all thought about the world. (1964, 28)

In many ways, Coetzee's literary project shares with phenomenological philosophy this sense of *formulating an experience of the world*. The experience of the literary text does not formulate the world, it does not replicate the world in any simple way; rather, it is its own "philosofictional" project that gives voice to what Merleau-Ponty calls *the experience of the world*:

> When one is concerned with giving voice to the experience of the world and showing how consciousness escapes into the world, one can no longer credit oneself with attaining a perfect transparence of expression. Philosophical expression assumes the same ambiguities as literary expression, if the world is such that it cannot be expressed except in "stories" and, as it were, pointed at. (1964, 28)

Through a complex web of engagement and estrangement, Coetzee's oeuvre points to the world in a phenomenological way, relying on ambiguity, on the provisional, and on the productive mystification that has been key to his writing from his first published work.

His ambiguous worlds force the reader to take careful steps through them, to hold tight to the characters and remain open to the narratives' winding ways. The content and the form of Coetzee's texts work in close alignment to relate an experience of the world which engenders a form of slow reading and, possibly, a form of meditative thinking. Continually, the works carve out space for thought and for reflection. Through their very composition, they provoke a rereading and rethinking of text and world. By holding up an ideal to be as receptive to a text as one is to the only world one has, in an open and in a meditative way, one may begin a philosophical analysis of this slow and estranging world of fiction.

In the end, perhaps, the image from this chapter's beginning may be modified. A text need not be thought of as a stranger so as to be responded to ethically and phenomenologically, through diligent care and with an acute sense for detail and deep thinking. Perhaps a text may be thought of rather as a slow man, a man who may not be pushed toward where he is bound, but in whose presence one may come to appreciate an experience of meditative reflection.

3

A Goblin: Why?—Coetzee's Questions

They buy a vacuum cleaner. Every morning his mother trails the vacuum cleaner from room to room, sucking up the dust into the roaring belly on which a smiling red goblin leaps as if over a hurdle. A goblin: why? (SPL 4)

The first question in the first instalment of Coetzee's trilogy of self-reflexive memoirs (or *autrebiographies*[1]) seems casual rather than pensive. At the beginning of *Boyhood*, from which the foregoing passage is taken, the narrator informs us that the mother of the ten-year-old focalizer John is endlessly engaged in "sweep[ing] and tidy[ing]" (*SPL* 3), in a battle against the sway of dust which ceaselessly whirls into their new house (*SPL* 4)—that is, until the addition of a vacuum cleaner to the household. John's question as to why there should be a goblin's likeness on the appliance serves different functions for the reading, functions which are not casual at all, but instead highlight the deep reflexivity and inquiring nature I have spoken of earlier regarding Coetzee's entire oeuvre.

A goblin: why? Up until this question the first paragraphs of *Boyhood* have been a phenomenological account of the boy's consciousness registering the home in Worcester where the Coetzee family has moved, as well as his responses to the new surroundings.[2] This deceptively casual question subtly suggests the boy's mindset and his curious and questioning worldview; his way of thinking seems meditative from the start.[3] Later in the text when "a boy from his class" comes upon him as John is "lying on his back under a chair" and asks what he

---

[1] As mentioned earlier, the term *autrebiography* is Coetzee's own, but it is significant that he has used it before any of his autrebiographies were written. See *DtP* 394.

[2] For the biographical details behind this period, see Kannemeyer (2012, 34–62). However, one should be aware of Coetzee's caution that "[a]ll autobiography is storytelling, all writing is autobiography" (*DtP* 391).

[3] Arguably, Coetzee's three Johns, in *Boyhood*, *Youth*, and *Summertime*, are his most deeply reflexive characters, which may not (only) be owed to the fact that the author is writing about his own life, but to the generally reflexive nature of the memoir. For Coetzee's thoughts on autobiography, see his essay "Confession and Double Thoughts: Tolstoy, Rousseau, Dostoevsky" (1985), collected in *Doubling the Point*, as well as the related interview with Attwell in the same volume. Also see his uncollected lecture "Truth in Autobiography" (1984).

is doing there, he replies curtly: "Thinking [...]. I like thinking" (*SPL* 25). As is frequently the case in Coetzee's oeuvre, thinking is once more deliberately linked to a moment of physical stillness here, though it is also connected to the child's inquiring character, which I will explore in the following. The tendency to think in this particularly inquiring way is emphasized in the "slightly mature version" (*DtP* 394) of John in the second autrebiography, *Youth*, about which Attridge argues that it "may well have a higher count of questions per page than any of Coetzee's works to date" (2004a, 58).

The questions throughout *Boyhood* essentially relate the meditative character of John's mind, staging the boy's proclivity for thinking through the sheer abundance of questions directly asked by the narrator. There is hardly a page without a question similar in kind to the first one, *A goblin: why?* These questions are asked in a customarily terse style and they are almost never answered. This way, the questions themselves constitute pauses in the text, since an answer is expected but withheld, and thus a reflection (or even an answer) is provoked in the reader's mind. The reader is invited not only to consider these questions reflexively, but also to think about her own faculties of meaning-making in the process, since meaning made from and through questions is approached differently and evaluated differently than meaning made by the text in the way of a presented argument or a given statement to which the reader could simply agree or disagree. The question is more involving than the assertion, since it makes the reader a more direct agent in the text's development and in the development of the character. The reader is also brought closer to a character through a character's meditative questions. The reader of *Boyhood* does not only reflect about John, she is also engaged in a reflexive dialogue with John about the world in his inquiring way. Attridge highlights this by arguing that

> [m]editative questions are a particularly effective way of drawing the reader into a character's experience—they invite us to share a moment of uncertainty or curiosity without arriving at a conclusion. (2004a, 58)

So, this meditative mode has the effect of giving the character and the text as a whole a reflexive quality, while also opening up a space of reflection in the reader. This is achieved by keeping questions raised, leaving them generally unanswered and at the same time conveying very distinctly that their asking is important to the narrative and to the characters or focalizers. When John is alone in the yard playing with a cricket ball, the text—and so John—asks:

What is the true trajectory of the ball: is it going straight up and straight down, as he sees it, or is it rising and falling in loops, as a motionless bystander would see it? When he talks to his mother about this, he sees a desperate look in her eyes: she knows things like this are important to him, and wants to understand why, but cannot. (*SPL* 31f.)

Because John's mother is unable to answer the question and because the narrator does not answer it, the ball is, nearly literally, in the reader's court (or yard). The reader is asked to reflect on this question. She is herself brought into an inquiring mode of the kind that John demonstrates, while she is provoked to reflect on perspective. Which perspective does she assume in her reading, the perspective of the focalizer John, or the perspective of an outside observer, outside of John's mind, outside of the book's world? By asking herself such questions, she is, of course, already deep inside the book's world and perhaps deep inside John's mind. It is less important what kind of question John has and more important that *things like this are important to him*, and that the reader may thus pause to ask herself why they are important to John, what this reveals about his character. Moreover, the reader is compelled to ask if such questions are important to her as well, whether only for the reading of the text or in a more general way.

Many times these questions are of the kind that I have referred to earlier, in Gottfried Benn's expression, as "the children's query" (1987, 255), referring to fundamental questions asked in a straightforward and often naïve way. These questions convey a sense of wonder and defamiliarization regarding what they inquire into. They are often questions *not easily answered, or not answerable at all*, as mentioned earlier. While the goblin-question, for example, is easily answered by an adult, especially one whose feelers extend via the World Wide Web—the British company manufacturing the appliances was simply called Goblin Vacuum Cleaners—for a young boy, especially one living in 1940s South Africa, it would be entirely astonishing—possibly entirely incomprehensible— why there should be a goblin on his mother's electrical cleaning apparatus. *A goblin: why?* shows the singularly childish interest in detail, and so this question, as insignificant as it may seem, immediately focuses the reader's attention to the child's point of view, the childish gaze at the world.

The narrator simply asks *A goblin: why?* and lets the question linger. This way the text aptly represents the young boy's lasting fascination with the bewildering appliance. Shortly after, the reader learns that "he plays with the vacuum cleaner, tearing up paper and watching the strips fly up the pipe like leaves in the wind" (*SPL* 4). The boy's response to this puzzling new machine is conveyed by effecting a different kind of bewilderment in the reader as well, one that stems from the subtly defamiliarizing view at simple, very ordinary phenomena in a new way. This is very much related to Shklovsky's argument about a chief technique in Tolstoy's works, namely the description of a phenomenon "as if it were perceived for the first time" ([1925] 1991, 6). Coetzee's works achieve a similar effect, although not through descriptions but through questions, which relate the focalizer's incredulity about phenomena, as if the object, the person, the goblin were *perceived for the first time*. So, a straightforward answer becomes more complicated and necessitates a slower reflection.

The technique of asking a question and withholding an answer is simple enough and a key of rhetoric, but Coetzee's work is unique for the sheer number of questions in the texts and for the fact that most of these questions are not rhetorical ones. Rhetorical questions do not slow down the reading in the way I argue, because they already contain their answer. The questions so frequent in Coetzee do not contain answers at all; they are literal questions that convey the focalizer's and narrator's uncertainty or reflexivity and repeat this reflexivity and uncertainty in the reader in a slowing way. The goblin-question from *Boyhood* reverberates in the reader's mind longer than a "mere" narrating of the goblin's effect on John could do, because a question asked in this way draws the reader in much more directly: A question that is not put to another character in dialogue seems to be put first to the reader.

This way, the reader is sucked into the narrative like those paper slips into the vacuum cleaner. Had the passage ended with a mere description of the goblin jumping over its imaginary hurdle—which was actually the lettering of the company name—the reader might see little need to reflect on this vacuum cleaner (and on John) more deeply. And had the question been asked in a more specific way, it would not have allowed the characterization of John in the deeply reflexive sense that it does now. In an early draft from 1987 when Coetzee began work on the memoir, the sentence read very differently: "It is a Goblin vacuum cleaner; but why?"[4] Here, then, the boy merely wonders why the *company* is called Goblin Vacuum Cleaners, or why the family *has* a Goblin vacuum cleaner; the question is concrete to the point of banality. In the published version, the shorter form of the question makes the object of inquiry less concrete, while the shorter sentence seems more direct. The clipped sentence conveys the more wide-reaching nature of John's inquiry, and so replicates in the reader's mind the urgency behind John's question and the mystery of the object of inquiry. This way John's comportment to the world around him appears naïve as well as

---

[4]   HRC, container 27, folder 1, p. 1/8. (The unusual pagination is due to loose pages collected as early drafts and notes toward an autobiography.)

meditative, and these aspects of asking and reflecting echo in the reader's mind when engaging with this question. The fascination John has with the vacuum cleaner is not only told to the reader, but it is experienced by the reader through a question which subtly but urgently defamiliarizes what it inquires into. Coetzee uses the question as a rhetorical device to convey the child's naïve reflection as well as to make the reader recur to what has been said before, stimulating her to reconsider what she has just read and to reflect in the slow, astonished way a child reflects on the strange image of a goblin on a vacuum cleaner. Why a goblin, indeed.

The question is arguably the most frequently and most subtly used device in Coetzee's works to slow the reading into a reflexive mode. Questions highlight the self-reflexivity and self-consciousness of all of Coetzee's characters and narrators in different ways, and they align their points of view with the reader's, even if the narrators are not homodiegetic but heterodiegetic. Especially the unusual narrative situation of the autrebiographical works *Boyhood* and *Youth*, the present continuous tense combined with the third person, complicates the reader's simple inference that John asks these questions only of himself and during the narrated time, and the reader is thus provoked to reflect on the questions with the character as well as about the position from which these questions are asked.

This will become clear by briefly looking at this specific narrative situation, the third person and the present continuous tense, which becomes Coetzee's "trademark fictional mode" (Head 2009, 3). Some of the works before *Boyhood* already use the present continuous tense. However, this very unique *fictional mode* is previously used only in *The Master of Petersburg* (1994), the work published directly before *Boyhood*.[5] In the memoirs, it is arguably employed in the most effective way, since this particular narrative situation and point of view raise direct epistemic questions about the focalizer's position, whether his view of the world is appropriate to a young person, or whether it is a point of view appropriated by an adult consciousness. Particularly in *Boyhood* and *Youth*, it creates a productive in-betweenness that keeps the reader in uncertainties.

One of Coetzee's notes for *Boyhood* is collected in a typed page of reflection which the author draws on during the conception of *Youth*. It comments on the young focalizer of *Boyhood* and illuminates the in-betweenness created

---

[5]   So far, this now *trademark fictional mode* has only been altered in *Diary of a Bad Year* (2007) and *Summertime* (2009), where the mix of voices also creates mixed narrative situations.

by this very specific narrative situation, as well as the middle position that the autrebiographies assume, between autobiography and fiction:

> Question of narration. Even novels that believe they are past "realism" adhere to an elementary realism of narration, in the sense that the narrative position at any given moment is either inside or outside. Thus the source of the narrative can be realistically conceptualized as the position of the narrator, inside or outside the action. What I need to do is to invent a position between the two that does not belong to realism, a position that is in effect itself a fictional construct. Neither a ten year old incapable yet of reflecting on himself nor the same child grown up, looking back, seeing implications. (5/12/94)[6]

The frequency of questions in *Boyhood* and the defamiliarizing form in which these are asked very distinctly shape this position that is somewhere between inside and outside. The narrative situation is effectively realized only in conjunction with the reader, since the question draws the reader into the text and momentarily confines her to the immature point of view, but then makes her oscillate back into her own position from which she considers the questions raised in the narrative but from which she also questions the focalizer's position from which these questions are asked.

This narrative situation and form of questioning create a way of reading that is itself fundamentally inquiring, so that the reader is held still in uncertainties, and forced to tarry with the text. This way of reading created by the text mirrors the indecisive or unpredictable existential positions that the focalizers find themselves in, since they too are in essential uncertainty as to where they are, who they are, and why such questions are relevant. This sense of existential uncertainty is felt most fiercely in *Youth*, as John leads an unexceptional life in London, to which he has travelled from South Africa after the Sharpeville massacre and in search of poetic inspiration. During the time of global political unrest in the 1960s, the sense of political fluctuation is turned into an existential uncertainty, which is related to the reader in the way John's questions drill deep into the heart of everything. During the Cuban Missile Crisis he attends a political rally in Trafalgar Square and reflects:

> The rally ends. He goes back to his room. He ought to be reading *The Golden Bowl* or working on his poems, but what would be the point, what is the point of anything? (*SPL* 215)

The specific question *what would be the point* blows up into the universal question *what is the point of anything*, and is thus asked in such a straightforward

---

[6]   HRC, container 45, 1, p. Y-FNNV01 1. The pagination refers to Coetzee's private pagination system.

and all-encompassing way that the reader is provoked to reflect on the existential implications of this question in a more fundamental sense. Many times in Coetzee's works questions are asked in such a direct way that they create the sense of a naïvely unafraid reflection on the world, a reflection from the here and now, from where reflection is possible, but from which retrospective implications cannot yet be perceived. Grand questions are frequently asked in a sweeping way, and the swift answering of such questions by the reader becomes as problematic as if the reader were in the moment with the character's limited point of view.

Arguably, Coetzee's memoirs have the highest frequency of questions asked, even though all of his works—especially from *Waiting for the Barbarians* onward and until his latest novel to date, *The Childhood of Jesus*—use the question as a rhetorical device to generate slow reading and explore philosophical ideas in a meditative way. The aforementioned sense of naïve questioning can be found in a variety of characters in Coetzee's oeuvre and is not limited to his immature "selves" in the memoirs. Attridge argues in this direction by drawing comparisons between the first two memoirs and *Life & Times of Michael K*:

> John in *Boyhood* and *Youth* is perhaps the closest to K in the kinds of questions he asks, often in extreme bemusement, as he tries to make sense of an enigmatic and often hostile world. (2004a, 58)

Attridge's link between John and Michael K is further illuminated by a remark about the elusive K, whose "questions [...] reflect his somewhat bemused attitude to the events that befall him, the natural consequence of his naïve outlook" (2004a, 58).

John's questions in the memoirs are usually asked in this attitude of *bemusement* and *naïveté*, although their naïve character is usually limited to the way *how* the questions are asked rather than to *what* they inquire into, since John is a very rational, highly intelligent character. Most of the time his questions are of this bemused nature because of his position as an outsider, something which is true of K as well, and which is an important motif in most of Coetzee's works.[7] Coetzee's outsiders are often capable of a very discerning view onto the phenomena surrounding them, on society, and even on history. The

---

[7] Head contextualizes this by commenting on Coetzee's national identity, which bears on the outsider position of John in the memoirs:

> The question of identity, as a literary as well as an ethnic matter, has proved problematic for many white South African writers, especially those who, like Coetzee, have been based in South Africa. Coetzee is not an Afrikaner, but a white South African inhabiting a very particular margin, since his background partly distances him from both Afrikaner as well as English affiliations. (2009, 3)

I return to this later.

outsider's position in Coetzee's works is usually one of meditative, composed contemplation, because the marginal position allows the more neutral reflection on that of which the outsider is not a part.

However, the outsider's view should not be romanticized, since David Lurie in *Disgrace*, for example, is certainly also an outsider after he is ostracized from the university, and his position as an outsider allows him for a long time to look with an indifferent arrogance upon the people and creatures around him. Nevertheless, the outsider's position brings about a change even in Lurie, although the novel does not explicate this and it has to be inferred from his actions, for example his problematic care of the dogs. It is important to see how the position as outsiders forces many of Coetzee's characters to reflect not only on what they perceive as the center of which they are excluded, but how this exclusion also forces them fundamentally to reflect upon themselves.

In *Youth*, for example, the outsider John observes London society with a contemplative and estranged look, and while his meditative questions about Londoners are inflected with an implicit critique of what he perceives as *unexamined lives* around him, his inquiring gaze is also loaded with a sense of naïve, but melancholic envy at the perceived easiness of a life that is not dominated by the sovereignty of reason. In a rumination on dancing, he thinks:

> Dancing makes sense only when it is interpreted as something else, something that people prefer not to admit. That *something else* is the real thing: the dance is merely a cover. Inviting a girl to dance stands for inviting her to have intercourse; accepting the invitation stands for agreeing to have intercourse; and dancing is miming and foreshadowing intercourse. So obvious are the correspondences that he wonders why people bother with dancing at all. Why the dressing up, why the ritual motions; why the huge sham? (*SPL* 219; original emphasis)

The voice is simultaneously stupefyingly perceptive and stupendously naïve. The hyperbolic description of the logics of intercourse through the expression *so obvious* highlights how alienated John feels from his contemporaries during this time in his life, and the fundamental question at the end of this passage allows us to see the real pain he experiences in isolation, while it also underlines his contemplative and observant character. The naïveté of this position creates a sense of bemusement and estrangement, which in the reader enables a challenging reflection on the phenomena inquired into.

The estranging look at phenomena exhibited by John is thus underscored not only by the unusual narrative position mentioned before, but also by the social position from which these questions are asked, namely that of the outsider. These positions are important to understand the inquiring, discerning character of Coetzee's work as a whole, since the outsider's view allows estranging and questioning, which give rise to reflections about whatever it is that is being estranged or questioned during the reading. Therefore, it is important to consider the position of the outsider as being charged with a political dimension. K is the most obviously explicit outsider, who is continually othered by the society he is (not) part of. And yet, even a white middle class character like Mrs. Curren can suddenly find herself in an ontological margin-position because of her terminal illness, as the ranks of the healthy drift ever more into an indeterminate space cordoned off to the diseased. In *Boyhood* John is an outsider because he likes thinking, because he lies in school about his religion, because of his love for the Russians over the Americans, because of his closeness to his mother, because of

> the physical isolation [of the Coetzee family] in Worcester [...] and [...] [because of John's] uncertain identity: as neither English nor Afrikaner South African, as of the farm but not of the farm, as an outsider shut out of the comfort of belonging to a designated group in his own motherland. (Kossew 2011, 12)

Especially this latter aspect is relevant, the lonely sense in which John learns that boyhood is also a state of outsiderhood[8] with a political and existential tinge, that which in *Youth* "is the painful and shameful nature of his South Africanness [...] as well as his apparent sexual ineptitude" (Kossew 2011, 12). Tim Mehigan contextualizes this by speaking of

> Coetzee's interest in the position of the outsider [...] [which] appear[s] to constitute a response to the vexed question of how to assume a position from which to speak politically through imaginative literature. (2011, 4)

The prevalence of questions in Coetzee's oeuvre allows his work to crabwalk a fine line between engaging with the political and avoiding the dangers of turning fiction into merely *supplementing history*, to echo Coetzee's "The Novel Today," in which he presents a poetological manifesto of sorts, namely the aforementioned avowal of a rivalry between the novel and history (*NT* 3f.). This rivalry between literature and socio-politics should not be seen as a hostile rivalry by which one is outdoing the other, but rather as one of discursive overlapping. Such a view of rivalry allows the contemplation of a productive rivalry also between literature

---

8   Consider, for example, the endearingly sad moment when John looks up *childhood* in the encyclopedia:

> Childhood, says the *Children's Encyclopaedia*, is a time of innocent joy, to be spent in the meadows amid buttercups and bunny-rabbits or at the hearthside absorbed in a storybook. It is a vision of childhood utterly alien to him. Nothing he experiences in Worcester, at home or at school leads him to think that childhood is anything but a time of gritting the teeth and enduring. (*SPL* 12)

and philosophy in a similarly discursive way. This rivalry, which Coetzee has never put into so many words, should not be understood as an acrimonious antagonism either, let alone a reanimation of the ancient quarrel. On the contrary, it should be viewed as a serious and complex form of engagement between two forms of discourse which address the world and its phenomena in an inquiring, reflexive way. While doubtless generalizing, such a productive rivalry between literature and philosophy helps us to explore the often elusive character of Coetzee's works more generally, as well as the profusion of questions therein more specifically.

Coetzee manages to engage with the political in a non-Lukácsian (and so a non-Gordimerian[9]) way by inclining toward allegory[10] rather than bearing witness or narrating history in the realist mode. Coetzee's works are situated against a literary realism that embraces historical representation, and

> the immature tension [in the memoirs] between the felt political straitjacket and the desire for unfettered creativity is the tension that informs the work of the mature artist. (Head 2009, 14)

This tension between the political and the literary also bears directly on the literary and the philosophical, since the disinclination toward realism raises the question summed up by Head elsewhere:

> Is it possible, in other words, to engage simultaneously with the sophisticated literary questions posed by the poststructuralist/postmodernist turn and, directly, with the key social and political issues of the day? (1997, 8)

The short answer to this question is yes. The more prolix answer has to begin by considering Head's word *directly* and might have to question if realism has the monopoly on *direct engagement*. In *Boyhood* history is narrated from the perspective of a ten- to thirteen-year-old boy, so it is doubtful that the realist ideal of directness can be achieved, since a child's views arguably cannot represent

---

[9]   The odd coinage is not mine, though I shoulder the blame in reproducing it from Dominic Head (1994, 187).

[10] An unfortunate term and here used merely *faute de mieux* to make a point. Still, some qualifications are in order. Attridge provocatively deconstructs Lukácsian allegory by noting:

> My reservations about allegory should not be construed as echoing Lukács's attack [...] on what he sees as the allegorical method of modernism: Lukács's own approach to realistic fiction, which seeks to translate particular detail into historical and social types, and subjects the alterity and singularity of the works it reads to an existing master-narrative, is, in the sense in which I am using the term, highly allegorical. (2004a, 39n17)

The way in which Attridge is using the term includes "the urge to treat elements in the text as symbols or metaphors for broader ideas or entities" (2004a, 39n17). By *inclining toward allegory*, then, I mean the complex eliding of historical realism without claiming Coetzee's "allegories" are *national allegories* in Jameson's sense, for example.

history or politics *directly*, when *directly* means that politics are *explicated*. If one assumes, however, that *directly* can mean that politics are *experienced*, then there is little reason to presume a simplistic hierarchy of representational modes by which realist representations are "right" and modernist, late modernist, or postmodernist ones "wrong." In *Boyhood* the political climate of the time and setting are filtered through the boy's worldview and epistemic horizon. Rather than engaging in an eliding of history, the work addresses history in a naïve way from the focalizer's perspective, such as when young John reflects on the paradoxical "mild racism"—the term is itself an oxymoron, like the euphemistic "manslaughter" which extenuates circumstances in the courts of law but brings no relief in the realms of ontology where *'tis death, and death, and death indeed*[11]—the racism John perceives in his mother and her sisters (*SPL* 32); or when on John's birthday he and his friends are enjoying ice-cream sundaes and "the occasion would be a marvellous success, were it not spoiled by the ragged Coloured children standing at the window looking at them" (*SPL* 61).[12] Here, then, the segregation under apartheid is related through an experience, not an explication. It may be ill-fitting to the consciousness of a young boy to think or speak of apartheid in a way that an adult conscious could, and so the reader is met with situations in which John expresses his bemusement and his incredulity at what he witnesses. This way, the reader engages with the political situation, but she has to engage with it through John's bemused and questioning view at the world, and thus has to reflect not only on *what* the text engages with, but also on *how*.

Something very similar is at work regarding the philosophical dimensions of Coetzee's oeuvre, in that the philosophical aspects are usually not highlighted through explicit references to philosophy either, but rather embedded and staged in the form of the work. In *Boyhood*, the questions asked inquire into the nature of the world's phenomena and into ethical, epistemic, and even ontological matters, and so highlight the deeply philosophical reflexivity of the young boy,

---

[11] I echo the poem "The Man of Double Deed" by Anonymous with its spiraling into death, like the house that Jack built. Coetzee has copied the poem into his notebook on *Life & Times of Michael K* (HRC, container 33, folder 5, p. 67).

[12] Generally, I explore this naïve perspective in light of its potential for reflection, but I caution against an idealization of such a position. For the problems involved regarding the childish point of view in Coetzee's memoirs, see Attridge's considerations of the example in *Boyhood* when John writes: "One can dismiss the Natives, perhaps, but one cannot dismiss the Coloured people. The Natives can be argued away because they are latecomers, invaders from the north, and have no right to be there" (*SPL* 52). Attridge comments: "At other times, the boy's unquestioning reproduction of racist thinking [...] can be read as sadly inevitable; an indication of the potency of ideology rather than any failing in the boy" (2004a, 150). The example of John's dismissal of *the Natives* echoes Coetzee's intimation of the early Cape explorers' othering the Khoikhoi as a lazy people, which Coetzee deconstructs in "Idleness in Africa".

and even more substantially of the text. Whereas the inclinations toward a more elusive and "allegorical" expression of space may signal toward a depoliticizing literature, they are, in fact, a very political engagement by different means, by rivalling means which not only make political readings valid but also implicitly question the literary representation of history. And whereas the generally elusive and inconclusive nature of philosophical debates and ideas in the works, such as in *The Lives of Animals* and *Elizabeth Costello*, might signal toward a Platonic rift between literature and philosophy, they are in fact a very direct engagement with the themes and ideas of philosophy through the forms available to imaginative writing.

The bemused question focalized through a naïve or immature character is one of the most basic ways to address philosophical concerns in a productively rivalling way, for example in the crucial moment which ends *Boyhood*, when John reflects: "He alone is left to do the thinking. How will he keep them all in his head, all the books, all the people, all the stories? And if he does not remember them, who will?" (*SPL* 140). This kind of inquiry makes use of the most basic aspect of narrative, of point of view, for an imaginative exploration of philosophical and literary questions, and this reflexive engagement with ideas is entirely unbound by the jargon of disciplines and the terminology of movements.[13] Instead, John's bemused questioning affords a reflexive and defamiliarizing view of phenomena and ideas important to him, and this way the text prepares the reader to question and reflect in a similarly bemused way.

It is this kind of naïve questioning apparent especially in Coetzee's memoirs that contributes to what I call *Coetzee's boyish imagination*, an aspect of his work that contributes to the philosophical character of the works. The term is borrowed from Richard Marggraf Turley's fascinating 2004 study *Keats's Boyish Imagination*, some of whose arguments resonate through my conception of the bemused questioning in Coetzee. One of Turley's key points is that "Keats deploy[s] juvenility as a system of interruptions" (Turley 2004, 1)—a point that may equally be made about

---

[13] This is not true for the entire oeuvre, however. Coetzee's first two works, for example, use philosophical writings as explicit intertextual references, or as moments of interruption, where philosophical phrases mix or clash with the narrative voices. See, for example, Dovey's analysis of Magda's reference to Hegel's master–slave dialectic (1988, 23) in *In the Heart of the Country*, as well as Pippin's excellent analysis of Nietzsche's expression "the pathos of its distances" in the novel (2010, 31).

In the notes toward the novel Coetzee conceives of his narrative along the lines of a very literal philosophical name-dropping. On "8.1.75" he notes a sentence apparently in Magda's voice: "'Someone has been dropping scraps of paper around the farm. Who can it be?' (Scraps contain quotations of Hegel, etc.)" (HRC, container 33, folder 3, n.p.).

Coetzee's work. It is particularly the boyish point of view through the focalizer who shares Coetzee's name in *Boyhood* and *Youth* that assumes an interruptive tendency. This is realized by "infantilizing the viewing subject" (Turley 2004, 74). As in Keats, the boyish point of view in Coetzee is used for comic as well as philosophical effect, for questioning and defamiliarizing the world's phenomena—and to indicate to the reader the possibility of deconstructing these very phenomena or norms by engendering a reflection on them.[14] An example of how this is realized can be found in John's already mentioned lie concerning his family's religion.

John comes from a secular Protestant family ("In religion they are certainly nothing" [*SPL* 16]).[15] But he shares a secret with the reader, namely that "he has become a Catholic" (*SPL* 16). When he is asked "[o]n the first morning at his new school" (*SPL* 16) about his religion, he reacts with a question to this question, but in his mind. Before he answers, the text relates John's bemused thoughts: "He glances left and right. What is the right answer? What religions are there to choose from?" (*SPL* 16). The question is presented in the simple, naïve way that a child would ask it to make sense of the world in a pragmatic way. And yet, in the unabashed generality that a child can muster in asking questions of the largest scope, in the simplest way possible, the text raises a question not only about religions John could *choose from* on his first day of school (that is, which religions are accepted in this school?) but about the nature of religion more generally (that is, why are there different religions in the first place?). The reader is stimulated to reflect on these questions both in the literal way that John asks them and in the more philosophical way of a subtly suggested auctorial

---

[14] This boyishness also has a subversive tendency, both in Keats and in Coetzee, which may be brought to bear on the deconstructing view of the outsider. Turley argues:

> Immaturity is a frequently disregarded and misunderstood feature of Keats's challenge to authority. Yet boyish pranks and infantile responses, which I argue function as a system of interruption, prove a powerfully strategic means of disturbing the "adult" focus of eighteenth-century aestheticians [...]. There is a deeply subversive purpose in Keats's politically freighted portrayal of himself as a "naughty boy" who "could not quiet be" (Turley 2004, 74).

(The poem alluded to is Keats's "A Song about Myself.")

A similarly subversive challenge to authority is apparent in Coetzee's works, not only in his autrebiographical figures but also in Michael K, who appears as the eternal son, even after his mother's death, and whose response to the world can best be described as *boyish*. Viewed in this light, K's slow resistance can be regarded as a childish resistance. His behavior of building a make-shift house and hiding could likewise be considered infantile behavior. While these aspects are important to an understanding of many of Coetzee's characters—Paul Rayment's life at the end is explicitly infantilized when he likens his tricycle to a perambulator, "a perambulator with a grizzled old baby in it" (*S* 256)—these aspects must be explored elsewhere in more detail.

[15] In *Doubling the Point* Coetzee describes himself—in the third person—as "a Protestant enrolled in a Catholic high school, with Jewish and Greek friends" (*DtP* 393).

consciousness behind these texts (suggested most strongly through the use of the third person). John lies that he is a Roman Catholic because he likes the Romans, and so he turns himself into an outsider in the Dutch Reformed town he lives in. This leads him to develop a deep reflection on lying, which ends in an ontological cul-de-sac:

> He knows he is a liar, knows he is bad, but he refuses to change. He does not change because he does not want to change. His difference from other boys may be bound up with his mother and his unnatural family, but is bound up with his lying too. If he stopped lying he would have to polish his shoes and talk politely and do everything that normal boys do. In that case he would no longer be himself. If he were no longer himself, what point would there be in living? (*SPL* 30)

Again, John's thinking here is a pragmatic self-reflection, but the seemingly rhetorical question at the end of the passage swells up to philosophical proportions by its signaling of the ontological dimension that informs it. The question is treacherously simple but infinitely complex, since it is looped up in the paradoxical allusiveness so frequent in Coetzee's writing. *If he were no longer himself, what point would there be in living?* The question is plain enough, but it actually condenses many related questions, such as: *How could he know that he were no longer himself? Can one live without a self? And who could tell if there were any "point" to it?* And so, a simple instrumental logic is debunked the way a child debunks the grand questions of life and existence. The contextualization of such a question in a pragmatic context, while allowing the question to open a wider realm of philosophical debate, permits the viewing of such a question as an interruption in the text, which provokes fundamental reflections by the reader.

When John has grown older in *Youth* he still asks questions in such a boyish way. Aside from the slowing force perhaps inherent in every reflexive question, the questions in the second memoir frequently open up an even more complex reflexive realm than those in the first one, since here they are often asked in a more piercing and more self-denigrating way (usually by expounding on the admission that "[i]n misery he is still top of the class" [*SPL* 199]). The questions in *Youth* may be described by what George Steiner calls a "ceaseless, circling, inward-driving query" (1989, 36), and this way John's self-questioning also contributes to an experienced isolation, as he dwindles more and more into his own mind, which the narrator reflects through questions in free indirect discourse. Just before John decides he will quit his mundane office job at IBM, which will make him a permanent drifter without a resident permit in London, he imagines a dialogue with a faceless official from England's Home Office:

> He is not a refugee; or rather, a claim on his part to be a refugee will get him nowhere with the Home Office. Who is oppressing you, the Home Office will say? From what are you fleeing? From boredom, he will reply. From philistinism. From atrophy of the moral life. From shame. Where will such a plea get him? (*SPL* 231)

Even when in his interior dialogue John answers his questions, or rather the questions by the imagined government official, the questioning mode circles around to become a quite existential doubt. John's boyishness is foregrounded both through the uncertainty that the questions reveal and through the shifting and fearsome sense of breaking down at the end with the final question, *Where will such a plea get him?* This crack in the defiant, logical stability of the voice is conveyed in the last question, and once again, it comes in the guise of a rhetorical question, which, however, belies the reflexive realm that it opens up: where, indeed, will such a plea get one? Are artists—what John so desperately wishes to become—exempt from the concrete logics of politics? Are artists somehow above reality, above history? And what will, ultimately, happen to John, what will become of him, how will he wind out of the morass of monotony and mundanity?

Such inquiry gains in naïveté when the reader brings to the text the knowledge that a version of John will eventually become the world-renowned writer J. M. Coetzee. The reader herself might ask when he will indeed become the artist, the writer, whose memoir she is, after all, reading during all this worrying about the outcome. Supposing that the reader asks this question, it is the reader herself who is provoked to confront a degree of her own naïveté, since John's worrying is quite realistic as he does not possess future knowledge by which he could divine the outcome of life's ways as a retrospective narrative of a life might; and since this narrative of a life is precisely that, a narrative, a story, not a mimetic mirror to the nature of the real J. M. Coetzee, but an imaginative and defamiliarizing exploration of the "massive autobiographical writing-enterprise that fills a life, this enterprise of self-construction" (*DtP* 17), this enterprise which has brought forth the character "John." Coetzee's autrebiographical project in all three *Scenes from Provincial Life (Boyhood, Youth, Summertime)* confronts the reader with estranging life-stories of Coetzee's "youthful self in as poor a light as possible" (Head 2009, 15), so that the reader is kept in perpetual suspense about how this less than perfect, less than impressive character will become the artist whose portrait she is reading. In a review, John Updike notes that *Youth* "has an overriding, suspenseful issue: when and how will our hero find his vocation, evident to us readers if not yet to him, as a world-class novelist?" (2007, 372).[16] This has the effect that the reader is held in a mode of questioning, of uncertainty comparable to what the character John himself feels about his own future. The use of the aforementioned narrative situation, particularly the present tense, is arguably put to the most effective use in Coetzee's memoirs, since here it has the function of making the reader pass through this "life" of the subject while the subject is himself passing through it.

This way, any inferential answer to John's uncertainties, which the reader might give on account of what she believes to know about the real author J. M. Coetzee—any such answer is interrupted through Coetzee's boyish imagination in the memoirs, by which I mean both the character John's view of the world that is narrated in the text, and the diegetic world that is imagined by the text. These aspects combined convey a boy's sense of "fundamental astonishment which is the necessary source of philosophical questioning" (Steiner 1989, 65).

It seems as if the trilogy of memoirs heralded a higher frequency of questions in Coetzee's oeuvre, and particularly questions which are ever simpler, and which thus mandate ever more complicated questions in the reader. The third instalment of this autrebiographical trilogy, *Summertime*, presents the peculiar case of a work structured by inquiry. While it is not a text written entirely in questions, like Padgett Powell's *The Interrogative Mood: A Novel?* (2009), the work's form owes its structure to the idea and the function of the question. *Summertime* is structured around a young academic's endeavor to write a critical biography about the late John Coetzee, and he pursues this goal by interviewing the people who have known the deceased writer. This questioning mode keeps the narrative's flow in a discursive oscillation between accelerative propulsion and halting slowness, or to echo the aforementioned expression from the text itself: "*Movement in stillness, stillness in movement*" (*SPL* 418; original emphasis).

In Coetzee's third work of autrebiography, the question as a device for slow reflection is thus translated from the minds of the two Johns in *Boyhood* and *Youth* to the very structure of the work in an explicit way. This foregrounds the question as a tactic to kindle reflexivity in a very different way, while transmuting it more explicitly into the formal arrangement of the work, and so inching the memoir away from more realist forms of autobiography even more strongly than the autrebiographical mode of the two previous memoirs have done. Now

---

[16] Only in *Summertime* is John already a practicing writer, if only at the very beginning of his career, having just published *Dusklands*.

it is no longer John who, via the narrator, is inquiring into his own life and self (and thus *constructing* a self or counter-self), but it is other characters who inquire into his life and so create a self that the reader accepts as a counter-self, because it is not filtered solely through the focalizing subject. The structure of the interview and the questions asked about the late John Coetzee thus caution us from the beginning that the answers given will only be approaches to the real J. M. Coetzee, and this distorts preconceived characterizations the reader may have of the real author on account of the previous memoirs or the interpretation of the public intellectual.

This way, the third autrebiography seems like an estranging response (or challenge) to the two previous works, which complicates a straightforward instrumental reading of the text in general and of the character John Coetzee as being equivalent to the real J. M. Coetzee in particular. When the interviewees answer the interviewer's questions, their answers frequently assume narrative qualities, but often adopt the inquiring mode of the interviewer themselves. So, the text creates a multilayered web of questions that is seemingly self-perpetuating, while it provokes the reader to be in a questioning mood also.

This questioning functions as a slowing device that is also reflected upon in the typographical layout of the text. The reader may sometimes forget—during a longer narrative passage—that what she is reading is an interview, and so the longer narrative passages are sharply interrupted by the interviewer with a startling silence, which is represented as "[Silence.]" in the text (for example, *SPL* 412),[17] which is once followed by an incredulous "And?" (*SPL* 412). Like *Diary of a Bad Year* the third memoir also contributes to the reader's questioning and estranged response through the typographical arrangement of the text on the page.[18] While long stretches of the work are narrative, many pages are visually fragmented and riven by questions. This way, the reader is continually pulled out of the narrative mode by a question, but then pushed back into the narrative as one of the interviewees responds to a question by the interviewer. The visual layout, then, emphasizes the function of the question in Coetzee as well, namely that it defamiliarizes, that it pulls the reader momentarily out of the text and makes her reflect in a more fundamental way about what a question implies. This is frequently achieved through the aforementioned boyish character of the question, the bemusement that it relates to the reader. David in *The Childhood*

---

[17] All five interview sections (Julia, Margot, Adriana, Martin, and Sophie) feature these moments of "[Silence.]" many times.

[18] For a deeper exploration of the typographical layout of *Diary of a Bad Year*, see the chapter on gaps of this study.

of Jesus seems like a poetological summation of the boyish inquirer in Coetzee's oeuvre, since the explicitness and the frequency of the why-questions force both Simón and the reader to reflect long and hard about the interruption the question represents (consider again the above-mentioned example of David's naïve question "What is human nature?" [*CoJ* 48]). The boyish sense of asking questions has the added effect of allowing the reader to join the philosophical debates in the texts much more readily, since a naïve way of asking a question, especially if it is asked by a child, as in the example from *The Childhood of Jesus*, steers clear of philosophical vernacular and allows a philosophizing even by those untrained in philosophy, simply by creating ambiguity that demands reflection, and by making strange what may otherwise be unconsidered, for example by asking a fundamental question, such as *What is human nature?*

The direct way of asking has the effect of eliciting a bemused response in the reader and so to put her into a meditative mood, allowing her to roam into philosophical terrain without the need for specialized language. The works usually do not treat philosophical inquiry as limited to philosophical terms and philosophers, but rather make all characters, regardless of background or age, philosophers, or rather philosophizers. Even if Costello's daughter-in-law, Norma, "find[s] [Costello's] philosophizing rather difficult to take" (*EC* 91) and calls her arguments "pseudo-philosophical" (*EC* 113), Costello, nevertheless, asks her sweeping questions about animal ethics in a naïve way. Costello's usually sweeping questions about ethics and reason are continually kept in check by Norma's comments.[19] This has the effect that the novel can ask those very large questions while also safeguarding itself against the accusation of naïveté, or uninformed dabbling at philosophy. Costello usually asks her questions in naïve fashion, whether she asks deceptively simple questions, such as "If there were no difference, what would become of our desire?" (*EC* 23); "Does the mind by nature prefer sensations to ideas, the tangible to the abstract?" (*EC* 24); or when she awakes during the night in a hotel room and wonders "*Where am I?* [...] *Who am I?*" (*EC* 117; original emphases). Particularly this last question confronts head on one of the biggest questions of all, the ontological white whale, *Who am I?* In microcosm one can see here how the novel operates on a

---

[19]   In his reflections on the lectures in *The Lives of Animals*, Peter Singer notes:

> Coetzee's fictional device enables him to distance himself from them. And he has this character, Norma, Costello's daughter-in-law, who makes all the obvious objections to what Costello is saying. It's a marvellous device, really. Costello can blithely criticize the use of reason, or the need to have any clear principles or proscriptions, without Coetzee really committing himself to these claims. Maybe he really shares Norma's very proper doubts about them. (1999, 91)

larger scale as well. The two questions, *Where am I?* and *Who am I?*, are asked by Costello when she is woken by the telephone in a hotel room. So, her question *Who am I?* may be read metaphorically and put in perspective as a question by a person gradually orienting herself in the night in a hotel room away from home and slowly awaking from a dream. However, by the time the reader comes to this question, she has already read Costello's utterance two pages earlier: "It's that I no longer know where I am" (*EC* 114). Here, what she means is to be understood not in a spatial way but in a social or possibly existential way, and so the novel provides the larger ontological interpretation of Costello's nocturnal reflections, while also permitting a metaphorical reading of her gradual awakening in the night.

The key aspect of Coetzee's meditative questions is their innocence, while this does not entail any less serious character of his works' meditative questioning, since these questions matter a great deal to the characters and the texts, the way the question about the cricket-ball is important to John. It is part and parcel of the immature mind to ask innocent questions, and thus to allow a more innocent, a more fundamental, engagement with these questions also.

When little Alice has tumbled down the rabbit-hole and has deemed the underground world of Wonderland "curiouser and curiouser" (Carroll [1865] 1992, 13), she is in pursuit of the ontological white whale as well: "'Who in the world am I?' Ah, *that's* the great puzzle!" (Carroll [1865] 1992, 15; original emphasis). It is probably not curiouser and curiouser that *Elizabeth Costello*—apart from its ethical and aesthetic reflections so caught up with ontology and epistemology and the rational (or non-rational) grasp of the self—should indicate Lewis Carroll's *Alice's Adventures in Wonderland* (1865) explicitly toward the end, just as Costello is confronted with ever more perplexing questions, and just as she is forced to assume a girlish vision herself, when she is in the face of indecipherable perplexity: "Her first impression was right: a court of Kafka or *Alice in Wonderland*, a court of paradox" (*EC* 223).[20] The aforementioned bemusement experienced by Michael K in the face of the world's phenomena is experienced by Costello in the face of the courtroom in the novel's final chapter. The scene plays up the allegorical potential of constituting a paradisiacal fantasy of the aging writer Costello at heaven's gates, where she argues her case at much higher stakes than before an academic audience. The intertextual connection

---

[20] Immediately afterwards, the narrator uses one of Tweedledee's staple words, "contrariwise" (*EC* 223). And before, Costello reflects on the absurdity of the court she is facing and admits that it may not, after all, be a courtroom from a children's novel: "Not the Mad Hatter's tea party" (*EC* 203). See also (Doniger 1999, 104) and Lamb (2010, 181) for small references to the *Alice* novels regarding Costello.

with Carroll's *Alice* books emphasizes the childish view at the world, which many of Coetzee's characters experience upon gazing at or inquiring into the world's phenomena. Generally, Coetzee's focalizers share a childish appreciation of the world, which always allows the asking of questions, even if they are considered naïve. These childish views allow Coetzee's texts to express a sense of sheer incredulity in the face of human and non-human suffering, for example.

Earlier I have argued that the inquiring nature behind Coetzee's focalizers and his works as a whole is related to an understanding of boyishness. The stance adopted by the reader is related to this boyishness as well. The texts might be seen as suggesting to the reader to adopt a similarly childish view as well, if *childish* is invested with the positive potential of *astonishment*, *naïve questioning*, and *bemusement*, but also a good dose of *incredulity*, that is a willingness to repeat ceaselessly *the children's query*. Along a simultaneity of these, slow reading can take place, a reading that is bemused and fascinated, unafraid to be in uncertainty, mystery, and doubt. Ultimately, Coetzee's works ask the reader to remain in negative capability, Keats's potentiality of "being in uncertainties, mysteries, doubts, without any irritable reaching after fact and reason" (1901, 50). Through the various devices explored in this study, Coetzee's works continually motion the reader to read attentively, responsively and responsibly without giving way to the itch for generating final answers. Coetzee's works recruit the reader in the co-production of the texts, and they do so without claiming that the authority of the writer is any less certain than the reader herself, whether the writer is a child or an adolescent who will grow to be a Nobel Prize winner, or whether the writer is Elizabeth Costello, part fish and part fowl, part writer and part thinker. Elizabeth Costello shares her own thoughts about writing, which are related to what I mean by slow reading when she sees herself as a *secretary of the invisible*:

> When I claim to be a secretary clean of belief I refer to my ideal self, a self capable of holding opinions and prejudices at bay while the word which it is her function to conduct passes through her. (*EC* 200)

Appropriately, one of the judges, who must have some knowledge of literary history—one would expect no less from a judge in a court out of Kafka or Carroll—catches Costello's drift and asks her: "Is it negative capability what you have in mind, what you claim to possess?" (*EC* 200). Costello replies: "Yes, if you like"(*EC* 200). Coetzee's works, in their inquiring nature, provoke an approaching of the world's phenomena and their representation and expression in literature in a way that owes to negative capability, an approaching attentively, inquisitively, inquiringly, and finally meditatively without the irritable domination of *fact and reason*, as Keats has it, without the desire for instrumentality, as Attridge has it.

Coetzee's works turn even the most sophisticated and rational reader into a bemused child, who is forced to look closely at the text she is reading, possibly even to re-read the work to reflect on what has been experienced. The texts make the reader appreciate that the answer might not be the point, but that the point is an ongoing *doubling the point*, since that which keeps reflection going may just be *the children's query*, the asking of very simple questions. And while these can quite possibly lead to grand questions about human nature, they might simply begin with *a goblin: why?*

4

What Matters Is that the Contest Is Staged—Coetzee's Slowing Syntax

"For a man of his age, fifty-two, divorced, he has, to his mind, solved the problem of sex rather well" (*Dis* 1). The seemingly effortless flow of the opening line to *Disgrace* is startling. The vocabulary is unobtrusive, the tone cool, unemotional, but not restrained. There is almost a subtle cheeriness to the words, a nonchalant sense of accomplishment. Beginning with a prepositional phrase, the sentence creates expectation; it prepares for a poignant resolution to the opening created by the preposition *for*. But the growing tension is immediately decelerated, and thereby intensified, through the qualifying parentheses, until the sentence is finally punctuated by the light-hearted expression *rather well*, which suggests more of a casual gladness than a euphoric climax, a phenomenon that might be termed unusual regarding the sentence's topic.[1] Michael Douthwaite notes:

> The first sentence of the novel is clearly a topical sentence. The topic is announced as being that of sex. The lexical choice immediately highlights a physical aspect of life, a basic drive that must be satisfied to ensure the functional integrity of the system. (2005, 43)

At this point in the narrated life of David Lurie, *the functional integrity of the system* seems to be ensured not by the body, but by the mind. Sex and passion, the sentence suggests, have been dealt with entirely rationally. Lurie's life, one might infer, must be as rigorously compartmentalized as this first sentence is rigorously structured. A few pages later, that which is subtly alluded to in this first sentence on a microscopic level, is echoed as an authorial comment: "He

---

[1] In his article "Time, Tense, and Aspect in Kafka's 'The Burrow'" Coetzee comments on the beginning of Kafka's story as laying out "the culmination of a certain past, in order to retrace the history leading up to this moment" (*DtP* 228). He argues: "The first sentence of 'The Burrow' seems to promise a similar project: 'I have completed the construction of my burrow and it seems to be successful.' But the project turns out to be riddled with problems" (*DtP* 229). In a similar way, one might say *Disgrace* opens with a first sentence that seems to promise a successful, conclusive solution, and it implicitly sets up the consequent deconstruction of this solution, how sex will, in fact, become what riddles his life with problems.

is all for double lives, triple lives, lives lived in compartments" (*Dis* 6). Like the protagonist's life and like the first sentence of the novel, this example sentence, too, is divided into compartments. Its fluid readability is fragmented by the parenthesis "triple lives," which seems emphatic and firm, and it seems to evoke more than it actually states. The chiastic and rhythmic lingering on *lives* is itself a doubling and mirroring of this character's life, and it invites reflection not only on the part but also on the whole.

Coetzee's sentences are frequently structured like this. Comma-spliced into small units, they might be seen as cells stocked with a wealth of information, arranged in such a way that individual phrases or parentheses complement and often even contest one another. Surely, syntactical arrangements are meant to be complementary and constitutive of sentences proper, but the layout of Coetzee's sentences often creates gaps between syntactical compartments. These gaps are a result of the density of the individual phrases from which the scaffold of a sentence is assembled, as if the sheer density of the text were better to be perused around breathing moments. The lacunae between individual phrases are often achieved through syntactical and rhythmical arrangement, as in the earlier example, where the twice repeated noun *lives* forces the reader's voice—aural or mental—to hesitate in the reading. The intervals between syntactically separate semantic and sonic units function like the pauses in music do, where silence is of equal importance as sound. These pauses can have the greatest effects for slowing down the reading process and allowing for reflexive space in reading, if one is attentive to these pauses.

"For a man of his age, fifty-two, divorced, he has, to his mind, solved the problem of sex rather well." The individual units of the sentence unfold slowly through their syntactically lengthening presentation and the condensed information therein, as if the sentence were a bowl of water and each phrase one of the Japanese paper flowers, pressed tightly together and unfurling more and more when dropped into water. In just twenty words the first sentence of *Disgrace* seems to contain, in crystallized form, everything about Lurie's character that later determines a large part of the story's incidents. On a thematic level, the suggestion is clear: to Lurie's mind sex is a near-banality. Sex used to be a cause for worry, but now the worrying is over, its real implications (emotional, passional, political) do not even warrant further thought. And yet, the very function of the sentence is to engage with sex, to such a degree that sex takes thematic precedence over everything else. This precedence alone complicates a straightforward reading of sex as a problem that has been solved, since it would not be the first conjuration by the focalizer if it had been solved *rather well*. What the sentence conjures into existence is not the solution to a problem, but the problem's continuation through negation. "The worst is not/So long as we can say 'This is the worst'" (IV.i.29–30), says *King Lear*'s Edgar. So long as the mind is compelled by the impetus to nullify a problem through utterance, so long the utterance elevates the problem into expressed reality. Could the mind's more radical solution to a problem not be to remain silent about it? Or is the mind so in need of verification, is it so fearful of the problem that it needs to pacify it through self-affirmation by way of uttering the problem away, which cannot be anything but an uttering into presence?

In any case, David Lurie's problem of sex is that the problem of sex remains. The sheer control he seems to exert over sex—note how he relishes Soraya's apartment as "functional, clean, well regulated" (*Dis* 5)—his sheer obsessive-compulsive domestication of sexuality suggests a wild beast brooding under the tranquil surface, and because thematically sex takes center stage through the novel's first sentence, the topic of sex will equally brood in the reader's mind as she reads along. Arguably, a reader will think back to this first sentence, to the very statement it makes about sex and about Lurie's smugness to think in such a way. So, any swift moving past this obstacle of sex is inhibited by the thematic implications of the first sentence alone. But it is equally powerfully suggested in the sentence's syntax that sex is a problem to stay.

"For a man of his age, fifty-two, divorced, he has, to his mind, solved the problem of sex rather well." The glaring word *sex* clouds the fact that the word order of this first sentence might suggest that what is negotiated here is not so much sex as it is ratio. The sentence's prime topic seems to be *sex*. However, this is undermined by the sentence's syntactic layout, through which *mind* takes chronological precedence over *sex*. The first sentence as a microcosm of the novel evokes an interactive dualism of mind and body on the syntactic level alone.[2] Before the "fall," Lurie believes he has found a solution to the mind–body problem; here, the dualism is interestingly eclipsed by *the problem of*

---

[2] The novel negotiates a Cartesian interactive dualism, which may be gleaned from Lurie's implied faith in rational control and the foregrounding of the body. This may first be seen in the way Lurie's problems only arise after his encroaching on Soraya's personal life and her resulting retreat. If one wishes to see his "fall" as a continuation from the bad judgment of seducing a student, then one might see this bad judgment as the collapse of a rational system whose power has been undermined by the needs of the body. The question arises if this can still be called a rational system at all? Note also the novel's preoccupation with the soul and Romanticism. One may perceive the staple Romantic phenomena of the *soul* and the *imagination* as negotiated in Lurie's attempts to harmonize mind and body. This attempt is dealt with not so much because he realizes rationally that his affair with a student was a bad choice, but only after his body (and his daughter's body) has been the site of an attack that further stages the impotence of the mind. Note the way Lurie "is not himself" (*Dis* 94) when he has been attacked and locked in the lavatory, and how, when he reflects on his "day

sex, which implicitly accords more power to the body than to reason. Sex is the body's first offense. If the mind were master over the body, surely it could prevent *the problem of sex* ever to become a problem at all by being nipped in the bud (pun definitely intended). So, implicitly the body seems to have started as master of the mind, but has been tamed by Lurie's mental faculties. And so, in his ritualized dealings with Soraya, Lurie's mind seems in full control of the needs of his body, even if the choice of language, *the problem of sex*, signals an implicit power of body over mind.

The first sentence, then, subtly characterizes Lurie's complex mind, his complicated thinking, not so much topically as formally, through the choice of words and through the syntactic structure of the first sentence, the reader's first encounter with *his mind*. The syntactic arrangement of the sentence, the words in succession as well as the intrusion of smaller phrase-units into the even flow of the sentence relate a sense of Lurie's mind as a convoluted sphere, where a sentence cannot be expressed without pauses and interruptions that suggest a controlled reflective mode.

On the second page one encounters a similar syntactic layout with regard to sex: "In the field of sex, his temperament, though intense, has never been passionate" (*Dis* 2). Insertions, such as the concessive clause *though intense* here, may be read as a harking back, a return to ideas evoked at the sentence's outset; they can qualify further or keep statements and allusions in check; and such insertions can anticipate and simultaneously challenge a reader's response to them. The insertions of phrases and clauses give a sense of doubleness to Lurie's voice, which mirrors his belief in "double lives, triple lives, lives lived in compartments" (*Dis* 6). This doubleness of the voice should be understood via Mikhail Bakhtin, who sees all of language as essentially "double," that each word is "double-voiced, in each word an argument" ([1929] 1984, 73).[3] Coetzee's syntax shows how a sentence can bring words or syntactic units in dialogue with one another and thus stimulate growing reflection in the reader. The aforementioned sentences thus negotiate different aspects of Lurie's character by

---

of testing" (*Dis* 94), he comes to understand: "He speaks Italian, he speaks French, but Italian and French will not save him here in the darkest Africa" (*Dis* 95). Language (as metonymic for the mind) is useless. For further engagements with the mind–body dualism in Coetzee's works, see Elizabeth Costello's notions of "reject[ing] a Cartesian dualism and the hegemony of reason" (O'Neill 2009, 226). See *EC* 66f.; 78f. See also Woessner (2010). More generally, one may be reminded of Beckett being reminded of Schopenhauer in his *Proust* (1930): "And we are reminded of Schopenhauer's definition of the artistic procedure as 'the contemplation of the world independently of the principle of reason'" ([1930] 1965, 87).

[3] The idea of a *double voice* is central to my understanding of dialogue in Chapter 7, "The legacy of Socrates—Dialogue in and with Coetzee."

expressing a history of rationalization in an extremely small space. This process can transfer to the reader's mind upon reading, and so it can productively slow down and stimulate reflection.

The mind that is evoked by such a complex system of syntactic organization is highly reflexive, a mind that keeps itself in check constantly, that corrects, qualifies its mental utterances as they occur, or even inhibits them as they arise. This might be seen in the stylistic device of restricting through syntactic intrusion, and may already be found in *Disgrace's* first sentence, where, arguably, it instigates an immediate slowing down, even as the novel begins *in medias res*. Such a sentence performs a double function of catalyzing the narrative while slowing down a swift moving past the reflexive realm evoked at the sentence's outset. Sentences like the opening to *Disgrace* might then be understood as moments of *dynamic stillness* mentioned earlier, accelerating the narrative firmly into motion through a staggering confrontation with a voice or a topic (the cool voice talking calmly about the problem of sex), and simultaneously decelerating the flow of this voice to stimulate thinking and to evoke a character ill at ease with himself despite his attesting to the contrary.

"For a man of his age, fifty-two, divorced, he has, to his mind, solved the problem of sex rather well." The parenthetical insertions (*fifty-two*; *divorced*; *to his mind*) come to the reader in seemingly unobtrusive fashion. Embraced by commas, they seem of a non-restrictive nature, supplying mere *additional* information, when their presentation belies their significance. The two appositions *fifty-two* and *divorced* "are phrases upshifted to the level of clause, as is the first phrase ['For a man of his age']" (Douthwaite 2005, 45). Such an upgrading of phrase to clause gives more meaning to the linguistic unit, to a mere throw-away phrase that seems to impart additional information, thus creating more textual density and allusive potential. Douthwaite continues:

> Coetzee could have written more simply, "For a divorced man of 52." This would have avoided promoting the phrase to clause, and would consequently have attributed far less importance to the information conveyed by these units. (2005, 45)

Through its specific syntactic organization the sentence becomes layered with signification. As Douthwaite shows, the aforementioned parenthetical insertions are all "modalizing [...] expressions" (2005, 45). This has the following effect:

> Lurie's objective in employing these expressions is to exhibit confidence in his opinion. To the reader, however, they signal Lurie's smugness. More importantly, the very fact that Lurie should include epistemic modal expressions [...] conveys

the locutionary force that he is actually only expressing an opinion. Opinions are not the same as facts. Consequently, Lurie is undermining his assertion of confidence by unwittingly drawing attention to the fact that he is indeed only expressing personal opinion, a very particular opinion at that. This, in turn, automatically makes the reader question the validity of Lurie's assertions. (Douthwaite 2005, 46)

From the first sentence onward, the reader is cautioned to reflect on everything the narrator relates to us, cautioned to consider thinking the text against the narrator's (and the focalizer's) smug presentation, a phenomenon that slows down the processing of the text by very subtly highlighting the double nature of the voice; the reader has, in effect, to read very rigorously and cautiously.

All that is related is mediated through the focalizer Lurie; the reader infers that the narrative is filtered through or produced by his mind, so one might at last consider more closely the phrase *to his mind*. Daniel Kiefer argues for the sly use of the phrase and its function to foreground Lurie's reliance on ratio: "The opening sentence of the novel offers the phrase 'to his mind' as a kind of conversational aside, but the muttering emphasizes David's reliance on his own self-reflection" (2009, 266). Earlier, I have pointed out the importance of this phrase if it is read in connection with or in opposition to the word *sex*. The way the phrase *to his mind* intrudes into the syntax, thematically one could argue Lurie's mind intrudes into his life, which evokes unsettling ideas about reason in a more general way. Without arguing that Lurie is crippled by his mind like Dostoevsky's underground man, for example, his thinking can still be regarded as contributing to his downfall, despite his reliance on self-reflection and precisely because of his reliance on the supremacy of the mind. While physical desire might be responsible for his pursuit of Soraya and Melanie, surely one cannot discount the fact that it is his mind that upsets his routine and his purported control over his life. It is his obsessive reliance on the sense that all *can* be regulated rationally that causes his descent; he "pays a detective agency to track [Soraya] down" (*Dis* 9); he thinks with envy of Soraya's husband, "the husband he has never seen" (*Dis* 10); and he consciously gives Melanie credit for insufficient academic work (*Dis* 48). All these are rational but ill judgments that riddle his life with problems later. Reading Lurie's very calculated subsequent actions against the smug demeanor indicated in the beginning of the text, one has the feeling that his mind has not mastered his body so much as his mind has, above all else, vanquished itself. To witness him making such bad judgments, then, suggests that his mind is an obstacle to itself. While the reader can witness a foregrounding of the breakdown of Lurie's rational faculties on a more thematic level as the novel progresses, this is already indicated in the very first sentence. Douthwaite again:

> Lurie is a professor of literature and communication. He is thus a master of language. The sophisticated writing technique proves this. Yet Lurie fails to control his writing (and therefore himself) fully, and in so doing inadvertently questions his own existence. (2005, 47)

The spliced-up nature of the first sentence may already hint at the complex shambles in which Lurie's mind is. However, the deceleration evident in the syntactic organization may be charged with further philosophical resonance. First, a deceleration carries the positive aspect of slowing down the sentence for a more reflexive, even meditative perusal that works along the lines of evocation rather than of statement. Second, the syntactic fragmentation rich with qualifiers signals the character's obsessive attempt at controlling language. This might be charged with an existential urgency, because if control, even linguistic control, is relinquished, the house of cards might collapse fully. In this argumentation, the syntax must be rigorously controlled and compartmentalized so as to remain manageable by the character (here: Lurie). It might also be argued that the rigorous control over language is a mask used by Lurie to keep at bay the more uncontrollable urges of his character, such as desire.

The fragmentation of the first sentence's syntax anticipates the slowly rupturing mind of David Lurie, it may highlight the existential necessity of a mind's slowness, while also evoking a deceleration of the reading process to provoke reflection. The sentence's fragmentation may be viewed in light of a "*deceleration* and change in intonation pattern caused by the insertion of 'to his mind'" (Douthwaite 2005, 47; added emphasis). The syntactic fragmentation "creates a sense of interruption" (Douthwaite 2005, 47). The form of Lurie's sentence undermines the easy, quick problem-solving which he purports. While Douthwaite concludes that "form negates content" (Douthwaite 2005, 47), the form actually points up beforehand what the content will reveal later in the narrative. The syntactic fragmentation of the first sentence, then, comments on the focalizer David Lurie's mind, while also decelerating the text.[4]

---

[4] Douthwaite identifies further fascinating linguistic devices in the first sentence. For example, he notes that "coldness and matter-of-factness," which the novel's beginning evokes, "have a distancing effect" (2005, 43). This distancing effect may also be linked to a sense of slowing down, since a distancing device may productively stimulate a deeper engagement with a text, as anything from Brecht to abstract expressionism will testify. In the latter example, it is interesting to note that the foregrounding of form productively complicates interpretation (in a solely hermeneutic understanding).

To give some examples of the different possibilities of ordering the novel's crucial first sentence syntactically, let us look at the various manuscript revisions which the opening to *Disgrace* has undergone from the first extant draft until the published work. In a draft version dated "19 August 1995," the opening line reads: "For someone of his age and temperament, he has solved the sexual business rather well."[5] The prepositional setup is already in place, as is the focus on Lurie's temperament, which in the published version will only be dealt with on the following page. However, the sentence is not decelerated rhythmically because of the absence of parentheses, and the reading is not complicated by any qualifiers that could suggest that the idea of a sex-problem-solution is merely David's *opinion*. In a revision stage dated "2 April 1996," the sentence becomes: "For a man in his fifties, divorced, alone, not particularly well-off, he has resolved the sexual business rather well, he thinks."[6] The parentheses are now in place, three in number, as well as an added qualifier in the end, like an afterthought that concludes—quite anti-climactically—that this statement should be considered Lurie's personal opinion and not a hard fact.

In the first typed version, titled *Version 1*, the sentence remains as in the revision of 2 April 1996, until it is revised, dated "21 May 1996," when *he thinks* at the end is cut and the sentence reads: "For a man in his fifties, divorced, alone, he has resolved the sexual business rather well."[7] The expression *not particularly well-off* has been cut, arguably because of a subtle indecisiveness suggested by the use of the adverb, an indecisiveness that seems counter to David's smugness. Because the second parenthesis seems rhythmically swifter than the first, the slow tension-building sense of the published sentence is lacking. In the second typed version, *Version 2*, dated "21 May 1996," the sentence is intact in its form from *Version 1*, but is extensively altered in the next revision called "Revision to September 1996": "For a man of his age, fifty-two, divorced, and with no intention of getting trapped by a woman again, he has solved the problem of sex rather well, he ~~thinks~~ believes."[8] Comparing the revision to *Version 1* with the revisions to *Version 2* one notes the subtle change from *For a man in his fifties* to the more fluid rhythm of *For a man of his age*. Now, the sentence delays specifics for a moment to create interest in the precise age of this man, which is answered in the first parenthesis, *fifty-two*. The phrase *fifty-two* is now used "as a redundancy," which means that "concepts are duplicated ('age' equals 'fifty-two')" (Douthwaite

---

5   HRC, container 35, folders 4–5, p. 1.
6   Ibid.
7   HRC, container 35, folder 6, p. 1.
8   HRC, container 35, folder 7, p. 1.

2005, 46), the effect of which is a further deceleration through repetition.[9] One can see how, in miniscule form, specifics are delayed and then paid off. This creates a sense of both slowness and movement, both of which are only possible because of the delaying of specific information. The long interjection *and with no intention of getting trapped by a woman again* seems agitated and aggressive in its explicitness and its rhythm. It makes one think of an altogether different David Lurie, a character who does not keep his emotions in check, but voices them quite openly and in crude fashion. Arguably, this statement also details too specifically what is at the core of David Lurie, not a problem of sex so much as a problem with women. Such notions are certainly present in the published novel, however in a transmuted way, choosing evocation over explicitness.

The statement is deleted from *Version 3*, dated "7 September 1996": "For a man of his age, fifty-two, divorced, of moderate means, he has solved the problem of sex rather well, he thinks."[10] The afterthought *he thinks* is reinstalled again, along with the new addition of the parenthesis *of moderate means*. Arguably, the third qualifier following directly after the second creates *too* much of a sense of hesitation, decelerates the sentence in an unbalanced way. In the revised version, dated "31 January 1997" it is cut: "For a man of his age, fifty-two, divorced, he has solved the problem of sex rather well, in his opinion."[11] The afterthought *he thinks* is changed to foreground Lurie's subjectivity through the word *opinion*, and this highlights his self-reliance. The phrase *in his opinion*, then, evokes how the problem of sex (and its attested solution) exists in Lurie's mind alone and is, thankfully, not a universal fact. The expression *opinion*, more so than *thinks*, connotes action and choice rather than a "mere" thought. The reader is thus more readily invited to distance herself from Lurie.

In *Version 4*, dated "31 January 1997" the syntax of *Version 3* is rearranged only very slightly, but already approaches the rhythmic and syntactic qualities of the published form: "For a man of his age, fifty-two, divorced, he has, in his opinion, solved the problem of sex rather well."[12] Particularly the shifting of *in his opinion* from the end to the middle of the sentence foregrounds Lurie's mind, since the words signaling his rational faculties are placed so as to intrude into the order of the sentence and into his ordered life.

---

[9] Note that Douthwaite's argument here is originally limited to the published version of the sentence, but may be applied here also. Further insight into the functions of repetition in Coetzee, functions which may include the decelerating force of his style, may be found in Zimbler's perceptive reading of *In the Heart of the Country*, pp. 56–86.

[10] HRC, container 35, folder 8, p. 1.

[11] Ibid.

[12] HRC, container 36, folder 1, p. 1.

It might be argued that rhythmically the qualifier *in his opinion* is too polysyllabic and constitutes too much of a delay to gel syntactically and that the reference to ratio is too tacit yet. The first page of *Version 4* shows only one revision, dated "4 Feb. 1997"—it is: "For a man of his age, fifty-two, divorced, he has, to his mind, solved the problem of sex rather well." There are eleven further full manuscripts in the Coetzee Papers, each exhibiting substantial revisions, along with two versions without the first five chapters. All of the manuscript material from *Version 4* onward conserves the first sentence as it reads in the published novel.[13] Lurie's *mind* is there to stay.

For a visual overview of the manuscript revisions I reproduce the development of the sentence:

For someone of his age and temperament, he has solved the sexual business rather well. (draft "19 August 1995")

For a man in his fifties, divorced, alone, not particularly well-off, he has resolved the sexual business rather well, he thinks. (draft revision "2 April 1996")

For a man in his fifties, divorced, alone, he has resolved the sexual business rather well. (*Version 1* revision "21 May 1996")

For a man of his age, fifty-two, divorced, and with no intention of getting trapped by a woman again, he has solved the problem of sex rather well, he ~~thinks~~ believes. (*Version 2* revision "to September 1996")

For a man of his age, fifty-two, divorced, of moderate means, he has solved the problem of sex rather well, he thinks. (*Version 3*, 7 September 1996)

For a man of his age, fifty-two, divorced, he has solved the problem of sex rather well, in his opinion. (*Version 3* revision, "31 January 1997")

For a man of his age, fifty-two, divorced, he has, in his opinion, solved the problem of sex rather well. (*Version 4*, "31 January 1997")

For a man of his age, fifty-two, divorced, he has, to his mind, solved the problem of sex rather well. (*Version 4* revision, "4 Feb. 1997")

For a man of his age, fifty-two, divorced, he has, to his mind, solved the problem of sex rather well. (published version)

---

[13] The versions as dated and catalogued at the HRC: *Version 5*, ("5–6 February 1997") and revision ("15 March 1997") (Container 36, folder 2); *Version 6* ("21–22, 24 March 1997") and revision "8–9 June 1997" (Container 36, folder 3); *Version 7* ("10–11 June 1997") and revision ("16 July 1997"/"3 Sept 1997") (Container 36, folder 4); *Version 8* ("3–4 September 1997") and revision ("4 Nov. 1997") (Container 36, folder 5); *Version 9* ("20 November 1997") and revision ("3 February 1998") (Container 36, folder 6); *Version 10* ("4 February 1998") and revision ("23 March 1998") (Container 36, folder 7); *Version 11* ("3 April 1998") and revision ("30 April 1998") (Container 37, folder); *Version 12* ("30 April 1998") and revision ("4 June 1998") (Container 37, folder 2); *Version 13* ("4 June 1998") and revision ("22 July 1998") (Container 37, folder 3); *Version 14* ("22 July 1998") and revision ("5/8/98") (Container 37, folder 4). *Versions 15–16* do not include the first five chapters (July–August 1998); *Version 17* undated with dated corrections ("11 Feb 1999"/"5 March 1999") (Container 37, folder 6).

Syntactically *to his mind* is foregrounded, the way thematically Lurie's mind is given central importance in a reading of *Disgrace*. The foregrounding of the mind in *Disgrace* is, however, far from a reverent celebration of the mind and rather an emphasis of the persistent possibility of rational collapse at every corner. Kevin O'Neill goes so far as to note a generality, what he calls "Coetzee's rejection of Western rationalism" (2009, 202). However, while thematically *Disgrace* (and, to a degree, Coetzee's entire oeuvre) negotiates a paradoxical skepticism of the possibility to be skeptical, through its interrogation of the mind, Coetzee's work also maps inner landscapes in a way that is not altogether skeptical or suspicious of rationalism, let alone nihilistic about it. Rather, the narratives cultivate an open engagement with mental processes and rationalism as a whole to produce the aforementioned "unusual degree of *reflexivity*, meaning thereby a reflective distance to the conventional understanding of everything" (Leist and Singer 2010, 6f.; original emphasis). What I have outlined earlier suggests that this *unusual degree of reflexivity* is not owed solely to the thematic implications but also aesthetic choices. It might be said that the syntax and grammar of the writing suggest a complementary or oppositional narrative to the developments of plot and character, commenting on these and contesting them in as subtle and evocative a way as the many mystifying thematic suggestions for signification do.

Nevertheless, it is possible to select various moments in the narratives where a sense of slowness on the level of the plot works in congruence with formal deceleration to evoke a texture of reflexivity that seems constituted by moments of hesitation rather than haste. It may seem no coincidence that the incidents in *Disgrace* that disrupt Lurie's existence are caesura-moments when the otherwise fluid progression of a life of routine is halted and the sharp deceleration forces him to think in a different way.

Both Jarad Zimbler and Gillian Dooley discuss the stylistic sparseness of Coetzee's prose as loci for moments of piercing intensity to stand out more sharply. With reference to Dawn's violence in *Dusklands* Zimbler writes:

[B]ecause of the ways moments of violence are positioned in the narrative, they are prioritized structurally and thematically. The fact that the writing is noticeably bare in such moments is a means both of ensuring the descriptions are vivid and intense, and of suggesting a particular relationship between violence and bare prose. (2014, 54)[14]

---

[14] Zimbler's core argument that Coetzee's clear "bare prose" accentuates its pointed and poignant effects are relevant to my concerns also. When he observes that "the syntax [of *Dusklands*] is regular and simple—clauses are relatively short, subordination and embedding are restricted" (2014, 40), or when he argues that the piercing effect of *In the Heart of the Country* is due to, not in spite of, its

And Dooley argues that

> extended flights are most likely to occur in those scenes when a character is
> alone, ruminating on his situation, whereas the business of narrating events and
> describing settings and other characters are couched in sparer prose. (2010, 98)

Among other scenes, Dooley considers the moment in *Disgrace* when after the
attack on the farm on the previous day, Lurie is sitting by himself, contemplating
his life in a moment of tranquility after the exasperation of the violence against
Lucy and himself:

> It is past eleven, but Lucy shows no sign of emerging. Aimlessly he roams about
> the garden. A grey mood is settling on him. It is not just that he does not know
> what to do with himself. The events of yesterday have shocked him to the depths.
> The trembling, the weakness are only the first and most superficial signs of that
> shock. He has a sense that, inside him, a vital organ has been bruised, abused—
> perhaps even his heart. For the first time he has a taste of what it will be like to
> be an old man, tired to the bone, without hopes, without desires, indifferent to
> the future. Slumped on a plastic chair amid the stench of chicken feathers and
> rotting apples, he feels his interest in the world draining from him drop by drop.
> It may take weeks, it may take months before he is bled dry, but he is bleeding.
> When that is finished, he will be like a fly casing in a spiderweb, brittle to the
> touch, lighter than rice-chaff, ready to fly away. (*Dis* 107)

The passage begins with a reference to passed time, as if this moment were
already too late, and so it gives a sense of urgency, almost a sense of haste, but
then the focus shifts to an elimination of any sense of urgency and fastness with
the reference to Lucy's absence, which puts Lurie in a state of waiting. In the
beginning, this moment alters between evocations of restlessness, with Lurie
wandering *aimlessly about the garden*, and echoes of slowness, the reflexive state
of Lurie's mind, when this man of routine suddenly *does not know what to do
with himself*. From what the narrator imparts about Lurie, this alienation from
the self seems owed to the recent attack, but the language and syntax might also
point to an emptiness within Lurie's character, the vacuity of which has been
unveiled by the attack on the farm. *The events of yesterday have shocked him to
the depths* signals a more existential isolation from the self than *to his depths*

"taut and spare" syntax (2014, 69), he is pushing toward an argument for the powerful effect of a
style related to minimalism. While Coetzee is hardly a minimalist, his deceptively simple style has
the effect of provoking similar reflections as do the silent compositions of John Cage, Beckett's late
stories, or Ad Reinhardt's black paintings. Their aesthetics raise questions about aesthetics, but also
about epistemology and phenomenology—what is there, how do I know what is there, and what is
my response to something that is there only "barely," meaning *subtly* as well as *near-absent*?

might suggest. The absence of the possessive adjective implies a rupture of the cohesive knowledge of a self in the first place.

> He has a sense that, inside him, a vital organ has been bruised, abused—perhaps even his heart. For the first time he has a taste of what it will be like to be an old man, tired to the bone, without hopes, without desires, indifferent to the future. (*Dis* 107)

These two sentences make further use of syntactical deceleration through fragmentation, which foregrounds character development, or, in Lurie's case, gradual character dissolution. The phrase *inside him* again intrudes through the use of redundancy, since where else but inside him could his vital organs be? The phrase slows down the reading and begins to turn both the narrative and the reader to Lurie's interior, *to his mind*. This moment in the narrative, then, recalls the first sentence of the novel, if the first sentence is understood as metonymic of Lurie's attitude regarding his own mental capabilities before the "fall." It is for the *first time* that this sense of reflection has hit him; in tone, the quoted passage is staggeringly devoid of any sense of smugness and rather weighed down by a sense of defeat, which the vocabulary also evokes. The slow draining away of Lurie's blood, which is later evoked in the repetition of the word *drop*, is already anticipated in the rhythmic slowing down evoked by the internal rhyme *bruised, abused*.

The second sentence considered more closely is captivating for its syntactic arrangement also, though in a different way: "For the first time he has a taste of what it will be like to be an old man, tired to the bone, without hopes, without desires, indifferent to the future." The sentence begins with a main clause and is then extended by further phrases, in a way which mirrors a groping for suitable expressions, examples to comment on and deepen what the main clause has begun to intimate. The phrases *tired to the bone, without hopes, without desires, indifferent to the future* are more far-reaching and yet, through their syntactic arrangement, feel more like deceleration, a slow succession of step after step down toward the defeat evoked in the preceding clause. The deceleration is achieved again through the use of syntactic redundancy, since the phrases after the main clause present Lurie's degrees of humiliation in the form of a list. And once again, the constituent parts are far from redundant; they do not merely supply additional information but flesh out Lurie's character in a wholly original way. Nowhere before in the narrative has he been this candid about himself, nowhere before has this man whose mind has always been highly engaged and highly controlled had the slow time to reflect meditatively rather than focusing simply on problem solving. Nowhere before has his mind been forced to reflect only on itself.

While Lurie's mind may be involved in a dangerous deconstruction of itself, while Lurie's thoughts may be interrogating themselves, while his thinking begins to think against itself, his thought process is nevertheless engaged in a thinking that may be viewed as charged with more positive value than the content suggests. Surely, the above-quoted passage is one of the lowest points at which Lurie has been. Nonetheless, his thinking is set in motion in a very different way than before, a way that may be, *for the first time*, honest about how Lurie feels at this point. Slumped on the plastic chair and alone, he may at last have begun to let go of his posturing smugness and allowed a more "honest" (deeper, heartfelt, unaffected, but not necessarily more "truthful") voice to seep out. The slow groping expressions after the main clause may be an indication of this. The rhythm slows down, and this could be read as Lurie's voice relinquishing something that would have been syntactically stopped by the Lurie of the novel's beginning. Here, the quadruple emphasis on Lurie's low spirits—*tired to the bone, without hopes, without desires, indifferent to the future*—seems less obsessional in its syntactic control and drops rather freely away until it ends on the words *indifferent to the future*. The David Lurie of the beginning, it seems, would not have tolerated indifference, would rather have tried to exercise control even over the most insignificant of matters. So, without trying to romanticize the many evocations of despair in the above-mentioned passage, Lurie's thinking is altered in a way that might be called a more serious engagement with himself (his life, his mind, his body) and the living moment he is part of (his existence, other creatures, history, the world). Lurie has yet to go through many more struggles and a lot more despair, but it *is* despair, it is *something* rather than the numb, sterile, obsessive-compulsive control of the man's life in the beginning, when despite his rigorous routine he and the world around him were locked in a relationship that might more readily warrant the word *indifferent* than the moment described here.

These moments are no rarity in Coetzee's oeuvre; scenes when slow self-contemplation, ruminative chafing away at a character's core mark all of his narratives. In such moments, characters' attentions are turned—to invoke a phrase by Mrs. Curren "all inward"—as if the brittle exterior world briefly fell away and the characters were immediately confronted with their own existences. In the dialing down of incident, the style is frequently used to decelerate in preparation for the opening up of a moment when a character is called to turn inward, not to hide there in solipsistic navel-gazing, but to find there the aforementioned "reflective distance to the conventional understanding of everything" (Leist and Singer 2010, 6f.), which includes a *reflective distance* to the self.

Many times in Coetzee's work such a *reflective distance* is expressed in the way the characters suddenly begin to think more meditatively and less calculatively. Many such moments are marked by a feeling of a discursive motion of thought performed by the characters, or forced upon them. Thought turns inward, to the self in the present moment, *to the depths*, but then it opens up to the outside, as if transcending the solid confines of the ego. Many such moments of mental agility occur when the characters' bodies are slowed down. In *Disgrace* it occurs when Lurie's body has not only been slowed down by sitting on the plastic chair, but when his body has been slowed down more profoundly by the attack of the previous day. This slowness of the body may ultimately require the mind to engage in thinking, as if to take stock, to reconsider, to reevaluate itself. By being slowed down, the characters begin to get close to themselves, which, in turn, first allows them to create a significant sense of reflective distance to themselves.

It is complex and problematic to consider the sense in which Coetzee's characters at times approach a more wholesome, philosophical and meditative way of thinking after their bodies have been slowed down or even harmed. One should be careful not to infer any corollary: If his characters begin to think in a meditative way after they have been harmed physically, it remains ultimately irresolvable if this thinking occurs *because* of their physical pains alone, and, in any case, one must not deduce the kind of argument that Colonel Joll and his "empire of pain" (*WfB* 24) would advocate, in other words that "[p]ain is truth" (*WfB* 5), that physical pain should be able to burn out a more "authentic" truth than any peaceful conduct. Rather, the slowness that is created after an attack on the body—Paul Rayment's amputation, the Magistrate's torture, Mrs. Curren's terminal illness—is a physical slowness that interrupts the general instrumental, and often unconsidered, forward-movement in which they have existed hitherto. Moments of physical pain or physical suffering then irrupt into these existences which are unexamined in the Platonic sense. Because the sudden change that physical suffering brings with it in an utterly irrational way, their minds are often forced to think in a radically different way, and therefore to consider different actions developed from this thinking. The thinking that ensues might be called meditative, while this does not mean that it is, in any way, *better* thinking.

The shift from a more straightforwardly instrumental thinking to a radically different kind of reflection can be illuminated well through an example from *The Master of Petersburg*, where it is provoked not by the physical suffering of the one doing the thinking, but by thinking suffering in general, or rather by the impossibility of thinking the suffering of another. After the death of his stepson, Pavel, Fyodor Dostoevsky finds himself in a deadening stupor in a city he cannot leave behind, because that city, Petersburg, is the site of Pavel's death. In the night, when Petersburg is still, when life in the city has slowed down, death irrupts into Dostoevsky's mind: "It is the dead of night, the whole house is still" (*MoP* 79). The expression *dead of night* and the double meaning of *still* impart forcefully what is on the focalizer's mind, and after he contemplates that what he hears is the voice of his dead stepson calling for him, he understands that "[i]t is the unhappy wail of a dog" (*MoP* 79). During this slow moment in the narrative, when Dostoevsky is entirely alone and entirely still, he enters into an astoundingly complex cascade of thinking, which begins in a wholly instrumental way, but, as his thoughts scrabble on, undermines instrumentality, as Dostoevsky contemplates whether he should go out and help the dog:

> The dog howls again. No hint of empty plains and silver light: a dog, not a wolf; a dog, not his son. Therefore? Therefore he must throw off his lethargy! *Because* it is not his son he must not go back to bed but must get dressed and answer the call. If he expects his son to come as a thief in the night, and listens only for the call of the thief, he will never see him. If he expects his son to speak in the voice of the unexpected, he will never hear him. As long as he expects what he does not expect, what he does not expect will not come. Therefore—paradox within paradox, darkness swaddled in darkness—he must answer to what he does not expect. (*MoP* 80; original emphasis)

The reading of this passage is very directly slowed down through the profuse use of repetition upon repetition, as well as through the paradoxical way of thinking staged in the sentences, which represents aptly the kind of thinking that hovers somewhere between the clarity and confusion of a man who has just come out of a realm of dreams. The initial question of *Therefore?* suggests that the only recourse available to the thinking agent at this point is instrumentality. The mechanized matter-of-factness of this question is only gradually countered by the intrusion of conditionals (twice *if* and *as long as*). And toward the end of the passage, the swift teleological rationalism initially implied is kept in check through a dual parenthetical intrusion (*paradox within paradox, darkness swaddled in darkness*) within the sentence. It seems that the focalizer attained a reasoning of a different kind, since at the end of this passage he is fully aware of how paradoxical his thinking is. Following this passage, he is out in the street looking for the dog. The urgent answer to his question (*Therefore?*), namely to *throw off his lethargy*, is brought about—*paradox within paradox*—by a moment of lethargy itself, since his decision to change his course and help the dog was prepared by lying in bed and by an entailed breaking out of lethargic instrumental thinking.

Moments of physical slowness in Coetzee's work, such as this one, frequently introduce a more agile mental tenor to a character's thinking, and this may, in turn, transmit to the reader's mind as well. In moments of slowness, whether self-imposed or inflicted by others, Coetzee's characters begin to reflect in another way—and frequently also in a different way about an other. Before he finally goes out to look for the dog, and before the earlier passage stages a complicated questioning of instrumental thinking, Dostoevksy referred carelessly to the dog as "only a thing that does not concern him, a dog howling for its father" (*MoP* 80). Thereupon, he ambulates between the kind of instrumental reasoning he is used to and a different way of thinking, and so realizes:

> Pavel will not be saved till he has freed the dog and brought it into his bed, brought *the least thing*, the beggarmen and the beggarwomen too, and much else he does not yet know of; and even then there will be no certainty. (*MoP* 82; original emphasis)

This realization is to be savored by the reader, and so the important change in Dostoevsky's thinking toward what might be called an irrational reasoning in this instance is once again conveyed to the reader through a syntactically slowing construction in a sentence rich with intruding syntactic units that play up repetition (*brought—brought*; *and—and*; *beggarmen—beggarwomen*). It is no coincidence that in a novel so much concerned with holding on and deferring—deferring grief so as not to end grief, which is after all the last string binding to the departed—that in such a novel Dostoevsky's thinking also evades thinking toward the end. In the earlier example, this complex aspect of the focalizer's mind is mirrored at the level of just one sentence at a crucial point in the narrative, in a sentence that seems hesitant to come to its end (shown through the accumulation of the word *and*).

Across the oeuvre Coetzee's sentences may assume such shapes at important instances, and such slowing syntactic structures can highlight important moments which are not given central attention by the plot alone. Whereas the attack in *Disgrace* or Eugene Dawn's stabbing of his child in *Dusklands* are explicitly emphasized as central by their content, the syntactic structures of sentences can grant quieter moments in the plot central importance in the narratives, for the conveyance of a character's inner life, and for provoking the reader's deep reflexive involvement in the text. In *Disgrace* the attack on Lucy and her father is narrated in a swift pace that is mirrored in short paragraphs and a more prevalent use of parataxis. The sense one gets is that in the later works it is less a violent act itself that is at the center, and rather the repercussions of violent acts, the thinking that arises as a result. The earlier narratives show an interest in focusing on the inner landscapes of characters, on their thoughts, *while* they are committing a violent act. In Coetzee's first two works, *Dusklands* and *In the Heart of the Country*, the narratives slow down and record, through detailed descriptions of the malefactor's thoughts, violence in slow motion. This is particularly striking in *Dusklands'* "The Vietnam Project" when Dawn attempts to stab his son, Martin, with a fruit-knife. The moments—at most a few minutes and more likely seconds—before he stabs the child are narrated in excruciating and estranging slowness, such as when the police break into his room, a moment which lasts no more than mere seconds in clock-time:

> I don't think it is fair that I should be burst in on like this, but I cannot say it to him, I am beyond talking. I don't want to think about it, but I think I am really in the soup. Fortunately I am beginning to drift, and my body to go numb as I level it. My mouth opens, I am aware, if that is awareness, of two cold parted slabs that must be my lips, and of a hole that must be the mouth itself, and of a thing, the tongue, which I can push out of the hole, as I do now. I hope I am not going to be called on to say anything because besides going numb I am also sweating a lot and turning white, in a fishy way. Also, something which I usually think of as my consciousness is shooting backwards, at a geometrically accelerating pace, according to a certain formula, out of the back of my head, and I am not sure I will be able to stay with it. (*Dusk* 41f.)

Here, the form of the passage is entirely opposite to the content, since slowness is created through the chiastic and hypotactic arrangement, which continually doubles back in on itself, in phrases such as *I don't want to think about it, but I think* or *I am aware, if that is awareness, of two cold parted slabs that must be my lips*. The intense emphasis on the self (*I, I am, my*) as well as the slowing syntactic arrangements are used here to convey the feverish hyperconscious awareness of Dawn's madness, while, as Zimbler points out, the passage also describes "an impairment of consciousness, which yet proceeds in a measured, collected fashion" (2014, 62). He sees the hypotactic character of the prose here as an indicator that "Dawn's derangement impinges on the syntax" (2014, 62). The style in this passage is an expression and conveyance of Dawn's mind breaking apart, scattering or racing off, *deranging*, and the convoluted syntax used to convey this causes the reader to read and experience this moment in a slower and so perhaps more intense way.

The style conveys Dawn's estrangement from the situation he is in—his drifting into a state that is nearly unconscious and fully unconscionable—and it evokes an ethically complicated response by the reader through the use of defamiliarization. On the one hand, the slowing defamiliarization involves the reader in the text and so in Dawn's mind, while, on the other hand, the reader becomes estranged by Dawn's growing insanity that leads him to stab his son in the following paragraphs.

The slowness of the narrative is used in a confrontational way, forcing the reader's ethical reflection on the acts narrated *and* on ethical reading. Is it permissible to read acts of violence in a deeply ethical way, that is by involving oneself deeply and openly in a text and accepting the text as it is? Does the form that mediates such violent acts function as a caveat against deeply involved reading? Or is the accepting and attentive reading evoked by the form quite necessary on moral grounds, because a quick scanning of the text could be in danger not only of missing what Dawn's mania drives him to, but also of trivializing the deranged mental state that is articulated through the blowing up of a short moment in this way?

Similar questions are provoked in segment 26 of *In the Heart of the Country*, which narrates Magda's (perhaps imagined) killing of her father. The segment begins with the following sentence:

> My father lies on his back, naked, the fingers of his right hand twined in the fingers of her left, the jaw slack, the dark eyes closed on all their fire and lightning, a liquid rattle coming from the throat, the tired blind fish, cause of all my woe, lolling in his groin (would that it had been dragged out long ago with all its roots and bulbs!). (*ItH* 12)

Here, the list of descriptions of the sleeping "couple"[15] and its specific focus on Magda's father lay out the scene in a gradual way, holding the plot's movement in an eerie suspension. And once again, the sentence structure evinces a sense of hesitation to end. Beginning with an independent clause, *My father lies on his back*, the sentence builds detail upon detail, thus evoking a slow reading which has the effect not only of heightening the suspense but also implicitly relating Magda's own hesitancy to go through with her violent killing, which she commences with the next sentence: "The axe sweeps up over my shoulder" (*ItH* 12). This sentence is effectively paratactic, and its form mirrors what it describes, the swift sense of *sweeping*. Magda's hesitancy, which is mirrored in

---

[15] This passage narrates the killing of the father, though Magda seems to be seeing a woman with her father—"his new bride" (*ItH* 1)—a woman who may only be a figment of Magda's distraught imagination, and thus contributing to her unreliable narration. See Pippin (2010, 33).

the preceding sentence and which is felt in so many of Magda's reflections, is an important aspect of her voice and so of her character, since her voice, like Beckett's *Unnamable*, conflates character and voice in a phenomenological way ("I create myself in words that create me" [*ItH* 8]). This means that from the silence of her voice follows the "death" of her character. To be silent will be to cease being, which is why the ending of the novel is so decidedly unwilling to let go, defiant of ending, and why Magda's monologue has such a plodding and tarrying character. The lull in pace before the killing of her father, then, is not only a hesitancy to end another person's life, but also a technique to accumulate words, to prolong her voice, and thus prolong her own existence.[16]

It is important to see a developing trajectory in the use of these slowing syntactic techniques in Coetzee's earlier works and his later ones. While the style of the sentences is often similar, rich in relative clauses and ellipses, in early works like *Dusklands* and *In the Heart of the Country* the syntax often accumulates words and phrases to show, through manic monologizing, the deranged shape that instrumental thinking can assume. The slowing syntactic arrangement in Coetzee's first two works explores the violent undercurrents of instrumental thinking, while in later works syntactic slowness is much more readily a locus of meditative thinking.[17]

In general, however, it is important to note that slowness, whether topical or formal (here, syntactic), is always linked to reflexivity, that it gives rise to reflexivity in characters or provokes reflexivity by the readers. Like Walther resting on his stone or Dante's Belacqua against his, a limber mind may be the product of slowness. In *De Anima* Aristotle half-accepts Plato's argument that "the movement of the mind is thinking" (407*a*), but objects that "thinking is more like a kind of rest and standing still than a movement" (*ItH* 8). I use this idea simply to illuminate a paradoxical discursivity inherent in thinking, an oscillation between movement and stillness that is at the heart of the kind of reflexivity found in Coetzee's characters. It is an oscillatory way of thinking that frequently expresses an altered contemplation of the world around the characters from a vantage point of repose.

---

[16] This is, ultimately, related to her ontological resistance to finding an ending to her story, as much as she desires it. See Strauss (1984) and Pippin (2010).

[17] Necessarily, these are generalizing claims and should not be understood as commenting on all works in exactly the same way, nor that there exists a clearly discernible demarcation line between "early" and "late" works. *Life & Times of Michael K*, for example, already accords a supreme meditative depth to moments of slowness and syntactic slowness, especially when K is in his burrow. Generally, however, it can be said that when Coetzee lets go of narrating violence in close detail and from within, that is violence carried out by first person narrators or through a focalizer, that the syntactic slowing mirrors less the dangerous derangement of radically instrumental thinking and more a thinking of meditative proportions.

If one follows the critical consensus that Coetzee's texts explore, among other things, alternatives to rationalism[18]—dealt with explicitly in *Elizabeth Costello*—one might be tempted to infer a privileging of the body over the mind. Such a reading becomes even more attractive when considering those examples in his works where a mind becomes attuned to a new way of thinking through physical pain, which is present in the early work *Waiting for the Barbarians*, but becomes much more accentuated in *Age of Iron*. This would revert to a simplistic notion of a mind–body dualism that privileges the physical potential for inducing reflexion over the mental. Such an argumentation does not long stand to scrutiny with regard to Coetzee's fiction, however, as so little does. While it might be said that *Slow Man*'s Paul Rayment is set on a course to a more meditative thinking, which culminates in a more ethical life as the narrative progresses, and while Mrs. Curren's narrative may be regarded as an oration against the collapse of her body, and indeed all bodies—while such arguments have their merits, one should counter them with the argument that it is not solely the failing of their bodies which sparks meditative thinking. More pragmatically, their sufferings are used as aspects of the plot to provoke the reader's reflection. The way physical suffering can make a character think in a different way in the diegetic world, so physical suffering is staged formally in a way that forces the reader to think deeply about this character's suffering as well. There would simply be no reflexive involvement in the narrative of *Slow Man* if it were not for Paul Rayment's accident, because there would be no narrative without "[t]he blow [that] catches him from the right" (*S* 1), and no narrative of Elizabeth Curren if it were not for "[her] body that has betrayed [her]" (*AoI* 12).

It might, then, be said that Coetzee's work stages neither a simplistic privileging of body over mind nor of mind over body, but that it choreographs currents between the two and renders an opening out of the one into the other, and vice versa. Rather than privileging, Coetzee's work is a rejection of privilege. Neither body nor mind takes over in any simple way, but they counter or counter-stimulate each other. Mind and body are staged in a complex relationship in Coetzee's fiction, in as complex a way as in philosophy or—dare one say it?—in life. As so much in Coetzee's work, a simple answer is not given through this contest. Instead: "What matters is that the contest is staged" (*DtP* 250), as Coetzee remarks about other matters elsewhere. In his fiction, often inner contests are related, characters who reflect in a slow way about themselves

---

[18] See O'Neill (2009), Aaltola (2010), Crary (2010), Leist (2010), Vermeulen (2010), and Woessner (2010).

and about the world. Even at the level of the syntax this contest is staged formally and fundamentally time and again. It is staged there in such a way that the reader is, first of all, provoked to read slowly. But this slow reading is only the beginning of slow reflection, a reflection which is in part effected by very small formal choices, such as a repetition or the elliptic insertion of a phrase such as *to his mind*. These small aspects have enormous consequence for bringing about a *turning inward*, but a turning inward not only into the character's but also into the reader's *mind*.

5

Meerlust—Coetzee and Literalness

In his chapter "Against Allegory" in *J. M. Coetzee and the Ethics of Reading: Literature in the Event*, Derek Attridge argues polemically against a mode of reading allegorically: "My purpose is to deny the valuable insights that this mode of reading has produced and no doubt will continue to produce" (2004a, 33). Attridge does not limit his understanding of the allegorical mode to reading characters or situations as standing for generic types or universal ideas, but he also speaks of a more general "urge to treat elements in the text as symbols or metaphors for broader ideas or entities" (2004a, 39). Attridge's form of ethical reading, which he calls *literal reading*, denies the "impulse to allegorize" (2004a, 35), aiming at taking the text literally rather than figuratively:

> I want to ask what happens if we *resist* the allegorical reading that [Coetzee's] novels seem half to solicit, half to problematize, and take them, as it were, at their word. (2004a, 35; original emphasis)

In the following I will explore how Coetzee's works *half solicit* and *half problematize* not only the allegorical (or figurative) realm but also the literal realm. As will become apparent, it is the unique way in which Coetzee's works activate both a figurative and a literal approach to the texts that the act of reading is slowed down and the act of reflexive responding is intensified. To begin this exploration of taking Coetzee's works *at their word* it is useful to take Attridge at his word and to explore first what could be understood as *reading literally*.

A small but illustrative example from *Disgrace* will get us started. Quite early in the novel, as David Lurie invites his student Melanie Isaacs "in for a drink" (*Dis* 12), the narrator—and so the focalizer Lurie—reflects: "Does she know he has an eye on her? Probably. Women are sensitive to it, to the weight of the *desiring* gaze" (*Dis* 12; added emphasis). The focalizer's desiring eye mediates Lurie's fascination with Melanie's beauty through the acute sense of detail: "There are raindrops on her hair. He stares, frankly ravished" (*Dis* 12). At this point, the narrator has already informed us that "barely a term passes when [Lurie] does not fall for one or other of his charges" (*Dis* 11f.).[1] And so it goes; shortly after Melanie has entered his house, Lurie "opens a bottle of Meerlust and sets out biscuits and cheese" (*Dis* 12). While *biscuits* and *cheese* are referred to only generically, the *bottle* is specified by the name *Meerlust*.[2]

Meerlust. How can this be read literally? The reader may take the word by the word, taking it by the letter. Andrew van der Vlies glosses the term: "Dutch for desire (*lust*) for the sea (*meer*), understood too in Afrikaans (in which desire or vitality is *lus*)" (2010, 100). Van der Vlies also notes: "It can be heard in English as a homonym for *mere lust*, adding to its ironic use in the novel" (2010, 100). Van der Vlies's explanations are very helpful, but there are a few more crucial allusions contained in this telling signifier *Meerlust*. The Dutch word *meer* also translates as the adjective *mere* in English (which van der Vlies notes regarding the homonym), as well as the determiner *more*. This would allow the signifier *Meerlust* to allude to *mere lust* but also *more lust*. Is it *mere lust* or is it *more lust*, and what is the function of this specific signifier in the text? Does it characterize Lurie, who opens the bottle of wine? Either the text suggests that Lurie desires (lusts after) *more lust* (especially after he has just lost Soraya); or Lurie feels *mere lust* for Melanie, and so these stirrings should not be exaggerated: there is nothing to it, it is only lust, after all—after all, Lurie is merely "a servant of Eros" (*Dis* 52). At the same time, *mere lust* could be viewed as an ironic metafictional comment on what a large part of this multilayered novel is "about": *mere lust*.

Even the English speaking reader can make meaning from the signifier *Meerlust* to some degree, especially since the loaded word *desiring* was mentioned just a few paragraphs earlier. So, the word *Meerlust* steers the reader toward viewing the signifier's allusions as commenting on Lurie's character and on the novel's topoi of desire, lust, and Eros by way of inference. Desire has been mentioned explicitly just before and might then seem like the guiding force behind Lurie's character at this point in the novel.

---

[1] As will be seen later, Coetzee's works continually make use of what Bakhtin calls *double-voiced words* ([1975] 1981, 360; [1929] 1984, 265), which may estrange through their allusive potential or enrich through their double meanings. *Charge* is a typical example, since the noun carries connotations of *guardian*, as well as *to pay* and *to attack* when read as a verb. All of these are meanings which bear on Lurie's character, since it could be argued that he replaces the prostitute Soraya with Melanie and that he essentially assails her.

[2] For a comprehensive exploration of names and the allusive space of their historical referents in Coetzee's works, see Clarkson's chapter "Names" in *Countervoices*, where she considers how "fiction clashes with history in a name" (2009, 134), though she is less interested in the reader's response to these than to the ethical "challenges facing the *writer* in using familiar names that may or may not evoke associations for the reader" (2009, 136; original emphasis). Clarkson concludes that "a question of names has less to do with the geography of the place than it has to do with the history of those who have chosen, who use and recognize the names" (2009, 152).

Dooley argues against such a consideration when she notes that the novel's topics seem to be less sex, love, and desire and more the political ramifications behind matters of Eros (2010, 128). She is certainly right to argue that sex and desire are (possibly inextricably) linked with the political in *Disgrace*. However, the text's allusions to *mere lust* (even to *more lust*) challenge an overtly political reading of desire as representative of something else, especially when following Attridge's skepticism of figurative readings of this kind. At the same time, reading *Meerlust* "literally" as taking the word by the word and interpreting it as *mere lust* is far from depoliticizing desire and lust in the novel. Instead, it brings in the political dimension *ex negativo*, as this simple signifier mirrors the novel's voice, which either dismisses the political or does not mention it at all. The language of the text itself, then, could be viewed as being saturated with Lurie's conceited voice: "No, it's neither noble nor ignoble to take *charge* of Melanie in this way, we're just having a bottle of *mere lust*." The reader who takes to this small word in this way might almost invariably disagree with the voice's insistence on *mere lust* and has already taken a position toward the novel that is inherently political. But is this taking the word *Meerlust* as standing for *mere lust* really to take it literally? Or rather: Is this the *only* way to take it literally?

The irony of the word *Meerlust* and thus the ironic reading of David Lurie as a creature of *mere lust* emphasizes the necessity to reflect on the very feasibility of *mere anything*: Is there such a thing as mere lust in the first place, or is lust always bound up with something else?[3] If one follows the allusion to *mere lust* in *Meerlust*, one might think that *Meerlust* is being taken literally, since one sees the word's two phonemes as standing for the character's interest in *mere lust* (or *more lust* if translated from the Dutch). The reader who proceeds in this way reflects on the word *Meerlust* and tests it for its signifying potential when reading the novel's character. But what other *literal* reading of Meerlust might exist? Meerlust is, of course, simply the real name of one of the most popular wine farms of South Africa. In my earlier quotation from Van der Vlies's gloss I have omitted his important addition: "[T]he name of a well-known wine estate" (2010, 100). Is what the text refers to literally, then, neither *more lust* nor *mere lust* but rather mere *Meerlust*?

---

[3] In the Lannan Interview with Coetzee Peter Sacks steers the conversation to matters "beyond questions of mere landscape." Here Coetzee politely—but firmly—interrupts saying: "There's no mere landscape." When Sacks questions the author if he means that there is no landscape that is free of social, historical, and political powers, Coetzee elucidates that what is more important is the writer's ever-present *emotional* attachment to landscape, which influences his writing of landscape. Here once again, Coetzee evades giving politics and history the primary role in literature, and he softly signals toward matters that precede, transcend, or challenge the historical (Coetzee and Sacks 2001).

While a non-South African reader might understand the phonemes inherent in the word *Meerlust* and find here an ironic comment on Lurie's character through his choice of wine (regardless whether the estate exists or not), a reader from South Africa (or a sommelier) will most likely find here a direct reference to the real South African context. A reader from South Africa, possibly more so than a non-South African reader, might also be aware of the fact that *Meerlust* is one of the *oldest* wine farms of the country, the estate dating back to 1693 (Dooling 2007, 1). In Lurie's choice of wine, then, a reader might find an allusion to the beginnings of wine production in the early days of the Cape Colony and to the high time of colonialism in the Western Cape. Lurie's choice of the traditional brand of *Meerlust* can be linked to the importance of the burgeoning wine trade and its reliance on slavery for the success of the Cape Colony in the nineteenth century.[4] But does one wish to brand any aficionado of Cape wine an advocate of colonial ideology? On the other hand, is the person who adheres to an unethical ideology unknowingly not just as instrumental in its persistence as the one who perpetuates its principles consciously? A further turn of the screw: when dealing with literature, are such arguments not unsophisticated historicizing, and the upshot of rather unrefined instrumental reading? Is it productive for the reading of the novel to establish these links, or *only* these links?

Construing a historical reality inherent in a signifier like *Meerlust* is not simplistic allegorical historicizing, since the reader is dealing with historical realities signaled by a text, even if in the subtlest of ways. Allowing the political context to resonate even in an understated reference to one of the oldest wine estates in colonized South Africa is part of my understanding of a meditative reading, because the reader does not stop there, and the reader does not stop there because the text signifies much more than that, since the word *Meerlust* works in many different directions. The reader is directly invited to draw connections between the allusive force of *Meerlust* (both the word and the brand) and David Lurie. There are very little markers in the text which allow us to know anything about Lurie's political or even philosophical disposition, for example; we are never given his explicit background, where he was during the apartheid era or what his ethical views are, for example. Therefore, the reader is directly invited

---

[4] "The wine boom could not have taken place without intensified exploitation of slave labour" (Dooling 2007, 82). Dooling even makes the claim that it was the wine farms, and their reliance on slavery until 1838 (that is four years *after* the official abolition of slavery [see Feinstein 2005, 52]), which "went some way towards rescuing the Colony from insolvency [in the early nineteenth century]" (Dooling 2007, 81). Feinstein argues: "Perhaps the main gain to the economic life of the colony from its absorption into the British Empire was the stimulus given to wine farms" (Feinstein 2005, 28).

to pounce on the few specific proper names of this kind. If the reader draws connections between *Meerlust's* allusions and David Lurie, she is confronted with her own hermeneutic and epistemological choices, because she is provoked to reflect whether it is prudent to draw connections between a bottle of wine and a linguistics professor, and to reflect if such connections are productively drawn when reading a work of literature. The text deploys the wine's name in such an off-handed way that it might seem insignificant. However, the word is such an allusive signifier that the reader's attention is concentrated on it. The reader is alone with how to respond to this, she is continually forced to weigh her choices. Can something seemingly insignificant in the world of the text be of such great significance in the reading? What is significant and insignificant in the first place when considering a text?

Which kind of answers the reader finds to these questions, whether she infers from *Meerlust* an allusive meaning or historicizes it in the way I have suggested, is ultimately to do with the reader's disposition. However, the novel plays with the reader's impulse to draw such connections, and so it heightens the reader's receptiveness to political, historical, and philosophical dimensions. In a novel which is so sparing in its use of brand names,[5] the appearance of *Meerlust* stands out very distinctly and elicits various different responses simultaneously.

Disgrace uses a number of allusions like this one, for example in the novel's telling names—Lurie (*lurid, alluring*), Petrus (its biblical implications), Pollux (its reference to the Greek myth),[6] or Melanie, whose name the narrator translates as "the dark one" (*Dis* 164).[7] Especially the use of the name *Melanie* makes the reader oscillate between (at least) two readings. The novel's glossing of the name's etymology is significant for being the only hint that Melanie is

---

[5] The case of Lurie's car is a good example to highlight the importance of the few brand names found in the novel. They are only given when they signify something. Although the car figures prominently in Lurie's seduction of Melanie, its make remains unknown. Only when the car has been stolen from Lucy's farm and the incident has been reported in the newspaper, is it identified as a Toyota Corolla (*Dis* 116). All of the brand names in the novel correspond to real brands and thus anchor the text in a specific time and place, but all of the brand names are also telling names. The newspapers *Argus* and *Herald* are named, the former just before Lurie is under the scrutiny of the committee where a "student observer" (*Dis* 48) is present; the latter just after the attack when a new time in Lurie's life is heralded. And while it is only a small crown, the king's corolla is gone for good. Or maybe it just means this: all that has been stolen is a car.

[6] Carrol Clarkson argues: "The name 'Pollux', evoking as it does a Greek myth with its associated European cultural heritage, does not effect the 'measured arm's length' that Lurie would have liked in the distance he would have had through a name he found unpronounceable" (2009, 145).

[7] In *Life & Times of Michael K* Coetzee uses a similar technique to create ambiguity about K's ethnicity—as he does here concerning Melanie's—and about how to read K. The only literal reference to K's ethnicity may be the information on his Jakkalsdrif charge sheet: "Michael Visagie—CM—40—NFA—Unemployed" (*K* 70). Poyner decodes these abbreviations: "CM" as short for *Coloured Male*, and "NFA" as an acronym for *No Fixed Abode* (2009, 69).

colored, by which the relationship between David and Melanie gains a decided political resonance. The novel's glossing may, however, also simply characterize the linguistics professor David Lurie as having a literal look at the name's etymology, at the word. Clarkson notes that

> [s]everal of Coetzee's characters (for the most part intellectuals, writers, academics) find themselves staring at words, exploring the possibility of a necessary—perhaps even a primal—link between a name and its referent. (2009, 153)

This aspect to the characters is significant, since it highlights an interest in *literal reading* as being innate in the works rather than being imposed externally. However, while this latter reading seems like a purely literal reading of the signifier *Melanie*, Lurie actually reads it figuratively, since the literal attention to the name sparks an allusion to the name's roots in Greek (*melaia*, "dark"). So, the reader is implicitly authorized by the text to read in a similar way too. It is also significant that Lurie's etymological gloss of the signifier *Melanie* occurs toward the end of the novel and not at the beginning, so that the reader may be authorized to perform a similar gloss of the signifier *Meerlust* from the novel's beginning only at a later stage.[8]

Dooley criticizes such strongly formalist readings of *Disgrace* (her disagreement is to do mainly with Douthwaite's analysis of the novel's first chapter). She argues that Douthwaite's formalist take on the book "leads to a literal interpretation which is not necessarily supported by a reading of the novel as a whole" (2010, 128). In my view, Dooley's criticism draws a generally too narrow distinction between formalism and historicism, since form does not exist in a vacuum. Dooley does not take into account that the literal reading is, at least partly, provoked by the text and that the literal also has political and philosophical resonance, even if one refrains from reading allegorically, as the *Meerlust* example has shown. The literal dimension called up by Coetzee's finely chiseled prose[9] is explored by the texts similarly to the way they engage with the figurative dimension. As becomes apparent from the earlier examples, a figurative and a literal reading are not always clearly separable; and, in fact, in Coetzee's work it is productive that they are not. The figurative and the literal

---

[8]   In Chapter 8 of this book I return to similar techniques, which may indicate the pertinence of re-readings.

[9]   See Dooley (2010, 127f) for a reflection on Coetzee's craft; as well as Douthwaite (2005, 47). See also Attridge's more sophisticated arguments that it is precisely the formal exactitude and stylistic prowess of Coetzee's writings—in other words, their *singularity*—which constitute his works' "effectiveness as literature" (2004a, 7), by which Attridge also indicates their political resonance. See also 2004a, 36; 61f.

always shade back into each other and so make the reader go back and forth between different readings as well. As can be seen, the construal of telling names and, more generally, the examination of a text's linguistic material, do not close off the political realm, but they instead open it up to the reader through the concrete phenomena of the text.

More generally, the examples show that formalist analyses need not depoliticize. By a close consideration of *what's in a word* the reader comes to reflect on which socio-historical and philosophical resonances are called up by that word: How is it that in the name of a wine we find allusions to lust, to desire, to history? And which position do we take when we construe words like *Meerlust* in our reading? How does this shape our reading experience as a whole? Let us see what Elizabeth Costello has to say on these matters.

In her considerations of the philosopher Thomas Nagel's reflections in the famous essay "What Is It Like to Be a Bat?" Costello acknowledges that Nagel uses examples of Martian and pteropine cognition as provocative ways to ask "questions [...] about the nature of consciousness" (*EC* 76). She notes that Nagel uses the contemplation of bats as ways to speak not only of bat-consciousness, but of consciousness more generally, and she contrasts herself to Nagel by adding: "[L]ike most writers, I have a literal cast of mind" (*EC* 76). Costello explains this by drawing on her own experiences and techniques less as a writer than as a reader: "When Kafka writes about an ape, I take him to be talking in the first place about an ape; when Nagel writes about a bat, I take him to be writing, in the first place, about a bat" (*EC* 76). When reading, Costello remains, first of all, with the text in a literal way, and without following any impetus to read figuratively, that is to get beneath or beyond the text—she seems to be a surface reader, a literal reader. One moves into the realm of speculation by claiming too hastily that Costello is uninterested in psychoanalytical or Marxist readings, which yoke the biographical or the social into the signification of the literary text, but it might be pertinent to reflect on whether such readings of *Elizabeth Costello* the novel are not misguided, since they are too prone to seeing J. M. Coetzee's silhouette shading through the mask of Elizabeth Costello. At the same time, it is important to take into account whether any strictly literal, or strictly formalist, reading is even possible, since language is by nature allusive. Would not the exclusive denial of all figurative meaning entail to shut out the signifying potential of language? Would such a reading not be just as instrumental and unproductive as an allegorical one, since the extremely *literal cast of mind* advocated by Costello would make of *Meerlust* a signifier which has nothing to do with desire, nothing to do with South Africa and only to do with wine?

The very basic problem with reading *only* allegorically is that a slippery slope emerges very easily by which soon anything goes, and the very basic problem with reading *only* literally is that very quickly very little may go at all. A slow reading, therefore, has to be open *both* to the figurative and to the literal realms, going back and forth between them without the need to favor either one, or the urge to cohere the two into a fixed whole. Slow reading is receptive precisely to how Coetzee's work *half solicits* and *half problematizes* the figurative, or the allegorical realm, but also how it engages and escapes the literal realm.

Let me consider how the specifically allegorical realm is simultaneously activated and restricted in Coetzee's work by turning to a title in the oeuvre which situates itself in a hybrid space that is both historically concrete and allegorically abstract, in that the novel is set in South Africa but in a historically "inaccurate" South Africa, in which an unspecified civil war devastates Cape Town. The novel is, of course, *Life & Times of Michael K*, and it also makes use of a single signifier around which the allegorical and the literal circulate: the novel's references to *the Castle* (*K* 152; 155; 160). Given that the protagonist shares the single-lettered surname with two protagonists in Kafka's oeuvre, the readiest way to read this novel may be to see the Castle reference as an intertextual allusion to Kafka's *Das Schloß* (*The Castle*, 1926) and so to read Coetzee's text as a rewriting or adaptation of the apparently allegorical (or parabolic) nature of Kafka's work.[10] However, the references to the Castle literally bind the novel, first of all, to a South African context. The Castle of Good Hope is a real building in Cape Town and it is used as an administrative institution by the military, just in the way the medical officer suggests. As is apparent, a reading of the Castle reference becomes very complicated and necessitates a cyclical query through various possibilities of what it signifies.[11]

More generally, the novel also makes explicit reference to allegory,[12] that is *allegory* itself becomes a signifier in the text. In his final monologue addressed to K after K is gone, the medical officer claims that Michael K's "stay in the camp was merely an allegory" (*K* 166). It is this moment which Attridge concentrates on following his claim that the reader

---

[10] It is similarly problematic to view Kafka's works as only allegories or only parables.

[11] For further information on the historical Castle of Good Hope, see, for example, Thompson (2001, 39f.; 51). See also Attridge's critique of Christopher Lehmann-Haupt's criticism in his review in the *New York Times*, where the reviewer sees only the allegorical allusion to Kafka and deems it obtrusive. Attridge claims that "anyone who has visited Cape Town knows this is a real enough building" (2004a, 51).

[12] So do *Waiting for the Barbarians* (*WfB* 122), *In the Heart of the Country* (*ItH* 143), *Age of Iron* (*AoI* 90), *The Master of Petersburg* (*MoP* 218), *Elizabeth Costello* (*EC* 217), *Slow Man* (*S* 33).

need[s] to ask how allegory is thematized in the fiction, and whether this staging of allegory as an *issue* provides any guidance in talking about Coetzee's *use* of allegory (and about allegory more generally). (2004a, 33f.; original emphases)

Attridge is right in this, although his drift is—arguably because of the reactive and polemical nature of his arguments against a simplified allegorization of Coetzee—a bit too distinctly away from the allegorical and therefore in danger of favoring literal readings exclusively. Attridge sees the direct reference to allegory as a rupture in the text. He writes that although

> there is [...] no generic rule that prohibits allegories from referring to allegory, these moments in the texts inevitably have the effect of puncturing any consistent experience of extraliteral correspondences, just as those moments when Shakespeare's characters talk about acting in a play suspend for an instant our suspension of disbelief. (2004a, 34)

When speaking about *Age of Iron* Attridge weighs Mrs. Curren's allegorical reading of Vercueil as the angel of death against her "*rejection* [...] of this allegory" (2004a, 35; original emphasis). Attridge's subsequent criticism of the allegorical mode of reading is carried out "[w]ith [...] encouragement from the fiction itself" (2004a, 35). While Attridge is fully aware that many different readings may be performed at the same time (2004a, 39), his important arguments about reading *with encouragement from the fiction itself* needs to include the allegorical realm in such a way that it can exist simultaneously with the literal realm, since the fiction only *half problematizes* the allegorical dimension, as he claims, while also *half soliciting* it (2004a, 35). If we are speaking of halves, is it not problematic to say one half is more important than the other?

So as to perform a slow reading as a meditative reading that prolongs and increases reflection on the texts, it is important not to exclude the allegorical categorically. Attridge is right that the rejection of allegory within the diegetic world forces the reader to question allegory's value here, but it is important to understand how Coetzee's works remain ambiguous whether the allegorical or the literal should take precedence in reading.

The literal reference to allegory in *Life & Times of Michael K* at once undermines and underlines an allegorical reading. A direct reference to allegory need not only *puncture a consistent experience of extraliteral correspondences*, as Attridge claims, but it may also enforce it, since a reference to allegory in an allegory would be metafictional and thereby quite explicitly external to the fiction. While some readers may indeed see in a text's explicit reference to allegory an impulse to be skeptical of an allegorical reading, others may indeed view it as justification to read allegorically. Most importantly, Attridge's claims against an allegorical reading are directed against instrumental readings. The only suggestion I posit as a recasting of Attridge's original arguments is that the allegorical realm of Coetzee's fiction is not situated on a hierarchically lower level than the literal one. If the reader is as ethically open to the text as I have outlined earlier, she will be appreciative of the way in which many of Coetzee's works both undermine and underline their allegorical potentiality and come to explore the acute allusiveness of his works by reflecting on the historical, philosophical, or psychological significance of the texts simultaneously or by oscillating between their different meanings. The polyvalent space of resonance which Coetzee's works open up to the reader inspires such an oscillatory reading, a reading that becomes meditative, a reading that becomes slow.

Attridge's argument of a resistance to allegory *with encouragement from the fiction* must now be qualified further. While, for example, Mrs. Curren's opinion of allegory remains ambiguous, and while Mrs. Costello advocates an inclination toward literalness, a turn to *Summertime* forces a modulation of the resistance to allegory *with encouragement from the fiction*, and it does this by a resistance to literalness. In one of the notebooks John Coetzee has left after his fictional death, he reflects on his performance during a job interview at the University of Stellenbosch. Like his real author, he writes about himself in the third person:

> *He has taken the question too literally. That has always been a fault of his: taking questions too literally, responding too briefly. These people don't want brief answers. They want something more leisurely, more expansive, something that will allow them to work out what kind of fellow they have before them.* (SPL 440; original emphasis)

What I have outlined earlier with regard to a single signifier within one text is thus also staged at the level of the oeuvre, namely in a dialogue between mutually exclusive ideas across individual texts. Whereas Costello propounds the literal, John challenges it. This creates a productive contradictoriness when considering the oeuvre as a whole, and this contradictoriness across individual texts repeats the contradictoriness that is activated in the reader's mind by individual signifiers. In a poststructuralist understanding of the signifier's arbitrariness, one is moved to see that a certain contradictoriness is always already part of language, and so of literature. If, however, this contradictoriness—in the allusion to different signifieds, in the use of clashing narrative voices, conflicting ideas, or colliding readings—if this contradictoriness is to become productive in reading, it has to draw attention to itself.

In Coetzee's texts this is continually the case, as the example of Meerlust shows, and as the conflicting "views" of allegory and literalness emphasize. The textual phenomena of Coetzee's works, be they topical or formal, seem to hover in an ambiguous space by way of their relation to conflicting textual phenomena. This technique, which can be exploited at the level of the oeuvre in a writer's later career, when the oeuvre is considerable enough and when, as Costello says, "a small critical industry" (*EC* 1) has grown about a writer—but it was already present at the smaller level of individual words and can be seen as part of an apparent project of increasing the text's polyvalence. Such polyvalence allows the works to tap various realms of signification and to enable many different readings by different readers in different situations and contexts, and to allow many of these readings to exist side by side rather than on their own.[13]

This technique of increasing the ambiguous force of a text is directly geared at the reader, but it is also geared at making the reader reflect on reading. The earlier examples are telling instances of how Coetzee's works lay many tracks that may become traps. Because the reader continually has a reading experience of interruptions, whereby each interpretation seems merely provisional, the reflection on reading is kept alive. Each signification found is qualified by a clashing signification, and so the reader is impelled to ask herself if an interpretation, or her reading, holds for the rest of the novel. This keeps the reader in a reading experience that compels her to be open and responsive and to remain with the text in a phenomenologically and epistemologically attentive way. While the above-noted connotations in the signifier *Meerlust* are provocative, the reader who follows any of them has all her work ahead of her, since the question how these allusions are meant to signify remain unanswered—they persist as questions to the reader or give rise to further questions to the text by the reader, and so prompt her to wait in curiosity for the text's development. The oscillatory dance between the literal and the figural, then, holds the reader in the productive state of being somewhere between these different, and possibly exclusive, poles. Rather than proclaiming the way toward signification, Coetzee's works simply emancipate the reader to become her own mediator.

For this to take place, Coetzee's works increasingly use single signifiers in punning ways, signaling a sense of uncanniness in language and making the

---

[13] Michael Chapman interprets these aspects of Coetzee's work in a way that has relevance regarding a global marketplace of South African writing when he comments on Coetzee's earlier work by highlighting the "difficulty of a writer's dual commitment to the troubled society and to the art of writing itself" (2003, 387). While the use of the word *commitment* is problematic for its suggestion of an intentional agency or a directive behind the writing, Chapman has a point in his suggestion of a double-edged relevance to Coetzee's fiction.

reader reflect more meditatively not only on the allusions of a word, but on language's epistemic status more generally. The vexing uses of the names *Marijana* and *Marianna* or the *Faucherys* and their *forgeries* in *Slow Man* highlight an essential strangeness of language. And the way the word *Meerlust* sends the reader away to search out its allusions, it is also a word that makes her strangely aware of the word itself, and so it binds her to the strangeness that is inherent in the word's linguistic construction and its allusions. Regardless of what the allusions signify, the word foregrounds the very fact that it has these allusions, it highlights the strange duplicity of words in general, and indicates reflection on the words themselves in the way Dostoevsky in *The Master of Petersburg* reflects about them before he acknowledges, in exasperation, the Bakhtinian notion: "Every word double" (*MoP* 219):

> This is the third time he has sat down to read Pavel's papers. What makes the reading so difficult he cannot say, but his attention keeps wandering from the sense of the words to the words themselves, to the letters on the paper, to the trace in ink of the hand's movements, the shadings left by the pressure of the fingers. (*MoP* 216)[14]

While this moment in the novel explores the psychological suffering experienced by Dostoevsky when reading his dead stepson's diary, the passage also highlights the immediate attention to language and writing that Coetzee's works explore and indicate to the reader. This moment in *The Master of Petersburg* engages quite literally with the act of reading. It does this topically, since Dostoevsky is engaged in the act of reading. Then, in the next paragraph Dostoevsky reflects on his reluctance to read Pavel's papers: "There is something ugly in this intrusion on Pavel, and indeed something obscene in the idea of the *Nachlass* of a child" (*MoP* 216). The use of the German word *Nachlass* is consistent with the fictional Dostoevsky's character, since he knows German and has just returned from Dresden to Petersburg in the wake of his loss.[15] But the German word is itself an intrusion into the English syntax of the passage, and functions as a subtle form of estrangement that slows down the reading of the text. This intrusiveness and the slowness involved in the reading are mirrored in the novel's topical engagement at this point in the narrative: Dostoevsky is reluctant to read his son's papers; he is afraid, it seems, both of what he may read out of the papers as what he may read into them.

---

[14] This instance also highlights the materiality of writing and reading, which will be analyzed further in the following chapter on gaps.

[15] The OED dates the German Word *Nachlass* as having its first recorded use in English in 1842, that is before the fictional time of the narrative in 1869, making its use in the diegetic world plausible.

There is something subtly estranging about the appearance of the word, but there is also something peculiarly uncanny to reading about a character reading, since one is suddenly "mirrored" by the text in the process one is engaged in—a process which is often not deeply reflected upon while a reader (especially a non-academic one) is perusing a text. In the example from *The Master of Petersburg* the reader is implicitly motioned to read more slowly, mirroring the way Dostoevsky reads not so much because the reader witnesses Dostoevsky reading slowly, but because she stumbles over a foreign word and has to pause.[16] While a highly receptive reader may adopt the kind of reading discussed topically in this passage, it is even more the formal construction of the passage that stimulates a more direct engagement with the text's language. The form achieves this chiefly through the use of repetitions.[17] Therefore, let me repeat the passage, extend it slightly, and respond to the slowing devices employed therein:

> This is the third time he has sat down to <u>read</u> Pavel's papers. What makes the <u>reading</u> so difficult he cannot say, but his attention keeps wandering from the sense <u>of the words to the words</u> themselves, <u>to the</u> letters on the paper, <u>to the</u> trace <u>in ink of the</u> hand's movements, the shadings left by the pressure <u>of the</u> fingers. There are moments when he closes his eyes and touches his lips <u>to the</u> page. <u>Dear</u>: every scratch <u>on the</u> paper <u>dear to me</u>, he tells himself. (*MoP* 216; added emphases)

The passage begins with a cluster of alliterations (underlined) and assonances (bold) in the first sentence: "<u>th</u>is <u>i</u>s <u>th</u>e <u>th</u>ird <u>t</u>ime" and "<u>P</u>avel's **p**a**p**ers," while *papers* is also repeated in one sentence.[18] This subtly introduces repetition as a rhetorical device, which resonates throughout; it can even be heard in "**in i**nk" and in "clos**es h**i**s** ey**es** and touch**es h**i**s** lips." The use of repetitions is then carried over into the actual repetition of words and phrases. The passage uses four major sets of literal repetitions: direct repetition of words (*word*, *dear*); repetition of phrases (*of the*; *to the*); figura etymologica (*read—reading*); and the insistence

---

[16] This pause may be a very short one, especially if one pictures a German reader or a reader with some knowledge of the term *Nachlass*. A German reader, however, still engages in some form of translating and integrating this word into the English language narrative that surrounds it. A reader who is not familiar with this word, of course, contemplates it much longer, or consults a dictionary.

[17] Repetition should here be understood as signifying the rhetorical device, but the word's etymology should be kept in mind. The Greek word *repetitiō* signifies the "act of going back or returning, act of demanding or claiming back, right to claim back, action for reclamation [...]" (OED)—repetition as a form of returning, of bringing back, a form of prolonging. As will be seen, this understanding resonates with the novel's topical engagement.

[18] I am tweaking the term assonance here slightly, since an assonance is per definition phonetic rather than graphic; it may not be finally answerable whether the assonances are merely seen here rather than heard. Then again, as William H. Gass has pointed out, when reading one is listening with one's eyes anyway, so perhaps there is even such a thing as a graphical assonance.

on running through various prepositions in the phrases *from the, to the, on the, by the,* until this ends with the cancelling out of the repeated article *the* and the chiastic reorganization of the once repeated preposition *to,* in the phrase *to me.* The combination of repetitions with slight alterations conveys Dostoevsky's paradoxical impasse in Petersburg formally, the sense of "[*m*]*ovement in stillness, stillness in movement*" (*SPL* 418; original emphasis), which defines the character's existential condition. The Master is a checkmated king, a stalemate character unable to leave Russia and return to Germany, yet desiring to depart the pre-revolutionary Petersburg and return to his life in Dresden. The sinuous changing of the prepositions seems to imply a spiraling progression, or a vortical fall, a sense of momentum as well as a sense of stagnation: beginning with *from the sense of the words* the preposition-progression falls to end with *to me.* The fall here is shown in the tumble of the prepositions down the page from *from* to *me*—from an unspecified origin down to concreteness, to the self.

A reading of this passage as a microcosmic and formal representation of falling is motivated by the novel's plot, since Dostoevsky's stepson Pavel has died by falling from Petersburg's shot tower.[19] During the conception of the novel, Coetzee "had wanted to call it *Falling,* [which] show[s] how crucial the theme of the fall is for him in this novel" (Kannemeyer 2012, 458).[20] The novel uses the repetition of the word *fall* and its derivatives as formal reminders of Pavel's literal fall a full 42 times,[21] thus suffusing the narrative's language with *falling,* the way the focalizer's mind is contaminated with the images and echoes of his falling stepson. In the beginning of the novel, expressions such as "fall silent" (*MoP* 4), "dusk is falling" (*MoP* 4), or "falling asleep" (*MoP* 6) are used in a conventionally metaphorical and seemingly innocent way, until the reader is told that Pavel has died from falling. Afterwards, an expression such as "he has fallen into a trap" (*MoP* 203) slowly erodes the metaphorical realm by alluding also to Pavel's actual fall. The reader is now provoked to reflect on the philosophical and psychological implications that this word has to Dostoevsky. As the novel progresses, the metaphorical use of the word *fall* is progressively

[19] Attwell points out that there is no shot tower in Petersburg, and that there has not been one during the time the novel is set, in his chapter "The Shot Tower" in *J. M. Coetzee and the Life of Writing: Face to Face with Time* (2015, 187–210). This is another instance of Coetzee's teasing de-literalizing of real space. For further explorations of this phenomenon, see the final chapter of this study, on worlds.

[20] In the novel Coetzee seems to engage with the death of his own son, Nicolas, from a fall from the balcony of his flat in Johannesburg in 1988, while Coetzee was at "the Johns Hopkins University in Baltimore to lecture for a semester" (Kannemeyer 2012, 455) and returned to South Africa for the funeral. Kannemeyer's biography of Coetzee recounts this tragic event in Coetzee's life; see Kannemeyer (2012, 452–457). See also Attwell's aforementioned chapter (2015, 187–210).

[21] My arithmetic includes two instances of the word *waterfall* (*MoP* 6; 83). These are pertinent also for linking the crucial first chapter to the pivotal "Ivanov" chapter.

cancelled out, until at the end of the novel Dostoevsky is actually high up on the shot tower from which his stepson has fallen to his death. In the end, the narrative uses the word *fall* to indicate Pavel's fall in a direct way rather than through allusions. The novel—a topic of which is Dostoevsky's being blocked in his writing—thus conveys formally how the death of his stepson by falling, has robbed Dostoevsky of the innocent and guiltless use of a word, has robbed him of part of his language.

In the tumble of the prepositions in the earlier passage that ends with *to me* one can hear a mournful signifying of the self, which is an uttering into existence of seclusion, isolation, and loneliness. A rarity in this text narrated in the third person and closely focalized through Dostoevsky, his *to me* is a painful *without him*. At the same time, it could very well imply a final possibility on Dostoevsky's part of saying the self, of reaching some kind of closure about his existential vacuum. This, however, is immediately undermined by the tag that follows, *he tells himself*, where a further figura etymologica (*he—himself*), through the sheer doubling of the third person singular, overpowers the first person and returns Dostoevsky back to *himself*, to a more complicated saying of the self, namely saying it as an other.

So, the paradoxical oscillation that is part of Dostoevsky's character, the vortical yet slow drifting through Petersburg and through his existence, emerges upon a detailed consideration of this passage's form. The formal arrangement of the paragraph makes use of repetition as a way of stalling and as a technique to involve the reader more slowly and more philosophically. At the simplest level, "[t]here is pleasure to be reaped from repetition" (Eagleton 2007, 131), since the reader is involved in recognizing repetitions; yet, repetitions also explicitly emphasize a given phenomenon. Repetition highlights a phenomenon's relevance, increases a reader's response to it, and points up the importance of its becoming an object of reflection. As a form of linguistic reiteration repetition is a way of marking time, a formal tiptoeing in one place, a stylistic experience of slowness and reluctance.

In the earlier example, this reluctance is staged through the form before it is literally defined as reluctance in the following paragraph: "But there is more to his *reluctance* than that" (*MoP* 216; added emphasis). This way, a visceral sense of reluctance is conveyed to the reader in an immediate way before it is stated literally. The sense of reluctance which Dostoevsky experiences about himself in his act of reading may compel the reader to reflect on her own act of reading. This is emphasized by a form which directly slows down the reading process in subtle but distinct ways.

The use of the word *fall* in a punning way and frequently as a figura etymologica throughout the novel highlights the uncanniness of language and the allusive force of a signifier, while it creates a web of signification across the novel that continually reminds the reader of Pavel's death by falling. Each time the reader happens across the word or its derivatives, she has to pause over it and decide, individually in each case, if she reads it as containing only a meaning about what it seems literally to refer to, or if she allows it to resonate with the cause of Pavel's death as well.

One instance like this, during the crucial moment in the narrative when Dostoevsky hears the wailing dog in the night, illuminates how the reader is brought into a meditative way of reading by being confronted with precisely these different modes of interpreting an occasion of figura etymologica built around the signifier *fall*. Dostoevsky hears the wailing dog during the night and goes out into the street because he establishes a connection between Pavel and this wailing dog. Yet, this connection does not satisfy him, and he becomes dispirited:

> He gives a great groan of despair. *What am I to do?* he thinks. If I were only in touch with my heart, might it be given to me to know? Yet it is not his heart he has lost touch with but the truth. Or—the other side of the same thought—it is not the truth he has lost touch with at all: on the contrary, truth has been pouring down upon him like a waterfall, without moderation, till now he is drowning in it. And then he thinks (reverse the thought and reverse the reversal too: by such Jesuitical tricks must one think nowadays!): Drowning under the falls, what is it that I need? More water, more flood, a deeper drowning. (*MoP* 82f.; original emphasis)

Here, then, the signifiers *waterfall* and *falls* are used metaphorically, but not in a way that relates to Pavel's death. At the same time, this passage teases the reader to draw a connection between these signifiers and Pavel's death, to reflect on death and grief, on whether Dostoevsky's admission that what he needs does not refer only to the metaphorical waterfalls, but to more thoughts about the fall, more *falls*, a hard, literal consideration of the fall, so that he can finally begin grieving his son, which he has deferred again and again until this point. At the same time, the reader may become suspicious of such connections—*suspicious of suspiciousness*—because of the questionable connection that Dostoevsky establishes between his dead stepson and the dog preceding this passage (a connection which he is himself suspicious of). What is going through the slow reader's mind here may be similar to Dostoevsky's reversal upon reversal, a continuing circular motion through the different ways of reading such a passage and through what its signifiers suggest and allude to.

In this example, as in those given earlier, the reader is shown an interpretive direction. She must remain with the text in a slow way, oscillate between the different meanings, and reflect continuously on the multiplicity of signification staged in the event of reading. Coetzee's works compel the reader to perform different readings at the same time or in succession in a way that forces the reader into a slow consideration of *what is there*. Figurative readings may very well be very important to a consideration of the text, but there are different kinds of figurative readings. Those that enrich the reading experience and thus keep the reader within the textual world, such as the figurative uses of the signifier *fall* and its derivatives in *The Master of Petersburg*; and there are those figurative readings, those simplistically allegorical readings, which get the reader out of the literal text and maybe never back in it, such as a Jamesonian national allegory or a Lukácsian typification might be said to do. Nevertheless, even these allegorical readings have heuristic value. A slow reading which focuses in as close a way as possible on the text might make productive use of such allegorical readings. However, slow reading is aware that these are happening never finally but rather simultaneously, or maybe even merely as a first step on a long way of reading a text. To illuminate this, it is useful to return to the aforementioned moments in *The Master of Petersburg*.

When Dostoevsky reads Pavel's papers he happens upon an idea his stepson jotted down. Dostoevsky reflects on it: "An idea for a fable, an allegory, not for a story. No life of its own, no centre. No spirit" (*MoP* 218). *No centre*. Pure allegory, more so than the fable, more so even than the parable, tries to get beyond or beneath the text. Dostoevsky is very aware of this sense in which allegory lacks a center, because its meanings are located elsewhere. When he establishes a connection between the wailing dog and Pavel, he essentially allegorizes the dog, he reads the world in an allegorical way, and what is lacking to Dostoevsky is clearly his dead stepson, the former center of his life. He tries to locate the dog's significance elsewhere, and it can be argued that this is an unethical response to the dog, since he does not respond to the dog as dog. It is a despairing move, though perhaps a natural response (as Coetzee explores in "He and His Man" also), since the text communicates quite clearly that Dostoevsky is shown as a man at the end of his tether, depressed, lost (*MoP* 82). His reading of the dog in this way, then, may be called a *helpless reading*. Not knowing how to respond to the dog, while its persistent wail clearly demands a response, Dostoevsky clutches at the first straw available, the first thing that comes to his mind: his missing center, Pavel.

The much greater question, which cannot and should not be answered hastily, is why readers frequently respond to texts by allegorizing them, by reading suspiciously. One might venture a theory, which is that behind the allegorical reading there lurks a *helpless* impetus, as it does in Dostoevsky's character. The stranger a text is, the more likely the reader may respond by allegorizing some aspects of it, so as to gain epistemic insights into the text, to control its allusive (and elusive) force, to get close to it. The fact that the most unproductive forms of allegorizing, indeed, take the reader away from the text must be seen as an unfortunate paradox, but a paradox that may be circumvented by slow reading. My claim that allegorical responses to texts are *helpless* does not imply that allegorical reading is less intelligent, or even necessarily less perceptive than any other reading. It merely shows that allegorizing can be an initial reaction, which should not be seen as an end, but rather as a beginning, since any response to a text only brings up the much more fascinating question which techniques the text deployed that such a response has been kindled.

For a productive use of allegorical readings, the reader might use them as first reactions, acknowledge them as *helpless* first responses, and by *first* I do not mean that the allegorical reading need to take chronological precedence over other kinds of reading—I merely mean to suggest that the allegorical reading should be seen as provisional and should be reflected on and considered against other responses, other readings. The literal and the allegorical modes are in a complex balance in Coetzee's works, and while I remain highly sympathetic to Attridge's arguments *against allegory*, it is more productive, more ethically responsive to the text, to see allegory as *first* in the way I describe it, as a first and heuristically valid reaction. When reading Coetzee's works, let the allegorical not receive all the credit, but let it receive *some* credit for being *first*, like first kisses, first lovers, or first books. And then, let us move on.

6

We Make a Leap—Coetzee's Gaps

In his talk "Eight Ways of Looking at Samuel Beckett" rather than segueing smoothly from topic to topic, Coetzee uses rough breaks between ideas to give a fragmentary form to his talk and perhaps to let meaning emerge in the listener's (and later reader's) flickering back and forth between the individual ways of looking at Beckett's work. He addresses this technique explicitly when saying: "We make a leap. Leave it to some other occasion to reflect on what this leap consists in" (*EW* 24). The talk's title echoes that of Wallace Stevens's poem "Thirteen Ways of Looking at a Blackbird" from *Harmonium* (1923) and with it the cubist sensibility of that work. The form of Coetzee's structure here seems akin to Barthes' aphoristic, concise structuring of works such as *S/Z* (1975) or *The Preparation of the Novel* (2011), and it illuminates a formal interest in the collision of seemingly disjointed parts in Coetzee's work as a whole, disconnected parts built around the curious and very productive middle phenomenon of gaps.

The previous chapters on questions, sentences, and literalness have explored facets of Coetzee's complex oeuvre, which owes much of its effects to various causal, temporal, syntactic, and most of all semantic gaps,[1] moments in which the works introduce blanks, moments of hesitation and ambiguity, as well as direct silences. These instances are occasions in the works to prompt various leaps on the part of the reader. Let this chapter, then, be an occasion to reflect on what these leaps may consist in, to reflect on an elementary form of gaps (or blanks)[2] used in two of Coetzee's works and to point out the functions and effects of further kinds of gaps and their larger implications for the oeuvre as a whole. As will be seen, the chapters following this one, on dialogue, endings, and worlds, owe a great deal to various configurations of gaps also, and while in the

---

[1] For a discussion of such gaps, see Iser (1989, 15).

[2] Iser, on whose theories my subsequent understanding of gaps is based, alternates between the terms *gap* and *blank*, his own English translations (in *The Act of Reading* [1978]) of the German term *Leerstelle* (in *Der Akt des Lesens: Theorie ästhetischer Wirkung* [1976]). *Leerstelle* literally translates as *blank space*, hence Iser's frequent explication of gaps as *places of indeterminacy* (see esp. 1978, 170–178).

previous and subsequent analyses gaps are understood in metaphorical ways, here I will address only a very literal implementation of gaps in Coetzee's works, that is the textual use of *visual* or *typographical gaps*.

These visual gaps will be taken as a primary strategy for effecting slow reading, a strategy so simple that hardly an analysis of Coetzee's works has explored their relevance in an explicit way. Before considering the gaps in *In the Heart of the Country* and *Diary of a Bad Year*, it will be necessary to consider a few theoretical contexts for an exploration of gaps. Let me first illuminate my understanding of gaps, which is situated against what Grant Farred notes critically about Lurie's increased reflections after the attack on his daughter and himself in *Disgrace*:

> It is [...] when Lurie poses, albeit tentatively, these kinds of questions about the machinations of violence against women that *Disgrace* offers a brief disruption of mundane thinking, a moment when the narrative reveals its gaps, its unevenness, its vulnerability to interrogation. (2002, 361)

What Farred criticizes as Coetzee's *lack* of "posit[ing] morality as an active social and ideological force" (2002, 361) will be reconfigured here as an entirely positive force which quite explicitly disrupts *mundane thinking*, that is petrified thinking about philosophical, political, and even poetological questions. In my understanding, the protean gaps implemented in Coetzee's narratives—regarding *Disgrace* the reticence to engage in active ethical normativeness—deliberately urge the reader to take reflexive action and develop her own ways of thinking as well as her own ways of reading.

To address in what way Coetzee's texts make active demands on the readers by using gaps, it will be prudent to return to Iser's theorizing of gaps as places of indeterminacy,[3] which, according to Iser, are central to every work of literature. He writes:

> Gaps are bound to open up, and they offer a free play in the interpretation of the specific ways in which the various views can be connected with one another. These gaps give the reader the chance to build his own bridges [...]. It is quite impossible for the text itself to fill the gaps. (Iser 1989, 9)

Here, Iser's reference to gaps is limited to the way in which indeterminate or ambiguous aspects of a text give a work of literature its highly signifying character.[4] Iser's argument is important to emphasize how the text–reader relationship is deepened through gaps and how they enable a wide variety of

---

[3] Iser develops this from Roman Ingarden's central idea that every work of art invariably features spots of indeterminacy, which the reader fills when reading (1978, 170–172).

[4] See also ibid., 22.

interpretations, since interpretation is always partly subjective. This also helps to illustrate how further kinds of gaps arise between different interpretations that may occur even during one reading by one reader, and how the balancing of each of these interpretations slows down the reading process. And while Iser's understanding of gaps is ultimately geared toward their filling,[5] he also argues against finding the *one* meaning to a text when he notes that "the interpreter's task should be to elucidate the potential meanings of a text, and not to restrict himself to just one" (1978, 22).[6] It is, however, the rhetoric of a *filling of gaps* that should be counterbalanced here, since it announces the end of inquiry, even if it is upheld merely as an ideal. In the following we will see that Coetzee's visual gaps are used as productive openings and as potentially infinite loci of signification. The productive potential of gaps is played up particularly in *In the Heart of the Country* and *Diary of a Bad Year*, where the implementation of typographical gaps underscores the already existent semantic gaps explored in these works. The topical and semantic gaps in these two texts are directly accentuated by the visual ones, the text's indeterminacies are increased further and highlighted in an explicit way, so that it becomes virtually impossible to close the texts' gaps in any final way.

The visual gaps under consideration here are opened up by Coetzee's ways of placing narrative segments side by side, or rather in vertical succession of the book's typographical arrangement. These narrative segments are juxtaposed or analogized rather than connected explicitly; it is their very tangible disconnection which imparts to the reader the sense that a connection is demanded, while simultaneously highlighting that a connection can only be provisional in the reader's mind, since an explicit connection could only be fulfilled by rearranging the book's typography. The reader who is confronted with visual gaps is made aware that a final filling of them is impossible and cannot be completed. Iser's comments on narrative segments may be applied here when he notes that "the need for completion is replaced here by the need for combination" (1978, 182).

The narrative segments in Coetzee's two novels under consideration here leave distinct gaps between them, which are immediately recognizable. And so is the need to combine them. Iser notes that "[w]herever there is an abrupt

---

[5] See, for example, Iser (1978, 9; 165; 172; 175; 194).

[6] Having said that, Iser's theory is also informed by an idea of getting beyond the text (such as when he speaks of "transcend[ing] [the words'] literal meaning" [Iser 1978, 226]). My method of slow reading is not interested in getting beyond the text (other than into the reader's mind); it desires to remain with and in the text in a reflexive way.

juxtaposition of segments, there must automatically be a blank, breaking up the expected order of the text" (1978, 195).[7] Upon registering a visual gap the reader is provoked to establish a connection between the two segments it separates, though in Coetzee the reader is left in the dark as to what shape this connection should take. Iser argues the following about the "blank as an empty space between segments" (1978, 195):

> If we are to grasp the unseen structure that regulates but does not formulate the connection or even the meaning, we must bear in mind the various forms in which the textual segments are presented to the reader's viewpoint. Their most elementary form is to be seen on the level of the story. (1978, 196)

It is Iser's last sentence in this quotation that interests me most with regard to Coetzee's gaps and their slowing function for the act of reading. Is Iser right here? Is the most elementary form of narrative segments really found on the level of the story, or could it not be argued that what may take precedence over the narrative element lies in a novel's typography? This cannot be answered finally, but one may consider whether before meaning-making and signification even begin on the narrative level, the reader (if she does not listen to an audio book) does not grasp the text visually, or as William H. Gass once put it, the reader "listen[s] with [her] eyes" (1985, 113). So accustomed is the reading eye to the act of reading that the typographical presentation of a text is often passed by. As will be seen, the two novels by Coetzee discussed here create gaps in the typography over which the reader stumbles.

Even a quick glance over the early novel *In the Heart of the Country* and the late work *Diary of a Bad Year* bring it home to the reader that a slower reflection on the texts' visual arrangements is demanded, a reflection on how these bear on the readings of the novels. A very distinct mode of arranging text visually is found in the 266 numbered segments that comprise *In the Heart of the Country*. In her futile attempts to write a philosophical account of her country life, Magda seems to have adopted a formal structuring of her narrative that might be borrowed from Wittgenstein's mode of textual succession in his *Tractatus logico philosophicus*, since her argumentation tries to proceed in an analytic and logically harmonious way, numbering her narrative segments for cohesion. This desire for cohesion apparent from the numbered segments is also informed by the political climate that forms the backdrop of the story, which takes place on a "veld farm," "a space resistant to colonial organization, a place where family relations, labour

---

[7] "The blank as an empty space between segments enables them to be joined together, thus constituting a field of vision for the wandering viewpoint" (Iser 1978, 197).

relations and sexual relations become disastrously confused" (Head 2009, 43f.). Magda's desire for cohesion and clarity is at once a legacy of the colonial project in this place, since it explicitly aims at cultivating and structuring, yet it is also an attempt to overcome the atrocious distortions of colonialism, paradoxically also through structuring and cultivating. What is enacted through the formal structuring of Magda's account affirms her status as "both perpetrator and victim of colonialism" (Head 2009, 43). Her "disruptive narrative" (Head 2009, 43) is informed by frequent new beginnings, by constant shifts, and erasures, which the blank spaces between the individual segments only emphasize. The numbering of the segments also plays with the reader's expectation that an enumeration reflects a logical design, and it triggers the reader's reflection on why the novel ends particularly at 266 rather than 270 or any other number. Even if 266 constitutes a mere coincidence, the concrete signifying attraction inherent in a number gets the reader to reflect on the number's meaning. The connections between the 266 individual segments of Magda's narrative are also often entirely elusive and wholly unsettling. Most of the segments are connected in a very vague way, but I shall concentrate on merely one example here:

190. This is no way to live.

191. Unable to sleep, I drift about the house at siesta time. I finger the strange clothes in the locked room. I look at myself in the mirror and try to smile. The face in the mirror smiles a haggard smile. Nothing has changed. I still do not like myself. Anna can wear these clothes but I cannot. From wearing black too long I have become a black person.

192. Hendrik is slaughtering a sheep a week. That is his way of claiming his due. (*ItH* 105)

The basic function of this perplexing segmentation is to fragment the narrative, to present flashing glimpses of Magda's life of boredom and inertia on the farm in a way that relates her stupor without using a drawn-out narrative style that might itself become inert. Coetzee's splitting the narrative into segments has the function of creating a distinct pace, while staging a complex and dense formal structure that conveys the slowness on the farm by presenting disconnected snippets far apart in narrated time. The quick pace is created by the fact that the gaps—and here I would speak of the visual as well as the semantic gaps between the segments—convey to the reader that considerable time must have passed between many segments. The resulting discontinuity between the segments begs a slow contemplation on how they might be connected or how a combination might be made. The explicit use of visually recognizable gaps creates tension and ambiguity, and these incite a momentary deautomatization of the process of meaning-making in the act of reading.

Reading slowly in an ethically and phenomenologically attentive way means to read these gaps not as representative of something that is not there and that it is the task of the reader to speculate what these absences could stand for, but rather to recognize them phenomenologically and seeing them not as standing for anything but for emptiness—and that this emptiness has an impact on one's reading.[8] Iser's comments on the effect of semantic gaps on the critic apply even more to visual gaps, when he argues that "this emptiness cannot be filled by a single referential meaning, and any attempt to reduce it in this way leads to nonsense" (1978, 8). Because visual gaps, even more than semantic gaps, directly confront the reader with explicit emptiness, the reader is forced to ask whether her filling of this emptiness with one *single referential meaning* is not, in fact, an act of arbitrating the text, or at the very least an act of reductive simplification. Rather than applying the interpretive forceps and reading meaning out of emptiness, the slow reader bridges the narrative segments across the blank space, tries out various forms of combination, and constantly reflects on her reading and on the value of her combinatory endeavor. How might this be realized in the example from *In the Heart of the Country*?

Whereas the transition from segment 190 to 191 is logical, a similar claim cannot be made so readily about the transition from 191 to 192. After reading the politically overdetermined last sentence of segment 191 about the Afrikaner Magda's claim that she has become a black person, the reader is suddenly confronted with the image of a sheep being slaughtered. While the reader is still in the process of reflecting on the political and ethical implications of her statement in 191, the jarring juxtaposition brought about by segment 192 pulls out the metaphorical rug beneath the reader and she is doubly slowed down in her reading: by trying to puzzle out whether Magda's statement is to be taken literally or figurally (and thus ideologically); and by reflecting how the segments 191 and 192 are related, that is by reflecting how the gap between them influences the reading rather than what this gap might "contain." It contains nothing so much as its function as a gap.

This small blank space can have the profoundest effect on an interpretation of Magda, while it also cautions the reader in her approach to the text. Let us say

---

[8]   This argument is informed by Best and Marcus's aforementioned claims against deep readings by way of a hermeneutics of suspicion, such as when they state quite matter-of-factly: "What is absent is simply not there [...]" (2009, 4).

we accept that the narrative is the representation of Magda's consciousness[9]—
does it follow, then, that in her mind the statement about being a black person
and slaughtering a sheep are somehow connected, and do we use this as a
way of characterizing Magda? The more fascinating—and the more ethically
pertinent—question is, what does it say about us that we even conceive of
drawing such a connection when the text quite literally does not? Arguably, we
are not wicked people if we do draw this connection, as the gap directly invites it.
At the same time, we should probably not be too content in pacifying ourselves
that we are only drawing this connection by way of conceiving of Magda's mind.
The text's arrangement plays with us here, it provokes us to draw this connection
very quickly, and only allows us to qualify it afterwards when we reflect upon
it. Especially Coetzee's earlier fiction explicitly draws attention to the very idea
of gaps, so as to heighten the reader's reflection on their significance to the text.
This is demonstrated, for example, in an astonishing passage early in *In the Heart
of the Country*, where Magda speaks about her relationship with her servants:

> I am spoken to not in words, which come to me quaint and veiled, but in signs, in
> conformations of face and tone, in *gaps and absences* whose grammar has never
> been recorded. Reading the brown folk I grope, as they grope reading me: for they
> too hear my words only dully, listening for those overtones of my voice, those
> subtleties of the eyebrows that tell them my true meaning "Beware do not cross me,"
> "What I say does not come from me." Across valleys of space and time we strain
> ourselves to catch the pale smoke of each other's signals. (*ItH* 8; added emphasis)

Here, Magda's direct reference to gaps is related to those instances in Coetzee's
oeuvre where allegory is mentioned explicitly, and in the reader a paradoxical
duality is triggered to read something into gaps in the text and to be skeptical
of reading too much into them. The foregoing example may be seen as part of a
general sense in which Coetzee's works often subsume critical responses to them.
This way, the reader who feels comfortable *filling* semantic gaps, for example, and
who thereby acknowledges that absences stand for something else, might here be
made to question her methods, not only because Magda draws explicit attention
to gaps, but also because once again her distinct reference to them is tainted by
a deplorable ideology. Is it permissible to read in the way Magda reads, when
she seems almost too accepting of the failure to communicate with her servants

---

[9]   This might be underscored as well as undermined by a comment such as this one: "I am a spinster
with a locked diary but I am more than that. I am an uneasy consciousness but I am more than that"
(*ItH* 4). Comments by Magda such as this one, in fact, tease the reader *not* to remain on the surface,
but rather to read suspiciously, in a Marxist or a Freudian tradition, for example. I do not contest
that such readings are void; I merely hold that remaining on the surface of Coetzee's works in no way
delimits (and frequently enriches) the powerful experience and the signification of his prose.

(who she denigrates as *brown folk*) on account of *gaps and absences*? And when she speaks about reading here, does she refer to reading in a metaphorical way that is limited to the diegetic world, or does she also speak to her real reader, the person reading the book *In the Heart of the Country*? Does her claim *What I say does not come from me* caution the reader to take this statement at face value, and does it make the reader ask from whom her statements come then, which would entail taking all else she says *not* at face value, since it would be standing for someone else's meaning? Or is the reader skeptical of her claim and does *not* take this cautioning statement at face value, which would entail taking all else she says as coming from her alone and thereby demanding a literal reading of all her utterances. *Paradox within paradox*. The fascinating aspect about Magda's statement is that the text as a whole complicates either of these choices. The reader of *In the Heart of the Country* is frequently forced to stop at a junction and decide: do I find in a statement, such as the reference to gaps or Magda's claim of caution, a *track* which may be pursued productively, or do I find in a track a *trap* and should therefore be wary of pursuing it? Whichever way the reader decides, a decision does not come without a price, without a reflexive investment in the text.

The use of visual gaps is a way of referencing the idea and the presence of gaps that is as explicit as Magda's direct reference to *gaps and absences*—the gaps are made explicit, but one is uncertain how to deal with them; no guidance is given as to how they function. This way, the gap of the text sets in motion a reflection on which effects a gap has in a text as well as which connections are drawn by the reader because of a gap. In examples such as the connections drawn between segments 191 and 192, then, the reader is tested, is provoked to deal with gaps and to decide whether her view on them is different from Magda's or related to hers, and what each view would imply. The gap between segments 191 and 192 forces the reader to consider if the connection she draws is a connection that the text invites or negates, and the reader is demanded to reflect on the ethical implications of the connection drawn. In this example, the reader's process of reasoning about the implications of a combination between Magda's claim that she has *become a black person* and the *slaughtering of a sheep* demands that the reader not only reflect on the text's ethical core, but also on her own. It is important to see that it is the text's literal blank space on the page that teases the reader to draw this connection,[10] and that it is the interplay of form and content (and context) that engenders reflection on what these effect in the reading.

---

[10] My subjective response to the succession of these two segments is very different when I conceive of them—or rearrange them using a word processor—as two successive paragraphs in a more conventional narrative arrangement, not least because then there are no numbers to intrude into

It is important to reiterate that the visual gaps here should not be seen as denoting absences that the reader is asked to fill with meaning, but that the reader is confronted with this emptiness simply as a present absence. Toward the end of *The Act of Reading* Iser moves too much toward a reading of absences as negative spaces containing meaning, which should be eschewed in light of the aforementioned ideas of *surface reading* and an awareness of problematic suspicious readings. As has been shown, the reader need not fill gaps in order to use them productively in her reading, simply by treating gaps as gaps, by considering their surfaces. Writing on *surface reading*, Best and Marcus argue against *symptomatic readings* that aim to see something as being present in absences, that is imposing meaning onto texts or extracting meaning from gaps (2009, 3f.), rather than accepting an absence simply as an absence and trying and using it in a way that emphasizes productive reflection on a text. Needless to say, a symptomatic reading is in peril of becoming instrumental or arbitrary. My proposed reading of gaps as present absences simply posits that during slow reading the gaps are not seen to represent something that is concealed and which may contain meaning, but that these absences are a presence in the text and that they need to be incorporated into the reading rather than being seen as something that needs to be argued away by being filled. These gaps do not indicate anything in a veiled way, they simply indicate themselves. It must be remembered that I limit these arguments first and foremost to the visual gaps in Coetzee's texts, even if a semantic gap or a text's deliberate silence about meaning need not be misconstrued as containing anything other than the fact that it does not contain anything either. In *Foe* Friday's silence should not be seen as standing for something else—a misreading that Barton engages in—but it should simply be understood as silence (and if we agree that his silence is the outcome of a colonial act of mutilation, then it does not even stand for that act, but rather for the outcome of that act, and maybe for the outcome of a history of violence). Reading Friday's silence this way is also a good example of seeing a gap as a narrative technique, the closing of which would curtail the narrative's tension and pace. It is because Friday's silence remains an absence that suspense is kindled and the reader's interest sustained.

Since it is the visual gap I am concerned with here, it is useful also to consider gaps in a visual medium, in cinema. First, the visual gap in a film is not perceived

---

the language and because of the decreased white space that cleaves the segments. At the same time, a direct stringing down the page of these lines would also give the narrative a disconnected feeling, even if one is arguably prone to read more slowly and to be involved more deeply when one is directly confronted with white space.

as visual at all, since the empty space between two images in a montage is the opposite of visuality, it is something that is simply not there, its essence is its immateriality, its immateriality is essential. Time is a crucial factor here, since the white space on a book page is a visual presence, whereas the gap between two images in a cinematic montage is not seen at all, it cannot even be visualized as a freeze frame. It is simply not there, and yet it exists, and it is essential to the viewer's meaning-making of the film.

In "The Filmic Fourth Dimension" Sergei Eisenstein, writing on montage, explains: "The dominating indications of two shots side by side produces [*sic*] one or another conflicting interrelation, resulting in another expressive effect [...]" (1949, 64). Eisenstein emphasizes the positive aspects of placing images in succession by describing an example montage:

> If we have even a *sequence* of montage pieces: A gray old man,/A gray old woman,/A white horse,/A snow-covered roof, we are still far from certain whether this sequence is working towards a dominating indication of "old age" or of "whiteness." (1949, 65; original emphasis)

Eisenstein's idea of the *conflicting interrelation* undermines a simple hierarchy between the successive images as well as a hierarchy of interpretations, what he calls the *dominating indication*. What is created instead is *another expressive effect*,[11] an opening of a wide realm of signification and potential for meaning-making by juxtaposing two shots, or, regarding a literary text, two narrative segments. In *In the Heart of the Country*, the juxtaposition of two segments (in vertical succession on the page) opens up a visual gap, which highlights the semantic and causal gaps that are opened up as well. The juxtaposed segments increase the density of a text since they present the reader with a wide array of possible signification, and the gaps also make it impossible to read in a simply teleological way, since the reader can never be entirely sure what has occurred in the emptiness that is constituted by one of these gaps. The visual gaps increase a text's complexity and density by pointing out to the reader that something has occurred in these gaps but withholding from her what this might have been. The productive disruption caused in the reader is an effect of the interplay between the visual and the causal gaps separating the segments.

In the introduction to *Doubling the Point* Attwell also makes the connection between the visual construction of *In the Heart of the Country* and cinematic

---

[11] Eisenstein's comments echo with Iser's reflection on gaps and how they "give the reader the chance to build his own bridges" (1989, 9).

montage (*DtP* 6).[12] And in Attwell's interview with Coetzee in the same volume, the author acknowledges a cinematic influence on his novel but qualifies it as follows:

> *In the Heart of the Country* is not a novel on the model of a screenplay, but it is constructed out of brief sequences, which are numbered as a way of pointing to what is not there between them. (*DtP* 59)[13]

And in the *Salmagundi* interview in conversation with Joanna Scott Coetzee mentions:

> I think at the formal level, the enabling device in *In the Heart of the Country* turned out to be the numbering of the sections, because they enabled me to drop all pretense of continuity. (Scott and Coetzee 1997, 89).

The use of gaps between the different segments "allow[s] Coetzee to construct a novel that dispense[s] with the paraphernalia of realism" (Wittenberg 2014, 9); and it is a device that disables a fluid reading process, though I would side with Coetzee (and Wittenberg) in arguing that this is not a *disabling* but an *enabling device*, since it facilitates slow reading and increases reflection. It is precisely the paradoxical simultaneity of the deft pacing that the cutting from segment to segment effects and the slow reading engendered by it that Coetzee implies when he comments on the numbered segments of his novel in more detail: "They enable a certain sharpness of transition, or lack of smooth transition" (Wittenberg 2014, 90).[14]

---

[12] See also *DtP* 143. For a comprehensive analysis of the representations of film in Coetzee's works, cinematic influences on his oeuvre, and adaptations of his work, see Dovey and Dovey (2010). See also Wittenberg's introduction to his edited collection of Coetzee's *Two Screenplays* (2014), one for *In the Heart of the Country* (filmed as *Dust* by Marion Hänsel [1985]) and one for the unrealized adaptation of *Waiting for the Barbarians*. During the writing of *Life & Times of Michael K* in 1980, Coetzee is struggling to find a form for the work and considers various options, including the aforementioned idea to rewrite Kleist's *Kohlhaas*. Before settling on the novel form, he toys with the idea of merging aspects of the novel with aspects of cinema, as when he notes: "14.vi.80 The whole has to be done as a screenplay, with extended descriptions of frozen stills" (HRC, container 33, folder 5, p. 6). And during a later bout of writer's block the possibility of incorporating visuality into the text still lingers in his mind, as he considers a development of the visual arrangement of *In the Heart of the Country*: "11.xii.80 [...] Formal remedy: to produce a text in blocks, somewhat like In the Heart .. but more radical. Think for the moment of a pictorial text, an exposition in which one moves along the wall from one block to the next. The order of blocks might as well be the order of composition as any other order" (HRC, container 33, folder 5, p. 12).

[13] Iser also refers to literature's kinship with cinema when he speaks of "the fact that each textual segment does not carry its own determinacy within itself, but will gain this in relation to other segments. Here literature may join hands with other media, such as the cinema" (Iser 1978, 195). However, it should not be forgotten that Iser again refers to narrative segments rather than visual ones.

[14] Note also Coetzee's introduction to Graham Greene's *Brighton Rock* (collected in *Inner Workings*), where he compares Greene's narrative style to film, noting among other things, "the tight cutting from scene to scene" (*InW* 164).

These clashing polarities inherent in the visual gap are also part of *Diary of a Bad Year*'s peculiar effect on the reader. The 2007 novel—or rather three-part invention of essay, diary, narrative—is effectively riven by gaps also. In the first five chapters of the text each page is split in two, and the two parts are separated by a thin black line in the middle. The upper part consists of essays by the aging writer JC, titled *Strong Opinions* soon to be published by Mittwoch Verlag GmbH in Berlin; the lower part consists of "a diary, perhaps"(McMahan 2010, 91), which details his meeting of a young Brazilian woman, Anya. Beginning with Chapter 6, titled "On Guidance Systems," JC has employed Anya "[a]s a typist pure and simple" (*DoB* 25). In this chapter, JC ruminates on weaponry and warfare during the Cold War and notes how "the Russians fell so far behind the Americans in weapons technology that, if it had come to all-out nuclear warfare, they would have been annihilated" (*DoB* 25). The advance of the Americans over the Russians is glossed as "*interruptions in equilibrium*" (*DoB* 25; added emphasis), and it is in this chapter that Anya commences a direct interruption in the equilibrium of JC's life, of his narrative, and a literal interruption of the page. The first page of Chapter 5 splits the page in three; JC's diary is pushed to the middle of the page and Anya's narrative occupies the lower third. We can regard this formal layout as a *guidance system* of a kind, which steers us toward a reflection on the text's visual gaps and toward the combinatory endeavor of making meaning from the way the three segments relate to each other—and to our reading. At this point even the name of the fictional Berlin publishing house gains added significance, since *Mittwoch* is German for *Wednesday*, even if the German word translates literally as *middle-of-the-week*, a not entirely unimportant name in a novel in which the protagonist's diary of the title is placed in the *middle* of the page after his contact with Anya.

Contrary to *In the Heart of the Country*, here the gaps between the segments are emphasized visually as thin black lines, which enables a more straightforward reading of their standing not *for* anything specific but of simply denoting their functions as gaps, that is as separators between the different narratives. Quite simply, the visual gaps of the novel serve the most direct function of decelerating the act of reading, while the visual arrangement of each page also has the direct function of emphasizing that one is reading a book. The visual gaps point to the book's materiality, since the reader actually has to pause and reflect and try out how to handle this book, how to read. At a very simple level, this reminds the reader not only of the book's literariness, but first and foremost of its literalness. What she is holding in her hands is a book, and it invites her to reflect whether from this book should be inferred anything in the way of a reading beneath the surface, as many critics have done and thus made the mistake of reading out of the text a far too simplistic connection between the character JC and the real J. M. Coetzee.[15] Such readings are complicated by one of JC's essays, "On Al Qaida," which attacks a hermeneutic of suspicion for its resonance regarding culture as a whole. Writing on suspicion and persecution, JC notes:

> Where did prosecutors learn to think in such a way? The answer: in literature classes in the United States of the 1980s and 1990s, where they were taught that in criticism suspiciousness is the chief virtue, that the critic must accept nothing whatsoever at face value. (*DoB* 33)

The emphasis on the book's materiality through the visual gaps and the resulting leafing back and forth through *Diary of a Bad Year* signals toward a reading that takes the text *at face value.*

Reading this novel takes time and responsibility, because the reader is not told how to process each chapter, whether to read the three segments of one page, then turn the page and do the same, or whether to read one chapter's segment at a time—in any case, a lot of handling of pages is involved and so the materiality of the book is drawn attention to. The use of visual gaps reminds the reader that she is not "only" reading a *novel*, but that she is reading, in the first place, a *book*. This way, the reader's relationship with the book is highlighted in a very different way from drawing her into the narrative through techniques such as using sympathy-increasing devices in characterization or tight plotting. It is tempting to argue that the abstract philosophical discussions in the novel about Darwinism, Zeno, or about the body are embedded in the reader's lives in a tangible way, since the book continually alerts her to the book's own materiality and so points to the act of reading in a way that involves both the reader's mind and body, even if only to a small degree. What the effects of this are on the individual reader can only remain the subject of conjecture here, though in the day and age of electronic reading the drawing attention to the materiality of a book is not unimportant, especially when considering that while some of Coetzee's texts do exist as e-books, *Diary of a Bad Year* does not. Furthermore, an e-book would also allow the reader to rearrange the pages, such as when she might increase the size of the type, which would destroy the important ordering of the work's three segments.[16] And while the explicit highlighting of the text's

---

[15] See Bradshaw for a contextualization (2010, 18f.).

[16] The preceding comments on the materiality of the book in the age of electronic reading is addressed by Coetzee in the Auster correspondence, when he writes to his friend on August 18, 2010 about his recent reading of "an alumnus magazine from a university in South Africa": "It included an article celebrating the opening of the new university library, with computer stations and study cubicles and

typography makes the book resistant to becoming an e-book, it also complicates its being turned into an audio-book, since the text continually draws attention to its existence as a *written* document.

These concerns are pertinent when considering that the text explores how the writing of a book of essays is embedded in a writer's daily life. This sense of embeddedness is related less topically than it is expressed formally, in the structuring of the novel through its visual gaps. In a discussion of the work, Jonathan Lear explores this by considering the ways in which one reads the novel. Lear addresses two possible readings which the novel invites, "two broad movements" (2010, 70). The first is what he calls "the *dialectic of responsibility*" (2010, 70; original emphasis), that is the reading across of JC's *Strong Opinions* in one go, and subsequently reading the diary and Anya's narrative. The second is what Lear calls "a *spectacle of embedding*" (2010, 70; original emphasis), that is the reading vertically down the page and appreciating "how the moral stances that are officially to be presented in book form are embedded in the fantasies, happenings, musings, and struggles of the author's day-to-day life" (2010, 70). Here, it becomes apparent that the visual gaps, which create a sense of montage in the book, also have semantic relevance, since the reader is invited to reflect on how the highly intellectual ideas by a writer connect, for example, with his desiring of his typist's behind.

This aspect of the novel represents one facet of Coetzee's multiform explorations of how philosophizing, reflecting, thinking are not confined to the ivy-clad ivory-towers of institutions of higher learning, but that they occur in the realm of the quotidian.[17] By juxtaposing the "high" and the "low" (quite literally JC's intellectual essays are high on the page, while the more ordinary aspects of life, such as doing laundry, are placed low on the page), the text

---

seminar rooms and work spaces too many to count. I read the article, reread it to make sure. I was right. The word *book* did not occur once" (*H&N* 179). The excerpt shows Coetzee as a slow reader, as a re-reader, and as concerned with the materiality of books. He emphasizes this through an anecdote about his purchase of a volume of *War and Peace* as a young man and how he has "sentimental relations with it—not with Tolstoy's *War and Peace* […], but with the object […]" (*H&N* 180).

17 In Coetzee's worlds, philosophizing and intense reflection are never limited to educated "thinkers"— the simple-minded K is the epitome of a meditative thinker; the policeman Ivanov philosophizes with Dostoevsky (*MoP* 89); and the boy John in *Boyhood* is not only wise beyond his years, but explicitly "left to do the thinking" (*SPL* 140). As mentioned before, it is often around the outsiders of these worlds that philosophical meaning-making is indicated to the reader. Frequently, this meaning-making is charged with a moral and political force, since the deconstruction of colonization and subjugation is shifted to the reader. This also highlights the importance of slow reading, since the slow reader who involves herself fully responds to the text's calling for being taken at face value, such as when she does not skip past Klawer's return after having been killed (even if he dies a second time afterwards), but takes it as a locus for signification. If her attention does skate past it, however, Klawer has died once, and once and for all Jacobus exults unbidden and undisturbed in his servant's death. Then, Klawer's death is no more than the depressing demise of a subjected man.

produces the effect of our going back and forth between the individual segments of the text, enabling us to reflect on the connection of intellectual thinking and bodily being through the use of gaps on the page. The separation between "high" and "low" might indicate that the public intellectual JC's domain is the lofty realm of thought, while Anya's realm is that of the body. However, as the text progresses, the reader witnesses that Anya is much more in control of JC than he thinks, not only when she plays up the features of her—as she calls it—"delicious behind" (*DoB* 25), but also how, when Anya's husband Alan proposes to steal money from JC, she is the one whose moral center is developed the most; it is Anya who reflects most astutely on the immorality of stealing from him (*DoB* 49f.). Shortly after her discussion with Alan, Anya also tells of a moment with JC when she voices a criticism about a choice of idiom found in his writing and she attests his slight misuse to the fact that English is not his "mother tongue," to which JC replies: "What does that mean, mother tongue?" (*DoB* 51). When Anya explains the expression *mother tongue* he goes on to claim that he very well knows what the expression means but that "it is [Anya's] choice of metaphor that [he is] querying" (*DoB* 51). A gap will open up between this moment and a much later *strong opinion* essay by JC titled "On the mother tongue" (*DoB* 195f.), where he takes up what Anya provoked him to think about when she glossed the term mother tongue as meaning "the tongue you learned at your mother's knee" (*DoB* 51).

This is but one example of how Anya is frequently responsible for the essays he writes, the directions his thoughts take, the way his life in writing is shaped. Nevertheless, the reader never finds out exactly in what way an idea, a thought, a reflection by Anya makes its way into his essays—the reader merely infers that it has happened this way because of the gaps between something Anya says or does and what JC writes about. In the same way, the reader is never told how the different segments of one page are connected, and so each reader forms her own combinations. This way, each reader is given more authority (but also more responsibility) in reading and reflecting than in those texts which, through their typographical layout, guide the reading in a simple way from top to bottom and from page to page.

While the suggestion of being slowed down by the typographical arrangement of the text seems to hint at a loss of freedom about how to read, the reverse is the case. Clarkson notes: "In the first place, the reader of *Diary of a Bad Year* has to *choose* which band of text to follow: which voice to listen to" (2009, 98; original emphasis). If the reader accepts the invitation to *choose*, if she takes the time to consider the text at face value, how the pages are laid out and how she incorporates the presence of the novel's gaps into her reading, she gains a great deal of freedom about her own acts of reading and meaning-making, without imposing anything arbitrary on the text. By the introduction of visual gaps on the page and the ensuing necessity to devise an individual technique of reading, the reader is implicitly encouraged to develop her own method of reading as well.

The visual gaps in *Diary of a Bad Year* are an explicit technique to disrupt customary reading habits that proceed in an unreflective way from left to right and from top to bottom (at least in the Latin script). By pointing to these visual disruptions, one may see how they also bear on the semantic and signifying potential of disruptions on different levels of discourse, for example in the many forms of productive estrangement that informs so much of Coetzee's work.[18]

Most elementary and most directly, the visual gaps in *Diary of a Bad Year* point out the impact of a text's typographical presentation on the reader's response and the extreme unconventionality of this novel. Certainly, this unconventionality appears greater when viewing *Diary of a Bad Year* against the other works in Coetzee's oeuvre than against those novels in literary history which make use of visual tools, of which Laurence Sterne's *The Life and Opinions of Tristram Shandy, Gentleman* (1759–67) is the gold standard in English language literature—with its black pages, the disruption of the type by clusters of asterisks and fence-like structures of dashes, or the not-so-straight lines that the gentleman of the title draws amid his text, even if he attests that he will be able to continue with his story "in a tolerable straight line" ([1767] 1998, 379).[19] In Sterne's novel the drawing attention to the text's typographical aspects causes confusion in the reading, and in *Diary of a Bad Year* the use of typographical gaps is a similar technique to highlight that the reader is dealing with an unusual, a confusing text as well, and this has the effect of getting the reader most directly and from the beginning into a mode of awareness that transcends habits of reading instrumentally and swiftly.[20] Opening the book, the reader immediately notices the gap as a

---

[18] JC's "On the Slaughter of Animals" explicitly references Shklovsky and the overall ethical importance of "seeing with an estranged eye" (*DoB* 63).

[19] Coetzee's works never mention Sterne's novels explicitly, although Coetzee's play with the reader is arguably indebted to Sterne, not only in the use of visual tools, but also in the works' digressions, and, most importantly, in the self-referentiality especially of Coetzee's later texts. Lisa McNally points out that *Diary of a Bad Year* is also related to *Tristram Shandy* because of the way Sterne's novel integrates the act of narrating the novel into the narration of the novel (2013, 32).

[20] Contemporary comic books and graphic novels, of course, make use of this as well, such as when they arrange panels without lines in between them or by upsetting customary Western reading habits of reading from left to right, from top to bottom. For Coetzee's interest in the medium of comic books, see his essay "Captain America in American Mythology" (1976), collected in *Doubling the Point*.

rupture in ordinary typography and is invited to pause upon this rupture. When looking at these ruptures more closely, it is noteworthy that not one of the two respective parts in the first five chapters continues individually to the next page in midsentence. This way, the text demands a decision by the reader: to read each page on its own or each section. The same is true of the respective three parts from Chapters 6 through 9, although this suddenly changes in Chapter 10, titled "On National Shame." There, for the first time in the novel, Anya's narrative carries a sentence across the page, when she writes of JC:

> The pages of writing he hands over are no use to me, no practical use. He forms his letters clearly enough, m's and n's and w's included, but when he has to write a whole passage he can't keep // the line straight, it dips like a plane nosediving into the sea or a baritone running out of breath. (*DoB* 42f.)

While this passage can function as a prototype for an understanding of how Coetzee's form and content are never to be thought of as separate, it also shows us how distinctly the text ruptures our reading. Let us assume that a reader develops her own technique of reading this novel over the first 41 pages of the text, and that this technique consists of reading each page on its own, then proceeding to the next page and so on. While the typographical arrangement through the gaps already creates ruptures, suddenly, then, the text introduces a further rupture, with the effect that now the reader has to reconsider the technique of reading she has used. Moreover, she is directly made aware of the connections between form and content, since the text claims that JC cannot *keep the line straight*, while the form of the novel quite literally does not keep it straight—similar to the way in which Gentleman Shandy does not keep it *tolerably straight* either.

Afterwards Anya's narrative does this continually. Anya herself becomes a rupture in JC's life, in the controlled narrative of his life, in his narrative, and in his writing life. And suddenly, in the tell-tale thirteenth chapter,[21] titled "On the body"—suddenly and for the first time, *his* narrative also crosses over the gap of the page: "These thoughts about a body occur not in the abstract but in // relation to a specific person, X, unnamed" (*DoB* 60f.). Here, the aforementioned connection between mind and body as well as the embodiedness and embeddedness of intellectual work are actually staged and shown formally, while the literal gap in the sentence might alert the reader to the fact that JC's mind has paused for a moment and reflected upon what to write next, or it might raise the question whether this rupture reveals anything about his character in general,

---

[21] In *Slow Man* it is also the thirteenth chapter that the pestering Elizabeth Costello begins to interrupt Paul Rayment's life and narrative.

about being easily influenced by a woman, easily distracted, for example, or about his complicated relation to *the relation to a specific person*. The reader begins to reflect on JC, on Anya's influence on him, and on the nature and genre of these essays, on the ways in which life leaves its traces in writing.

A similar rupture occurs in the aforementioned fourteenth chapter, "On the slaughter of animals." Here, it is important that the midsentence rupture occurs in the middle segment of the page for the first time, in JC's possible diary. The rupture Anya represents now spreads to his entire existence, and even beyond, since the rupture in Chapter 14 reads as follows:

> If I had been told that the last of my infatuations would be with a girl with provocative manners and cathouse connections (*a cathouse—you know, a home for cats*), I would have supposed I was destined to suffer one of those derided deaths in which the patron of the house of ill repute has a heart attack *in medias res* and his corpse has to be hastily dressed and smuggled out and // dumped in an alley. But no, if the new dream is to be trusted it will not be like that. I will expire in my own bed and be discovered by my typist, who will close my eyes and pick up the telephone to make her report. (*DoB* 64f.; original emphases)

Thus, Anya inhabits his projected imagination even beyond the confines of his existence and beyond his death; so she is deliberately linked to his mortality, and by way of this ultimate act of the body (or ultimate undoing of all that is bodily), she becomes viewed in *relation to* his body pure and simple. Because the carrying over of one sentence to the next page has been begun by Anya, it is the form that mirrors how Anya slowly takes over JC's life and work here. These ruptures represent visual and semantic gaps, as do the gaps between the different segments of each page, and so they continually enforce a renewed reflection on how to read this text. This way it is the gaps which stage a dialogic relationship between the different segments.[22]

The arrangement of the text in this way liberates the novel from the hegemony of a successive reading (down the page) by which what is read at the top of the page might (even if unconsciously) be privileged over that which is read

---

[22] There are further ruptures of this kind. Top section: 74f., 76f., 90f., 92f., 94f., 98f., 122f., 146f., 208f. Middle section: 78f., 80f., 88f., 104f., 112f., 116f., 120f., 124f., 126f., 132f., 136f., 140f., 146f. Lower section: 80f., 92f., 124f., 149f. As can be seen, all numbers are even, which means that these ruptures always occur when reading the left side of a page, so that one need merely look across to the right page to finish, thus not being strongly confused, but only subtly estranged. Only one time does the rupture occur so that one has to turn the page. It is when Anya reports on a conversation she has with Alan. She writes of a moment when she wants to say something: "Because—//He interrupts me" (*DoB* 149f.). Bradshaw also illuminates the dialogicity involved in the novel's formal arrangement and its function for undermining the privileging of the "protagonist's viewpoint," saying that "[t]he very layout of the new novel works against that supposition" (2010, 17).

afterwards at the bottom of the page. Chapter 14 shows quite deliberately how this is broken up through the carrying of one sentence across the page within one segment. Because the reader's security to read in the customary way is disrupted, she is unable to say whether the connection of JC's thoughts about animal death are related to thoughts about the end of his own life as well. It is entirely unclear if his essay about animal death has been prompted by thoughts about his own mortality, or the other way around, and yet the reader is provoked to combine these two segments and thus to reflect on the values of such a combination. An oscillation between the two segments and their signification is what Iser calls the "wandering viewpoint" (1978, 116), that is the passing from one meaning to another and from one narrative segment to another. Precisely through this *wandering viewpoint* the reader becomes more involved in the text, the reading process is slowed down and the text-reader relationship is increased, since "[the acts] of apprehension brought about by the wandering viewpoint organize the transfer of the text into the reader's conscious mind" (1978, 135). Regarding the earlier example, the reader, at the very least, comes to reflect on death, animal death and its possible connections to human death, death in a book and death in the world, possibly even her own death.

This indication toward a reflection on death simply through the formal arrangement is increased when the text uses a further rupture, only this time not through a visual gap but through the closing of one. Chapter 31 is titled "On the afterlife" and it is the first and only time that two successive pages are entirely filled, made up only of JC's essay. And once again, the formal closing of the visual gap is also addressed topically, when during his rumination on the death and the persistence of the soul after the termination of bodily being, JC wonders why the idea of an afterlife continues to engage thought:

> It is surprising that the notion of an individual afterlife persists in intellectually respectable versions of Christianity. It so transparently *fills a lack*—an incapacity to think of a world from which the thinker is absent—that religion ought simply to note such incapacity as part of the human condition and leave it at that. (*DoB* 154; added emphasis)

After this chapter, part two of the novel begins, titled "Second Diary," which returns to the division of each page into sets of three, although for the first four chapters a vacant white gap "fills" the middle section, as if JC were bereft of thoughts, as if there were a direct gap, a lack in his life which the visual emptiness underscores formally. Shortly afterwards he describes the end of his relationship with Anya and the middle segment narrates the moment when he "saw Anya for the last time" (*DoB* 169). His resuming descriptions, then, fill the gap in the middle of the page, and we are made to reflect whether in Anya's absence the only thing he can do is take this lack, this gap, this absence in his life at face value as well, and simply describe that she is gone.

Through the use of typographical gaps in the two novels discussed here, the works push at the boundaries of the novel genre by subsuming ideas of literary theory into the very form of the works. In this way, these theoretical considerations are normalized and used for an enrichment of the genre of the novel and an enrichment of our reading, even if we "attend to the surfaces of texts [in the most literal way conceivable] rather than plumb their depths" (Best and Marcus 2009, 1f.).

In closing of this middle chapter and to "get us from where we are," as *Elizabeth Costello* has it, "to the far bank" (*EC* 1) of the following slow readings, it will be useful to reflect again on my use of the arguably problematically charged term *enrichment* with regard to reading. I highlight this term here as a point of connecting my method of slow reading with Heather Love's aforementioned considerations of a sociological descriptive reading as juxtaposed against a humanist instrumental one, and whether the former strips the text of a *richness* that the latter is argued to emphasize. Ultimately, Love argues for the importance of description by performing a descriptive reading of the literary forms of description in Tony Morrison's novel, *Beloved*. Love holds:

> Good descriptions are in a sense rich, but not because they truck with imponderables like human experience or human nature. They are close, but they are not deep; rather than adding anything "extra" to the description, they account for the real variety that is already there. (2010, 377)

As has been shown, Love's arguments are important to my study both for her emphasis on phenomenological description and her mimetic link between her descriptive method and an aspect of the text under analysis. This resonates with my own method of slow reading, which is promulgated by the form of the text while being mirrored in many representations of slowness at the level of the content. The only addition to Love's argument would be this: A descriptive method of reading—even if this means to take the very basic element of a book's visual layout at face value—not only enriches our reading if we understand reading as an intellectual grasp of a text, but it also enriches our reading if we understand simply the reader's relationship with a book, whichever shape this relationship takes, whichever level of education the reader has.

7

The Legacy of Socrates—Dialogue in and with Coetzee

Coetzee is a writer whose oeuvre seems ever more interested in various forms of dialogue. His first published novel *Dusklands* contrasts two narratives in a dialogic way, while his *Foe* and *The Master of Petersburg* as well as his Nobel Lecture "He and His Man" address forms of dialogue and communication intra-diegetically, and he makes use of the way narrative segments speak to one another in a dialogic way in *In the Heart of the Country* and *Diary of a Bad Year* (as I have argued in the previous chapter). Even in his later writing life, it seems the oeuvre has not exhausted the dialogic potential of narrative, as *The Lives of Animals* and *Elizabeth Costello* make use of the structure of a dialogue between interlocutors in the way that Plato's Socrates did.[1] And in *The Childhood of Jesus*, his characters quite explicitly engage in philosophical dialogue in a Socratic (or mock-Socratic) way. Even his recently published works of correspondence with Paul Auster (*Here and Now*, 2013), Berlinde De Bruyckere (*Cripplewood/Kreupelhout*, 2013), and Arabella Kurtz (*The Good Story: Exchanges on Truth, Fiction and Psychoanalytic Psychotherapy*, 2015) seem to give a philosophical, Socratic construction of dialogue and reflection to the epistolary form.

This inclination toward dialogue may be owed to the fact that Coetzee's work seems, above all, an inquiring oeuvre, as I have argued before. The deceleration through inquiry accelerates philosophizing and reflection on the texts and the

---

[1] To my knowledge, only Richard Alan Northover attempts an analysis of a Coetzee character as a Socratic figure, when he compares Elizabeth Costello to the various Socratic interlocutors; he limits himself mostly to the topical similarities discernible, but argues convincingly that "[t]he Platonic dialogue is the perfect medium for the combination of the rational and the imaginative" (2012, 40). Northover refers to *The Lives of Animals* and also draws pertinent connections between Socrates, Coetzee, and Bakhtin, though his argument is ultimately self-defeating, as he claims that the polyphony which Coetzee achieves through the Socratic dialogue precludes "critics and reviewers […] to work out his own views on the issue of animal rights" (2012, 53), when he himself claims that the success of the "Bakhtinian polyphony" blurs the "many opinions Coetzee holds" (2012, 41). Either, Coetzee was not as successful as Northover claims, if he is, in fact, able to work out that the opinions are Coetzee's own, or Northover has fallen prey to a slightly intentionalist argument, perhaps because Coetzee's opinions were so imaginatively wrought that they must be his own.

issues raised or implied therein. Coetzee's narrators' and focalizers' foremost way of reflection is through self-questioning, which the texts realize through free indirect discourse or interior monologue, what Mikhail Bakhtin terms "dialogized interior monologue"[2] or "*microdialogue*" ([1929] 1984, 74; original emphasis).[3] In Coetzee's fiction, characters seem more inclined to be in dialogue with themselves than with others, both because many of the characters are outsiders and loners and because understanding between human beings is often staged as an encounter of misunderstanding or of silence. However, silence and the thwarting of fluid conversation actively foster a more engaged text–reader dialogue. Where the text is silent the reader is herself moved to engage in her own dialogized interior monologue, in her own *microdialogue* about the text.

A large part of Coetzee's oeuvre is shaped dialogically in the Bakhtinian and dialectically in the Socratic[4] sense;[5] it is frequently characterized by direct questioning between characters in monologue or dialogue. The questioning of another character has an ethical resonance concerning another subject; one is moved to ask, for example, is it morally permissible or ethically necessary to make K or Friday yield their stories? But the reverberations of inquiry in Coetzee transcend ethics and inform the reader's reflections about communication more generally, about the possibilities of mutual understanding. Dialogue between characters in Coetzee often has the function of discursively opening up arenas

---

[2] Philosophically, it is useful to speak of dialogue when concerned with monologue as well, since philosophically the idea of pure monologue, of a single whole voice, unrelated or uninfluenced by other voices, is questionable. It is therefore as a literary term that I use the word monologue when referring to a form of conversation that a character engages in with herself.

[3] Bakhtin's notion of dialogicity extends toward a conception of viewing each word as a microcosm of philosophical reflection. Each word is "double-voiced, in each word an argument (a microdialogue)" (Bakhtin [1929] 1984, 73). And "[l]ike the word, the idea is by nature dialogic, and monologue is merely the conventional compositional form of its expression, a form that emerged out of the ideological monologism of modern times" (Bakhtin [1929] 1984, 88).

[4] It is the Socratic method I refer to here, in the full knowledge that not only Socrates (viz. Plato) has used dialogue as philosophical inquiry. Prominent examples are found in Bruno, Erasmus, Diderot, or Hume.

[5] In her preface to *Problems of Dostoevsky's Poetics* (1929) Caryl Emerson cautions that "for [Bakhtin] the *word* 'dialectical,' like the word 'rhetoric,' generally has pejorative overtones" ([1929] 1984, xxvi; original emphasis). Emerson explains that

> for Bakhtin 'dialogic' does not mean 'dialectic'; his universe owes much more to Kant than to Hegel. [...] Consider, for example, this note jotted down in 1970–71 [from his private *Jottings 1970-1971*]: 'Dialogue and dialectics. Take a dialogue and remove the voices ... remove the intonations ... carve out abstract concepts and judgments from living words and responses, cram everything into one abstract consciousness—and that's how you get dialectics.' [...] In place of the comfortable patterns of synthesis and *Aufhebung*, Bakhtin posits a dualistic universe of *permanent* dialogue. Life in language is in fact dependent upon the preservation of a gap. Two speakers must not, and never do, completely understand each other; they must remain only partially satisfied with each other's replies, because the continuation of dialogue is in a large part dependent on neither party knowing exactly what the other means. (1984, xxxii; original emphases)

of thinking and philosophizing, and of engaging different voices in exploring,[6] searching, and encircling various opinions, positions, and points of view. Many times in Coetzee's works the characters do not seem to communicate instrumentally, that is they do not ask questions as a means toward an end (Could you pass the salt? Are you a conservative or a liberal?). At the same time, their communication is hardly phatic or expressive (How do you do? There's a lot of snow this year!). Rather, his characters exchange positions and ideas either directly to make their dialogue philosophical, or implicitly to prompt a philosophical dialogue between the text and the reader.[7] It is important not to think of philosophical conversations by the characters as trying to work toward a conclusion in a calculative way, but that ideas are exchanged in a ruminative and often searching fashion that is reminiscent of philosophical inquiry. In Coetzee's texts this form of inquiry is dispersed among different voices in dialogue and the various narrative levels characteristic of the novel genre.[8] Arguments, opinions, and ideas are distributed in a polyphonic way through the text and between the characters, rather than assigned to one character who is deemed philosophical.

The characters' ruminative discourse may be viewed as a form of slow dialogicity[9] that is conducive to activating a slow reflexive text–reader dialogue

[6] In the following it will become clear that my understanding of dialogue begins from an idea of dialogue as a form of exploration, which is often motivated by a sense of unknowing, complication, or indeterminacy. Needless to say, this exploration is to be distinguished from the kind of exploring that Jacobus Coetzee is associated with, when he "speculates on the unknowability of the South African people he has moved among" (Attridge 2004a, 84): "I am an explorer. My essence is to open what is closed, to bring to light what is dark. If the Hottentots comprise an immense world of delight, it is an impenetrable world, impenetrable to men like me, who must either skirt it, which is to evade our mission, or clear it out of the way" (*Dusk* 106). It will not be going too far to hear in this rhetoric the violence wreaked by the colonizer as well as the "violence" wreaked by the "colonizer" of the text, the suspicious reader discussed earlier.

[7] Examples can be found in the post-lecture discussions in *Elizabeth Costello*; in Lurie and Lucy's discussions of desire and rape, before as well as after the attack on the farm); or when Mrs. Curren is in the transformed agora of the township, a moment to which I return later. Northover makes a similar point, arguing that the dialogic form of *The Lives of Animals* aims "to encourage readers to work through the issues themselves rather than subscribe dogmatically to some principle or position" (2012, 41).

[8] Bakhtin limits this to the genre of what he calls the "polyphonic novel" heralded by Dostoevsky (1984, 7), although modern literary theory is more inclusive of texts predating Dostoevsky's work, as well as going beyond Bakhtin's view that merely the novel is polyphonic and heteroglossic (Richter 2007, 15n1). For Bakhtin's full discussion of heteroglossia (*raznorečie*) see the essay "Discourse in the Novel" in *The Dialogic Imagination* (1975), where he explains: "The novel orchestrates all its themes, the totality of the world of objects and ideas depicted and expressed in it, by means of the social diversity of speech types [*raznorečie*] and by the differing individual voices that flourish under such conditions" ([1975] 1981, 263). See also Bakhtin ([1975] 1981, 301–331).

[9] My idea of *slow dialogicity* is based on Bakhtin's sense of a *permanent dialogue* mentioned earlier, especially about a text–reader relationship that is increased and lengthened through the engagement with a complex literary work. What Bakhtin has to say about the reader who is drawn into the dialogic world of the novel ([1929] 1984, 18) is relevant with regard to the above-mentioned notions

and a slow microdialogue in the reader's mind as well.[10] Coetzee's works continually foreground the dialogic relationship between the reader and the text by mandating the reader to ask questions, to work with gaps, and to co-construct the work. Because of the discursive nature of this relationship and the often enigmatic and open-ended quality of Coetzee's texts, this reader–text dialogue is a locus for particularly productive kinds of reflection. Clarkson's work is illuminating here, when she considers the competing voices in Coetzee's works and speaks about the sense in which Coetzee "play[s] up the dialogic potential of writing, instead of trying to suppress it [and] raises a countervoice, producing a discourse inflected by an invisible interlocutor" (2009, 7).

In Coetzee's works the reader–text dialogue is also spurred on by the explicit integration of argument and reflection into the narrative through characters who are discussing and reasoning in conversation or in microdialogue.[11] Because philosophical questions are raised in the texts topically, the reader is likewise moved to reflect on them, but reflection and argument are also

---

by Poulet of thinking the thoughts of another, but thinking them as one's own (1980, 44). About the reader and Dostoevsky's works, Bakhtin writes:

> Every true reader of Dostoevsky, who perceives his novels not in the monologic mode and who is capable of rising to Dostoevsky's new authorial position, can sense this peculiar active broadening of his consciousness, not solely in the sense of an assimilation of new objects (human types, character, natural and social phenomena), but primarily in the sense of a special dialogic mode of communication with the autonomous consciousnesses of others, something never before experienced, an active dialogic penetration into the unfinalizable depths of man. ([1929] 1984, 68)

I am most interested in Bakhtin's sense of *permanence* and *unfinalizability* for my conception of a slow dialogicity and for the explorations of endings in the following chapter.

[10] About Dostoevsky's novels Bakhtin writes what may be brought to bear on the text–reader dialogue in Coetzee's work as well:

> [The novel] is constructed not as the whole of a single consciousness, absorbing other consciousnesses as objects into itself, but as a whole formed by the interaction of several consciousnesses, none of which entirely becomes an object for the other; this interaction provides no support for the viewer who would objectify an entire event according to some ordinary monologic category (thematically, lyrically or cognitively)—and this consequently makes the viewer also a participant. ([1929] 1984, 18)

See also Attridge's thoughts on the reader–text dialogue, which permeates his ideas on the singularity of literature; especially his considerations of the reader's response to works of literature and her co-construction of the text (2004b, 79–93).

[11] A good example is the aforementioned moment in *Life & Times of Michael K*, where K is alone in his burrow and thinks deeply philosophical thoughts in microdialogue about the master–slave dialectic by allegorizing it as the relationship between a parasite and a sheep (*K* 116), which is borrowed from Hillis Miller's "The Critic as Host" ([1979] 2004), though Miller uses it in a very different context. The example shows how Coetzee integrates such highly philosophical or theoretical thinking into the worlds and minds of ordinary people. Philosophy is not something practiced in the lecture halls of universities, philosophy is the way Coetzee's people think. In his notebook on the composition of *Life & Times of Michael K* Coetzee glosses this passage after it was written: "19.ix.81 [...] I seem to have found something interesting to say, as a manifesto. The host–parasite idea comes from the essay by J. Hillis Miller in Deconstruction + Criticism" (HRC, container 33, folder 5, p. 47).

stimulated formally through slowing devices such as the ones explored in the previous chapters. Dialogue between characters contributes to the decelerating style of Coetzee's works in an essential way, such as when dialogue or monologue themselves assume a tarrying or even frustrating quality. The complicated, non-teleological dialogue between the medical officer and K in part two of *Life & Times of Michael K* is a prime example of this. In the following, I will explore how such non-teleological dialogue is mirrored in the complex non-teleological *permanent dialogue* between the reader and the text. This dialogue does not yield any facts or "truths," but provokes a lasting dialogic intimacy pointing even beyond the diegetic world.[12]

The dialogue between Coetzee's characters appears as highly argumentative, reflexive, and explorative. The exploratory, searching nature of Coetzee's dialogue is often owed to the fact that character exchanges are marked not primarily by statements and postulations but by suggestions and questions, and it is owed to the linguistic choices inherent in dialogue and the arrangement of dialogue on the page. The characters' dialogue is presented in a seemingly simple and clear language, which belies its complexity.[13] The clarity of the characters' speech invites the reader to join in the dialogue, while the implied complexities emerge when considering the issues left unresolved in the characters' conversations. As an example, let us look at a pivotal moment in *Age of Iron*, when Mrs. Curren (the first person narrator) is among the people in Gugulethu. Amid the burning shacks of the township, and in search of Bheki, the son of Curren's maid Florence, the reader witnesses an exchange between the former teacher, Mrs. Curren, and Florence's cousin, Mr. Thabane. After a while, a man from the cluster of people around them joins their dialogue:

> "You want to go home," he [Thabane] said. "But what of the people who live here? When they want to go home, this is where they must go. What do you think of that?" [...]
> "I have no answer," I said. "It is terrible."
> "It is not just terrible," he said, "it is a crime. When you see a crime being committed in front of your eyes, what do you say? Do you say, 'I have seen enough, I didn't come to see sights, I want to go home'? [...] No, you don't," he said. "Correct. Then what do you say? What sort of crime is it that you see? What is its name?"

---

[12] This phenomenon will be explored further in the following chapter on endings.

[13] Bradshaw comments on this notion regarding Coetzee's work in general. About *Disgrace* he notes the novel "might at first seem deceptively simple. The chapters are short, each with a single focus that advances a linear storyline [...]. Yet, the novel's difficulties and challenges appear as soon as we find ourselves trying to grasp the non-linear relations between its different constituents" (2010, 15).

He is a teacher, I thought: that is why he speaks so well. What he is doing to me he has practiced in the classroom. It is the trick one uses to make one's own answer seem to come from the child. Ventriloquism, the legacy of Socrates, as oppressive in Africa as it was in Athens.

"There are many things I am sure I could say, Mr. Thabane," I said. "But then they must truly come from me. When one speaks under duress—you should know this—one rarely speaks the truth."

He was going to respond, but I stopped him.

"Wait. Give me a minute. I am not evading your question. There are terrible things going on here. But what I think of them I must say in my own way."

"Then let us hear what you have to say! We are listening! We are waiting." He raised his hands for silence. The crowd murmured approval.

"These are terrible sights," I repeated, faltering. "They are to be condemned. But I cannot denounce them in other people's words. I must find my own words, from myself. Otherwise it is not the truth. That is all I can say now."

"This woman talks shit," said a man in the crowd. He looked around. "Shit," he said. No one contradicted him. […]

"Yes," I said, speaking directly to him. "You are right, what you say is true." (*AoI* 97–99)

The passage highlights how questions outnumber the answers, leaving gaps for the reader to address, and how a withheld answer (*I have no answer*) actually engenders further dialogue, both in the diegetic world, where it causes frustration and angered response, and in the reader's mind, who is provoked to reflect on Curren's position at this moment and whether her responses and her thoughts are acceptable. The already hesitant dialogue between the characters—because Curren is uncertain what to say—is further interrupted by her reflections, moments of microdialogue inserted into the characters' exchanges. The interplay of these voices along with the resulting sense of hesitation gives the passage as a whole their tarrying quality. This is shown in Mrs. Curren's method of stalling (*Wait*; *I am not evading your question*; her repetition), which only provokes the reactions from Thabane and the man in the crowd.

The scene stages a dialogic encounter on various levels: on the level of the combating characters; on the level of the different voices of Curren (her direct speech and her interior monologue, which are very different in tone); and on the text–reader level, since the reader is prompted to reflect on the validity of Mrs. Curren's final admission that the man in the crowd is right, that what he says is *true*. The reader is urged to reflect on what her admission signifies about truth,[14] which she has claimed will not be spoken under duress, and on what this says about the relationship between self and other, since Mrs. Curren admits that another person has spoken more truthfully about her present situation than she could at this point. Through the failure of understanding, a more complex form of conversation is staged between the characters, and a complex form of reflection is instigated in the reader.

In Coetzee's dialogue the hesitant quality of the characters' exchanges and the resulting effect of instigating reflection are also owed to the frequent use of *perhapses* and *on the other hands* in character exchanges. This gives the dialogue a simple conversational form to which the reader can easily relate, yet this, too, belies the complex mode of presenting counter-ideas, interjections, and new propositions, a mode which characterizes Coetzee's style across the board. Finally, dialogue is often left without speech tags to delineate unequivocally the addresser and addressee, causing the reader to turn back the pages (or count back the lines) to grasp who is speaking. The latter point has the very simple function of making the reader puzzle out who said what. The ending of *The Childhood of Jesus* is a good example of this:

"Did you like Dr García?" he, Simón, inquires.

"He's OK," says the boy. "He has hairs on his fingers like a werewolf."

"Why did you want him to come along to Estrellita?"

"Because."

"You can't just invite every stranger you meet to come with us," says Inés.

"Why not?"

"Because there is no room in the car."

"There is room. Bolívar can sit on my lap, can't you, Bolívar?" A pause. "What are we going to do when we get to Estrellita?"

"It's a long way yet to Estrellita. Be patient."

"But what are we going to *do* there?"

"We are going to find the Relocation Centre and we are going to present ourselves at the desk, you and Inés and I, and –"

"And Juan. You didn't say Juan. And Bolívar."

"You and Inés and Juan and Bolívar and I, and we are going to say, *Good morning, we are new arrivals, and we are looking for somewhere to stay.*"

"And?"

"That's all. *Looking for somewhere to stay, to start our new life.*" (*CoJ* 277; original emphases)

---

[14] "When one speaks under duress [...] one rarely speaks the truth" (*AoI* 98). Mrs. Curren's statement here about truth seems like a simplistic truism, but its missing explication may also trigger reflection. A turn to a later novel in the oeuvre might give further mental nourishment, when in *Slow Man* Paul reflects: "Truth is not spoken in anger. Truth is spoken, if it ever comes to be spoken, in love" (*S* 161).

The dialogue features few speech tags and thus makes it difficult to delineate who is speaking to David (who is asking the questions) in any quick way. Furthermore, the boy addresses Bolívar, the dog, directly, as children do, but by doing so he also bends the boundaries of dialogue. Especially the line following the address to the dog (*It's a long way yet to Estrellita. Be patient.*) makes it very difficult to say whether this is uttered by Inés or Simón. This technique quite simply slows down the reading process, as one retraces the lines to see whose turn it is to speak. Yet, this use of dialogue has further political and philosophical functions. Without the addenda *he said/she said* the hierarchies of who is entitled to speak on account of race, gender, age, class, etc. are momentarily blurred. And by the time the reader picks apart who does speak, her involvement in the text and her deepened characterization have already begun. The philosophical functions involved become apparent when considering dialogicity again, since the rift between subjects is momentarily macerated as well. This philosophical dimension is explicitly addressed by Michael K when he thinks about thinking:

> It seemed more like Robert than like him, as he knew himself, to think like that. Would he have to say that the thought was Robert's and had merely found a home in him, or could he say that though the seed had come from Robert, the thought, having grown up inside him, was now his own? He did not know. (*K* 95)

What K addresses explicitly here is often implied formally in Coetzee's work, as in the earlier example from *Age of Iron* where Mrs. Curren explicitly adopts (or borrows) another character's utterance (*Shit*) and uses it as her own.

Such mixing of voices fleshes out a topic, an idea, even a thought, in a more multidimensional way, and thus implicitly proposes to the reader a way of reading and reflecting on the texts herself. An exploration of a phenomenon in this multidimensional way is often achieved by a sense of fragmentation underlying the dialogue. First, in the sense that ideas and arguments are left open-ended, that they are not or cannot be cohered into one final meaning. Second, in the sense that differing opinions by two or more characters as well as the dialogic negotiation of differing views by one character through microdialogue deconstruct the whole idea of a "whole idea."[15] This way the hard Truth, the very idea of an ontological fact, is countered by a diffraction

---

[15] Behind this idea is the aforementioned explicit emphasis of the dialogicity of a text and so the challenging of the idea whether any voice can ever be fully authorial or whole. Coetzee reflects on this in his review of Joseph Frank's fourth volume of his biography of Dostoevsky, *The Miraculous Years, 1865–1871*: "A fully dialogic novel is one in which there is no dominating, central authorial consciousness, and therefore no claim to truth or authority, only competing voices and discourses" (*StS* 123). See also Clarkson (2009, 7–9) and Clarkson (2011, 230).

of opinions, views, and meanings. The philosophical discussions between the stevedores in *The Childhood of Jesus* show this quite well, though the two most fascinating instances might be found in the constructions of *Diary of a Bad Year* and *Summertime*. While in the former novel the division between the different segments and voices on one page interact dialogically and even competitively, the latter, Coetzee's third memoir, is written almost entirely in dialogue form. It consists of different interviews with different characters which through the course of the novel are geared toward achieving a near cubist portrayal of one subject: the late John Coetzee. Through such dialogic fragmentations, a wide spectrum of philosophical reflections is suggested to the reader and philosophical meaning-making is continually inspired, both when the reader reflects on *what* the characters discuss and when she considers *how* the characters and the texts go about their discussions.

As in Plato's Socratic dialogues, meaning emerges from the moments where communication and understanding momentarily pause, and where understanding is slowed down for the productive activation of reflection. In Coetzee, meaning-making is provoked by the cracks between utterances, where ideas collide, where views clash, or opinions need to be weighed, evaluated, and reconsidered by the reader. However, when juxtaposing the modes of Plato and Coetzee, one comes to appreciate how different Coetzee's dialogic method is from that of Socrates in Plato's dialogues, even if their aspirations seem similar. Plato's Socrates is a provocateur and a coaxer, coercing his interlocutors into exposing their flaws in reasoning, teaching cogent thought, and moving very clearly and distinctly toward knowledge and Truth. Because Socrates appears as the most discerning and persuasive intelligent thinker of his time, in dialogue he is the one in charge. This is one of the reasons why Socrates was put on trial for corrupting the young by his ignorant accuser Meletus;[16] and while the dying classicist Mrs. Curren does not seem likely to welcome Socrates's facing trial, his persuasiveness might be a reason why she finds the Socratic method so "oppressive" (*AoI* 98). Socrates can single-handedly steer his opponents' thoughts through an argument by using coercive statements and questions, and he can confidently win every argument in the end. The strong didactic streak, the hierarchy of the interlocutors, and the teleological impetus are missing from Coetzee's dialogue, or they are challenged and diffracted by a more complex dialogic structure.

---

[16] See the *Apology* 24*b*–26*a*, where Socrates exposes Meletus's ignorance through a persuasive session of cross-examination of his accuser—and all while Socrates is the one being cross-examined.

The didactic impulse in Plato's Socrates is difficult to label. While both Plato and Socrates seem strongly opposed to a didacticism that professes in any finger-wagging way, Socrates's ultimate goal is the delineation of truth, coming to wisdom, or seeing "the good," as he calls it in "The Simile of the Cave" (*The Republic* 514*a*–521*b*). *The Republic* as a whole places a strong emphasis on education, and Part VIII specifically outlines the education of the philosopher. The chapter "Dialectic" (531*d*–534*e*) gives a good overview of Socrates's dialectic method as "the only procedure which proceeds by the destruction of assumptions to the very first principle, so as to give itself a firm base" (533*d*). Socrates's dialectic is on the road to essences, to knowledge, wisdom, to the grasping of truth "by pure thought" (532*a*). Coetzee's writing is vastly different from this. It simply does not teach through a straightforward didacticism. Even if *characters* seem to lecture, the dialogic structure of his works subvert or qualify the didactic impulses of his people, such as when in *Elizabeth Costello* or *Diary of a Bad Year*, for example, the didactic statements by Costello or JC are countered through a polyphony of other views, other opinions.[17] At the same time, the reader may be likely to side with a character like Elizabeth Costello because she too seems as if on trial, like Socrates, when she has to defend her provocative ideas, and because the reader may simply pity her, for her loneliness or even just for her "white shoes with which there is nothing wrong yet which somehow make her look like Daisy Duck" (*EC* 4).

Whereas in Coetzee's works sympathy for characters might be said occasionally to steer the reader in a didactic way, in Plato's dialogues Socrates guides the argument through coaxing questions and ironic comments throughout, and he offers a secure opinion that is worked toward, even if this becomes clear only in retrospect. In contrast, the dialogic structure of Coetzee's texts and the individual opinions, thoughts, ideas expressed therein dispense arguments, offer views (such as Costello's problematic Holocaust analogy), but immediately challenge these by equally valid counterarguments and alternative views (such as Abraham Stern's letter of protest). Because these theses and antitheses are not cohered into solid syntheses, the reader is invited into the agora where the characters are engaged in discussions, and she is invited to join the swirl of voices that is a novel. This means, however, that Coetzee's works could still be called didactic. By withholding exegesis, by denying the argumentative synthesis present in Plato, Coetzee's dialectic forces the reader to think for herself, not merely to follow the thoughts expressed by a character.

---

[17] See Clarkson (2009, 7–9) and Northover (2012, 41).

While Socrates's method may also provoke slow reading, Plato's dialogues do this in a crucially different way from Coetzee's works. In Plato the reader also shares in the dialogue and is also asked to weigh her ideas against those presented by Socrates and his interlocutors.[18] Coleridge sees in Socrates's method less a finding of Truth and more a stimulation of thought, so the interlocutor may come to attain a truth on her own (1818, 177). Coleridge aligns the philosopher in the Socratic tradition with the writer of literature; it is here that his definitions of the "philosophic poet" and the "poetic philosopher" (1818, 176) converge: "[T]he purpose of the writer is not so much to establish any particular truth, as to remove the obstacles, the continuance of which is preclusive to all truth" (1818, 177). The sharp distinction between the Socratic method in Plato and Coetzee's Socratic literature, then, is a difference in epistemological impact. In the Socratic method the reader is asked to think for herself and then, after a negotiation of ideas has occurred, to *learn* the truth—and to learn it by proxy, since the first student of Socrates is always his interlocutor. While the interlocutor is involved in thinking and questioning his[19] epistemic talents and epistemology in general while in dialogue, a more passive involvement is demanded of the reader, since Socrates is always there as a firm guide. Socrates knows the outcome of the argument, or he could not question in the persuasive manner that he does. Coetzee's Socratic method is likewise involved in a *removal of the obstacles*, but it is so, paradoxically, by first putting obstacles in place and making the reader deal with these obstacles intellectually. Contrary to Plato's dialogues, Coetzee's works do not remove these obstacles *in the text*, but highlight their presence and so provoke the reader to reflect on what these obstacles signify. The reader is left alone with these obstacles, with gaps, with the manifold defamiliarizations, and indeed with disparate arguments in dialogue by different characters, without being shown resolutions to these arguments. The onus is entirely on the reader to delineate and to work with these and, in effect, to learn to read them.[20]

---

[18] See Tarrant (2003, xiii–xiv) for a discussion of this important characteristic of Plato's Socrates.

[19] While Socrates had a high opinion of women, there are no female interlocutors in Plato's world, a not unimportant problem with Plato's dialectic, especially when considering the high number of (and highly reflexive) female characters in Coetzee's oeuvre. For absorbing readings of Coetzee's female narrators, see Kossew (1998).

[20] One may recall Coetzee's implication that he views his work as a professor of literature not so much as consisting of teaching meaning but teaching reading: "As for the teaching of reading, I merely suggest that it is a good idea for students to be exposed to the spectacle of someone else reading intently and intensively, particularly if what emerges from that reading fosters in the student a respect for close reading" (*DtP* 429). While he is clearly referring to his pedagogy in the university, the dialectic method of his works allows the reemphasis of this study, namely that his works are *teachers of slow reading*.

In the dialogue with the text, the reader is stimulated to think meditatively about the textual significations as they fall upon her consciousness, while the simultaneously beckoning and confronting complexity of the works continually forces the reader to question her own epistemology during the reading. Coetzee's dialogue stimulates slower and more philosophical reading by holding in a rocky balance complex or possibly mutually exclusive arguments. One may turn to Elizabeth Costello to emphasize the epistemological impetus behind this enterprise, when she simply states: "We understand by immersing ourselves and our intelligence in complexity" (*EC* 108).

One fundamental way in which this complexity is kept alive in Coetzee's fiction is through the many ways in which dialogue between characters peters out, in which communication falters. The conversations have an essentially slowing feature through their open-ended quality, which is often to do with the general disinterest or inability by Coetzee's characters to function purely rationally and purely instrumentally. Very often his characters seem either unwilling or unable to follow simple instrumental reason, to function along the lines of calculative thinking. Michael K is the key example of a character who seems simply incapable of thinking and acting in the way that institutions (governments, camps) function and demand, that is instrumentally.[21] Question asked—question answered? Not quite. Michael K's response to the medical officer's entreating is rather like that man's from New York who says "I would prefer not to."[22] Indeed, K would prefer not to, not to give answers, not to engage in the simple teleological communication the medical officer seems to have in mind, not to share in the simplistic Aristotelian story-telling, not to play the game—especially the game of war. A good example of how dialogue functions as a firm stoppage is when K, after being spoken to about the war, curtly responds: "I am not in the war" (*K* 138). War as a concept of instrumental, state-driven teleology (its objective being victory for the one, defeat for the other) is wholly beyond K's rational system.[23] As a result, K's radical rational idiosyncrasy naturally

---

[21] Attwell notes:

> [I]n *Life and* [sic] *Times of Michael K* we have a lavishly specific account of a civil war into which is inserted a leading protagonist who is able not to feel the weight of that history bearing down upon him. The interest lies precisely in the tension between the closely realized social texture and the literary re-working of that ground in the name of another, transformative level of consciousness. (1998, 174)

[22] On 13 March 1982 J. M. Coetzee explicitly refers to Melville's *Bartleby* with regard to *Life & Times of Michael K*, when he writes in his composition diary: "Michaels is like that man in New York who said, 'I prefer not to'..." (HRC, container 33, folder 5, p. 61).

[23] Note also the dissociation with war and instrumental society in general when K is in his burrow: "Once or twice the other time in which the war had its existence reminded itself to him as the jet fighters whistled high overhead. But for the rest he was living beyond the reach of calendar and clock

contributes to the breakdown of communication in the narrative dialogue about concepts like war. At the same time, his way of thinking (and so his way of speaking) is also charged with an ethics of quiet (and idle) disobedience to any form of complicity, or even compliance.[24] The subaltern, in this regard, does not speak; instead, he chooses an ethics of silence and restraint and so forces the reader to think. Paradoxically, the silences of K and other characters in Coetzee may be viewed as an insistent invitation to the reader to listen ever more closely to these enigmatic, elusive characters.

Coetzee's texts use silences to keep the reader interested in the narratives, since the reader listens to these characters' silences the way other characters are listening, such as the medical officer or Susan Barton in *Foe*. In the way these listening characters respond to the silent characters, however, the reader is shown that a reading for the answer to a question, the reading for a filling of silences is misguided, and that another response is needed. The reader who responds phenomenologically to K's silence slowly begins to think differently about the character's reticence and understands his silent retreat as a resistance to instrumentality. This way a deconstructive reversal is indicated, what one might call—slightly flippantly—a *postcolonial flip*, following what Robert J. C. Young identifies as one of the basic tenets of postcolonialism, namely the idea of "turning the world upside down" (2003, 2). Here, it is initiated through the text–reader dialogue, since the reversal in Coetzee is quite different from letting the silenced speak, supplying power to the subjugated by giving them an active voice, a voice to talk back, which would essentially always be a supplied voice, a false voice, the voice of the *ventriloquist*. In Coetzee the opposite is the case, since it is often precisely because the silenced cannot (or will not) speak that a dialogue with them is sought. Paradoxically, his characters assume agency more through their passive, slinking evasion than through an aggressive taking of the floor. The effect is that the reader works *with* the gaps of silence in the works, rather than merely filling them. Once more, one may repeat Poulet's cross-current of mental activity, the idea of *thinking the thought of another as one's own*.[25]

---

in a blessedly neglected corner, half awake, half asleep" (*K* 115f.). For further considerations of the deceleration of time and the acceleration of reflection in *Life & Times of Michael K* with regard to his burrow, see Meljac (2008).

[24] See also Head (2009, 57).

[25] One may likewise illuminate this through Iser: "[I]n supplying all the missing links, [the reader] must think in terms of experiences different from his own; indeed, it is only by leaving behind the familiar world of his own experience that the reader can truly participate in the adventure the literary text offers him" (1980, 57).

Poulet's argument may be reversed and read with the ethical resonance it entails, when one considers that otherness intrudes into every reader's thoughts, always. Coetzee's texts continually force the reader to make herself deputy to this otherness, to the silent, resistant character in an ethical way, or, as Elizabeth Costello would say, by way of Cesław Miłosz's, to be a "secretary of the invisible" (*EC* 199).[26] The reader is concurrently authorized by the text and in service to it, involving herself in the complexity of an enigmatic character, entering into a philosophical dialogue with a character who is, in the socio-historic world of the narrative, a powerless person. It is the reading that gives momentum to the character, but it is the character's elusiveness that gives resonance to the reader's thinking.

Through the various dislocations and defamiliarizations staged in Coetzee's work, a reversal also frequently occurs at the level of the reader–text relationship. Time and again Coetzee's works use destabilizations of epistemology—such as Klawer's twofold death in *Dusklands* or the death and return and death of Magda's father *In the Heart of the Country*—to increase *the ethics of reading* in Attridge's or Miller's sense, to heighten the text–reader dialogue. This increase in the dialogue is often brought about in the way that the reader is provoked to submit herself to the text in her reading. In Coetzee, this submission is all the more significant because it is often brought about not by commonly authoritarian characters, but by characters who have themselves been subject to a history of submission, political or otherwise. It is not irrelevant that the above-mentioned rupture in *Duskland*'s epistemic stability is linked to Klawer, a slave. Here as in other texts by Coetzee, the deepening of the dialogue between reader and text is linked to the marginalized. Klawer, Magda, Michael K, the "barbarian" girl, Susan Barton *and* Friday,[27] Vercueil, perhaps Ivanov, Petrus, Marijana—these characters have the profoundest effects not only on the focalizers' views of the world and their own epistemologies, but especially on those of the reader. It is as if these characters' presences exercised their direct power over the reader precisely because they are othered in the diegetic world, and because they

---

[26] This may be interpreted with the full force of attentive listening, imagining, reading, and writing, as acts which are only possible when undertaken slowly. The original phrase in Miłosz's poem does not end where Costello ends it. Miłosz's "Secretaries" begins: "I am no more than a secretary of the invisible thing/That is dictated to me and a few others" (Miłosz 2001, 325). Costello seems to use the clipped expression deliberately, as a *secretary of the invisible* seems to conform more to her idea of sympathy with another (an other) creature, whereas a *secretary of the invisible thing* might signify a thinking into other things (objects as well as ideas) rather than "merely" other human and non-human animals.

[27] Head notes that both Susan Barton and Friday are the novel's "two marginalized figures" (2009, 63).

possess a veritable agency of resisting being drawn back into neatly rationalized stock characters or categories.

Because of these characters' silences—whether their silences are figural or literal—and because of their challenges to set ways of character or narrative, even to dialogue, the text–reader dialogue is heightened. It is a deeply complex and endlessly fascinating aspect of Coetzee's paradoxical oeuvre that the dialogue between text and reader is stimulated most profoundly by its opposite. As the slowness in Coetzee's characters and form quickens meditative thinking, so is the reader's dialogic involvement in the narrative and in the voicing of signification paradoxically stimulated by the texts' and the characters' silences.

What materializes between the text and the reader is dealt with between two characters in *Foe*, in the relationship between Susan Barton and Friday, and in the way the text moves toward an alternative way of conceiving of dialogue. Friday's silence teases the reader with the allegorical potential of its standing for "the repression of the black majority in South Africa" (Head 2009, 64), [28] which Coetzee later and even more explicitly explores in "He and His Man." As in the Nobel Lecture, the allegorical reading of *Foe* comes with the two complications of (a) Barton's trying to teach Friday to speak and (b) Friday's remaining silent. If (a) "connotes the dilemma of the South African liberal" (Head 2009, 64), then (a) also ridicules the liberal's simplistic instrumentality of "giving voice to the oppressed"—something that always sounds vulgarly similar to the white man's burden anyway—simply because Friday, quite literally, cannot be "given a voice": his tongue has been cut out, his voice has been taken from him. And so, (b) ultimately forces Barton to devise an alternative to her instrumental idea of solving the problem of Friday's silence by making him speak. This alternative is not presented as a solution at all, but it rather appears in the narrative through a slow change in Barton's calculative thinking brought about by Friday's unyielding silence. It is again a paradox of Coetzee's work that Susan's insistence to make Friday speak or understand only foregrounds his silence more sharply, and this conversely brings about the change in her thinking. This change, then, bears on the reader's thinking as well.

An instance in *Foe* that illustrates her burgeoning change in thinking about Friday is the music scene, when she surreptitiously lays out a recorder for Friday to find, and he soon begins to play it. At this point, Susan's thoughts when Friday plays the flute remain trapped in a thinking of alterity, when she says:

---

[28] On the many views and treatments of allegory in *Foe*, see, for example, Attwell (1993, 104f.), Head (1997, 118f.), Attridge (2004a, 80), Poyner (2009, 82f.), and Caracciolo (2012).

> How like a savage to master a strange instrument—to the extent that he is able
> without a tongue—and then be content forever to play one tune upon it! It is a
> form of incuriosity, is it not, of sloth. (*F* 95)

At the same time, what she deems slothful seems to jumpstart a reversal
nonetheless, since it is soon Barton herself who becomes curious and who
follows Friday in playing the instrument:

> [I]t occurred to me that if there were any language accessible to Friday, it would
> be the language of music. So I closed the door and practised the blowing and
> the fingering as I had seen people do, *till I could play Friday's little tune* tolerably
> well […]. (*F* 96; added emphasis)

This encounter through music, when Barton *follows* Friday in playing "Friday's
tune" (*F* 96), heralds the transformation of her thinking in an extraordinarily
dense passage:

> I thought: It is true, I am not conversing with Friday, but is this not as good? Is
> conversation not simply a species of music in which first the one takes up the
> refrain and then the other? Does it matter what the refrain of our conversation is
> any more than it matters what tune it is we play? And I asked myself further: Are
> not both music and conversation like love? Who would venture to say that what
> passes between lovers is of substance (I refer to their lovemaking, not their talk),
> yet is it not true that something is passed between them, back and forth, and
> they come away refreshed and healed for a while of their loneliness? As long as I
> have music in common with Friday, perhaps he and I will need no language. […]
> For that hour in your kitchen I believe I was at ease with the life that has befallen
> me. (*F* 96f.)

Barton's reference to Friday and herself as *we* and to a form of *conversation* in the
etymological sense of the word, that is a living among, a familiarity with, clearly
heralds a change in thinking. But things are not as simple as that, and Barton
concedes the failure to engage with Friday:

> But alas, just as we cannot exchange forever the same utterances—"Good day",
> sir—"Good day"—and believe we are conversing, or perform forever the same
> motion and call it lovemaking, so it is with music: we cannot forever play the
> same tune and be content. Or so at least it is with civilized people. (*F* 97)

Friday's missing tongue remains the literal gap—the "hole" in Barton's story
(*F* 121)[29]—the literal lack which Barton desperately tries to fill, still failing to
understand that the filling of gaps and lacks is not the only response to their

---

[29] See also Attridge (2004a, 81f.).

cleaving indeterminacy, and that all gaps and lacks may, in fact, be integrated into one's thinking and may be worked with in possibly ever more complex progressions, accepted as facts of life. My semantics are slowly shifting to a more general level of discourse and to the side of the reader here. But let Barton for a moment be understood as a reader, as it were, a reader of the silence of Friday. It is obvious that a central aspect of *Foe* deals with writing; it is also, of course, a novel about reading. This seems to have been incorporated into the novel's allusive structure during the conception. In Coetzee's composition diary on *Foe* one comes across an entry to illuminate this:

> 1.vi.83 When I think of writing this book, I am struck by the fact that there is no core subject, just a technical exercise. I could write it and there would be nothing worth reading. The core will have to be provided by Friday, by Friday as Susan secretly reads him.[30]

It seems as if Coetzee's fears that *there would be nothing worth reading* have been subsumed into Susan's thinking about Friday in the form of a catalytic question, such as, *is there anything to Friday worth reading?* Susan's initial inability to overcome othering Friday is entirely consistent with the novel's logic of time and place, but it is also a precondition to her beginning comportment toward him. It is almost unnecessary to draw attention to this, and one must be careful not to develop a simplistic corollary here (such as, it is beneficial to other since this prepares for an overcoming of othering). But, as with the Magistrate in *Waiting for the Barbarians*, and solely in narrative terms, it is important that Barton's thinking be of a colonist mindset, so that the novel can enact a transgression of this thinking with profound effects on the reader. In a related thought Attridge notes that "it is important to remember that it is only from the point of view of his oppressors (however well meaning) that Friday figures as an absolute absence" (2004a, 83).[31]

Barton's desire to teach Friday to speak (and later to write) and Foe's desire to make him yield his story are geared toward rectifying this absolute absence, solving the problem of Friday. Since these desires are finally frustrated, the responsibility of how to respond to Friday is passed to the reader, how to react epistemologically and ethically to the gap that has resulted from his mutilation, "the shadow whose lack you feel is there: [...] the loss of Friday's tongue" (*F* 117). Implicitly, the reader is provoked again not by the one doing the mastering, but

---

[30] HRC, container 33, folder 6, p. 7.

[31] Attridge continues: "Included among those oppressors are Coetzee and the reader, and hence it is only by indirection that the substantiality of Friday's own world (in which he is not, of course, 'Friday'—perhaps not even 'he') can be suggested" (2004a, 83).

by the servant, the other, to whom the reader stands as Miłosz's (and Costello's) secretary does to the invisible.

Attwell raises a relevant question, which is whether the novel's ending "might not represent merely another attempt to make Friday speak in the name of interests that are not his own" (1993, 115). The reader is not exempt from such criticism. The ethical reading suggested here is one whose primary concern is the dialogue between text and reader and whose second concern is to do with the ethical *epistēmē* the novel explores. The reader who reads slowly may come to appreciate the roaming thoughts that Friday's silence engenders in Barton, without the need to cohere them into a solution, without appropriating Friday's silence. The slow reader waits with the text and resists the desire to turn a diegetic event into "the tool to an unproductive closure" (Spivak 1991, 169). Slow reading resists any temptation to graft onto the text meaning that is unwarranted. The silences of the text are not filled, but rather described phenomenologically and reflected philosophically *as silences*. This means, concretely, that meaning-making never stops, since stopping would mean the "problem" that Friday's silence represents were "solved," or that it no longer mattered.

The slow reader appreciates the aporetic dilemma of Friday's silence without trying to end her reflection on the character and the colonial othering that has marked (and mutilated) his life. The slow reader acknowledges what Hayes argues about the dialogic quality of the various interpretive instances involved in the signification of *Foe*:

> The main energies of *Foe* are […] devoted to complicating, both in literary and political terms, what we mean by "the foe." The text won't let us join together as "friends" to decide the issue—instead, it hunts out ways of tripping up our judgment, and in so doing, of keeping divergent political impulses, and divergent sympathies, *in a productive tension*. (2010, 128; added emphasis)

As a slow reader one is responsive to this *productive tension*, aware of the inconclusive nature of all of Coetzee's texts and responsive to their complex ethico-political reverberations in an effort to take an insoluble aporia in a text as a productive impetus for philosophical reflection. This does not mean to dismiss with a shrug a finally complicated text; instead, the slow reader enthusiastically takes the plunge into complication, into a text such as *Foe*, and demonstrates the novel's infinitely signifying character.

As argued before, it is the fissures in understanding and the failures in communication that encourage this type of reader–text dialogue. Friday's silence stimulates Barton's microdialogue, but this microdialogue transpires with him in attendance, so that the failed communication with Friday takes on the form of a reflexive dialogue turned inward, and so a dialogue with the reader in Friday's presence. Again, this questions Barton's ethical position to him, as this kind of talk about Friday seems on par with that of parents sharing the humbling details of their child's misbehavior, referring to the child in the third person while the oblivious youngster is playing with toy blocks in the corner of the room. But is the child oblivious? Is Friday oblivious? Witnessing this, reading this, we are forced to question our own position to Friday and reflect in the way Attridge does, when he asks whether as a reader one is not merely another oppressor of Friday (2004a, 83). That said, Barton's microdialogue itself shows how the intense gaze at Friday (and his intense gaze back at her)—initiated precisely by his resistance to being "solved"—how this encounter, which is like two mirrors facing each other, paradoxically provokes ever deeper involvement with him and with herself.

What does this suggest? In a larger cultural context, it might present the grim message that deep involvement may only be possible through misunderstanding. And yet, this message is not as grim as it sounds when presupposing that a deep encounter between human beings starts from a point of difference, as Bakhtin argues. With regard to literature, this simply recalls well-known ideas about literary discourse: that misunderstanding is a form of tension which gives rise to productive dramaturgy and characterization; and that misunderstanding of the kind explored in Coetzee triggers a reflection on understanding and knowledge about matters literary and philosophical.

An example of Barton's triggered and deepened reflection occurs when the woman, who in England goes by the faux name of Mrs. Cruso, tries to "teach [Friday] the names of things" (*F* 57). With obviously matronizing (and Biblical) connotations, Barton doggedly talks to Friday, calling out "'Spoon, Friday!' […] 'Fork! Knife!'" (*F* 57) as she holds up the same, and Friday remains entirely unresponsive to her calls. (It is important to see here that his unresponsiveness need not be interpreted as an *inability* to understand and that it is entirely possible that Friday simply sees an impossibly hysterical woman waving spoons as if *she* were illiterate.) So, Barton fills the blanks where Friday's utterances might occur with her own words. At first, she simply tries to "make the air around him thick with words," although she hopes that

> memories will be reborn in him which died under Cruso's rule, and with them the recognition that to live in silence is to live like the whales, great castles of flesh floating leagues apart one from another, or like spiders, sitting each alone at the heart of his web, which to him is the entire world. (*F* 59)

While Barton claims she fills Friday's silence, what she is primarily doing, of course, is to fill her own silence, with thoughts. Friday's silence is a great affront to a talking head like Barton,[32] a woman who initially seems all story; and against this affront she reacts in the only way natural to her, by producing language. It should be noted here that this behavior need not necessarily be equaled to speaking *for* Friday, since her speaking might simply be a case of nervousness about silence in general. If this is the case, we might surmise that Barton's excessive chatter (in thought) is a paradoxical defense mechanism against a fear of silence, a fear of her own thoughts. It would then be even more resonant to see that it is Friday's silence which paradoxically initiates a reflection of her own.

While her goal may be end-oriented—to teach Friday language—in her microdialogue Barton thinks very meditatively about Friday:

> What I fear most is that after years of speechlessness the very notion of speech may be lost to him. When I take the spoon from his hand (but is it truly a spoon to him, or a mere thing?—I do not know), and say *Spoon*, how can I be sure he does not think I am chattering to myself as a magpie or an ape does, for the pleasure of hearing the noise I make, and feeling the play of my tongue, as he himself used to find pleasure in flute playing? (*F* 57; original emphasis)

Barton's thoughts become meditative as they float into philosophical inquiry (*is it truly a spoon to him, or a mere thing?*), and their reflexive nature is mirrored in the formal deceleration through the hypotactic and parenthetic arrangement of her syntax. Her thoughts become slower when she interacts with Friday and when she ruminates on his silence.

To some extent, Barton initially falls prey to the same kind of othering that those travel writers have fallen prey to and whom Coetzee considers in "Idleness in South Africa," that is to the failure to engage in an ethically responsive dialogue, even to consider the Khoikhoi on their own terms. This is even shown in the way she views Friday's flute playing as the aforementioned form of sloth, the way the travel writers of whom Coetzee speaks viewed the Khoikhoi as a lazy people. For a moment, I wish to use the term *dialogue* in a metaphorical way here and understand it simply as a sense of regard that stirs the imagination into a

---

[32] Caroline Rody calls Magda in *In the Heart of the Country* a "talking head straight out of Beckett" (1994, 161). Beckett's talking heads, while all cranium, are far from being decapitated heads passed around on silver platters to the amusement of a crazed minx. They are—like Coetzee's talking heads, Magda, Barton, Mrs. Curren, Costello to some degree—represented as all mind, in the sense that their voices conflate with their textual presences: the three talking heads of *Play* (1963), for example, Winnie of *Happy Days* (1961), especially *The Unnamable* (1953 [F]; 1958 [GB]).

direction where othering is no longer possible, or no longer necessary. The travel writers' limiting view of the Khoikhoi as a lazy people is initially repeated by Barton when she views Friday on her own terms without trying to perceive his disregarding nature as "the mere outward aspect of a profound [...] contemplative life" (*WW* 18).[33] At the same time, a difference is discernible in Barton: through her failed communication with and her subsequent meditative advance toward Friday, slowly there appears the careful impetus of a deconstructive reversal or a postcolonial flip, without these being brought to a full revolution in the book's narrated time. This potential for reversal is heralded by Barton's discursive going back and forth between, on the one hand, regarding Friday as an animal (whale, spider) that she watches and, on the other, regarding herself as an animal that is being watched by him (magpie, ape).

The encounter with Friday is thus carefully dialogic without materializing in character dialogue, and the novel presents an extreme example of how withheld dialogue in the narrative actually increases the text–reader dialogue. In her encounters with Friday, Barton begins to regard him more carefully, with a deeper ethical and phenomenological concern, which derives directly from the stalled communication itself. Very carefully she begins to move sympathetically toward Friday to try and regard him on his terms, or rather *their* terms, which might be the best she can do, the best anyone can do. This is shown very subtly through her use of the pronouns *I* and *we* and her use of Friday's name in conjunction with her *I*. Initially, she refers to Friday as an other (early on the island he is referred to as "the Negro"), and later his name is rarely allowed admittance to a sentence which also uses the pronoun *I*—Friday and she are separate. But soon, at a linguistic level a dialogic encounter between Friday's name and her *I* occurs after she begins to consider him in her microdialogue, and after having moved slightly toward him through a more ethical regard of who he is. Only then does one of her sentences construct a dialogue between him and her, when she refers explicitly to "Friday and I" (*F* 65). When she regards Friday more carefully and tries to project herself toward him, she allows into her account of her time in England—an account which is dominated by the pronoun *I*—the advance of the pronoun *we* (*F* 64f.).

While it is uncertain whether Barton ultimately surpasses seeing Friday as an other, she slowly approaches him when she asks questions about epistemology

---

[33] It must be repeated that Friday has most likely been subject to lingual mutilation, and his silence is therefore not a voluntary silence that would allow for this kind of view. At the same time, Barton's deductive mistake is that because Friday is dumb in the older sense of the word (*speechless*), he must also be dumb in the newer sense of the word (*stupid*).

and ethics with regard to the possibility or impossibility of knowing another person more generally. She begins to feel closer to him, even if a distance remains:

> If Friday had been anyone else, I would have wished him to take me in his arms and comfort me […]. […] I have no doubt that amongst Africans the human sympathies move as readily as amongst us. (*F* 70)

So, while an us/them binary persists in her thinking, the potential for a deconstruction of this binary is indicated through her encounters with Friday, through the form of her text, through the implied microdialogue in the subtly introduced words *we* and *us*.

The novel's form relates this beginning change most emphatically at the end of the text, when a different narrative voice intrudes "in the novel's metafictional frame"[34] during the "culminating 'event'" of the novel (Head 1997, 124)—"in the 'voicing' of Friday's silence" (Head 1997, 126). Critics have sometimes yielded to the temptation to read this final voice in the narrative as Coetzee's own.[35] It is much more prudent to view this narrative change not as a shift to the author's voice,[36] but rather as an entirely ambiguous voice intruding into the narrative. This view prevents the reader's seeing in the novel's end a solution to the dilemma of Friday's silence, or seeing in the final narrator a version of Barton herself and reading the ending as her finally being touched by Friday.[37] Rather, the ending ensnares the reader in the persistent problem of representing empire in a postcolonial register by using the register of empire (Spivak 1991, 162f.; Attridge 2004a, 83). And by this view, the ending of the novel may be regarded as an attempt to sound, through a voice that seems simultaneously interior and exterior to the world of the text,[38] not "only" the voice of Friday (or not at all), and rather a polyphony of voices to represent "the ambiguous condition of postcoloniality" (Attwell 1993, 108).

---

[34] See also Attwell (1993, 114f.).

[35] See, for example, Gräbe (1989, 150); Head (1997, 123); Head (2009, 65). In the *Salmagundi* interview Joanna Scott makes the mistake of asking Coetzee a direct (one might say an unfortunately calculative) question regarding *Foe*'s last voice: "Who is speaking at the end of the novel? I'm not sure I know. Is it the author? A narrator?" (Coetzee and Scott 1997, 99). Coetzee's answer: "Goodness knows. I don't know" (Coetzee and Scott 1997, 99).

[36] Anyway, which author? Foe, Defoe, Barton? The final two manuscripts addressed in the novel's ending seem to allow for at least four authors (including the implied author Coetzee), while reading *Foe* against the Nobel Lecture "He and His Man" would allow the inclusion of Friday as a possible narrator of the novel's ending as well.

[37] The following chapter will deal with this idea and the ending of *Foe* as a whole more thoroughly than is possible here.

[38] This does not mean that this voice has a wholly objective grasp of the text, nor that it claims to, or indeed that it is itself *wholly* exterior to the text, such as a real author might be (but then again might not). This voice's grasp of the text is not an objective one, it is, of course, part of the diegetic world,

The novel's foregrounding of polyphony and heteroglossia conveys an ambiguous and complex web of voices that relates the complexities of difference involved in any dialogic encounter with another person and, in extension, with any linguistic event, a word, an utterance, a novel. *Foe*'s ending subverts the idea of a single "whole" voice by keeping open a "hole" in the text. This is mirrored literally at the end of the novel when the unnamed narrator of the last section "enter[s] the hole [in a wrecked ship]" (*F* 156) to find the "home of Friday" (*F* 157), where a different phenomenological regard of Friday's "voice" is possible, and by implication a different reading. Friday must remain silent so that the reader may engage with him. Friday's silence is the paradoxical question that every reader must answer on her own. This way Friday is an anti-Socrates, a teacher of a kind, but a silent teacher, a teacher who *leaves you behind*. One may remember the image of Bach the teacher at the keyboard, who leaves behind the boy as whom Coetzee pictures himself, and one may conceive of *Foe* (and possibly each of Coetzee's novels) as

> leading readers into the problem the novel itself poses. How might the realist tradition respond when confronted by Friday? What would be lost in political and ethical terms if the cultural processes engendered by the novel were to be discarded? Or perhaps most tellingly—what kind of status can Susan's literary genre find in a world in which it is ever harder to pretend its story can be told without also telling the story of Friday? By creating a text through which these questions must be kept in play, *Foe* refuses to allow its readers to "sail across the surface and come ashore none the wiser, and resume our old lives, and sleep without dreaming, like babes". (Hayes 2010, 128f.; quoting from *F* 141)

In a Socratic understanding of dialectic, every dialogue always leaves traces in the interlocutor's mind. Coetzee's works, through their cleaving gaps and their unsettling silences, leave traces in the reader, and then leave the reader behind to follow these traces into her own mind and toward philosophical reflection. Like a stimulant dialogue, Coetzee's works ring out long after the interlocutors have fallen silent, as the reader is held still within the world of the text, provoked to read slowly and think sprightly. As will be seen shortly, the endings to Coetzee's works, those moments where the text's voices fall silent, are merely the inception of the reader's dialogue with the text.

---

and any ethical and epistemological statements it makes on the text should be considered with this in mind. What John Gray, in a different context, says about the moral point of view may also bear on epistemology with regard to literary texts in this instance: "There is no view from nowhere which is 'the moral point of view'; there are only diverse moralities and value perspectives" (Gray 1992, 168). There can be no external perspective onto a text from within a text, the way, as Costello is cautioned, there can be no perspective on reason from a place outside of reason.

8

Dark and Unending—Coetzee's
Open-Ended Endings

Shortly after finishing *Life & Times of Michael K* and even before its publication in 1983, Coetzee begins a new project toward the end of 1982. This project will become the 1986 novel *Foe*. The composition is slow but steady. In October 1983, the author reflects on the writing in a diary:

> 18.x.83 The only hope for this book is if it moves to a climax. That is to say, it will have to justify itself at the end (<u>Michael K</u> justified itself somewhere in the middle).[1]

Arguably, the intensity of *Foe*'s closing moments fulfills this longing for the climactic, ending with its (supposed) acts of violence, the following eerie lull, the dream-like flavors of magic realism, and the perplexing questions regarding authorship and signification. The justification to which Coetzee refers can be seen in the ending's final frustration of a simple hermeneutic grasp on the narrative and in a powerful thrust reversal that impels the reader to return to the narrative in an act of reflection or rereading.

In a reflection on Coetzee's endings Dooley argues for the poignant and transformative character of the final moments in Coetzee's works (2010, 172; 183), and she reads in the ending of *Foe* a desire for a different outcome, for change (2010, 172; 183). I see in *Foe*'s ending less a wish for a transformation than the staging of a return to the novel's beginning as well as the stimulus for a deeper immersion into the narrative as a whole. The return is explicated through the expressions "[a]t last I could row no further" and "making barely a splash," both of which appear on the novel's first page and are echoed at the very end (*F* 1; 155). The possibility for the reader's deeper immersion in the text is indicated by a moment where the literal mixes with the figural at the very end, when the new narrator takes a plunge into the world of the text in

[1] HRC, container 33, folder 6, p. 27.

Daniel (De-)Foe's quarters and suddenly finds himself or herself submerged in an underwater world (*F* 1; 155). The effect on the reader is one of confusion, especially concerning questions of setting; does one find oneself in the literal or in the figural realm here, "in the realm of the whales and eternal ice" (*F* 155) or in "the home of Friday" (*F* 157), a realm "where bodies are their own signs" (*F* 157)?[2] By mingling the literal and the figural, the text ensures that reading does not stop even at the narrative's end; further reflection is indicated, possibly even a rereading. In this chapter, these ideas will be pursued to elucidate how slow reading need not slacken to a standstill even at the end of Coetzee's works, and to show how his endings function as ways toward new beginnings, of reading and of reflection.

Dooley is helpful here, even if her ideas are hardly specific enough, when she suggests that the endings "are often enigmatic, though they never jar" (Dooley 2010, 198). Her first point is accurate; her second misguided. The endings *do* jar quite distinctly, and in the case of *Foe* one comes across an ending that jars both metaphorically and literally. The novel ends on the gaping mouth of Friday from which "comes a slow stream, without breath, without interruption," a stream that is all-encompassing, "dark and unending" (*F* 157). Next to the literal jarring of Friday's mouth, of course, the ending is metaphorically jarring through its "unendingness." It opens more doors than it closes, something which is again echoed in the final moments, when the unidentified narrator of the last part reports:

> I come to a bulkhead and a stairway. The door at the head of the stairway is closed; but when I put a shoulder to it and push, the wall of water yields and I can enter. (*F* 156)

The literal door that the narrator comes to turns into a figurative wall of water, as the reader finds herself in the uncertain space of the narrative. The underwater atmosphere—the submerged floating relayed by the narrator—aptly mirrors the reader's feelings in these unsettling and mystifying final moments, where a grasp on signification is highly complicated. This feeling is emphasized by the introduction of the new narrative situation, which gives Attwell occasion to argue that "we are now in the realm of narration per se, and the addressee is simply the reader, the one who holds the book" (1993, 115). In this realm, where *bodies are their own signs*, signs have a bodily concreteness that does not yield

---

[2] For more on these vexing semiotic implications, see, for example, Dovey (1988, 396–402) and Attwell (1993, 116f.).

signification and thus continues to jar; it creates its own gap. Let us look at the moment of jarring more closely to see what the text stages:

> His mouth opens. From inside him comes a slow stream, without breath, without interruption. It flows up through his body and out upon me; it passes through the cabin, through the wreck; washing the cliffs and shores of the island, it runs northward and southward to the ends of the earth. Soft and cold, dark and unending, it beats against my eyelids, against the skin of my face. (*F* 157)

Here the novel ends. Attridge argues that "[t]he final paragraphs of *Foe* achieve their power in large measure as a result of their relation to what has gone before" (2004a, 65). The final moments when Friday's mouth opens allow Friday to assume a "voice," a radically singular way of establishing contact with the narrator or with the reader. It is important that Friday's silence as the result of colonial mutilation remains—Friday does not speak in these final moments. Rather, his silence becomes a sign that goes well beyond the mark of mutilation, of which it has consisted before this ending. His silence becomes a *slow stream, without breath, without interruption*, an action, which metaphorically overwhelms the narrator and which literally touches him or her. The continually frustrated attempts of establishing contact with Friday, of which the narrator's here is "the last" (Attridge 2004a, 67)—and which was the concern of my previous chapter—is here made tactile, it is literalized, since the *slow stream* signals physicality, even visuality (like a silver string of bubbles under water rising toward the light); but the stream is also distinctly figuralized, since its far-reaching motion indicates political and philosophical dimensions spanning the entire *earth*. Attridge calls Friday's act here a "speechless speech" (2004a, 67). It is true that Friday remains *speechless*, but what occurs here is not *speech*, which is also why my word "voice" should be used with caution here. It is not a *voice*, it is not *speech*—and it is important that it is neither. Friday's contact with the narrator is linguistic only if we follow Attwell's idea that we are in the realm of narrative. But then, Friday's contact with us, the readers, has been linguistic all the time, since we have *heard* Susan Barton speak of him throughout. The narrator in the text, however, does not hear Friday at all; he is pure silence, and he remains silent. The contact between Friday and the narrator is wholly corporeal here, a sign that is bodily, or rather exudes from his body as a *slow stream* felt on the narrator's face. But if we remind ourselves again of Attwell's argument that "we are now in the realm of narration per se, and the addressee is simply the reader" (1993, 115), the question is, how do we, the readers, react to this silent contact between Friday and the narrator, and more importantly, how does this influence our own contact with Friday? How do we respond to this ending?

The final moments of the text, the mixing of literal and figural realms, the underwater space, Friday's perplexing *slow stream*—all these create a sense of *speechlessness in the reader*. It was Friday's silence which compelled Susan Barton to speak to him, to reflect on him, and to speak to herself, and so it is Friday's speechless ending here which creates a speechlessness about this baffling ending in the reader. The reader will reflect on her own speechlessness in the face of this ending, on why this ending cannot be readily put into an interpretive shape, why the question what the ending signifies cannot (and perhaps should not) be settled. Because of the baffling nature of the ending, the reader is not likely to put the book down and cease thinking about it. Rather, she is compelled to reflect on this ending's implications about Friday, and about Friday's significance to the text. By ending the novel on Friday's open mouth, Friday's silence and Friday are made even more central to the novel than they already were to Susan Barton. They are central to the reader because they are the reader's last impressions, and this may prompt her to remain in the book reflexively or to return to it by rereading.

This impetus is emphasized through the ending's loop to the beginning, which is indicated by the repeated phrases mentioned above. This technique is not specific to *Foe* but something that all of Coetzee's endings indicate in one way or another: they lead to beginnings.[3] Some of his works' endings return one directly to the texts' openings—next to *Foe* it is *Life & Times of Michael K* and the aforementioned *Slow Man* which explicitly reference their beginnings at

---

[3]   In the fascinating (if necessarily sketchy) early essay—written only after three of Coetzee's works had been published—Peter Strauss makes a helpful argument about *In the Heart of the Country*, many suggestions of which have proved valid even about Coetzee's subsequent works. On the ending of Coetzee's second novel Strauss writes:

> [Magda] makes beginning after beginning, she is constantly initiating action, but the consequences of her acts of freedom always have less to do with the acts themselves than with the trap she was in in the first place. [...] Coetzee is kept from finding a straightforward end to his story by a philosophy of action [...] which is hyperconscious of beginnings and less confident about consequences. (1984, 123)

Strauss could have written "philosophy of *in*-action" without bending the novel, as its action is an action of the imagination rather than physicality, and the continued beginnings of the novel are, in fact, caused by Magda's essentially idle character, in a Beckettian echoing of Aristotle's *sedendo et quiescendo anima efficitur prudens*. Like Beckett's talking heads, Coetzee's early characters are fearful of having *to end yet again* (as one of Beckett's *Fizzles* has it)—and they keep the end at bay by talking. This is true of Jacobus, Dawn, but especially of Magda, though reverberations of it are found, of course, in Elizabeth Curren and even in the other Elizabeth, the Costello woman. At the same time, in Coetzee's latest works, beginning with *Slow Man*, the endings are much more subdued in tone, less prone to evocations of violence or to the stubborn will to keep monologizing. Overall, the later works (perhaps post *Age of Iron*) are more concerned, it seems, with introducing tonally and topically moments of quieter beginnings for reflection to the reader rather than staging a character's desperately fighting his or her own end.

the end.[4] The endings may also indicate new beginnings in the characters' lives or minds, such as in both of the novellas of *Dusklands*, or in *Boyhood*. Or the endings function as suggestions for alternate readings of the narratives, such as the ending of *The Master of Petersburg* does, the final moments of which allow us to reinterpret the character of Dostoevsky and the narrative retrospectively. Finally, the endings trigger new philosophical beginnings in the readers' minds, reflections on beginnings and endings as such, whether in literature or in life. While this may be true of all of Coetzee's endings, it is most directly discerned in the endings of *Waiting for the Barbarians*, *Disgrace*, and *The Childhood of Jesus*.

His works usually build toward pinnacles of intensity, even if an ending seems anti-climactic, as the closing moments of *Disgrace* arguably do.[5] In the 1999 novel the force of the devastating ending is owed not to a climactic resolution but to a defeated giving up, which the novel's final line echoes (*Dis* 220). Likewise, the endings of the three autrebiographies (*Boyhood*, *Youth*, *Summertime*) leave off on notes of melancholy or failure, although they signal new beginnings by implication, new thoughts, new choices. The endings' intensities and their provocation of a rereading or rethinking of the works are often owed to the fact that Coetzee's works raise urgent philosophical and political questions and that these are left unanswered within the boundaries of the narrative worlds. This anti-Aristotelian mode leaves the knots that are tied in the beginnings of the

---

[4]   Head notes:

> [*Life & Times of Michael K*] ends with K's imagined return to the farm—not an event in the world of the novel—and the improvised use of a teaspoon to draw water from the damaged well [...]. This image of minimal existence surpasses all others in the novel, and installs a narrative loop, since the infant K, with his harelip, was fed with a teaspoon [...]. If K endures, the narrative loop implies, he does so by virtue of his persistent, minimal philosophy. (2009, 61)

The relevant passages in the novel are as follows. The ending:

> [...] Michael K [...] would produce a teaspoon from his pocket, a teaspoon and a long roll of string. He would clear the rubble from the mouth of the shaft, he would bend the handle of the teaspoon in a loop and tie the string to it, he would lower it down the shaft deep into the earth, and when he brought it up there would be water in the bowl of the spoon; and in that way, he would say, one can live. (*K* 183f.)

And back to the beginning: "The child could not suck from the breast and cried with hunger. She tried a bottle; when it could not suck from the bottle she fed it with a teaspoon, fretting with impatience when it coughed and spluttered and cried" (*K* 3). Note how the change from *it* to *he* is used to indicate Michael K has, even if only subtly, come into his own at the end. I will return to a similar change in pronouns, though in a different novel, later.

[5]   It may be specific to the genre of the printed book that the ending of a novel, even if it is wholly anti-climactic, has a special intensity. The very materiality of a printed novel, its pages receding under the perusing hands and eyes, emphasizes the narrative's closing moments in ways that supersede structural devices. Mullan notes: "Many readers will know how, as the sense of an impending ending becomes strong, the last pages of a novel take on a special intensity" (2006, 303). See also Lodge (1992, 224).

works intricately fastened beyond the works' closing moments. At times, a text's ending, such as *Disgrace*'s closing scene, can be a further tugging at the strings, a fanning of the flames that emphasizes the reader's productive puzzlement over the ending's suggestions.

However, Coetzee's endings are not only anti-climactic; they are also highly anti-cathartic, denying a straightforward externalization of discomfort onto the characters and stimulating instead a reflexive inward-turning on the part of the reader. If the works do not leave off on a note of tragedy, the final moments provoke the reader to reflect on the diegetic worlds, essentially to take the questions of the narrative along for a rereading of the text or for a reflection on what has just been read. This is realized by the endings' general open-endedness, by their denial of catharsis that would bring closure, by their sense of keeping the reader in the reflexive space opened up by the complexities and ambiguities of the final moments.

Dooley claims that Coetzee's "novels are always shapely objects, even those that seem most unlike novels" (2010, 198).[6] She argues that no ending is contrived regarding its story's logic. Yet, the philosophical questions raised in the works continue their uncomfortable sting long after their final lines, often giving the works a philosophical unwieldiness that demands an agile mind. Coetzee's endings do not free the reader from reflection by offering solutions and enabling a comfortable return to the real world, like turning away from a crime scene. On the contrary, Coetzee's endings stage an inability or an unwillingness to end, as if the reader were imprisoned[7] in the world of the text. What has happened to Pavel in *The Master of Petersburg*, what is Petrus's connection to Lucy's rapists, in what way will Michael K live, *will* he live at all? These questions are lengthily built up and driven toward resolutions, but resolutions never come, the answers remain absences, gaps, and since these propel the narrative, they also propel reflection

---

[6]   Dooley is right in arguing for a certain logical harmony to the narrative structure of Coetzee's works, but her argument is in peril of generalization and seems unreceptive of the larger late modernist tradition, as part of which Coetzee's texts should be read (2010, 171f.). It is not going too far to be skeptical of the notion of shapeliness (in Dooley's terms), even of harmony (in my own), when contextualizing the works in this way. Eagleton illuminates modernist endings by arguing that "[s]ome modernist works are [...] sceptical of the whole notion of narrative. Narrative suggests that there is a shapeliness to the world, an orderly procession of causes and effects" (2013, 106). Eagleton favors a rhizomic view of modernist literature, which bears on the understanding of Coetzee's endings: "Whereas realism views the world as unfolding, modernism tends to see it as text" (2013, 106).

[7]   I understand the term *imprisoned* positively by way of Coetzee's comments about Beckett: "Fiction is the only subject of fiction. Therefore, fictions are closed systems, prisons. The prisoner can spend his time writing on the walls *(The Unnamable)* or making magic jokes about their unreality *(Murphy)*. He remains imprisoned" *(DtP* 38). If fiction is the only subject of fiction, then the reader of fiction is as much part of this subject as is the character, which shows, however, that fiction is probably not the only subject of fiction, unless *everything* is fiction. This, of course, it may very well be.

after the narrative is over.[8] The movement toward resolutions is actually used in the texts to stymie the reading progress, allowing her to relish the excitement of approaching an answer.[9] At the end, however, the reader remains pinned down in a state of uncertainty, confronted with the acutely complicated paradoxes of the endings beyond the end. The reader is left alone to ask what are the implications of these endings, for example of the utter uprooting of what has gone before in *In the Heart of the Country*; or even to ask what has "really" occurred in the last moments of a novel, as in the baffling endings of *Foe, Age of Iron*, or *The Childhood of Jesus*? So, Coetzee's endings *give offense* to petrified expectations of narrative, and of closure more generally, through their unsettling of the reader's expected or demanded sense of an ending.[10] While the final moments of the texts do not corrupt the logics of the stories (as a *deus ex machina* might), the endings cause outrage in the reader nonetheless, ethical or epistemological outrage.[11]

It is a melancholy truth that reflection is commenced generally by that which causes outrage, which unsettles, disrupts, or jars. Coetzee's novels exploit this through their endings' lasting complications. The reflection stimulated through complexity, which the reader feels upon the novels' endings, is also explored intradiegetically and in the minds of the characters. While Coetzee's characters are generally highly reflexive from the beginning, their reflexivity assumes a more involved and involuted quality as the complications of the plot congeal. The characters' thinking is often focused on the ethical or the ontological by a downturn in their existences, a caesura, a gap, a stoppage. As mentioned above, it is Mrs. Curren's news of her life's imminent ending that kindles a new form of thinking; and it is the inertia and idleness of Vercueil and his dog which set in motion Mrs. Curren's meditative reflections and her deep reimmersion in literature, philosophy, and history. Facing the end, facing death, the former classics teacher returns to beginnings of an aesthetic and philosophical kind: to the classics. In Coetzee's own definition, the classics offer a thinking of endurance with an ontological force—they are beginnings without endings. In

---

[8] The sense of absence as being a catalyst of narrative is illuminated by Eagleton, who claims that very often "[i]t is absence which keeps the narrative going" (2013, 104). While Eagleton's materialist view signals more in the direction of a perceived absence in the text, what I mean by absences here are merely those parts of the diegetic material which are simply not there after the narrative has stopped. These absences might be said to keep the narrative going in the reader's mind.

[9] Mullan's idea on the reader's rising expectations toward the endings may be brought to bear on this: "[W]e might slow ourselves to relish a conclusion for which we have long prepared" (2006, 304).

[10] Eagleton writes that "the effect of many a modernist ending is to unsettle" (2013, 103).

[11] See Pippin's aforementioned claims about a frustrated epistemology regarding Klawer's death, which may also be made about the presence of Magda's father at the end of *In the Heart of the Country*, even if she has killed him in the beginning (2010, 29).

his essay "Zbigniew Herbert and the Censor" in *Giving Offense* (1996) Coetzee writes on the Polish author's poem "Why the Classics":

> The answer to the question proposed by the title—Why the classics?—is thus: The classics because they provide models of response to misfortune that [...] will outlast us; the classics because the classics give an answer to our appeal for a model of how to become a classic, that is, *how to endure*. (*GO* 151; added emphasis)

To Mrs. Curren the classics offer a symbolic way out of the dead end of her life, and her persistence to live by thinking and writing aims at defying being's compulsion to end; writing and reflecting to her means to endure. She writes: "Death may indeed be the last great foe of writing, but writing is also the foe of death" (*AoI* 115f.). To Mrs. Curren, making a narrative of her life is a ploy of keeping time at bay. She uses narrative as a way of "holding death at arm's length" (*AoI* 116), but she accomplishes this only by writing about death. Maurice Blanchot speaks of a related conception of writing about mortality as a way of keeping death *at arm's length*, of direct confrontation as a sly evasion: "[T]o write is to put oneself outside of life, it is to take pleasure in one's death through an imposture that will become a frightening reality" (2001, 261). To Blanchot the fiber of writing is always made brittle by death, but it is also writing about death that continually reinvigorates the fiber of life.[12]

It is perhaps a sentimental (yet no less significant) claim that our continued reading of or reflection on a text which deliberately defies ending, such as *Age of Iron*, has reverberations beyond the narrative implications of a work's finitude, extending toward ethics and ontology, and performing for a brief period an alternative to the cold certitude that a character, a narrative, a life has to end. It is as if Coetzee's works (or his characters) understood that the end of a narrative may be the end of a character's "life." Ending a book is ending a character. To make a book endure, then, is to keep a character "alive." Mrs. Curren depends on Vercueil to send her letter (her manuscript) to her daughter after her death, and she depends on us, the readers, to make her endure as a text by keeping our reflection on her "life" going.

The open-endedness of Coetzee's works gives them this distinct ontological potentiality. By impelling us to read a character into being through a slow and ethical response to the text and so to continue the characters' lives beyond the narrative boundaries, we make them endure, maybe even make them

---

[12] For further thoughts on Blanchot's engrossing thoughts on the links between literature, language, and death, see especially his "Literature and the Right to Death" in *The Work of Fire* (1949).

classics. Such a narrative elision of having to end is inherently philosophical. My understanding of the philosophical ideal is one of keeping reflection going, keeping language and thought circulating about the wealth of existent phenomena; to keep from ending, then, is to remain philosophical. This idea is illuminated by Derrida's understanding of *keeping* when he speaks about memory in an interview:

> [T]he philosopher is above all a guardian of memory: someone who asks himself questions about truth, Being, language, *in order to keep*, between truth and keeping. […] [T]he philosopher is someone who, having thought about keeping, says: one must first of all keep keeping if one wants to keep something. (1995, 145; original emphasis)

To Derrida, actual existential keeping is, of course, an impossibility considering the certainty of death (1995, 146). But precisely because keeping can never be realized with finality, can never bring closure, what is inscribed into keeping is endlessness. The need to keep, to remember, to conserve, to continue is so urgent precisely because it leads to "nothing" (Derrida 1995, 145). Derrida's notion of keeping may throw light on Coetzee's and my own notions of *enduring* as a way of prolonging philosophizing. The denial of closure in Coetzee makes the reader reflect ending as a phenomenon; and because closure is withheld, the reader is forced to find her own closure and signification. Coetzee's endings bid the reader to keep on and thus to respond to the works in a productively slow and lasting way.

So, it is merely one more paradoxical aspect of Coetzee's paradoxical oeuvre that it is the endings which offer ways out of dead ends social, historical, and philosophical by inciting and perpetuating reflections about an impasse, an aporia. First and foremost, Coetzee's endings suggest ways out of the realist dead ends of narrative endings by provoking the reader to endure with the texts and to endure the texts in a positive understanding of hardening the text against a final interpretation. Endurance, with its etymological resonances of hardening and continuing, is related to my ideas of slowness and meditativeness, and it echoes the sense of cyclicality of Coetzee's works I have indicated at the beginning of this chapter. As I have shown in my reading of *Slow Man*, only a deep involvement in the novel allows for the perception of the subtle loop at the end of the text. And the resulting continued rumination on the text facilitates a deep and meditative reflection on the political and philosophical implications of the work. *Slow Man*'s ending takes us back to Paul Rayment's childhood and thus comments less topically than formally on the aging man's mind. By being

taken back to Paul's childhood, to the beginning of his life, by implication we are
also provoked to reflect on his life's ending, even if the novel's ending does not
explicitly reference it.

While Coetzee's endings are frequently haunted by death, the works typically
begin with a fictional vagitus of throwing the readers into the diegetic worlds
with little exposition, creating a productive disorienting effect *in medias res*.[13]
After matter-of-fact or perplexing beginnings, which fire the works into being,
the disorienting qualities are carried through until the end, where the reader
is left behind with a host of questions to continue reflection, or to reevaluate
the implications of the text in the new light emanating from the endings. In
paradoxical instances of *dynamic stillness* the accelerative beginnings frequently
draw immediate attention to a kind of slowness, an impasse, and so alert us
to the final slowness looming in the near distance. The syntactically stalling
sentence that opens *Disgrace* (as shown above) realizes this oscillation between
the dynamic and the still formally, while the beginning of *Foe*, for example,
alludes to it topically with its explicit double emphasis on an impasse, indeed on
an ending that gets the novel going: "*At last* I could row *no further*" (*F* 1; added
emphases). And the opening of *The Master of Petersburg* also heralds an elegiac
slowing down through an arrival, a return:

> October 1869: A droshky passes *slowly* down a street in the Haymarket district
> of St Petersburg. Before a tall tenement building the driver *reins in his horse*.
> (*MoP* 1; added emphases)

These openings project a voice and the idea of a subject into the reader's mind
and provoke the asking of the narratological threshold questions, who speaks,
who sees? The beginning of *Diary of a Bad Year*, in turn, presents yet a different
kind of a discursive motion of *slowing acceleration* that is made use of in Coetzee's
works. In her review of the novel Hilary Mantel notes: "Some writers begin by
lulling their readers, some by shocking them. J. M. Coetzee begins by starting an
argument" (2008, n.p.).

It will not be going too far to start the argument that all of Coetzee's endings, in
one way or another, do not end an argument but rather start one. All of Coetzee's
works end by indicating a continuation of the arguments started in the text, by
introducing, at the latest possible moment, a new strand of argumentation, or by

---

[13] *Life & Times of Michael K* is an exception here. While it does nearly begin with a vagitus, shortly
after K's birth, it seems structured like a *bildungsroman* in the realist tradition. Here, this beginning
is used to lay out a comfortable ground upon which the following developments—and the form—of
the novel seem even more estranging by comparison.

indicating a soft announcement of hope that mandates further reflection by the reader or inspires a rereading under altered conditions. This is often accomplished by the location of plot or character development at the latest possible instance in the narrative and by a mere allusion to these just before the novel ends. By situating the possibility for a character's transformation at the latest moment in a narrative, the very idea of transformation begs further reflection, or even a rereading of the text, since it may only be verified by going back over the text and tracing its causes. Any transformation may, then, have to be produced by the reader herself. Examples for this effect may be found across the oeuvre, but the most tangible one is in the ending of *Disgrace*, when Lurie first reflects in a hopeful way on Lucy's future while watching her gardening (*Dis* 216f.),[14] and then, shortly afterwards, *gives up* the dog in an ethically ambiguous act (*Dis* 220). The ethical consequences of this final act continue to haunt and disturb the reader after the end of the book, since Lurie's action is left fully unexplained, some might say, fully unjustified.

Ostensibly, the final scene of the novel turns around any kind of hope that is brought up by Lurie's sentiments in the penultimate scene. It seems to explore a warped ethics that is a letting go, possibly signaling a form of love, but love whose motivation is *not* to hold on in a selfish way. Lurie knows that the dog will have to die (*Dis* 215), but he holds on to the animal nevertheless. The text implies this in Bev Shaw's last lines in the novel when she sees Lurie entering the surgery with the dog and says: "I thought you would save him for another week" (*Dis* 220). It can be inferred that this *saving* of the dog has continued for some time, and that Lurie either cannot bring himself to care for the dog fully, love the dog wholly, or that he holds on to him for reasons other than the dog's own (whatever they might be). This way, then, the letting go of the dog would be an unselfish act, and yet the act's ethical outrageousness would not be diminished. Regardless of what one takes the ending to signify, it remains ethically disturbing—and this is precisely the point. As Barnard writes: "The final scene [...] is not [...] readily processed; and it is essential that we do not, as it were, try to beat it into convenient shape with a critical shovel" (2003, 222). The ending stages how there may not be a way to rectify an ill, to turn an ill into a good, to resolve complicated situations too simply. Any act that is borne forth from suffering (here: the dog's), even if it is an entirely good act, cannot erase suffering; it can only attempt to grow something

---

[14] For a consideration of the complexities of pastoral and the possible hope in this penultimate scene see Barnard (2003, 219f.). For further insight into the novel's exploration of pastoral see also Van der Vlies (2010, 63–66). And for additional considerations of Coetzee's earlier works and the pastoral see, for example, Dovey (1988, 149–168), Attwell (1993, 59), and Head (2009, 45); as well as Coetzee's own contextualization of the pastoral in South African literature: see *WW*, esp. 63–81.

positive from it, while it necessarily carries the traces of the negative from which it was nurtured. The ending, in its complicated ethical quandary that it implies, shows this dramatically, and it has the added effect of complicating something possibly more important. The ethically paradoxical implications of the ending make it difficult to extract an ethical normativeness from this text; one can argue that the paradoxical staging of this novel's ending uses its moral complexity to complicate the extraction of any ethical norm in an instrumental way. The ethically confrontational ending has the potential of inciting a more meditative thinking which is forced to take into account the explored problems of instrumentality.

Originally, Coetzee had planned to end the novel simply with Lurie returning to Cape Town. In his notebook on *Disgrace* he writes: "<u>8 April 1997</u> It can only end with DL [David Lurie] going back to Cape Town to face ~~the~~ disgrace. The disgrace can only work if it is described in close detail."[15] This ending, however, would have brought a sense of closure. If Lurie had faced up to the charges against him, even if penance with an entailed repentance had not occurred, in the reader's mind an equilibrium would have been indicated, since Lurie's offense would have been resolved in the diegetic logic. Months later in the composition of *Disgrace* Coetzee moves toward the philosophical sense of (and possibly the dramatic need for) something *unresolved* pertaining to Lurie. On a trip to Paris, he jots down in his notebook:

<u>13 November 1997</u> (Paris)

[…] There is something unresolved in his life, connected with sex, ageing, with Melanie, with hurt pride, but also with Byron, creativity, not dying without leaving a mark.[16]

This sense of the *unresolved* as well as the urgent presence of death is, then, crystallized in the last line of the novel, the way Lurie's character was already crystallized in its first line. In January of the following year, then, Coetzee lets go of the idea of bringing closure to the novel, and of ending it with Lurie's return to Cape Town. He records two connected ideas:

<u>24 January 1998</u>

Make this the last chapter. […]
He calls the dog Byron (or George Gordon), gives in to Dot's (Lucy's?) argument that none of the dogs deserve to be saved, or all ('Pass one, pass all[']). Other

---

[15] HRC, container 35, folder 3, n.p.
[16] HRC, container 35, folder 3, n.p.

dogs pass through the yard whom he loves (he finds that he loves more and more easily) and kills.

    If I am to be God, he tells himself, I must learn to kill impartially[.]

    The dog Byron, before it goes in to be killed, behaves guiltily, creeping on the floor, flattening its ears. The shame of dying.[17]

28 January 1998

[…] Dot Shaw: "Are you going to give him up?"
He takes the dog in his arms. It licks his face, his lips, his eyes, his ears.
"Yes, I am going to give him up."
End of book.[18]

Much of what Coetzee writes here is condensed in the ending of the published version of the novel. While the dog is not named Byron but Driepoot—and hence somewhat shares Byron's infirmity—and while Dot Shaw becomes Bev Shaw, it is fascinating to perceive how the idea of disgrace looms over these moments, in the *shame of dying* exhibited by the dog, and the sense of injustice at saving merely one dog. Also, how the final idea of *giving up* may not only be perceived as a giving up of the dog, but also a *giving in* to arguments which are not Lurie's alone. This puts into perspective the radical choice not to save Driepoot in the end, since saving him, while an ethical gesture toward this individual dog, would be an unethical act against all the other dogs in the clinic. Nevertheless, such a justification constitutes a twisted utilitarianism which retains its unethical dimensions and prepares for the moral outrage one may feel about the published novel's ending. At the same time, Coetzee's reflections in his notebook (24 January) allow a reflection on Lurie by way of his justification. Even if one feels threatened and outraged by it, at least one understands more of what Lurie's position is. The ending of the published work, in contrast, omits Lurie's motives entirely, and this way the philosophical implications of the ending remain wholly open, and the effected outrage is even greater. This way the ending, which is so much *about* ending too, about the end of Driepoot's life, about David's *giving up*, is also about beginning.

    A radically new beginning is not only indicated through the philosophical reflection sparked in the reader, it is also invoked by the novel's allusions to Christian eschatology and its connection of endings and beginnings. The religious dimension of the ending that was still present very explicitly in

---

[17] HRC, container 35, folder 3, n.p.
[18] Ibid.

Coetzee's note from January 24, 1998 ("If I am to be God, he tells himself, I must learn to kill impartially") is now only implied through a small simile. Here are the two mentioned versions of the ending in comparison:

(28 January 1998)

[…] Dot Shaw: "Are you going to give him up?"
He takes the dog in his arms. It licks his face, his lips, his eyes, his ears.
"Yes, I am going to give him up." […][19]

(published version)

Bearing him in his arms, *like a lamb*, he reenters the surgery. "I thought you would save him for another week," says Bev Shaw. "Are you giving him up?"
"Yes, I am giving him up." (*Dis* 220; added emphasis)

Importantly, the religiously suggestive simile *like a lamb* is missing from the earlier version. And Lurie's explicit comparison to God mentioned earlier is entirely missing from the final novel, as if the lamb simile were all that was needed to imply the religious dimension of the ending. The religious dimension of the novel has been prepared throughout: in the Biblical allusions in Lurie's "fall," the exploration of the states of grace and disgrace,[20] as well the (failed) attempt at atonement and redemption at the Isaacs's family home. The animal simile *like a lamb* constitutes a very distinct conclusion to the religious aspects of the novel, even if this radical ending brings about a new beginning. This may be seen through the ending's reference to the *Book of Revelation*. A new beginning after the cataclysm is implied, and this cataclysm is partly symbolized by the giving up of Driepoot. Chris Danta argues that the animal simile does not reference the *Revelation* but rather the moment when Abraham "is about to sacrifice the ram in place of his beloved son Isaac in Genesis" (2007, 733). Danta conceives of this through a view of scapegoating, whereby Driepoot becomes a scapegoat for political ills explored in the novel (2007, 735).[21] I am deeply skeptical of such a view, not least because Danta has to deform the novel to suit his argument. He is fully aware that Lurie himself is deeply skeptical of the idea of scapegoating, when Lucy likens him to a scapegoat (2007, 732; see *Dis* 91). And while Danta's intertextual analogy to *Genesis* is heuristically worthwhile, it

---

[19] HRC, container 35, folder 3, n.p.
[20] See Attridge (2004a, 162–191) for an extended discussion of the states of grace and disgrace in the novel.
[21] For further reflections on the idea of the scapegoat in *Disgrace* and *Elizabeth Costello*, see Lamey (2010).

is not the only possible reading of the *lamb simile*, not least because the animal which Abraham finally offers up as a sacrifice by proxy is not a lamb, but a ram.[22] Moreover, it is not entirely clear whether the giving up of Driepoot has to be understood only as a sacrifice—it is quite possible that the lamb has a different allusive potential as well.

The ending's construction subtly emphasizes the lamb simile, even if it seems to hide it in a relative clause. The participial construction of the phrase *Bearing him in his arms* foreshadows the sentence's conclusion that will follow in the main clause. This gives the sentence a sense of determination that resonates with the novel's ending as a whole. At the same time, this determination is momentarily impeded through the incompleteness of the subordinate clause. The syntactic arrangement mirrors the quivering between hesitation and determination that is present in so much of Coetzee's writing and is tied up with the ending and beginning signaled by the *Revelation* allusion. The religious connotation in the simile *like a lamb* creates this connection by alluding to the complex signification of the *agnus dei*, which calls up the realm of the apocalypse, of death and resurrection, as well as of revelation, unveiling, and beginning.[23]

The *Revelation* links the lamb to sacrifice (Rev. 5.6), to something being *given up*, but it also makes the lamb itself a *bringer* of something: wrath (Rev. 6.16–17) as well as salvation (Rev. 7.10; Rev. 7.17). The lamb simile fulfills conflicting purposes at the end of *Disgrace*, in that the killing of the dog invokes the triune complexity of sacrifice, wrath, and potential salvation, without signifying any of the three in a conclusive way. The act of *giving him up* may be an act of sacrifice, but it is also an act of wrath, both against the dog (he will die) and against Lurie himself (he likes this dog, possibly loves it, and by killing it also punishes himself). The lamb simile, then, also turns the dog into a bringer of salvation and gives Driepoot, the unwanted other,[24] a centrality only at the very end of the text, the way the slave Friday is given the utmost centrality at the end of *Foe*, Vercueil as the messenger of the letter central importance at the end of

---

22 Gen. 22.13: "And Abraham looked up and saw a ram, caught in a thicket by its horns. Abraham went and took the ram and offered it up as a burnt offering instead of his son." Danta is not the victim of a translation error here, since Abraham also speaks about a lamb before, though not in the instance Danta is referring to.

23 Pamela Cooper notes that "the text entertains the grand narratives of birth, death, and (re) incarnation" (2005, 34).

24 It is not the first time in Coetzee's oeuvre that the text makes the reader question whether a dog is symbolic of something else. The aforementioned pivotal scene in *The Master of Petersburg*, when Dostoevsky hears the wailing dog in the night, asks such a question directly within the diegetic world. As has been seen above, it is prudent to be half-skeptical of simplistically figural readings of this kind. However, the delicate lamb simile may fulfill the purpose of drawing such connections, which Dostoevsky in *The Master of Petersburg* explores explicitly.

Age of Iron. Lurie's growing attachment to the dog may be read as an ethically deeply problematic form of caring for the other. Despite remaining problematic, this form of caring is clearly announced in the text's changing estimation of the dog toward the end, most directly in a change of the personal pronoun when referring to the dog.

Shortly before the last scene, the narrator registers Lurie's changing relationship with the dog in the expression that refers to Lurie's "particular fondness for *it*" (*Dis* 215; added emphasis). Shortly after the dog's first appearance at a very late stage in the narrative (*Dis* 214), the following paragraphs use *it* (and the determiner *its*) when referring to the dog a full thirteen times (the traditionally unlucky number may be a coincidence, but then again it may not). The reference to *it* changes suddenly when, in parenthesis, Bev Shaw mentions the dog's name *Driepoot* (*Dis* 215). After that the text alters between the expressions *it* and *the dog* when referring to Driepoot, thus reflecting Lurie's gradual acceptance of the dog as a creature rather than an object. It may not be insignificant that the dog only has three legs and that this number might signal the Holy Trinity indicated in the *Revelation*. At the same time, such readings may lead nowhere but to conclusions, which is, after all, not where this chapter wishes to go too easily, so one might better concentrate on how the reference to the name (for want of a better term) "humanizes" the dog to Lurie. The reference to the proper name *Driepoot* seems to usher in Lurie's later reflection on his relationship with the dog as a form of "love" (*Dis* 219). When the name of the dog has been mentioned, Lurie's regard and concern for *it* are changed. (One might ask: Is it possible to love an *it*, is it possible to speak of what one loves as *it*?) Immediately afterwards he shows a deeper awareness of the dog, something which is frequently found in Coetzee's characters after a drastic change in their lives,[25] a suddenly more ethical, more phenomenologically aware, more meditative regard for the world and its beings. In close detail the focalizer relates the dog's interaction with Lurie when he is playing music, how "the dog is fascinated by the sound of the banjo," how the dog "sits up, cocks its head, listens," and how "the dog smacks its lips and seems on the point of singing too, or howling" (*Dis* 215). The deeper regard for another being and the knowledge of the dog's proper name lay the ground for what Lurie "no longer has the difficulty in calling by its proper name: love" (*Dis* 219).

---

[25] Dostoevsky's concern for the dog and for the homeless man, Ivanov, after Pavel's death in *The Master of Petersburg*; Susan Barton's concern for Bheki and his friend, and for Vercueil and his dog are examples of this phenomenon. Needless to say, not all examples involve dogs.

Disgrace fundamentally complicates this kind of love not only by likening it to giving up, but also by deconstructing it a page later. Immediately after the explicit reference to Lurie's complicated form of love, this love is negated by the expression that it is "little enough, less than little: nothing" (*Dis* 220). But this negation is again not final, since it has been prophylactically deconstructed by the subtle change in pronouns I have hinted at above, a change which is registered just before Lurie takes the dog into the "room that is not a room but a hole where one leaks out of existence" (*Dis* 219). Lurie reflects:

> There is only the young dog left, the one who likes music, the one who, given half a chance, would already have lolloped after *his* comrades into the clinic building, into the theatre with its zinc-topped table where the rich, mixed smells still linger, including one *he* will not yet have met with in *his* life: the smell of expiration, the soft, short smell of the released soul. (*Dis* 219; added emphases)

Suddenly and subtly Driepoot is referred to as *he*, poignantly in the context of the sterile hints at the machinations of the killing-room. It is this use of *one* and *he* and *his* (and the emotional change implied) that enables Lurie to summarize his feelings for Driepoot as something like love.

The ruminations on love and on Driepoot stage the complex flux of emotions coursing through Lurie at this stage of the novel, and they deconstruct the reader's view of Lurie as a wholly unethical, uncaring person, even if it is done in so subtle a way that a slow reading is needed to register this deconstruction. Through the arrangement of the novel we seem initially inclined to read Lurie's understanding of love as entirely possessive and sexual, entirely physical. When in the end he *gives up* the *body* of the dog he may also be giving up this kind of love, a love which is as yet called both love *and* nothing. This simultaneity mirrors Lurie's oscillatory thoughts, and this simultaneity is transplanted into the reader's mind as well. At the end, the reader is no longer so sure who David Lurie really is. The assured character of Lurie's voice at the beginning is gone. Even if the novel's final line is decisive, the reader is invited to ask if this is the same arrogant, self-assured man from the beginning, the man who chased his desire, and is now giving up a form of love.

It is important to repeat that the final act of giving up Driepoot cannot be forced into signaling only a positive or only a negative meaning. Reading the above-mentioned passages on the emphasis of love in conjunction with the use of the personal pronoun for the dog (which is not revoked for the remainder of the novel), the reader may feel in Lurie's act a gesture of kindness as well as a gesture of defeat, and through the subtle religious connotations an indication of renewal[26] as well as a possible admission by Lurie of being in a moral dead end. The question remains whether a man who has come to some kind of understanding that his moral code may be unfit to care for this dog, even to love him, could have attained such an understanding if he were a wholly immoral person. A quick interpretation to reprimand Lurie for this final act is misguided, also because in the world of the novel (via Bev Shaw) it is not demonized. The reader's calculative thought process is stalled by this ending, because there is no *purpose* to the killing of Driepoot. It is hardly a killing *for*, and this complicates its being viewed as merely a sacrifice.

Much more than a killing *for*, it is a giving up *with*, since symbolically, Lurie is giving up himself as much as the dog. This is related through the syntactic closeness of subject and object in the final sentence, "Yes, I am giving him up" (*Dis* 220). Even if one does not go along with this reading, the progressive tense that concludes the novel indicates a continuation and conflates the sense of an ending in the suggestion of a perpetuation. If nothing else, the shock and the bleakness of the ending, in its mysterious and negative implications, may give the positive impulse to reread the text, to make the novel, its characters, its questions, and especially Driepoot endure.

In *Disgrace*'s ending one may, however, not only find an indication to reread; there also emerges a subtle reworking (or unworking) of tropes and ideas explored in earlier works of the oeuvre, which also highlights the intertextual dialogue of the author's texts with each other. Coetzee's endings, at times, echo previous endings, giving ideas, tropes, or topics in the oeuvre an obsessional quality that is reminiscent of Beckett's reworking and unworking of topoi and images across the works. One of these topics is the discussion of souls, which finds mention in another ending in Coetzee's oeuvre (though it is discussed most prominently in Elizabeth Costello's lectures making up "The Lives of Animals"). The aforementioned reflection on the smell of the soul in *Disgrace* ("the smell of expiration, the soft, short smell of the released soul" [*Dis* 219]) recalls a previous ending in Coetzee's corpus, where the soul is likewise linked to a sense-experience, namely to taste in the final line of *The Master of Petersburg*. The novel's last scene shares with the ending of *Disgrace* a poignant moment of dynamic stillness, where finitude is emphasized while through its determined

---

[26] Whether one reads this renewal as a renewal of Lurie's character, a salvation of the dog, or even as a more allegorical form of renewal with regard to the country of South Africa, it must be remembered that any such form of renewal does not solve anything but rather holds the hope for renewal in an uncertain balance. For the complex relation between the ending and the time and place the novel is set in, see Attridge (2004a, 162–191).

urgency an undercurrent of pleading (of hope for the future) is implied, a plea
that urges a continued response. The last line of *The Master of Petersburg* invokes
the topic of the soul through a sense-experience and carries the same defeated
sadness of giving up that is inherent in *Disgrace's* ending. The narrator speaks of
Dostoevsky's soul, which he seems to have lost or sold in the course of his life as
a writer. The novel ends: "Now he begins to taste it. It tastes like gall" (*MoP* 250).
In density and associative richness this ending has a very simple poetic quality,
though it is the mysterious emphasis on gall that stands out most strongly. It
calls up the ancient theory of the four humors, and there may be (at least) two
separate interpretations as to how Dostoevsky feels at the end of the novel, and
as to what shape his actions might take after we leave him behind. *Gall* evokes
both yellow and black bile and might cause one to diagnose Dostoevsky as
either a melancholic or a choleric,[27] if one were a medieval physician. In such a
reading, the use of the signifier *gall* evokes two entirely opposite interpretations
of Dostoevsky at the end of this text, urging us to weigh both interpretations
against the story and discourse that have gone before, and to view Dostoevsky,
at the end of the text, at the end of the line—riven by the death of his stepson
and used by the revolutionaries—as a man deeply torn apart and, in the simplest
meaning of the word, double.

There is, however, a further and subtler allusion that prefigures the religious
connotations in *Disgrace's* ending, and likewise conjures up the wholly
ambiguous simultaneity of negativity and positivity discussed before. The
references in the final line to *gall* and to *tasting* evoke another book of *The
New Testament*, the first gospel (first in canonical order before Mark, second in
historical composition after Mark), the gospel of Matthew. After Jesus has been
hounded up Calvary and before he is nailed to the cross we are informed: "They
gave him vinegar to drink mingled with *gall*: and when he had *tasted* thereof,
he would not drink" (Mt. 27.34; added emphases). In Bible-ese vinegar simply
denotes a cheap or bitter wine (Clarke 1837, 273), and gall could have been "any
bitter liquid, possibly the myrrh of Mk 15.23" (May and Metzger 1962, 1210f.).
At the time of the crucifixion, wine mingled with gall (or myrrh) constituted a
common "stupefying potion [...] [given] to condemned malefactors" (Clarke
1837, 273). Jesus, "determin[ed] [...] to endure the fulness of pain, refused to
take what was thus offered to him" (Clarke 1837, 273). The crux about this
offering at the crucial moment before the crucifixion is this: Had Jesus taken

---

[27] See Robert Burton's treatment in *The Anatomy of Melancholy* (1621), and his references to Galen:
esp. [(1621)] 1838, 93; 96; 110–112.

the *stupefying potion* his suffering would have been alleviated and—as the story goes—salvation would not have come. The reference to the tasting of gall at the very end of *The Master of Petersburg* indicates suffering as well as an imminent punishment, which Dostoevsky either accepts or does not. If we read his tasting literally and merely as *tasting*, that is as a refusal to drink, the way Jesus refuses to drink, then suffering—for the guilt Dostoevsky feels about his exploits as a writer, perhaps especially regarding Matrjona, about his stepson's death—would continue and bring salvation, his guilt would be lifted from his shoulders. If, however, his tasting of gall means that he is *drinking* some kind of stupefying potion, he alleviates his suffering, salvation will be postponed, and guilt will continue to burden him.

The Master of Petersburg is a novel written in the form of a confession, and so the novel's ending subtly points to absolution as a possibility, even if this possibility is not granted and remains ambiguously located outside of the diegetic frame. At the same time, the potential for salvation remains real, even if the immediate understanding of the ending seems to indicate defeat. Like the much more confrontational ending of *Disgrace*, the ending of *The Master of Petersburg* also closes by alluding to a moment of eschatology as a final moment which is neither only an ending nor only a beginning, neither only negative nor only positive. These endings challenge the reader to think simultaneities, to conceive of the philosophical and the interpretive possibility of the concept of *both*, of remaining in uncertainty and taking this as a productive opportunity for reflection on the text's wide variety of meanings.

In these endings the reader finds allusions to a religious desire for renewal, for an apocalypticism that brings about rebirth.[28] What can be read in them are echoes of the deconstructivist notion of a renunciation of ending and an avowal of infinite beginnings, of the positive potentiality of being in a state of undecidability,[29] on the part of the characters but especially on the part of the reader. At the narrative level, one can see the modernist renunciation of the

---

[28] In his study of ending, Frank Kermode points out that the human mind is characterized by a deeply entrenched thinking about the apocalyptic, that it is the simultaneity of ending and beginning inherent in apocalypse. Kermode describes it as a way of thinking which "continue[s] to lie under our ways of making sense of the world" (2000, 28).

[29] Derrida lays this out nicely in *Limited Inc* (1988), where he notes that the "undecidable opens the field of decision or of decidability," where undecidability is seen as the "necessary condition" of decidability (1988, 116). Elsewhere Derrida notes: "The only decision possible is the impossible decision. It is when it is not possible to *know* what must be done, when knowledge is not and cannot be determining that a decision is possible as such" (1995, 147; original emphasis). These ideas may be brought to bear on Coetzee's paradoxical fiction, which time and again, and especially in its endings, navigates the readers into dead ends, into moments of *undecidability*, from which, paradoxically, the reader constructs *ways out*, simply because she has to.

conclusiveness of realist narratives, the most succinct origins of which David Lodge locates in Henry James, who "pioneered the 'open' ending characteristic of modern fiction [...], leaving a phrase hanging resonantly, but ambiguously, in the air" (1992, 224).[30]

Coetzee's novels all end in such ambiguous ways, refusing the neat cohering of the various strands of a novel into a single, stable unity. A new possibility for action may be indicated; or a "narrative loop" may be staged, which links back to the beginning, signaling a rereading; or the text may literally point to the future, while signaling the past, such as the first part of *Dusklands* does in a grimly ironic way, when Eugene Dawn, stuck in a prison cell like Norman Bates upon his end, reflects: "[...] I ponder and ponder. I have high hopes of finding whose fault I am" (*Dusk* 49).[31] And then there are those endings which push the reader to a gaping abyss, forcing her to stare down a void, and so being thrown back upon herself to supply a reflection on emptiness, on the vacuity cleaving before one after the last line has been read.[32] The endings of *Disgrace*, *The Master of Petersburg*, *Foe*, *Age of Iron*, and to a lesser degree *Youth*, are clearly of that order, introducing a shock or a sensation of ostensible hopelessness that is suitable to the diegetic logic, but which, as Lodge claims of William Golding's endings, has the form of a shock that "throw[s] everything that has gone before into a new and surprising light" (1992, 224).

While Coetzee's endings introduce a final ambiguity to reverberate in the reader's mind after the closing of the book, it is important to see that the endings leave off in a complex way of gazing both backward and forward. The regret that is often emphasized in the endings signals a distinct glance backward, over memory, over a life's past, over the novel the reader is finishing. At the same time, the endings press on, exploring an unresolvedness, inconclusiveness, and fragmentariness[33] to the existences of the works' fictional lives. It is curious, then,

---

[30] In his notebooks James writes on the composition of *The Portrait of a Lady* in a way that anticipates modernist literature (as well as post-structural theory): "The *whole* of anything is never told; you can only take what groups together. What I have done has that unity—it groups together. It is complete in itself [...]" (1947, 18; original emphasis).

[31] Dawn's future-gazing is likewise indebted to a mining of the past, since he thinks: "There is still my entire childhood to work through before I can expect to get to the bottom of my story" (*Dusk* 49).

[32] I borrow the image of the abyss from Spivak's preface to her translation of Derrida's *Of Grammatology* (1967), where she elucidates Derrida's notions discussed above: "Deconstruction seems to offer a way out of the closure of knowledge. By inaugurating the open-ended indefiniteness of textuality—by thus 'placing in the abyss' [...]—it shows us the lure of the abyss as freedom" ([1967] 1997, lxxxvii). For Derrida's use of the abyss image in manifold ways, see, for example, his discussion of Rousseau in the same volume ([1967] 1997, 163f.).

[33] These terms (inconclusive, fragmentary) are borrowed from Hermione Lee's review of *Elizabeth Costello* in *The Guardian*, where she uses them to criticize the form and plot of the novel. Needless to say, I refer to them in a more heuristically productive way to view the endings of Coetzee's works merely as the beginnings of reflection. See Lee (2003).

that Coetzee's texts seem more to allude to death than to narrate it. Yet, this way they may be seen to explore the philosophical idea that death is strung through the fiber of life rather than a mere closing of the brackets at the end, and that all of life is given both its magnitude and its inconsequence by the final bookend looming uncertainly yet certainly in the distance. It is remarkable that not even one of Coetzee's endings closes with an explicit, unambiguously narrated death of a character. Not once is the reader witness to a protagonist's end of life. Even in *Age of Iron* the moment of death is an event that we do not witness *as death* in a literal way, and the fact that we are reading Elizabeth Curren's words about her death in this epistolary book of hers problematizes a reading of the book's final lines as constituting her death. Even if the author is dead, she cannot write about her death in the past tense. And while the ending of *Life & Times of Michael K* may hint at the undernourished man's death, actual death is deferred. *Elizabeth Costello* curiously appears in a Kafkaesque scene of being *ad portas*, possibly before the gates of heaven (or the gates of hell?). And yet, in a reworking of the Kafkan image, she is not admitted—does this mean she does not die but remains in a middle place, in limbo, like that other hero in Kafka, Hunter Gracchus? An affirmative answer to this question is given credibility by her reappearance in *Slow Man*—an intertextual technique which complicates the simple conclusion that either Elizabeth Costello or *Elizabeth Costello* have really ended. And even *Foe*'s death of Susan Barton is not naturalized to the reader but moved into the realms of metafiction, leaving the reader to think about death in a more fundamental way, without its being safely confined to the bounds of the diegetic world.[34]

Before ending this chapter, it will be useful to return to *The Master of Petersburg* and to *Disgrace*, and to end with *Age of Iron*. *The Master of Petersburg* is an elegiac novel for the acute sense of loss and death that tracks Dostoevsky's every step, like a dog (*MoP* 52); for the appalling shadow of guilt and regret that Pavel's death has cast over the man and the novel; and for the poignant quality of Dostoevsky's (increasingly futile) attempts to reimagine Pavel. The narrative is arranged along a line of deferrals,[35] since Dostoevsky is unable to bring himself to leave Petersburg and return to Dresden, to his young wife awaiting him there.[36]

---

[34] For a treatment of the always tempting analogy between a narrative's ending and the termination of the narrative of life, see especially Garrett Stewart's first chapter "Points of Departure" in his endlessly fascinating *Death Sentences: Styles of Dying in British Fiction* (1984).

[35] In an intertextual study concerned with the novel's inherent trope of *looking back*, Ottilia Veres argues that "the text [...] follows a discourse of displacement" (2008, 243).

[36] See, for example, the chapter "The Police" when, after having arranged to leave Petersburg, Dostoevsky returns to Anna Sergeyevna and explains: "I have put off my departure" (*MoP* 165).

The memory of Pavel binds him to the city of his death. To keep Pavel, to make him endure, Dostoevsky has to remain in Russia. Yet, in the structure of the text there is the indication that the novel is strung along these deferrals to counter the more philosophical dimensions of the ending of narrative in general. Despite the already neoteric qualities of the real Dostoevsky's works (one may think of the narrative structure of *Notes from Underground* [1864] or the moral ruptures of *Crime and Punishment* [1866] and *The Brothers Karamazov* [1880]), Coetzee still manages to peg a historical narrative to the clothesline of a modernist worldview and a modernist idea of narrative closure.

The plot's staged uncertainties, the Master's hesitancy and existential sluggishness are motivated intradiegetically as outcomes of the guilt emanating from Pavel's untimely death. Simultaneously, the arrangement of the plot along these hesitancies and deferrals as well as the Master's slowness are also reactions against the progressive acceleration of a growing modernity that is represented by the revolutionaries of the novel, who may or may not be involved in Pavel's death. As many other novels by Coetzee do, the form of *The Master of Petersburg* mirrors the focalizer's inner landscape. In a similar way, the arrangement of the plot of *Disgrace* shows the sudden stop to Lurie's industrious life after he leaves Cape Town to go to the country. Whereas much action is packed into the first six chapters playing out in Cape Town, the following thirteen chapters in the Eastern Cape seem literally to take their narrative time to spread out the story.[37] In a small amount of narrative time in the beginning in Cape Town, a large amount of narrated time is condensed; in the following chapters in the country, a larger amount of narrative time is used to cover a smaller amount of narrated time. This mirrors the slower country life as compared to that of the city, while it also conveys Lurie's inner state of drifting and of existential homelessness (in both space and time). This slowness also prepares for the two most powerful shocks in the narrative, the attack on the farm and the giving up of Driepoot. Both of these narrative shocks are stoppages in the progress of the plot and in the character's lives; they are end points (the latter is, of course, also the end point of the narrative)—but these shocks are powerful narrative techniques to accelerate philosophical meaning-making in the reader.

In *The Master of Petersburg* the ending prompts the reader's meaning-making very distinctly as well, teasing with the expectation of an explication of the final line, but since this is denied, the ending can only confront the reader with silence,

---

[37] Chapter 19 marks Lurie's return to the Western Cape, first to George, then to Cape Town. The return to the city is an intermission only, and Chapter 22 sees Lurie returning to the farm once again.

and thus convey Dostoevsky's loss over his dead stepson even more poignantly. As Dostoevsky puts it much earlier in the novel: "Mourning for a dead child has no end" (*MoP* 77). This way, it is only appropriate that the novel should not end in a conclusive way, since this would allow not only the closing of the book, but also the closing of the book on Pavel.[38] The ending of *The Master of Petersburg* is thus necessarily trapped in a dead end. In a moment of undecidability, it glances Janus-faced back over the preceding narrative and into an uncertain future, that, as the ending of *Waiting for the Barbarians* paradigmatically puts it, "may lead nowhere" (*WfB* 170), but that will doubtless lead somewhere. At the very least, these endings put the others center stage, be they former slaves, be they neglected mongrel dogs, or the dead. But the works put the others at the center only at the end, so that the reader has to reflect on whether and on how they may have been at the center all along. The readers have to decide on their own, in these final moments of undecidability.

By arranging endings which are undecidable in this way, Coetzee's works mirror the uncertainty of the characters looking into an uncertain future, while expressing a polarity of emotions to stymie the reading and mediating a more meditative thinking about the texts and the worlds they engage with. At the latest possible instances, the works stage one further moment of slowness in the reader, of static tension, provoking a final moment of slow reading under the sway of which the reader surfaces in the real world, with the traces of the text still awash in her mind.

In *Age of Iron* Mrs. Curren once writes about ending as a form of agency: "Between waiting in bed for the breathing to stop and going out to make one's own end, what a difference!" (*AoI* 116). By ending his novels as shown above, Coetzee implants the doubt in the reader's mind whether this statement by Mrs. Curren is confined to her thoughts on dying, or if it might not comment on the reader of his works as well, a reader who has to *make her own end* of these unending endings. It is with these arguments behind us that this chapter must conclude, maybe sentimentally (though hopefully no less significantly), that a work by Coetzee never ends. Roland Barthes famously said that the death of the author is the birth of the reader. With regard to Coetzee's oeuvre this chapter has tried to suggest that the endings of his texts are merely the beginning of readings.

---

[38] Significantly, Dostoevsky is incapable of even beginning to mourn for Pavel, since to him the work of mourning implies the end of mourning. Freud illuminates this in "Mourning and Melancholia" (1917): "[W]hen the work of mourning is completed the ego becomes free and uninhibited again" (1957, 245)—an outcome Dostoevsky could not wish for.

9

An Empty Cube—Coetzee's Irreal Worlds

About a third into *The Childhood of Jesus* and into the world of Novilla, in a dialogue with Elena, Simón ruminates on a memory about memory. He asks: "Do you remember how the other day you told me you didn't suffer from memories?" (*CoJ* 65). Fittingly, Elena cannot recall anything of the kind, while Simón remembers the conversation very clearly. He elaborates:

> I am not like you. I suffer from memories, or the shadows of memories. I know we are all supposed to be washed clean by the passage here, and it is true, I don't have a great repertoire to call on. But the shadows linger nevertheless. That is what I suffer from. Except that I don't use the word *suffer*. I hold onto them, those shadows. (*CoJ* 65; original emphasis)

In these comments, Simón initially speaks very explicitly about memories (he uses the word twice), and he connects memories with shadows (*shadows of memories*). But as he progresses, shadows and suffering gradually gain control of his discourse (he ends having used the words *shadows* and *suffer* thrice each). After he has spoken of the purging passage to Novilla, he merely speaks of shadows proper, no longer of shadows of memories, as if the speaking about memories had purged him from using the word and he could now merely refer to shadows. And the word *suffer* also looms on the horizon. Simón first says he suffers from memories, but after the word shadows has come to his mind, he seems to argue that what he is really suffering from are not memories at all, but rather the shadows of memories, the nebulous obscurity that clouds his clear vision of the past. *Except I don't use the word suffer*, he adds. Through this paralipsis Simón places emphasis on suffering by referring to it negatively. By saying he does not use the word *suffer*, he does, of course, use the word *suffer*. It is paradoxical to refer to something negatively, since it also refers to it positively; in a phenomenological way, a word that negates another word does not cancel out the other word but repeats and qualifies it. In the earlier example this alerts us to a complex and paradoxical play with signifiers in Coetzee's work more generally. The ambiguity of this passage is achieved not through complicated syntax or vocabulary; it is achieved through the altering significance that attaches to the signifiers *memories, shadows,* and *suffer.* This gives the text a quality which Coetzee has called an "allusive (connotative) force" (*H&N* 78).

In just over sixty words, one gets a microcosmic view of various aspects relevant to the philosophical implications of Coetzee's work, the first aspect of which is that one cannot quickly go past this passage if one wishes to do it justice—one has to reflect on it. It is as if the form of the text instructed the reader as Simón instructs David: "Please don't answer at once. Reflect" (*CoJ* 191). The passage's clear and simple style belies its ambiguity, and its repetition of words creates a sense of harmony, even if the passage is far from being easily grasped. Because of the combination of the deceptively simple language and complex formal strategies the reader is confused, and so she has to read slowly.

The Childhood of Jesus is Coetzee's latest work to date, and it is a summation of many of the estranging and ambiguity increasing techniques which have occupied his work from the beginning. This chapter will explore some of these techniques regarding the strange world which is represented in this work, and it will link aspects of this world to other worlds in Coetzee's oeuvre. *The Childhood of Jesus* clearly draws attention to its ambiguities, for example through the mystifying relations to intertexts such as Johann Christoph Friedrich Bach's *Die Kindheit Jesu* (1773), the Bible's *Apocrypha,* Cervantes's *Don Quixote* (1605/1615), or, in turn, Jorge Luis Borges's "Pierre Menard, Author of the *Quixote* (1939)." *The Childhood of Jesus* is a book as much about a new world as about reading, and the reader is invited to consider how to approach this novel, how to read this world, whether in the way David reads his children's version of *Don Quixote,* that is arbitrarily, or in the way Simón reads this new world, that is in estrangement. The text gives no answer, but rather stages the possibility of not having to read the narrative for the one final answer, and instead to experience it in a different way, in the ethical way this study has explored throughout. Simón reminds the reader of this possibility when he says: "For real reading you have to *submit* to what is written on the page" (*CoJ* 165; added emphasis).

By provoking slow reading, Coetzee's novel opens up spaces for a number of ethical, epistemological, and ontological questions and reflections. In beginning to explore how these are related to the strange world of Novilla, it may be prudent to begin not by looking at the *world* of Novilla but rather at the *word* Novilla. In its allusions to etymological origins in Latin and Romance languages, Novilla carries connotations of *novella,* etymologically referring to the new, to novelty. The obvious interpretation is that Novilla is a new village, part of a new world. But the new in Novilla also alludes to novel, novella, and so to narrative, which alerts us to the aspect of the work that is to do with reading. But the Spanish word *novilla* has a literal translation in English as well; it means *heifer*, that is a young female cow which has not reared a calf. This emphasizes the novel's preoccupations with virginity and youth. Through the novel's explicit use of the name *Novilla* combined with the strange place that it refers to, the reader is stimulated to think through the allusions in the word, and to reflect on the epistemological questions raised by its different meanings. As shown earlier in the chapter on literalness, the *allusive connotative force* of an individual signifier here, too, makes the reader go through the various different meanings and to play through a variety of readings enabled by merely one signifier. However, here such a word, which works in various directions, is used to refer to the very world in which the novel is set. This way the world of Novilla becomes difficult to place, while, at the same time, every reader will make a distinct place of this world of Novilla from whatever the allusions in the word provoke in her mind. The way Novilla is a word of many words, Novilla is also a world of many worlds.

What kinds of *worlds* are related to the reader, then, and how? Very subtly, Simón's statement earlier asks the reader what kind of a world she has entered upon beginning her perusal of the novel. What kind of a world is this, where memories have been purged from people's minds, though, it seems, not always successfully, what realm is the reader moving through, what realm are the characters moving through? That Simón is caught up with the shadows of memories from his past, must give the reader pause regarding the *epistēmē* of this world. Whatever the reader can know about the world of Novilla is focalized through Simón; but since Simón's mind may be plagued by the shadows of memories, the reader is challenged to reflect whether the world Simón focalizes to her is the "real" world of Novilla, a world superimposed over another world, or a world suffused with past memories or past worlds. The world of Novilla raises ontological, phenomenological, and epistemological questions: What world is there, how does this world appear to Simón, and what can the reader know about this world?

The most interesting statement to do with these questions, and with Simón's memories in Novilla, is made by Elena. When Simón has mentioned shadows and memories and how he will hold on to them, Elena comments: "That's good. [...] It takes all kinds to make a world" (*CoJ* 65).[1] This statement takes the reader into the philosophical terrain of worlds in various ways. It calls up the

---

[1] Later on in the novel Simón seems to be of a different opinion. Exasperated with David's many Why? questions, he tells the boy: "The world was not made for our convenience, my young friend. It is up to us to fit in" (*CoJ* 169). This statement engages with Elena's in a dialogue about the phenomenon of *worlds*, and the reader is implicitly invited to join.

constructivist idea of *worldmaking* as well as the ontological, phenomenological, and epistemological ideas of *world disclosure*. What kind of a world being made or to be made does Elena refer to? How will this world be distinguished from other worlds and how will it be recognized? What does she even mean by this? The fact that we ask such questions has already enmeshed us in the construction of the world of Novilla, and it has forced us to reflect what a world even is. How does one make a world? The fact that the world of Novilla is ambiguous immediately stimulates our constructive and reflexive faculties. Through ambiguity and defamiliarization, and through the slow reading that follows, not only *The Childhood of Jesus* but Coetzee's works more generally activate the reader's worldmaking and world disclosure in an important way.

Nelson Goodman, who has coined the term *worldmaking* in his work *Ways of Worldmaking* (1978), explores the many forms in which human beings, through thought and cultural activity, are always engaged in the making of worlds. Goodman argues that any world that the human mind has access to is not an absolute, dogmatic, ontological fact, but that each world is an individual world constructed inter-subjectively and from other worlds. The way each text may be thought of as being made from other texts in a post-structuralist understanding of intertextuality,[2] so, according to Goodman, each new world is a revision of a previous world and a contribution to the sum of possible worlds in the cultural reservoir of humanity. There is never one world; there are always as many "different world-versions" (Goodman 1978, 4) as there are human beings and cultural artifacts expressing, representing, or exemplifying worlds (Goodman 1978, 66). These *world-versions* are "contrasting *right* versions not all reducible to one" (Goodman 1978, 5; added emphasis). Goodman's idea of a plurality of worlds, then, is made up of community, a social and dialogic phenomenon, but one in which each individual world-version is its own whole world.[3]

The Childhood of Jesus presents many different ways of worldmaking and does so on different levels of discourse. First, the characters in the story are literally

---

[2]	My understanding of these ideas is informed by the Bakhtinian notion of textual dialogicity as developed by Julia Kristeva in her argument that "any text is constructed as a mosaic of quotations; any text is the absorption of another" (1989, 37). T. S. Eliot's ideas of modernist art discussed in "Tradition and the Individual Talent" are also relevant here. While Eliot contends that "novelty is better than repetition," he notes: "No poet, no artist of any art, has his complete meaning alone. His significance, his appreciation is the appreciation of his relation to the dead poets and artists" (1975, 38). Eliot describes Kristeva's intertextuality *avant la lettre* by stating: "[W]hat happens when a new work of art is created is something that happens simultaneously to all the works of art which preceded it" (1975, 38). Similarly, each new world made influences each world already made and likewise every world to come.

[3]	"We are not speaking in terms of multiple possible alternatives to a single actual world but of multiple actual worlds" (Goodman 1978, 2).

making a world, as they are trying to create a civilization in a new environment. Second, the novel as a cultural artifact is itself a world made through language. And third, the readers are making worlds while reading, constructing in their minds the world of the novel, and the reflection on the world of the novel resonates back as a form of worldmaking into the readers' real worlds. How do these ideas of worldmaking illuminate Coetzee's novel?

Reading Elena's statements about worldmaking literally, one could argue that *The Childhood of Jesus* is either a work of science fiction, or a form of the utopian or dystopian novel; or one could associate it with echoes in history of such events as the English Puritans arriving in the new world of America, for example. A group of disparate people, for reasons unknown to the reader (possibly unknown to the people themselves), have been sent to this brave new world of Novilla in order that a new society may flourish. But if we read it as a dystopia, what gives pause here is the fact that unlike classical dystopian worlds, Novilla does not seem to be ruled by a despot like Mustapha Mond in *Brave New World* (1932), or Big Brother in *Nineteen Eighty-four* (1949). And if we read it in a historically literal way we must see that unlike the English pilgrims the people of Novilla are not linked by an umbilical cord to a mother country. They are like the refugees from Coetzee's early drafts of *Waiting for the Barbarians*, uncertain how they got to where they are and uncertain when they may be able to leave. It seems as if the idea of the refugees on Robben Island from the earlier drafts of the earlier novel had been subsumed into the final draft of the later one, though in Novilla there is no Manos Milis, no Magistrate character, no insider who watches over them—here, all are on their own, strangers to this strange new world. They have arrived on these shores without knowledge of the past but have, as it were, built a city upon a hill there, and like the pilgrims of America they were presumably left to themselves. The reader is left in the dark with the characters as to who took them there and why.

It could be suggested that they have come from painful pasts, from societies at war, for example, that they really are refugees, and that their attempts at creating an ideal society is a reaction against a history of violence. But such an interpretation is immediately complicated, since we are told that they have no memory of the past—does this mean they have no history?[4] Is it possible to make a *better* world if what the new world is an improvement over is forgotten? Can

---

[4] See Simón's comment, to which I return later: "Like you I bring no history with me. What history I had I left behind. I am simply a new man in a new land, and that is a good thing. But I have not let go of the idea of history, the idea of change without beginning or end. Ideas cannot be washed out of us, not even by time. Ideas are everywhere" (*CoJ* 114f.).

worldmaking occur if one has no knowledge of other worlds? And if the direct opposite interpretation is chosen, that these people were brought to Novilla to create an ideal society, then are they not, in fact, prisoners or guinea pigs? But prisoners of whom, guinea pigs for what?

Clearly, the novel gives no answers to these questions, and this is the point: The reader is kept in the dark about this world as much as the people of Novilla are. To make the world of Novilla, if one followed the constructivist argument, one would have to pay very close attention to every detail of the text, since only through that could one ever hope to make a world of this strange empty place.

It takes all kinds to make a world. The literal creation and making of a new world in literature follows the long-standing philosophical tradition of man imagining an idealized world, be that the Elysian Fields imagined by Homer and Hesiod, Plato's paragon of a *Republic* or the Renaissance ideal of the Islands of the Blest, of which More's *Utopia* (1516) is the most well-known example. These texts are themselves instances of explicit worldmaking. *Utopia* makes a socialist world that rectifies the injustices of Renaissance society, and Plato's republic makes a philosophical world where philosopher kings govern in an idle, *laissez faire* way without the desire for personal gain or indeed for rule.

It takes all kinds to make a world. The novel also tempts the reader to understand this statement metaphorically, since Elena makes it in such a sweeping, normative way, thereby asking the reader to reflect on whether this seemingly universal point only refers to Novilla, or if it has larger implications? One may register political and ethical connotations here, namely that any community needs difference and cultural diversity if it is to function as a community, as a world. The novel, however, seems implicitly to negate this interpretation, and a slow reading of this novel must address the question of how Elena, who unlike Simon has no memories of the past whatsoever, could make a normative claim like this in the first place. Without even the shadows of memories, how could Elena's statement have any credibility? From which position does she make this claim? How could she imagine something into the future if she has no access to anything in her past? As we can see, reading her statement metaphorically leads to a hermeneutic dead end, from which an instrumental epistemology might not offer a way out. Since the novel complicates a straightforward allegorical reading of Novilla, a metaphorical reading of Elena's statements does not illuminate this alien world in a satisfying way; the reader remains alone with her questions. To consider them, then, she is invited to consider what is actually said, what is actually there on the surface of the world of Novilla.

The world of Novilla that the reader makes from what she is given by the text is a subsistence-based society, non-capitalist and socialist:[5] the buses are free (*CoJ* 10); everyone is polite and helpful (*CoJ* 16); one's mental and physical well-being is taken care of; there are philosophy courses in the recreation center, the Institute (*CoJ* 119–122); one eats margarine instead of butter, one does not drink or smoke (except for Señor Dagga), one does not eat meat or use salt (*CoJ* 26). Above anything, it seems, Novilla is a world without heart disease. But it is also a world without heart more generally, or as Simón says, it is "bloodless" (*CoJ* 30). Here, it seems the literal and the figural merge: Novilla's literal lack of salt is also a metaphorical lack of salt, of the spice of life; the literal lack of meat is also a metaphorical lack of physicality: there is no passion in this world (*CoJ* 63). The little sex there is is entirely end-oriented. Granted, to deserve the term pleasurable, sex usually tends to be that; in Novilla, however, it is entirely devoid of pleasure, so much so that it is even called "the business of sex" (*CoJ* 60). The expression recalls the opening line of Coetzee's *Disgrace*, where sex is seen in an equally functional way. The world of Novilla seems perfectly functional too; and yet, like David Lurie's sex life, it is fraught with problems. Something essential is always lacking in Novilla. While the easy politeness of the citizens of Novilla makes them disinterested, it also seems to make them uninterested in the people around them (*CoJ* 22). There are further problems sneaking into the easy functionalism of this world. For example, Novilla is a world infested with rats (*CoJ* 111f.); the rat overpopulation is the result of Novilla's hoarding endless amounts of grain, which are stored simply for the sake of it. And as one witnesses in the beginning of the novel, Novilla is structured through or indeed dominated by a bureaucracy that has little purpose despite its pure instrumental functionality. One has the feeling that in Novilla everything goes according to an unspoken normative ethics that is paradoxically flawed by its foundation in pure rationalism, without a deeper reflection on ethics and ratio. Because people have to eat, it is wise to store grain, which may be used to bake bread and feed the people. After all, the novel reiterates the Biblical truism that "[b]read is the staff of life" (*CoJ* 97).[6] Because it is good to store grain, a lot of grain will produce a lot of good. This is utilitarianism taken to an absurd extreme, and only little David seems to see through this topsy-turvy manna-mania, when he claims matter-of-factly: "I hate bread. Bread is boring. I like ice cream" (*CoJ* 245).

But while David's exclamation is childish—and why should it not be, he is a child after all—one has the feeling that in the world of Novilla the real children

---

[5]   See, for example, the critique of capitalism in the dialogue about not needing "a new bicycle every day" (*CoJ* 41).
[6]   See, for example, Lev. 26.26 or Isa. 3.1.

are the adult citizens, that they are, in fact, merely playing society, going through the motions of how a society should work in theory, but that they are not yet fit to make a world that is meaningful in practice. What is peculiar about these "children" is that they seem to have learned the techniques of rationalizing, although in a seemingly automatic and unexamined way. Indeed, everything in Novilla follows the logic of reason, and there is little room for emotion or imagination. It is a world the Stoics would have liked, a world without passions or irrational emotions, based entirely on rationalism, a world without ice cream.

There are, however, exceptions to this purely rationalist world, which cause a sense of disruption and uncanniness, both in the world of Novilla and in the reader. The biggest exception is, of course, little David. His references to miracles and his insistence on his own imaginative worldview clash with the strict logics of Novilla. In his childish and naïve way of looking at the world, David represents a worldview of a boyish imagination that includes wonder but also skepticism in the face of the world's phenomena. It seems that what clashes so readily with the society of Novilla later on in the novel is not what this *boyish imagination*, this boyish worldview, actually dreams up, but rather the mere possibility that such a way of thinking and imagining the world could exist at all. Despite its socialist character, this world is a kind of mathematical dystopia,[7] in which logic and rationalism dominate, while pluralism is prohibited—despite Elena's claim to the contrary. The one ideal world may not be an ideal world. A world of pure beauty would not be a beautiful world.

At the simplest level, a statement about the quality of the world of Novilla can only be made when comparing it to other fictional worlds or juxtaposing it against our own world(s). It is precisely this aspect through which Coetzee's text defamiliarizes and unsettles the reader most powerfully, since this artificial world seems simultaneously recognizable and entirely strange. Coetzee's text employs a duality of familiarizing and defamiliarizing to keep the reader ever engaged in an ongoing reflection on what this world is and how one could construct it so as to make sense of it. Through the interplay of familiarizing and defamiliarizing the textual world appears as a beckoning strangeness to the reader, provoking her to draw precisely the connections with the real world that it frustrates. Entering Coetzee's world the reader appreciates that the world of the text only seems familiar and unfamiliar when compared to another world, to her own. Defamiliarization in literature is always marked by dual desires: it makes strange the world of the text, but since any text bears at least some resemblance

---

[7] This becomes clear when considering David's alternative thinking to the unbending rules of mathematics and the repercussions this has in the world of Novilla—Simón asks: "What kind of crime is it for a child to say that two and two make three?" (*CoJ* 254).

to the real world, even a highly defamiliarized text also makes strange what it represents or expresses, constructs, or deconstructs. Any text is an affirmation of the world, even if it is a distinct negation of the world, such as the dystopia. One cannot, neither the philosopher, nor the novelist, nor the astronaut, get out of the ontological frame of the world.

In *The Childhood of Jesus* the reader encounters a world that is, to a great degree, familiar. Most importantly, the material world, its repertoire of objects, such as baby-prams, telephones, letters, ships, and buses—they can all be related to the reader's world very simply. One feels that this is a world-version which is plausible. At the same time, this material world is deeply estranging. Why, for example, in this day and age, where people do use cranes and telephones, do the stevedores operate horse-drawn carriages, and why do they only labor manually? Simón shares in our confusion at this perceived anachronism and says to his foreman: "If you were to bring in a crane, [...] you could get the unloading done in a tenth of the time" (*CoJ* 15), to which the foreman's answer is simply a rhetorical question: "But what would be the point?" (*CoJ* 15). This statement is a typical example of the paradoxical games Coetzee's works play. Since in this world of Novilla, where the mind is wholly dominated by the hegemony of instrumental thinking, the foreman's answer paradoxically undermines Simón's plea for a more efficient instrumentality, and it does this, in a further paradoxical twist, by asking for the instrumental purpose behind Simón's rather obvious suggestion. This paradoxical element extends to the world of Novilla as a whole, with its strangely anachronistic flavors. One cannot pin down this world in time and place, one cannot classify it easily and must therefore reflect constructively about this world as an *other* world, while recognizing it as a world *like* our own. The dual effect of this is that the world of the text seems uncanny to us—like our own world and not like our own world—and we begin to reflect on the world of the text as well as on our own world.

The technique of "anachronizing" the diegetic world has its precursors in Coetzee's oeuvre, for example in *In the Heart of the Country*, which seems to be set in feudal times, although in her growing madness Magda refers to "voices speak[ing] to me out of machines that fly in the sky" (*ItH* 137). Because Magda is dwindling toward insanity, it is difficult to say whether there are really airplanes traversing the sky or whether she is a woman in feudal times who has proto-industrial hallucinations. Pippin comments that

> it is difficult to pick an actual historical time for the events [of the novel], since we seem to range from horse and buggy days to the airplane, perhaps even the jet age. Or at least Magda cannot locate herself. Her sense of historical time seems dreamy, often fantastic. (2010, 32)

This *dreamy* and *fantastic* historical time, then, is also related to the reader's grasp of the diegetic world, since Magda is the focalizer through whom the world of the novel is mediated. Something similar is discernible in *Waiting for the Barbarians*, where the scenery and the objects of the border town likewise recall a feudal setting, even if the novel also suggests a more contemporary world, for example through its opening image of Colonel Joll's sunglasses:

> I have never seen anything like it: two little discs of glass suspended in front of his eyes in loops of wire. Is he blind? I could understand it if he wanted to hide blind eyes. But he is not blind. The discs are dark, they look opaque from the outside, but he can see through them. (*WfB* 1)

It is not unimportant that this novel about a world unfamiliar to us begins on a note of defamiliarization. Here as elsewhere Coetzee's technique is a phenomenological defamiliarizing through detailed description. Judith Butler, in a foreword to Maurice Natanson's study of phenomenology in literature (or rather phenomenological literature or literary phenomenology), helps to illuminate the phenomenological impetus at work in the "anachronizing" aspects of *Waiting for the Barbarians*: "[T]he fictive domain irrealizes the world, but it does not deny its reality; neither does it escape the world. Literary works perform this irrealization of the world [...]" (1998, xvf.). One may use these statements to shed light on Coetzee's worlds, as one may draw on Butler's mention of

> insights culled from the everyday that consistently disorient us with respect to what we take for granted. The literary texts recall a life-world that exceeds them, and yet the life-world is rediscovered in the literary text inflected as irreal. (1998, xvi)

An *irrealization of the world* occurs in moments of defamiliarization in Coetzee's works, as in the beginning of *Waiting for the Barbarians*. Such moments get the reader into a mood (and a mode) of reading, in which she has to process the phenomena described by the narrator-focalizer very carefully and slowly. The question remains whether this is an anachronistic world devoid of sunglasses, or whether the Magistrate is an anachronistic man, entirely at odds with modernity in his little outpost in the desert. Through the anachronistic description of objects that call up an historical world, the reader feels detached and estranged from this world, while the feeling remains that this world is very close to her own. It is a world in which modernity and feudality seem to coexist in perhaps an uncomfortable way. The discomfort comes from the fact that one is unable firmly to grasp this world, and therefore in need of engaging with it in a phenomenologically attentive way in the hope of grasping parts of it.

This points to a characteristic of Coetzee's work more generally. Like Beckett's characters, Coetzee's people also inhabit worlds that have complex relationships with the real world; both authors' worlds are indeed hard to define, they are real and unreal, they realize in fiction the irreality of the world and thus both represent and challenge history by rivalling it through the worlds of the novels. Especially Coetzee's earlier novels simultaneously represent and transform the real world very strongly. In his composition diary kept during the writing of *Waiting for the Barbarians* Coetzee comments on the anachronistic sense of his project. He writes: "25/12/77. [...] It is a wholly unreal enterprise I am engaged in. No matter what, this is a book that could have been written a hundred years ago."[8] During the various drafts of the novel, Coetzee slowly finds the unreal place suitable to the story, and gradually he seems to become convinced that the novel should be set in what is essentially a *hybrid time and place*.[9] Many of Coetzee's worlds exhibit a tenuous relationship with specific locales, because they are pluralized worlds, constructed from various disparate aspects of real worlds, like an assemblage of world-versions, an eclectic bricolage of disjunct world-elements, and because they do not *describe* worlds in a mimetically realist way, but rather *suggest* them. In the profile for Dutch television by Wim Kayzer as part of the series *Van de schoonheid en de troost* (Of Beauty and Consolation, 2000), Coetzee comments on his stance regarding the engagement with "the world" in fiction:

> [O]ne isn't in writing [...] transforming the world into the world as it should be [...]. That would be too much of a task if one undertook it every time. [...] No, I think that ... grasping the world as it is [...], putting it within a certain frame, taming it to a certain extent—that is quite enough of an ambition. (Coetzee and Kayzer 2000)

As usual, Coetzee's comment is quite perplexing, since the sense of *grasping the world as it is* seems to stand in contrast to the idea of *putting it within a certain frame* and *taming it*. The paradoxical aspect of this comment, however, may illuminate the very duality of Coetzee's worlds, that they are familiarizations

---

[8] HRC, container 33, folder 3, n.p.

[9] The expression "hybrid time" is Salman Rushdie's in his review of Christoph Ransmayr's *The Last World* (1992, 291). I add to its temporal hybridity a spatial one, which seems appropriate to describe many of Coetzee's worlds. In *The Childhood of Jesus* the sense of hybrid time is addressed in the novel not only through its anachronistic mingling of historical referents, but also through its explicit engagement with history, as in the aforementioned comment by Simón to David about the idea of history. The way memories and the past may, at times, come up in Simón's consciousness, so history may also surface in the novel. This means that the reader may read the work both literally and historically, since the novel's constructed hybrid time and place mean that these are both concrete and abstract, not Either-Or, but And-And, not only historically abstract, but also historically concrete—the former if the reader reads literally, the latter if she reads historically, and there seems little in the text itself to prevent the reader from mixing these two readings.

and defamiliarizations. The idea of putting the world within a certain frame is especially enlightening when considering the sparseness of description of setting in Coetzee's writing and how the novels and memoirs work more through allusion and suggestion to give a sense of a world rather than a representation of *the world as it is*.

In this way, Coetzee's defamiliarized worlds "perform[...] a paradoxical exercise, building up what is already there, at once layering what is disclosed, constituting the given" (Butler 1998, ixf.). Coetzee's worlds *build up* real worlds and thereby establish paradoxical and productive links between reality and fiction for the reader to reflect. Coetzee's works have just as much access to reality, as it were, than a novel in the mimetic realist tradition or as a photograph has of reality. The difference is that Coetzee's texts make worlds in different ways, through various defamiliarizing techniques. Generally, defamiliarization has just as valid a claim on expressing and representing "the world" as does familiarization, but defamiliarization adds a layer of reflection that is perhaps less accentuated in a realist tradition. A blurry photograph has the same ontological relation to the real world as a crystal clear image; the difference is an epistemological one—but the blurry photograph has the very simple effect of provoking a closer look.

When writing *Waiting for the Barbarians* Coetzee deliberately blurs his fictional world to suggest a different epistemological grasp to the reader. In his composition diary he notes: "28/4/78. Have begun, in desperation, on a new version. As I 'imagine' it, it is now set in a vaguely 18th–19th century Africa; but soon it is going to be snowing!"[10] By mixing disparate spatial markers, Coetzee creates an uncertain landscape that forces the reader into contemplation and reflection on the epistemological dimensions of a non-realist, (late) modernist literature, and conversely about the reality the text engages with. *How* Coetzee's literature engages with or explores a phenomenon, a topic, a place, a time always makes statements about *what* it is that is explored or engaged with. His techniques of mixing spatial and cultural markers in a liberal way make claims on the kind of world that is created—the very technique of mixing makes a world. Coetzee extends his ideas regarding the world of *Waiting for the Barbarians* and notes:

> 29/10/78. I must think seriously of giving some of these people Afrikaans names (Snyman/Schneemann, for example) and dropping the attempt to be consistent re northern/southern hemispheres.[11]

---

[10] HRC, container 33, folder 3, n.p.
[11] HRC, container 33, folder 3, n.p.

The idea to sprinkle Afrikaans names into this dislocated space is another gesture reminiscent of Beckett, whose mixing of Irish and French names in his prose combined with uncertain landscapes creates a similar sense of hybrid time and place, a related defamiliarization of place. A few more notes by Coetzee give further insight into his method of making, of assembling, a fictional world, as when he reflects further on subtly defamiliarizing the desert landscape.

(1) 2/10/78. Make the life of the desert more various. Little birds, tortoises.

(2) 31/10/78. [...] Give him more affection for the landscape. Give the landscape its own detailed life. The kind of white clay where nothing grows. Lizards.

(3) 23/2/79. [...] Make the "desert" more like the Karoo.[12]

Coetzee's impetus to emphasize the ambiguous time and place of the novel remains strong even when the book has been published and Coetzee reviews, with pencil in hand, the first translation into German by Brigitte Weidmann, which was published by Karl H. Henssel Verlag in 1984. (Incidentally, the book lists Coetzee's name as "J(ean) M(arie) Coetzee" in the author's note—an odd ambiguity Coetzee might have appreciated.[13]) Judging from his notes in the

---

[12] HRC, container 33, folder 3, n.p. Whereas the use of snow creates a sense of an unreal Karoo, here the Karoo is intimated to give a more realistic sense of place, which highlights the discursive force of familiarizing and defamiliarizing. An analogy may be pertinent here: this force is related to the larger Coetzeean project of a simultaneous alluding to and eliding of history that has been mentioned earlier. These historical ambiguities may, however, also be related to the novels' integration and placement in an increasingly globalized world of literature that Coetzee may have appreciated at the time of the writing. Michael J. F. Chapman has noted that "serious writers like Gordimer, Brink and Coetzee have had to retain a bifocal vision knowing that their local subject matter and preoccupations are going to be received more widely abroad than at home and, at home, by relatively few white 'literary' readers" (2003, 386). While Chapman's clustering of Gordimer, Brink and Coetzee is unfortunate, since the three are engaged in very different ways of exploring history, this is, however, an acute observation of Coetzee's work and its relation to the global marketplace of literature. Tim Parks comments on this sentiment in Coetzee by glossing a review Coetzee has written on Harry Mulisch's *The Discovery of Heaven*:

> Reviewing the novel favorably in these pages [of the NYRB], J. M. Coetzee [...] remarked that 'the chapters devoted to the internal squabbles of Dutch politics of the 1970s are largely wasted on the foreign reader,' suggesting a tension between Mulisch's desire to address his fellow Dutchmen and at the same time to write an effective novel for a wider audience. (2011, n.p.)

In a footnote Parks adds: "It's worth noting how attentive Coetzee is to this problem in his own novels, which frequently address (or addressed) the political situation in South Africa, but without ever entering into the kind of detail that would have required more than an ordinary newspaper reader's grasp of South African politics" (2011, n.p.). For Coetzee's review of Mulisch's novel, see *StS* 39–48. For a more general discussion of Coetzee in the global marketplace, see Brouillette (2007, 112–143).

[13] This was an odd running motif in criticism and scholarship until a decade ago; such mistakes have "even affect[ed] the interpretation of [Coetzee's] novels" (Kannemeyer 2012, 17). For a short account of the many mistakes, see Kannemeyer (2012, 17) and the related endnote, Kannemeyer (2012, 620). Ironically and irritatingly, in an account of misinformation and mistakes, Kannemeyer (or his translator) makes the mistake of misinforming us that Kafka's *The Trial* was, in the German original, called *Der Proze*.

margin, Coetzee seems often unhappy with the Weidmann translation (Reinhild Böhnke, his chief translator into German from 1995 onwards, translated the novel again in 2002). Frequently, Coetzee finds Weidman's phrases and syntactical constructions clumsy. Relevant to this discussion of worlds is a margin note on page 97 of the German manuscript. Weidmann translates the analogy between the Magistrate's torturer and the "surgeon" who "operates" on the victims' hearts (*WfB* 129) as "Herzspezialist" (*cardiologist*; a composite transliterated as *heart-specialist*). Coetzee appears as a very careful slow reader of Weidmann's translation and comments in the margin: "'Herzspezialist' too 20th century a term."[14] Such twentieth-century references are clearly against the grain of the historical ambiguity Coetzee has wrought into the novel, against his meticulous construction of a world that is assembled from different world referents liberated from the dominion of concrete historical data. So, *Waiting for the Barbarians* creates a no-place that is also, in part, a ubiquitous place, since it is so open to interpretation that the readers can fill (or reflect on) the gaps inherent in this world-version by lacing it with individual world-versions of their own.

Similar strategies of defamiliarization and of playing with the complexities of allegorization are at work in *The Childhood of Jesus*. The novel defamiliarizes the world of Novilla by withholding specific descriptions of what this world looks and feels like. Even more than in earlier works the reader is in the dark, in a blurred world, and she has to grope through an arcane landscape that is strange for its lack of descriptive literary worldliness. Where *Waiting for the Barbarians* lays out to the reader the physical world of the novel's uncertain place in a technique of clashing descriptions and aspects of places, the world of *The Childhood of Jesus* is a strange world from the beginning not only for unfamiliar or uncanny moments of difference between our world and the diegetic world, but more fundamentally for the sheer absence of concrete descriptions of Novilla.

If there are descriptions, they are sparse and usually overlaid with even further strangeness, as in the novel's first scenes when Simón and David have left the premises of the Centre and wait for Ana to return: "'Hush,' [Simón] says. 'Listen to the birds'. They listen to the *strange* birdsong, feel the *strange* wind on their skins" (*CoJ* 5; added emphases). The stylistic qualities of *The Childhood of Jesus* may be described by the definition of late style which Coetzee calls up in the Auster correspondence, where he refers to a "stripped-down style" (*H&N* 88),

---

[14]   HRC, container 6, folders 5–6, p. 97. Weidmann keeps the word for the published version (*Barbaren* 157). Böhnke is more careful, using simply *Arzt* (*doctor*) (*Warten* 218).

which is marked by "a simple, subdued, unornamented language" (*CoJ* 97). This makes the reader, from the very beginning, construct the world of Novilla for herself from the sparse allusions and suggestions supplied. The minimal construction of a literary world by the text paradoxically stimulates the reader's more active construction of this world.

The novel's near minimalist technique of alluding to place rather than describing it is related to poetry's condensed evocations of place in the way John in *Youth* views the distinctions between the two genres:

> There are other ways too, it appears, in which prose is not like poetry. In poetry the action can take place everywhere and nowhere: it does not matter whether the lonely wives of the fishermen live in Kalk Bay or Portugal or Maine. Prose, on the other hand, seems naggingly to demand a specific setting. (*SPL* 195)

The way *The Childhood of Jesus* sidesteps the *nagging demand of a specific setting*, one might think of it as approaching a poetic minimalism whose descriptive gaps mandate the reader continually to remain with the text in the attentive way outlined earlier, and to regard it as highly signifying as one does poetry—as well as to read it as slowly.

The novel's obstinate refusal to bow to the *nagging demand of specific setting* is particularly surprising when one considers that, upon entering this world for the first time as a reader, the focalizer Simón also enters it for the first time. So, a close description of Simón's and the reader's new surroundings would seem only natural. However, both the reader and Simón are simply confronted with strangeness. The novel is written in English and the characters speak English, but they have come to a world where Spanish is spoken and where institutions have Spanish names; we are told that Simón and David have come from a camp called Belstar (*CoJ* 2), the purpose and location of which are not explained; and that the two of them were *given* Spanish names (*CoJ* 2). What is particularly estranging is the already mentioned pastlessness one encounters from the beginning, which is emphasized further by the fact that David was not only given a name but also an age; he was assigned an age the way a foundling might be assigned an age.[15]

Because of the nature of this utopian or dystopian new world the reader might initially expect a close verisimilar description of Novilla, the way the look

---

[15] The feeling of pastlessness is indicated continually, as when we are told that Simón and David "share a birthday. That is to say, because they arrived on the same boat on the same day they have been assigned as their birth date the date of their joint arrival, their joint entry into a new life" (*CoJ* 201). See also *CoJ* 97; 106; 114; 143; 208. The sense of pastlessness is, of course, also related to the sense that the people of this world do not have parents—they have forgotten them. If parents ever constitute one's past, having no past means to have no parents—a further hint that the people of Novilla are (possibly perpetual) children.

and life of future London is laid out to the reader in *Brave New World*, or the bleakness of Oceania in *Nineteen Eighty-four*. A close description of the setting might seem all the more logical when remembering that the focalizer Simón is not only a newcomer to this world, like us, but that he also shares our ability to compare this world to other worlds. Would he not, the reader might wonder, try to make sense of this strange new world by carefully looking at it, by describing its strangeness in great detail, phenomenologically in the way the Magistrate in *Waiting for the Barbarians* describes the novelty of Joll's sunglasses in the novel's opening moments? Since Simón does not look closely, it is the reader who has to. The effect is that the reader may think this is a novel about every place, about a universal place. And yet, there lies a further paradox. The very fact that the reader thinks about this place as a universal place is a result of her filling this world's gaps with aspects from her own world and thus making the world of the novel not universal, but, in fact, highly subjective.

Such techniques are hardly singular to Coetzee's writing; they firmly accentuate modes of worldmaking at play in any reading of literary texts. It is hard to imagine a novel set in a universal space, since setting is by definition specific and does not exist in a vacuum. Universality can loom as an ideal, as a philosophical potential, but as soon as a pen touches paper or as eyes fall across a line universality is imagined away more than it is conjured up. Literary space, it seems, is unable to escape its most basic connections to the real world. Even Beckett's attempts to loose writing from corporeality and specific setting (especially in the post war trilogy) do not signal ontological universals—they do, however, point toward universality in their flattening out and defamiliarization of local and historical specifics. A novel may *feel* as though it were universal, even if it is not. Coetzee's use of very specific details of setting (such as the place and street names in *Life & Times of Michael K*) combined with the works' vague historical alliances (such as in *Waiting for the Barbarians*) gives the impression of an oeuvre signaling toward universality, or at the very least toward allegorical potentiality.

In the Lannan interview Coetzee indicates he would prefer to think of his novels in a more global way, but that one cannot write a novel set in a global space, that it has to be set somewhere (Coetzee and Sacks 2001). A novel can certainly take place in many places around the globe—like *Elizabeth Costello*— but it cannot be set in a place that is "globalness," since no place on the globe can stand metonymically for the globe in its entirety. And yet, Coetzee's novels continually demonstrate how his fiction can have the best of all worlds about this, how there can be a novel that is indeed set *somewhere* but that leaves enough of this *somewhere* uncertain so as to signal the global or the universal as a possibility. In *The Childhood of Jesus* Coetzee undermines realism and verisimilitude through a minimal description of the world we are entering with the characters, but he also undermines his previous ways of undermining realism, such as in *Waiting for the Barbarians*, for example. In *The Childhood of Jesus*, the look of this world's landscape is not even described to us negatively or unfamiliarly—it is hardly described at all. This has the paradoxical effect that the reader's desire to construct this place is heightened even more and that she may feel this place *could* be anywhere, because it could be her own.

The reader is moving as precariously through this world as the characters are, and she is estranged and confused with them, which in the reader may provoke the impetus to read slowly. It is with Simón that one moves cautiously through this uncanny space, shuffling through it as if through fog, or, to use an opposing image, through a dark room to which one's eyes adapt only gradually. In a letter to Paul Auster from November 11, 2010, Coetzee writes of descriptive gaps in his work:

> The room in which my fictional action takes place is a pretty bare place, an empty cube, in fact; I import a sofa only if it turns out to be needed (if someone is going to sit on it or look at it), and after that the dresser with the set of cutlery in the top left-hand drawer without which we cannot have the butter knife with which the heroine is going to butter her toast. (*H&N* 193)

The *bare place* of his novel's world is constructed slowly and phenomenologically during the reader's passing slowly through the chronology of the novel and through the world of Novilla, groping through fog or darkness. The setting, the place, the world emerge through their individual parts as they become significant during the reading. There is something cinematic to this way of gradually revealing the diegetic world, which does not begin with a long shot of the entire *mise-en-scène*, as a classical realist or naturalist novel might do in language, but it rather supplies us with various close-ups edited together; from the connections as much as from the gaps between them the reader then assembles the textual world. While the reader is engaged in the direct opposite of what the focalizer is engaged in (that is the construction of a world through its composite parts), the reader's experience of passing through a bare or blurry world that is strange and only disclosed slowly paradoxically mirrors the character's experience of this new world. So, the effect of the formal level on the reader mirrors the focalizer's experience at the level of the plot, but paradoxically only because the reader's way of making sense of this world is entirely different from the focalizer's. The reader tries to grasp this world in the opposite way of how Simón grasps it, namely by considering the details of the text very closely and slowly. She does this because Simón grasps this world (or fails to grasp it) by leaving vast gaps in the description of this world. The fascinating upshot of this is that Simón's and the reader's response to this world are very similar: both are estranged, albeit for very different reasons.

A large part of this world's estranging effect is to do with the complex question of this world's language. We are told that the characters have undergone language training at Belstar before coming to Novilla (*CoJ* 2). And while the characters speak English on the page, their English seems merely superimposed over the Spanish they are really speaking. This is accentuated most clearly in the novel's beginning, when Simón has to struggle to be understood or to understand, and when he attests that his Spanish is not good (*CoJ* 11). The Spanish that the characters are speaking in the diegetic world is an English that the reader is reading. Quite simply, and quite subtly, this means that whatever the reader is reading is somehow double, that there is something other even to the language of this world, and this text. At one point in the novel, Simón and David "are on the bus, heading out of the city into the countryside" (*CoJ* 66), and David begins to sing a song, a bastardized version of Goethe's poem "Erlkönig" of the same name:

> Wer reitet so spät durch Dampf und Wind?
> Er ist der Vater mit seinem Kind;
> Er halt den Knaben in dem Arm,
> Er füttert ihn Zucker, er küsst ihm warm. (*CoJ* 67)

To compare, Goethe's original goes like this:

> Wer reitet so spät durch Nacht und Wind?
> Es ist der Vater mit seinem Kind;
> Er hat den Knaben wohl in dem Arm,
> Er faßt ihn sicher, er hält ihn warm. (Goethe 2004, 248)

David's bowdlerization of the stanza is hardly alarming if we consider the child's vivid imagination and the fact that his memory may simply play a trick on him— we know, after all, that memory does not work too well in Novilla. The ballad's topic is more cause for discomfort, since it tells of a father's inability to save his son from the "Erlkönig," a mythical figure that ultimately claims the child's life. What is most estranging about this recital, however, occurs at the formal level. First of all, the typographical closeness between the two versions (Er—Es; halt—hat;

ihm—ihn) draws attention to the novel's textuality, and it suggests that what we are reading may, in fact, be a transcription or a translation of the narrative of David and Simón and the people of Novilla. This sense is further emphasized by the implied mistake of the "translator" of having somehow confused the boy with the horse of the poem, since the child is being fed sugar (*Zucker*). The translational interpretation is also highlighted by the text's insistence that what David has just sung is not German but English (*CoJ* 67).

This constitutes various forms of defamiliarizations at once. To an English-speaking reader, of course, the defamiliarization arises from the fact that what she is told is English is, in fact, not English. To a German-speaking reader who reads this in the English original, the defamiliarization is twofold, since she will share the English-speaker's sentiment; but added to this, she will find an occasion for humor in David's changes to the song. The English-speaking reader who speaks German or even the English-speaking reader who does not but knows one of Goethe's most famous poems, will share the German-speaking reader's bafflement. Each reader will experience a different sense of defamiliarization, but it seems that each reader will simply feel estranged when confronted with this palimpsestic use of languages. Through one simple moment in the text the entire diegetic world is dislocated, while it becomes even more complicated to guess David and Simón's origins. The way the characters have been washed clean of their pasts, so the text, through this converse layering of languages, erodes the characters' linguistic and geographical origins. One might surmise they could not have come from places where Spanish, English, or German are spoken. If one thinks about this more carefully, however, they may, of course, very well have come from any of these places, and that it was their passage to Novilla, their stay in the relocation camps that have purged them of their languages along with their pasts. The way languages are mixed here and cancelled out against one another, the space of Novilla and its anachronisms cancel each other out also, with the effect that the world is indefinable in any quick and conclusive way.

The strategies at play emphasize the text's mystification by suggesting that what we are reading is, in fact, a translated text, that this world is, metaphorically speaking, a *translated world* (and this despite the insistence that it is new). The issue of translation may be an implicit and internal justification of the flatness of description and of the many gaps that permeate the text, suggesting that something may, in fact, have been lost in translation. If we begin to infer that a fictive translation process has taken place before the text of *The Childhood of Jesus* has come into our hands, then the floodgates are opened for all kinds of speculations, since in a book where we are given to understand that Spanish is not Spanish, English not English and German not German, we can no longer be sure what else has been changed in the translation, what has been omitted and what has been added. If one simply entertains this as a thought experiment, even the explosive title of the text can be put into perspective. It may be the case that a fictional editor has stumbled upon this manuscript, like the narrator at the end of *Foe*, and simply given this work a name based on the plot, as Max Brod has done with so many of Kafka's works, for example.

These arguments imply that an act of translation necessarily loses something, whether meaning is lost in a literal act of literary translation, or distinct origins are lost in a metaphorical act of translating people from one place to another. Yet, one may just as well conceive of translation in the opposite way, namely as something *new*, and this might illuminate something very fundamental about Coetzee's use of defamiliarization more generally. In the essay "Imaginary Homelands" (1982) Salman Rushdie offers his own thoughts on a constructivist view of worldmaking with regard to the writing of fiction. Rushdie's essay, written from London about his childhood in Mumbai, explores the grasp on childhood memories when making fictional worlds, but it also reflects the construction of memory more generally. Here, it may help us to illustrate the reading of Coetzee's fragmentary, elusive texts, from which one may make meaning the way one does from memories that are riven with gaps. The metaphor Rushdie uses to describe the vision of the past is that of "broken mirrors, some of whose fragments have been irretrievably lost" (1992, 11). The past is shattered behind us and is constructed from the disparate fragments left and from the gaps between them. But let us take heart—Rushdie continues as follows: "[T]here is a paradox here. The broken mirror may actually be as valuable as the one which is supposedly unflawed" (1992, 11). Rushdie's most interesting statement of the essay is stored away in parentheses when he speaks about different languages adopted by the diasporic writer:

> (The word "translation" comes, etymologically, from the Latin for "bearing across". Having been borne across the world, we are translated men. It is normally supposed that something always gets lost in translation; I cling, obstinately, to the notion that something can also be gained.) (1992, 17)

Let us indeed take heart, then, and cling obstinately to the notion that something can be gained from translation by looking at *The Childhood of Jesus* as a work exploring literal and metaphorical kinds of translation. In one sense, all the citizens of Novilla are translated men and women. There are no indigenous people in this new world; they have all been borne across from one place to another, to Novilla. Our reading of the bare, fragmentary world of the novel may be thought as a form of translation itself, which adds something to the text—not at all by imposing wild interpretations, but simply by constructing, by giving our attention and our reflection to the text.

In *The Singularity of Literature* Attridge offers his own view on translation and how a work's singularity is "far from being opposed to translatability" and, in fact, "goes hand-in-hand with it" (2004b, 73). A work's singularity is increased through its translation, but a work's singularity is already also an outcome of a sense of translation behind the work as well as constitutive of a metaphorical translation with each new reading:

> The singular work is therefore not merely *available* for translation but is *constituted* in what may be thought of as an unending set of translations—for each new context in which it appears produces a further transformation. (2004b, 73; original emphases)

Attridge's view could be extended even further, since it may also be said that each literary text is not only translated by *each new context in which it* appears, but that it also translates this very context in which it appears, in the way it resonates back into the reader's own world. Gazing up from her book, the reader may willingly or unwillingly transform the real word in which she is reading, as if the reader brought to her own world the experiences from the world of the text, as if *bearing across* to her home the experiences from other places when returning from travel.

A constructivist idea of worldmaking always views worlds as being remade from other worlds and a post-structuralist idea of literature argues that every literary world is always in dialogue with other literary worlds and is, in fact, created (or translated) from other literary world-versions. So, every world, be it literary or literal, is always already a translation, and is always already a real, a right world-version. Reading as translating is a making of a world, and only if one drills holes into the text looking for its origins, for its author, for example, only then is something truly lost. Because then one must assume that literature as an act of communication always fails, since only a scrap of what an author has seen or heard or felt while writing could ever be communicated (or borne across) to the reader. If one does not, however, look for origins and looks instead to what is present, reading in as careful and attentive a way as a translator does by paying close attention to the text, then something will indeed be gained in translation, a whole world.

The Childhood of Jesus explores this idea by enrolling the reader in the construction of its world very actively. Through the myriad ways of defamiliarization, the reader is involved in the novel very deeply, and by giving the reader a world that is only hinted at, the reader becomes as integral a constructor of this world as the author and the characters. The novel's many mystifications work directly toward blurring reality, making it strange, breaking the mirror held up to nature to show the world in a very specific way. This way, the novel provokes the ethical involvement in the world of the text that I have spoken of from the beginning; it provokes a deep reflection on this world. And because this world gives a bifocal vision of a recognizable world as well as a strange world, the novel can freely explore literary and real worlds without being pigeonholed either to allegory or symbolism or to a concrete political realism and an ethical normativeness.

The slow reader who locks into the oscillation between familiarizing and defamiliarizing, the reader who reads attentively and stays with the reading in a phenomenological way, this reader may open herself to the disclosure of signification in the literary world merely through the forms of the texts, and possibly to a disclosure of the world in general through a deep engagement with a literary world. What I mean by this may be clarified first through an argument by Goodman and a related argument by Heidegger.

Goodman argues that the world appears to us, is disclosed to us, in objects and events as they appear in symbolizing works, such as works of literature. He explains a now standard conception of literature's epistemological functions when he says

> the arts must be taken no less seriously than the sciences as modes of discovery, creation, and enlargement of knowledge in the broad sense of advancement of the understanding, and thus [...] the philosophy of art should be conceived as an integral part of metaphysics and epistemology. (Goodman 1978, 102)

He continues to say:

> Works of fiction in literature and their counterparts in other arts obviously play a prominent role in worldmaking; our worlds are no more a heritage from scientists, biographers, and historians than from novelists, playwrights, and painters. (Goodman 1978, 103)

Coetzee's novels use aesthetic techniques to increase the reader's constructive possibilities and responsibilities by making her more responsive to the text. It may seem paradoxical that a person's grasp on the *epistēmē* of the world, on what can be known about the world, should be increased by a fictional engagement with the world and by supplying the reader with a world-version that is blank, bare, and strange. But the blank, the fragmentary, the defamiliarized has the potential to disclose what might otherwise go unseen. When something is not readily recognized, it demands a closer look in the hope of recognition. To grossly generalize, if there is any problem with a realist or a mimetic epistemology with regard to philosophical signification, it is this: When presented with something wholly recognizable (if such a thing exists), it does not logically follow on its own that one begins reflecting on it.

In *Being and Time* Heidegger maintains that it is the disruptions that disclose aspects of the world to us. He argues that the things of the world float past us in an unconsidered way as long as they fulfill a certain function to us, as long as they have a purpose, as long as we know what they are for. As long as things run smoothly, we do not consider them, we use them, then go about our business. We take a pen to write a sentence, when the sentence has been written, we put the pen away, perhaps without knowing what color the pen was, what it felt like in our hands, sometimes not even what color the ink was—sometimes not even what has been written. But let us say we have only this one pen and the urge to write is strong, but upon putting pen to paper, the pen does not work and we do not understand why. We might shake the pen, we might unscrew it to see if it is out of ink, we might become frustrated with it, knock it against the table, and so on. While we are doing this (and if we do not simply throw it away), we are no longer indifferent to it, we have begun regarding it slowly and meditatively. Even if only for a very short moment, this insignificant pen has become significant to us, it has become conspicuous because it has lost its purpose. Heidegger explains this: "When we discover [a thing's] unusability, the thing becomes conspicuous" ([1927] 2010, 72). Heidegger's terminology is notoriously difficult, as he continues to claim that "[c]onspicuousness presents the thing at hand in a certain unhandiness" ([1927] 2010, 72; original emphasis), but what this merely illuminates is that the distorted, the defamiliarized, the unrecognizable, the exceptional that is not immediately grasped or known, is what jumpstarts reflection. "When we notice [a thing's] unhandiness, what is at hand enters the mode of *obtrusiveness*" ([1927] 2010, 73; original emphasis). *Obtrusive* here simply means that something becomes noticeable in such a way that it cannot be disregarded. World is disclosed to us in moments of discord, in moments of uncanniness and defamiliarization. Through moments of disruption, moments of confusion, "we [...] have the possibility of catching sight of [the phenomena of the world]" ([1927] 2010, 73). The world's phenomena are disclosed to us when something goes wrong, when something does *not* make sense, when the fragmentary parts of a phenomenon do *not* add up.

> Something is unusable. This means that the constitutive reference of the in-order-to to a what-for has been disrupted. [...] [I]n a *disruption of reference*—in being unusable for ...—the reference becomes explicit. ([1927] 2010, 74; original emphasis)

Heidegger's complicated language contains a very simple idea, but the estranging language is, of course, part of the point he is making, since Heidegger's style is itself a form of defamiliarization whose objective is to activate reflection. Heidegger's paradoxical argument that it is disruption, discord, defamiliarization which disclose what they ostensibly do not disclose in a recognizable way is to do with the fundamental importance of reflection and thinking to Heidegger's project. As Maurice Merleau-Ponty has said, "Heidegger wants to reflect on the unreflected" (1964, 134).

Reflecting on the unreflected, examining the unexamined, and imagining the unimaginable are fundamental aspects of Coetzee's ways of worldmaking, of Coetzee's worlds. His works disclose worlds by making them strange, by obscuring our view onto their worlds. They force us to look closer, to involve ourselves more slowly, and always to take a step toward the text when the text seems to make us take a step back.

When All Else Fails, Philosophize.
A Failing, Philosophizing Conclusion

A letter arrives at the Swedish Academy in Stockholm in the early days of October 2003. The letter was sent from the University of Chicago, where J. M. Coetzee was teaching during an "annual three-month stint" (Kannemeyer 2012, 553). A few days earlier Coetzee, having just been made the recipient of the 2003 Nobel Prize in literature, was invited by the Permanent Secretary of the Swedish Academy, Horace Engdahl, to give the Nobel Lecture during the awards proceedings in December of that year. Engdahl asked Coetzee for the text of the lecture by mid-November. Coetzee's letter to Engdahl, most likely sent on October 7, 2003,[1] is written with expected aplomb. It is quoted here in full:

> Dear Mr Engdahl,
>
> Thank you for your letter of 2 October.
>
> My partner and I are happy to accept your invitation to dinner on 7 December.
>
> I am somewhat alarmed by the deadline of 17 November for submission of the text of my lecture. I am not sure I can meet it. I do not normally write in a rushed manner.
>
> > Yours sincerely,
> > John Coetzee[2]

And indeed, he does *not normally write in a rushed manner*. Coetzee's archival materials, the many drafts of *Disgrace* or the hovering over the right form of *Life & Times of Michael K*, confirm how Coetzee has described his writing process in the very short essay "Thematizing" in 1993:

> As I reflect on the process of writing and ask myself how themes enter that process, it seems to me that a certain back-and-forth motion takes place. First you give yourself to (or throw yourself into) the writing, and go where it takes

---

[1] HRC, container 90, folder 3, n.p. The letter, typed on a word-processor, is undated, but features the date "?7/10/2003" written in pencil in Coetzee's hand.

[2] HRC, container 90, folder 3, n.p.

you. Then you step back and ask yourself where you are, whether you really want to be there. This interrogation entails conceptualizing, and specifically thematizing what you have written (or what has been written out of you). (*T* 289)

Coetzee describes writing as a slow process, a steady *back-and-forth motion*, and he intimates a phenomenological contemplation by *stepping back* and reflecting on what is there, as his many drafts and notebooks show. He slowly explores an idea, begins to mold and modulate it, until it gradually crystallizes into a work which is itself characterized by a *back-and-forth motion*. His works let his characters tarry in uncertain situations and existences, and the works spark in the reader a similar sense of tarrying, of vibrating between an advance toward the text, a *throwing oneself into the writing*, and a retreat from the text, an inquiring *stepping back*. This study has explored how Coetzee's highly elusive as well as highly allusive works create these two antipodes in the act of reading, between familiarizing and defamiliarizing, and how this fluctuation gives rise to a productive slowness in reading.

Slowness, it seems, is at the heart of Coetzee's aesthetic project. It is central to the exploration of being, reason, ethics, and epistemology in his singularly reflexive works of fiction and memoir. Slowness makes of Coetzee's works a philosophical oeuvre. During moments when his characters are slowed down, their thinking becomes meditative, inquisitive, and roaming freely into philosophical terrain, as when Michael K is lying in his burrow and thinking about his life, his times, and "[o]nce or twice" about "the other time in which the war had its existence" (*K* 115f.). Many times, such meditative thinking in Coetzee is the upshot of a preceding crisis, an impasse, a moment of stasis that the characters have been maneuvered into; a more purely instrumental thinking is interrupted and suspended in moments where philosophical reflection becomes possible. When the Magistrate sees mirrored, in the suffering inflicted on the "barbarian" girl, his shameful alliance with the Empire, his thinking is shaken out of his habitual rut and his *unexamined life* changes direction. Martin Woessner interprets the inner workings of the Magistrate as follows:

[His] moral awakening [...] does not come quickly, but it would be incorrect to say that it is the product of slow and careful deliberation. There is no moral balance sheet to be drawn up, discussed, and debated. (2010, 23)

Woessner's choice of words must be looked at more carefully here, since the Magistrate's moral awakening certainly occurs slowly, as he goes back and forth from uncertainty to uncertainty on how to proceed, how to respond to what is plainly before his eyes. It is important to appreciate, however, that this moral awakening is not *deliberate* or in any way *calculated*; it slowly spreads in his mind in those slow moments when he is with the girl, washing her, waiting with her, being with her. The reflection Coetzee's characters engage in is a response to a suddenly altered world, and their thinking becomes an alternative, or other, way of looking at the world's phenomena, a slow reading of the world. Confronted with something in their lives that is profoundly new, fundamentally strange, an elemental rupture—Mrs. Curren's terminal illness, Paul Rayment's amputation, the unvarying world of Novilla—many of Coetzee's characters are stopped in their tracks of habitual or traditional thinking and compelled to seek different ways of addressing the phenomena surrounding them. It is then that they become philosophical. In *Disgrace* Lucy essentially anticipates this alteration of thinking in both her own and her father's lives shortly before the attack on them, and she says: "When all else fails, philosophize" (*Dis* 60).

In the grip of physical immobility or frozen in the face of a fractured worldview—shocked like the steenbok the men of the Voëlfontein farm hunt during the night by blinding it with the headlights of their Studebaker (*SPL* 75)—Coetzee's characters have no choice but to get themselves out of their ontological corners by thinking. *When all else fails, philosophize*—Coetzee's works explore how sometimes philosophizing is the last hope for damage control. Thus, topical slowness is often used to hold characters in existential dead ends where contemplation and reflection become ethical or ontological necessities, and where more engaged vantage points on the world's phenomena may be explored through the focalizers. What many times begins as moments of stasis becomes, through the process of meditative reflection, through tarrying, transformed into a thinking against instrumentality, against stasis, against the dead ends from where such thinking often takes its starting point. In the process Coetzee's characters become considerate, at times more caring of those in whose circle they move, whether human or non-human, as when Paul Rayment feels the urge to support the Jokićs, or when David Lurie begins his ethically complex engagement with the dogs at Bev Shaw's animal welfare clinic.

The key moment to illustrate this change toward a more meditative thinking is the aforementioned "signal event" (*SPL* 242) in *Youth*, when John has an experience on the Heath in London which he describes as a "moment of ecstatic unity with the All" (*SPL* 242). This is as transcendental as Coetzee's language becomes throughout the oeuvre, though it is less significant for a metaphysical consideration of the character John as it is helpful to illustrate what it highlights in the narrative of the memoir and the narrative of John's youth. The preceding two-thirds of the text see him following and failing to reach one goal, to become a poet. This is why he came to London, "to the great dark city to be tested and transformed" (*SPL* 242). The *signal event* in the "garden" of Hampstead Heath does transform him, it allows him a different view on his life, a view that is defined by the little word *ecstatic*, carrying within it as it does the simultaneity of "frenzy and stupor" (OED), the paradoxical being oneself while being outside oneself, of closeness and distance. In Coetzee's John this moment comes about when his obsessive self-absorption gives way, for a moment, to an openness that occurs when "he sinks into a sleep or half-sleep in which consciousness does not vanish but continues to hover" (*SPL* 242).

This moment has an analogue in Coetzee, and here one may speak both of his literary corpus and his autobiography. In his lecture "What is a Classic?" Coetzee describes a similar moment as "a revelation in the garden" (*StS* 8), where in a moment of standing still an unexpected openness occurs that allows the receiving subject to be utterly transformed, this time not by being in an *ecstatic unity with the all*, but being touched by a work of art. Coetzee is fully aware that "following an autobiographical path may be methodologically reckless" (*StS* 8), but he writes:

> One Sunday afternoon in the summer of 1955, when I was fifteen years old, I was mooning around our back garden in the suburbs of Cape Town, wondering what to do, boredom being the main problem of existence in those days, when from the house next door I heard music. As long as the music lasted, I was frozen, I dared not breathe. I was being spoken to by the music as music had never spoken to me. (*StS* 8)

Coetzee shares this moment of being touched to engage with the question posed by the title of his lecture. He follows this *autobiographical path* because of its "virtue of dramatizing the issue" (*StS* 8), namely why one is touched by an artwork, how such a touching occurs, and what it says about oneself and about the work of art (*StS* 15).

I follow an autobiographical path—as aware as Coetzee was about his own that it may be methodologically reckless—to describe my reading experience of Coetzee as one of being touched in a very similar way. My readings of Coetzee's works continue to be shaped by moments of rapture as well as moments of rupture. Reading his novels and memoirs, even his criticism, his many essays on literature, I am forced to pause over a turn of phrase, over an expression, over individual words. I have to put the book down to contemplate and let go of automatized hermeneutic processes that allow me comfortably to say what a work, a scene, even a single image *means*. Whatever I make of a work by Coetzee, whichever philosophical idea I find contained in it or resonating with it, whatever signification I glean from the work—I have to read slowly.

I leave behind now autobiographical paths—Coetzee's and my own—to recall the guiding impetus behind this study, which was to investigate the complex field of those techniques of Coetzee's work which have the effect of slowing down the act of reading. Such an investigation is inherently complex itself, because it pushes one to the precipice of paradox. How can one give answers about an oeuvre that is so very often decidedly shaped by the absence or the seeming impossibility of direct answers? In the encountering of Coetzee's elusive work, one may well be reminded of a sentiment Joseph Conrad voiced about Henry James, namely that "[t]he critical faculty hesitates before the magnitude of Henry James's work" (1949, 11). Nevertheless, this study has aimed at giving answers to why one's critical faculties *hesitate* before Coetzee's works also. It has explored the questions, *how does Coetzee's work slow down the reading process*, and *how does a slow reading experience heighten the sense in which Coetzee's work may be called philosophical?* To answer these intricate and interwoven questions, this study has set up a theoretical framework that enabled the detailed description of the formal techniques at work to deautomatize the interpretive process. In doing so, this study has itself avoided falling victim to instrumental readings, that is to detecting conclusive meanings which the oeuvre seems to challenge continuously. By building on reader-response theories, phenomenological and deconstructivist trends in Coetzee studies and in literary theory more generally, this study has explored the ways in which a slow reading experience shapes the philosophical character of Coetzee's oeuvre. What is slow about Coetzee's form, and what is philosophical about slow form?

In trying to elucidate these questions I have challenged readings of Coetzee's works which limit their grasp of the texts to distinctly topical, and especially ethical, concepts negotiated therein. While such matters are undoubtedly crucial to Coetzee's work—as this study regularly substantiates—a reading of exclusively ethical topics is in danger of becoming an unethical reading by being reductive about the texts' inquiry into matters aesthetic, epistemological, ontological, or even metaphysical. Moreover, such a reading is in danger of drifting back into a simplistic liberal humanist ethos of interpreting literature for its pragmatic moral functions.

The present study is not a "correction" of these trends, nor does it posit that there is anything wrong in pursuing them. Instead, it reflects on the ways in which Coetzee's work allows for a vast variety and heterogeneity of different and conflicting readings as well as similarly variegated ideas expressed or represented therein. Slow reading tolerates and, in fact, incites an estranging flux of different readings to occur simultaneously or in a cyclical way. This way, slow reading responds to the otherness inherent in a literary text and it allows this otherness to resonate productively rather than ironing it out or shoehorning it into habitual language or thinking.

Reading back through Coetzee's oeuvre from the vantage point of his latest work to date, many thoughts about the philosophical dimensions of his work have become clearer. In *The Childhood of Jesus*, philosophy is explicitly mocked as being too imperious, too abstract, too inducing of impatience. And yet, the characters are philosophizing constantly (and perhaps failing in doing so). By staging philosophizing on the docks or in the home in such a way, the novel normalizes it in a way that mirrors Cicero's verdict on Socrates, namely that he "called philosophy down from heaven, and gave it a place in cities, and introduced it even into men's homes" (1886, 257). But this statement is itself a bit too lofty and needs to be qualified by pointing out that Coetzee does not merely have his characters engage in philosophical discussions in the way that popular philosophical fiction does, that is explicitly (and therefore at best directly and at worst crudely). Rather, Coetzee's work normalizes philosophizing by bringing the reader into the elenctic agora through the various oscillations between familiarizing and defamiliarizing described earlier, through the fundamental ambiguity of his writing. This ambiguity demands of the reader to tolerate uncertainty and thus to consider which position the novel takes on philosophical questions. This goes so far that the reader is at times uncertain even if philosophizing is to be taken seriously, or if it has lost its relevance. The reader who responds to what the work indicates in this way, the reader who asks, maybe flippantly, whether philosophy has lost its significance or whether a different kind of thinking is possible—that reader who is made skeptical of philosophizing is engaging with a fundamental philosophical problem, namely the place of philosophy in the text and of philosophy and literature in the world.

To read slowly has proven productive to highlight these philosophical qualities of Coetzee's work as being entirely independent from referring to philosophy or philosophers explicitly and possibly crudely. It is hoped that none of the philosophical questions have been resolved in an instrumental way and that my philosophizing has productively failed, so that, since all has failed, philosophizing is, in turn, provoked by the (perhaps: slow) reader of this study.

The slow reading that has been developed in this study is built on the meditative responses which J. M. Coetzee's writings engender. Such a focus on one highly idiosyncratic author's oeuvre, then, brings up the question of method more generally. Is this reading method specific to Coetzee? Is the method useful for other works of literature that deal with slowness topically? Can it be adapted to other, maybe all, literary texts? Or are there literary works whose forms, whose styles generate similar responses and therefore permit productive slow readings? The answers to all of these questions include some variety of *Yes*.

Yes, the method is specific to Coetzee, but this does not mean that a version of slow reading, that a similar kind of *mind-frame* may not be useful more generally. *Yes*, the method is certainly receptive to topical slowness. As Attridge has once aptly put it, "the literary text in part constitutes its reader" (1992, 17). One does not revitalize thematic criticism by responding to a work's topical slowness and performing a slow reading of the text, which will also inquire into the formal characteristics of a work and see which responses and reflections are wrought by the text. For example, the method would be very useful for a reading of Olive Schreiner's *The Story of an African Farm*, not least because of the very different idle ways of Em and Lyndall's childhood and the detrimental and domineering slothfulness of Bonaparte Blenkins. A slow reading that sets out from the thematic representations of slowness in this work would necessarily interrogate the work's engagement (and challenging) of an idealized pastoralism in the context of colonized South Africa, and how this is expressed in the interplay of content, context, and form.[3] *Yes*, the method might be adapted to all literary texts, even if it is most receptive and most productive regarding texts that play up the poetic functions of their language in more complex ways than others.

The ultimate test for slow reading's productivity might have to be one that engages with a text whose form is ostensibly less complex and less receptive to reflection than the works of William Faulkner, Marcel Proust, or Virginia Woolf. These examples lead to a last *Yes*: There are certainly writers and writings more receptive to slow reading than others, and this might have most to do with the way they engage with or depart from realism. The formal, topical, and historical complexities, as well as the complexities of ideas and of ideology, concentrated in modernist, late modernist, and postmodernist literature are most receptive to slow reading, since the way the aforementioned characteristics are entangled in the works create a sense of productive perplexity in the act of reading. While one could defend the view that there is a sense of otherness to all literary texts, the writings of Kafka or Beckett, for example, seem fundamentally estranging and seem to solicit slow responses.

---

[3] Coetzee's *White Writing* deals with this across the various essays, though "Farm Novel and Plaasroman" explores the "antipastoral" of Schreiner's novel particularly.

An illustration of the reasons behind this can be found in Adorno's aforementioned notions about a politically "uncommitted" writing, since this kind of writing affords "experiences" rather than giving "explications":

> Kafka's prose and Beckett's plays and his genuinely colossal novel *The Unnamable* have an effect in comparison to which official works of committed art look like children's games—they arouse the anxiety that existentialism only talks about. ([1963] 1992, 90)

Though Adorno's quarrel here is with a Sartrian political commitment in art, something quite similar is the case with the philosophical dimensions of literary works. The reason why Kafka's or Beckett's texts remain so receptive to vastly different philosophical readings is that they do not wear their ideas on their sleeves. They do not postulate philosophical dogma, but contain philosophy as subsumed in their form; they dramatize philosophical problems and ideas aesthetically. As Adorno writes: "The substance of works is not the spirit that was pumped into them; if anything, it is the opposite" ([1963] 1992, 93). It is in the way these works of a (late) modernist tradition seem often to elude direct political as well as philosophical themes that they are most receptive to reflections about the positions they take to these and how both politics and philosophy may be directly there on the surface of a text, but in a different way than when a work of literature features a character marching along in a demonstration or when two characters discuss metaphysics over coffee.

These Adornian ideas are not only relevant when considering texts from an academic point of view, but they also influence one's possibly more primary engagement with literature as an encounter of excitement and joy. There is a delight in experiencing something that "is communicated in the shock of the unintelligible" ([1963] 1992, 79). And there is a delight in the encounter with a work of literature in a slow way because it allows the reader the time to have a lingering, gradually unfolding experience in the first place. To contemplate that one is in the company of something wholly singular, something other, and reflecting on what it means to be touched by a text, what it means to take the cue from a literary construct and suddenly reflect on one's position in a text, and one's place in the world—all of this does not occur lightly or suddenly. To be touched by a work of art, one cannot be on the run from it.

When talking about speed reading in an interview, William H. Gass reflects on Henry James:

> James [...] has to be played in the head. He becomes immediately clear for one thing ... marvellously resonant ... but who's going to sit down and really do

that? So we start to speed up and move a little faster. But that's like speeding up Mozart. [...] You get to the end faster, but you really never quite hear the music. And the music is [a] major part of it. (Gass and Swaim 1985)

The *music is a major part* of slow reading as well, as slow reading not only allows a highly productive academic engagement with texts, but enables the reader to tune into the text in an almost childish sense of being awed and estranged when touched by something singular, a sense that Coetzee fittingly crystallizes in the Augustinian moment in the garden when listening to Bach, which he describes as an event of "stunned overwhelmedness" (*StS* 12).

Stunned overwhelmedness can be enabled and prolonged by slowing down and listening to the music of the words, by playing the words in one's head. And both the academic and the general reader can take delight in a literary encounter which is reminiscent of a moment in Beckett's *Molloy*. In another, though much quieter, much slower, revelation in the garden, when the protagonist has returned to his beehives after a long journey, while he is standing before a dried out honeycomb, he remarks: "Here is something I can study all my life, and never understand" ([1955] 2009, 177). It is this sentiment which sustains the slow philosophy of J. M. Coetzee.

Bibliography

Works by J. M. Coetzee

Auster, Paul and J. M. Coetzee (2013), *Here and Now*, New York, NY: Viking Penguin.

Coetzee, J. M. (1984), *Truth in Autobiography*, Cape Town: University of Cape Town.

Coetzee, J. M. (1984), *Warten auf die Barbaren*, trans. Brigitte Weidmann, Berlin: Karl H. Henssel Verlag.

Coetzee, J. M. ([1983] 1985), *Life & Times of Michael K*, London: Penguin.

Coetzee, J. M. (1986), *Foe*, London: Penguin.

Coetzee, J. M. (1988), "The Novel Today," *Upstream*, 6 (1): 2–5.

Coetzee, J. M. (1988), *White Writing: On the Culture of Letters in South Africa*, New Haven, CT/London: Yale University Press.

Coetzee, J. M. (1990), *Age of Iron*, London: Penguin.

Coetzee, J. M. (1992), *Doubling the Point: Essays and Interviews*, ed. David Attwell, Cambridge, MA/London: Harvard University Press.

Coetzee, J. M. (1993), "Homage," *The Threepenny Review*, 53: 5–7.

Coetzee, J. M. (1993), "Thematizing," in Werner Sollors (ed.), *The Return of Thematic Criticism*, 289, Cambridge, MA/London: Harvard University Press.

Coetzee, J. M. (1996), *Giving Offense*, Chicago, IL/London: The University of Chicago Press.

Coetzee, J. M. ([1947] 1998), *Dusklands*, London: Vintage.

Coetzee, J. M. (1999), *Disgrace*, London: Vintage.

Coetzee, J. M. ([1977] 1999), *In the Heart of the Country*, London: Vintage.

Coetzee, J. M. (1999), *The Lives of Animals*, ed. Amy Gutmann, Princeton, NJ: Princeton University Press.

Coetzee, J. M. (2001), *Stranger Shores: Literary Essays*, London: Penguin.

Coetzee, J. M. (2002), *Warten auf die Barbaren*, trans. Reinhild Böhnke, Frankfurt am Main: Fischer Verlag.

Coetzee, J. M. (2003), *He and His Man: The Nobel Lecture in Literature, 2003*, London: Penguin.

Coetzee, J. M. ([2003] 2004), *Elizabeth Costello: Eight Lessons*, London: Vintage.

Coetzee, J. M. ([1994] 2004), *The Master of Petersburg*, London: Vintage.

Coetzee, J. M. ([1980] 2004), *Waiting for the Barbarians*, London: Vintage.

Coetzee, J. M. (2006), *L'homme ralenti*, trans. Catherine Lauga du Plessis, Paris: Éditions du Seuil.

Coetzee, J. M. ([2005] 2006), *Slow Man*, London: Vintage.

Coetzee, J. M. (2007), *Diary of a Bad Year*, London: Harvill Secker.

Coetzee, J. M. (2007), *Inner Workings: Literary Essays 2000–2005*, New York, NY: Viking Penguin.

Coetzee, J. M. (2008), "Eight Ways of Looking at Samuel Beckett," in Minako Okamuro, et al. (eds), *Borderless Beckett/Beckett Sans Frontières*, 19–31, Amsterdam/New York, NY: Rodopi.

Coetzee, J. M. (2011), *Scenes from Provincial Life: Boyhood, Youth, Summertime*, London: Penguin.

Coetzee, J. M. (2013), *The Childhood of Jesus*, London: Harvill Secker.

Coetzee, J. M. (2013), "JM Coetzee visits UCT to read from his new work" [Online video clip], *University of Cape Town South Africa*, *YouTube*, 5 February. Available online: https://www.youtube.com/watch?v=yXufoko-HgM (accessed September 1, 2015).

Coetzee, J. M. (2014), *Two Screenplays*, ed. Hermann Wittenberg, Cape Town: UCT Press.

De Bruyckere, Berlinde and J. M. Coetzee (2013), *Cripplewood/Kreupelhout*, Brussels and New Haven, CT/London: Mercatorfonds and Yale University Press.

Kurtz, Arabella and J. M. Coetzee (2015), *The Good Story: Exchanges on Truth, Fiction and Psychoanalytic Psychotherapy*, London: Harvill Secker.

Interviews with J. M. Coetzee

Coetzee, J. M. and David Attwell (2003), "An Exclusive Interview with J. M. Coetzee," *Kultur & Nöje*, 8 December. Available online: http://www.dn.se/kultur-noje/an -exclusive-interview-with-j-m-coetzee%5C (accessed September 1, 2015).

Coetzee, J. M. and Richard Begam (1992), "An Interview with J. M. Coetzee," *Contemporary Literature*, 33 (3): 419–431.

Coetzee, J. M. and Avril Herber (1979), "J. M. Coetzee," in *Conversations: Some People, Some Place, Some Time, South Africa*, 174–176, Johannesburg: Bateleur Press.

Coetzee, J. M. and Wim Kayzer (2000), "J. M. Coetzee," in *Van de schoonheid en de troost*, Hilversum: VPRO.

Coetzee, J. M. and Jane Poyner (2006), "J. M. Coetzee in Conversation with Jane Poyner," in *J. M. Coetzee and the Idea of the Public Intellectual*, 21–24, Athens, OH: Ohio University Press.

Coetzee, J. M. and Peter Sacks (2001), "Conversation" [Online video clip], *The Lannan Foundation*, 8 November. Available online: http://podcast.lannan.org/2010/06/28/j -m-coetzee-with-peter-sacks-conversation-8-november-2001-video (accessed September 1, 2015).

Coetzee, J. M. and Joanna Scott (1997), "An Interview with J. M. Coetzee," *Salmagundi*, 114/115: 82–102.

Coetzee, J. M. and André Viola (1992), "An Interview with J. M. Coetzee," *Commonwealth Essays and Studies*, 14 (2): 6.

Coetzee, J. M. and Stephen Watson (1978), "Speaking: J. M. Coetzee," *Speak*, 1 (3): 21–24.

Coetzee, J. M. and World Literature Today (1996), "An Interview with J. M. Coetzee," *World Literature Today*, 70 (1): 107–110.

Archival material

J. M. Coetzee Papers. The Harry Ransom Center, the University of Texas at Austin, TX. All material was accessed from February to April 2013. All archival material © J. M. Coetzee.

Container 1, folder 1. Long Works, 1960s–2012. Dusklands (Fiction, 1974). "Lies," handwritten draft with revisions and notes, June 11, 1972–February 13, 1973.

Container 5, folder 1. Long Works, 1960s–2012. Waiting for the Barbarians (Fiction, 1980). Early handwritten drafts, September 20, 1977–March 26, 1978.

Container 5, folder 2. Long Works, 1960s–2012. Waiting for the Barbarians (Fiction, 1980). Handwritten draft, "Version G," April 28, 1977–October 29, 1978.

Container 5, folder 3. Long Works, 1960s–2012. Waiting for the Barbarians (Fiction, 1980). Handwritten draft, "Version H," November 1, 1978–June 1, 1979.

Container 6, folder 1. Long Works, 1960s–2012. Waiting for the Barbarians (Fiction, 1980). Photocopy typed draft, "Versions J–K," chapters 1–3, with revisions, June 1–30, 1979.

Container 6, folders 5–6. Long Works, 1960s–2012. Waiting for the Barbarians (Fiction, 1980). German translation, photocopy typed draft, circa 1984.

Container 7, folder 1. Long Works, 1960s–2012. Life & Times of Michael K (Fiction, 1983). "Versions 1–4," handwritten draft with revisions, May 31, 1980–January 14, 1981.

Container 27, folder 1, Long works, 1960s–2012. Boyhood (Fictionalized autobiography, 1997). "Scenes from Provincial Life," early handwritten draft, 20 March–June 12, 1987.

Container 33, folder 3. Long Works, 1960s–2012. Waiting for the Barbarians (Fiction, 1980). Small spiral notebook, July 11, 1977–August 28, 1978.

Container 33, folder 3. Long Works, 1960s–2012. In the Heart of the Country (Fiction, 1977). Small notebook, March 16, 1974–February 9, 1976.

Container 33, folder 5. Long Works, 1960s–2012. Life & Times of Michael K (Fiction, 1983). Gray casebound notebook, includes notes on other subjects, 1972–1982.

Container 33, folder 6. Long Works, 1960s–2012. Foe (Fiction, 1986). Green casebound notebook with gilt edges, 1982–1985.

Container 35, folders 4–5. Long Works, 1960s–2012. Disgrace (Fiction, 1999). Handwritten early draft with extensive revisions, August 19, 1995–April 2, 1996.

Container 35, folder 6. Long Works, 1960s–2012. Disgrace (Fiction, 1999). "Version 1," with revisions, 3 April May 21, 1996.

Container 35, folder 7. Long Works, 1960s–2012. Disgrace (Fiction, 1999). "Version 2," with revisions, 21 May–September 1996.

Container 35, folder 8. Long Works, 1960s–2012. Disgrace (Fiction, 1999). "Version 3," with revisions, September 7, 1996–January 31, 1997.

Container 36, folder 1. Long Works, 1960s–2012. Disgrace (Fiction, 1999). "Version 4," with revisions, 31 January–February 4, 1997.

Container 36, folder 2. Long Works, 1960s–2012. Disgrace (Fiction, 1999). "Version 5," with revisions, March–July 1997.

Container 36, folder 3. Long Works, 1960s–2012. Disgrace (Fiction, 1999). "Version 6," with notes, fragments, and revisions, March–July 1997.

Container 36, folder 4. Long Works, 1960s–2012. Disgrace (Fiction, 1999). "Version 7," with notes, fragments, and revisions, March–July 1997.

Container 36, folder 5. Long Works, 1960s–2012. Disgrace (Fiction, 1999). "Version 8," with notes, fragments, and revisions, September 1997–January 1998.

Container 36, folder 6. Long Works, 1960s–2012. Disgrace (Fiction, 1999). "Version 9," with notes, fragments, and revisions, September 1997–January 1998.

Container 36, folder 7. Long Works, 1960s–2012. Disgrace (Fiction, 1999). "Version 10," with notes, fragments, and revisions, 4 September–March 23, 1998.

Container 37, folder 1. Long Works, 1960s–2012. Disgrace (Fiction, 1999). "Version 11," with notes, fragments, and revisions, 3 April–April 30, 1998.

Container 37, folder 2. Long Works, 1960s–2012. Disgrace (Fiction, 1999). "Version 12," with notes, fragments, corrections, and comments, 30 April–June 27, 1998.

Container 37, folder 3. Long Works, 1960s–2012. Disgrace (Fiction, 1999). "Version 13," with notes and revisions, 4 June–July 22, 1998.

Container 37, folder 4. Long Works, 1960s–2012. Disgrace (Fiction, 1999). "Version 14," with notes and revisions, July 1998.

Container 37, folder 5. Long Works, 1960s–2012. Disgrace (Fiction, 1999). "Versions 15–16," with notes and light revisions, July–August 1998.

Container 37, folder 6. Long Works, 1960s–2012. Disgrace (Fiction, 1999). "Versions 17," with revisions, February–March 1999.

Container 45, folder 1. Long Works, 1960s–2012. Youth (Fictionalized autobiography, 2002). Handwritten draft 1 with printout notes and fragments, October 11, 1996–December 28, 1998.

Container 69, folders 1–4. Business Correspondence, 1969–2006. February 1969–June 1981.

Container 90, folder 3. Business correspondence, 1969–2006. July 2003–February 2004.

Container 94, folder 10. Research materials, circa 1960s–2009. Caws–Crusoe, 1949–1995.

Container 97, folder 4. Research materials, circa 1960s–2009. Sokel–Szasz, 1925–2002.

Further works cited

Aaltola, Elisa (2010), "Coetzee and Alternative Animal Ethics," in Anton Leist and Peter Singer (eds), *J. M. Coetzee and Ethics: Philosophical Perspectives on Literature*, 119–144, New York, NY: Columbia University Press.

Ackerley, Chris (2011), "Style: Coetzee and Beckett," in Tim Mehigan (ed.), *A Companion to the Works of J. M. Coetzee*, 23–38, Rochester, NY: Camden House.

Adorno, Theodor W. ([1963] 1992), *Notes to Literature, Volume II*, trans. Shierry Weber Nicholsen, ed. Rolf Tiedemann, New York, NY: Columbia University Press.

Aristotle (1986), *De Anima (On the Soul)*, trans. Hugh Lawson-Tancred, London: Penguin.

Attridge, Derek (1992), "Introduction," in Derek Attridge (ed.), *Jacques Derrida, Acts of Literature*, 1–29, New York, NY/London: Routledge.

Attridge, Derek (2004a), *J. M. Coetzee and the Ethics of Reading: Literature in the Event*, Chicago, IL: The University of Chicago Press.

Attridge, Derek (2004b), *The Singularity of Literature*, London: Routledge.

Attridge, Derek (2009), "Sex, Comedy and Influence: Coetzee's Beckett," in Elleke Boehmer, Katy Iddiols, and Robert Eaglestone (eds), *J. M. Coetzee in Context and Theory*, 71–90, London/New York, NY: Continuum.

Attwell, David (1993), *J. M. Coetzee: South Africa and the Politics of Writing*, Berkeley, CA: University of California Press.

Attwell, David (1998), "'Dialogue' and 'fulfilment' in J. M. Coetzee's *Age of Iron*," in Derek Attridge and Rosemary Jolly (eds), *Writing South Africa: Literature, Apartheid, and Democracy, 1970–1995*, 166–179, Cambridge: Cambridge University Press.

Attwell, David (2006), "The Life and Times of Elizabeth Costello," in Jane Poyner (ed.), *J. M. Coetzee and the Idea of the Public Intellectual*, 25–41, Athens, OH: Ohio University Press.

Attwell, David (2013), "The Shot Tower: History, *Autre*-Biography and Madness in *The Master of Petersburg*," in Susanna Zinato and Assalisa Pes (eds), *Ex-centric Writing: Essays on Madness in Postcolonial Fiction*, 25–42, Newcastle upon Tyne: Cambridge Scholars Press.

Attwell, David (2015), *J. M. Coetzee & the Life of Writing: Face to Face with Time*, Oxford: Oxford University Press.

Ayer, A. J. (1999), "The Method of Philosophy," in Nigel Warburton (ed.), *Philosophy: Basic Readings*, 9–11, London: Routledge.

Bakhtin, Mikhail ([1975] 1981), *The Dialogic Imagination*, tans. Caryl Emerson and Michael Holquist, ed. Michael Holquist, Austin, TX: University of Texas Press.

Bakhtin, Mikhail ([1929] 1984), *Problems of Dostoevsky's Poetics*, trans. ed. Caryl Emerson, Minneapolis, MN/London: University of Minnesota Press.

Barnard, Rita (2003), "J. M. Coetzee's 'Disgrace' and the South African Pastoral," *Contemporary Literature*, 44 (2): 199–224.

Beckett, Samuel ([1930] 1965), *Proust and Three Dialogues with Georges Duthuit*, London: John Calder.

Beckett, Samuel ([1955] 2009), *Molloy*, ed. Shane Weller, London: Faber.

Beckett, Samuel ([1956] 2010), *Malone Dies*, ed. Peter Boxall, London: Faber.

Beckett, Samuel ([1958] 2010), *The Unnamable*, ed. Steven Connor, London: Faber.

Benn, Gottfried (1987), *Prose Essays Poems*, trans. E. B. Ashton, et al., ed. Volkmar Sander, New York, NY: Continuum.

Best, Stephen and Sharon Marcus (2009), "Surface Reading: An Introduction," *Representations*, 108 (1): 1–21.

Blackburn, Simon (1999), *Think: A Compelling Introduction to Philosophy*, Oxford: Oxford University Press.

Blanchot, Maurice ([1949] 1995), *The Work of Fire*, trans. Charlotte Mandell and Lydia Davis, Stanford, CA: Stanford University Press.

Blanchot, Maurice (2001), *Friendship*, trans. Elizabeth Rottenberg, Stanford, CA: Stanford University Press.

Bradshaw, Graham (2010), "Introduction: After 'Disgrace': Lord and Lady Chandos in Cape Town and Adelaide," in Graham Bradshaw and Michael Neill (eds), *J. M. Coetzee's Austerities*, 1–24, Farnham: Ashgate.

Brouillette, Sarah (2007), *Postcolonial Writers and the Global Literary Marketplace*, New York, NY: Palgrave.

Bryden, Mary (2004), "Beckett and the Dynamic Still," *Samuel Beckett Today/Aujourd'hui*, 14 (1): 179–192.

Burton, Robert (1838), *The Anatomy of Melancholy*, London: Blake.

Butler, Judith (1998), "Foreword," in Maurice Natanson, *The Erotic Bird: Phenomenology in Literature*, ix–xvi, Princeton, NJ: Princeton University Press.

Calvino, Italo (1998), *If on a Winter's Night a Traveller*, trans. William Weaver, London: Vintage.

Caracciolo, Marco (2012), "J. M. Coetzee's *Foe* and the Embodiment of Meaning," *Journal of Modern Literature*, 36 (1): 90–103.

Carroll, Lewis (1992), *Alice in Wonderland*, ed. Donald. J. Gray, New York, NY/London: W. W. Norton & Company.

Chapman, Michael J. F. (2003), *South African Literatures*, Scottsville: University of Natal Press.

Childs, Peter (2000), *Modernism*, London: Routledge.

Cicero (1886), *Tusculan Disputations*, trans. Andrew P. Peabody, Boston: Little, Brown, and Company.

Clarke, Adam (1837), *The New Testament of Our Lord and Saviour Jesus Christ. The Text Carefully Printed from the Most Correct Copies of the Present Authorized Translation, Including the Marginal Readings of Parallel Texts: With a Commentary and Critical Notes; Designed as a Help to a Better Understanding of the Sacred Writings. Vol. I*, New York: T. Mason & G. Lane.

Clarkson, Carrol (2009), *J. M. Coetzee: Countervoices*, New York, NY: Palgrave Macmillan.

Clarkson, Carrol (2011), "Coetzee's Criticism," in Tim Mehigan (ed.), *A Companion to the Works of J. M. Coetzee*, 222–234, Rochester, NY: Camden House.

Coleridge, Samuel Taylor (1818), *The Friend: A Series of Essays, Volume III*, London: Fenner.

Conrad, Joseph (1949), *Notes on Life and Letters*, London: Dent.

Cooper, Pamela (2005), "Metamorphosis and Sexuality: Reading the Strange Passions of *Disgrace*," *Research in African Literatures*, 36 (4): 22–39.

Craig, Edward (2002), *Philosophy*, Oxford: Oxford University Press.

Crary, Alice (2010), "J. M. Coetzee, Moral Thinker," in Anton Leist and Peter Singer (eds), *J. M. Coetzee and Ethics: Philosophical Perspectives on Literature*, 249–268, New York, NY: Columbia University Press.

Danta, Chris (2007), "'Like a Dog … like a Lamb': Becoming Sacrificial Animal in Kafka and Coetzee," *New Literary History*, 38 (4): 721–737.

Derrida, Jacques (1988), *Limited Inc*, trans. Samuel Weber, Evanston, IL: Northwestern University Press.

Derrida, Jacques (1995), *Points …: Interviews, 1974–1994*, trans. Peggy Kamuf, et al., ed. Elisabeth Weber, Stanford, CA: Stanford University Press.

Derrida, Jacques (1997), *Of Grammatology*, trans. Gayatri Chakravorty Spivak, Baltimore, MD: The Johns Hopkins University Press.

Doniger, Wendy (1999), "Reflections," in Amy Gutmann (ed.), J. M. Coetzee, *The Lives of Animals*, 93–106, Princeton, NJ: Princeton University Press.

Dooley, Gillian (2010), *J. M. Coetzee and the Power of Narrative*, Amherst, NY: Cambria Press.

Dooling, Wayne (2007), *Slavery, Emancipation and Colonial Rule in South Africa*, Athens, OH: Ohio University Press.

Douthwaite, John (2005), "Coetzee's *Disgrace*: A Linguistic Analysis of the Opening Chapter," in Geoffrey V. Davis, Peter H. Marsden, Bénédict Ledent and Marc Delrez (eds), *Towards a Transcultural Future: Literature and Society in a "Post"-Colonial World. ASNEL Papers 9.2*, 41–60, Amsterdam/New York, NY: Rodopi.

Dovey, Lindiwe and Teresa Dovey (2010), "Coetzee on Film," in Graham Bradshaw and Michael Neill (eds), *J. M. Coetzee's Austerities*, 57–78, Farnham: Ashgate.

Dovey, Teresa (1988), *The Novels of J. M. Coetzee: Lacanian Allegories*, Craighall: Donker.

Dreyfus, Hubert (1993), "Heidegger on the Connection between Nihilism, Art, Technology, and Politics," in Charles B. Guignon (ed.), *The Cambridge Companion to Heidegger*, 345–373, Cambridge: Cambridge University Press.

Dunne, Éamonn (2013), *Reading Theory Now: An ABC of Good Reading with J. Hillis Miller*, New York, NY/London: Bloomsbury.

Eagleton, Terry (2007), *How to Read a Poem*, Oxford: Blackwell.

Eagleton, Terry (2008), *Literary Theory: An Introduction*, Oxford: Blackwell.

Eagleton, Terry (2013), *How to Read Literature*, New Haven, CT/London: Yale University Press.

Eisenstein, Sergei (1949), *Film Form: Essays in Film Theory*, trans. ed. Jay Leyda, New York, NY: Harcourt Brace.

Eliot, T. S. (1975), *Selected Prose of T. S. Eliot*, ed. Frank Kermode, London: Faber.

Farred, Grant (2002), "The Mundanacity of Violence: Living in a State of Disgrace," *Interventions: International Journal of Postcolonial Studies*, 4 (5): 352–362.

Feinstein, Charles H. (2005), *An Economic History of South Africa: Conquest, Discrimination, and Development*, Cambridge: Cambridge University Press.

Felski, Rita (2008), *Uses of Literature*, Oxford: Blackwell.

Felski, Rita (2011), "Suspicious Minds," *Poetics Today*, 32 (3): 215–234.

Fish, Stanley (1980), *Is There a Text in This Class? The Authority of Interpretive Communities*, Cambridge, MA/London: Harvard University Press.

Freud, Sigmund (1957), *Standard Edition of the Complete Psychological Works of Sigmund Freud, Vol. XIV*, trans. ed. James Strachey, London: Hogarth Press.

Gary, Rosemary (1986), "J. M. Coetzee's *Dusklands*: Of War and War's Alarms," *Commonwealth Essays and Studies*, 9 (1): 32–43.

Gass, William H. (1985), *Habitations of the Word*, New York, NY: Simon and Schuster.

Gass, William H. and Don Swaim (1985), "Interview with William H. Gass" [Online audio clip], *Wired for Books, Ohio University*. Available online: http://www.wiredforbooks.org/mp3/WilliamGass1985.mp3 (accessed September 1, 2015).

Goethe, Johann Wolfgang (2004), *Goethes Gedichte in zeitlicher Folge*, Leipzig: Insel.

Goodman, Nelson (1978), *Ways of Worldmaking*, Indianapolis, IN: Hackett Publishing.

Gray, John (1992), *Enlightenment's Wake: Politics and Culture at the Close of the Modern Age*, London/New York, NY: Routledge.

Gurr, Jens Martin (2007), "Functions of Intertextuality and Metafiction in J. M. Coetzee's *Slow Man*," *Anglistik*, 18 (1): 95–112.

Hayes, Patrick (2010), *J. M. Coetzee and the Novel: Writing and Politics after Beckett*, Oxford: Oxford University Press.

Head, Dominic (1994), *Nadine Gordimer*, Cambridge: Cambridge University Press.

Head, Dominic (1997), *J. M. Coetzee*, Cambridge: Cambridge University Press.

Head, Dominic (2009), *The Cambridge Introduction to J. M. Coetzee*, Cambridge: Cambridge University Press.

Heidegger, Martin ([1959] 1966), *Discourse on Thinking*, trans. John M. Anderson and Hans E. Freund, New York, NY: Harper.

Heidegger, Martin ([1954] 1976), *What Is Called Thinking?* trans. J. Glenn Gray, New York, NY: Harper.

Heidegger, Martin ([1938] 1994), *The Fundamental Concepts of Metaphysics: World, Finitude, Solitude*, trans. William McNeill and Nicholas Walker, Bloomington, IN: Indiana University Press.

Heidegger, Martin ([1927] 2010), *Being and Time*, trans. Joan Stambaugh, Albany, NY: State University of New York Press.

Horn, Peter (2005), "Michael K: Pastiche, Parody or the Inversion of Michael Kohlhaas," *Current Writing*, 17 (2): 56–73.

Iser, Wolfgang (1976), *Der Akt des Lesens: Theorie ästhetischer Wirkung*, München: Wilhelm Fink.

Iser, Wolfgang (1978), *The Act of Reading: A Theory of Aesthetic Response*, Baltimore, MD: The Johns Hopkins University Press.

Iser, Wolfgang (1980), "The Reading Process," in Jane P. Tompkins (ed.), *Reader-Response Criticism: From Formalism to Post-Structuralism*, 50–69, Baltimore, MD: The Johns Hopkins University Press.

Iser, Wolfgang (1989), *Prospecting*, Baltimore, MD: The Johns Hopkins University Press.

James, Henry (1947), *The Notebooks of Henry James*, ed. F. O Matthiessen and Kenneth B. Murdock, New York, NY: Oxford University Press.

Jameson, Fredric (1986), "Third-World Literature in the Era of Multinational Capitalism," *Social Text*, 15: 65–88.

Jolly, Rosemary Jane (1996), *Colonization, Violence, and Narration in White South African Writing: André Brink, Breyten Breytenbach, and J. M. Coetzee*, Athens, OH: Ohio University Press.

Kannemeyer, J. C. (2012), *J. M. Coetzee: A Life in Writing*, trans. Michiel Heyns, Johannesburg/Cape Town: Jonathan Ball Publishers.

Keats, John (1901), *The Complete Works of John Keats, Volume IV: Letters 1814–January 1819*, Glasgow: Gowars & Gray.

Keats, John (2006), *The Complete Poems*, ed. John Barnard, London: Penguin.

Kermode, Frank (2000), *The Sense of an Ending*, Oxford: Oxford University Press.

Kiefer, Daniel (2009), "Sympathy for the Devil: On the Perversity of Teaching *Disgrace*," in Bill McDonald (ed.), *Encountering Disgrace: Reading and Teaching Coetzee's Novel*, 264–275, Rochester, NY: Camden House.

Kossew, Sue (1998), "'Women's Words': A Reading of J. M. Coetzee's Women Narrators," in Sue Kossew (ed.), *Critical Essays on J. M. Coetzee*, 166–179, New York, NY: G. K. Hall.

Kossew, Sue (2011), "*Scenes from Provincial Life* (1997–2009)," in Tim Mehigan (ed.), *A Companion to the Works of J. M. Coetzee*, 9–22, Rochester, NY: Camden House.

Kristeva, Julia (1989), *Desire in Language*, Oxford: Blackwell.

Lamb, Jonathan (2010), "'The True Words at Last from the Mind in Ruins': J.M Coetzee and Realism," in Graham Bradshaw and Michael Neill (eds), *J. M. Coetzee's Austerities*, 177–189, Farnham: Ashgate.

Lamb, Jonathan (2011), "Sympathy with Animals and Salvation of the Soul," *Eighteenth Century: Theory and Interpretation*, 52 (1): 69–85.

Lamey, Andy (2010), "Sympathy and Scapegoating in J. M. Coetzee," in Anton Leist and Peter Singer (eds), *J.M. Coetzee and Ethics: Philosophical Perspectives on Literature*, 171–193, New York, NY: Columbia University Press.

Lear, Jonathan (2010), "Ethical Thought and the Problem of Communication: A Strategy for Reading *Diary of a Bad Year*," in Anton Leist and Peter Singer (eds), *J. M. Coetzee and Ethics: Philosophical Perspectives on Literature*, 65–88, New York, HY: Columbia University Press.

Lee, Hermione (2003), "The Rest Is Silence," *The Guardian*, 30 August. Available online: http://www.theguardian.com/books/2003/aug/30/bookerprize2003.highereducation (accessed September 1, 2015).

Leist, Anton and Peter Singer (2010), "Introduction: Coetzee and Philosophy," in Anton Leist and Peter Singer (eds), *J. M. Coetzee and Ethics: Philosophical Perspectives on Literature*, 1–15, New York, NY: Columbia University Press.

Lodge, David (1992), *The Art of Fiction*, London: Vintage.

Love, Heather (2010), "Close but not Deep: Literary Ethics and the Descriptive Turn," *New Literary History*, 41 (2): 371–391.

Macaskill, Brian (1994), "Charting J. M. Coetzee's Middle Voice," *Contemporary Literature*, 35 (3): 441–475.

MacKay, Marina (2011), *The Cambridge Introduction to the Novel*, Cambridge: Cambridge University Press.

Mantel, Hilary (2008), "The Shadow Line," *New York Review of Books*, 17 January. Available online: http://nybooks.com/articles/archives/2008/jan/17/the-shadow -line/ (accessed September 1, 2015).

May, Herbert G. and Bruce M. Metzger, eds (1962), *The Oxford Annotated Bible*, Oxford: Oxford University Press.

McMahan, Jess (2010), "Torture and Collective Shame," in Anton Leist and Peter Singer (eds), *J. M. Coetzee and Ethics: Philosophical Perspectives on Literature*, 89–105, New York, NY: Columbia University Press.

McNally, Lisa (2013), *Reading Theories in Contemporary Fiction*, London/New York, NY: Bloomsbury.

Mehigan, Tim (2011), "Introduction," in Tim Mehigan (ed.), *A Companion to the Works of J. M. Coetzee*, 1–8, Rochester, NY: Camden House.

Meihuizen, N. C. T. (2011), "Beckett and Coetzee: Alternative Identities," *Literator*, 32 (1): 1–19.

Meljac, Eric Paul (2008), "The Poetics of Dwelling: A Consideration of Heidegger, Kafka, and Michael K," *Journal of Modern Literature*, 32 (1): 69–76.

Merleau-Ponty, Marcel (1964), *Sense and Non-Sense*, trans. Hubert Dreyfus and Patricia Allen Dreyfus, Evanston, IL: Northwestern University Press.

Miller, J. Hillis (1990), *Versions of Pygmalion*, Cambridge, MA: Harvard University Press.

Miller, J. Hillis (2002), *On Literature*. London: Routledge.

Miller, J. Hillis ([1979] 2004), "The Critic as Host," in Harold Bloom, Paul De Man, Jacques Derrida, Geoffrey Hartman, and J. Hillis Miller (eds), *Deconstruction and Criticism*, 177–207, London/New York, NY: Bloomsbury.

Miller, J. Hillis (2005), *The J. Hillis Miller Reader*, ed. Julian Wolfreys, Stanford, CA: Stanford University Press.

Miłosz, Cesław (2001), *New and Collected Poems, 1931–2001*, New York, NY: Ecco.

Mullan, John (2006), *How Novels Work*, Oxford: Oxford University Press.

Nagel, Thomas (1979), *Mortal Questions*, Cambridge: Cambridge University Press.

Nagel, Thomas (1987), *What Does It All Mean? A Very Short Introduction to Philosophy*, New York, NY/Oxford: Oxford University Press.

Neill, Michael (2010), "'The Language of the Heart': Confession, Metaphor and Grace in J. M. Coetzee's *Age of Iron*," in Graham Bradshaw and Michael Neill (eds), *J. M. Coetzee's Austerities*, 79–105, Farnham: Ashgate.

Nietzsche, Friedrich ([1881–] 1997), *Daybreak: Thoughts on the Prejudices of Morality*, trans. R. J. Hollingdale, ed. Maudemarie Clark and Brian Leiter, Cambridge: Cambridge University Press.

Northover, Richard Alan (2012), "Elizabeth Costello as a Socratic Figure," *English in Africa*, 39 (1): 37–55.

O'Neill, Kevin (2009), "The Dispossession of David Lurie," in Bill McDonald (ed.), *Encountering Disgrace: Reading and Teaching Coetzee's Novel*, 202–230, Rochester, NY: Camden House.

Parks, Tim (2011), "The Dutch Are Coming!," *New York Review of Books*, 27 October. Available online: http://www.nybooks.com/articles/archives/2011/oct/27/dutch-are -coming/ (accessed September 1, 2015).

Pellow, C. Kenneth (2009), "Intertextuality and Other Analogues in J. M. Coetzee's *Slow Man*," *Contemporary Literature*, 50 (3): 528–552.

Pippin, Robert (2010), "The Paradoxes of Power in the Early Novels of J. M. Coetzee," in Anton Leist and Peter Singer (eds), *J. M. Coetzee and Ethics: Philosophical Perspectives on Literature*, 19–41, New York, NY: Columbia University Press.

Plato (2003), *The Last Days of Socrates: Euthyphro, Apology, Crito, Phaedo*, trans. Hugh Tredennik and Harold Tarrant, London: Penguin.

Plato (2007), *The Republic*, trans. Desmond Lee, London: Penguin.

Poulet, Georges (1980), "Criticism and the Experience of Interiority," in Jane P. Tompkins (ed.), *Reader-Response Criticism: From Formalism to Post-Structuralism*, 41–49, Baltimore, MD: The Johns Hopkins University Press.

Poyner, Jane, ed. (2006), *J. M. Coetzee and the Idea of the Public Intellectual*, Athens, OH: Ohio University Press.

Poyner, Jane (2009), *J. M. Coetzee and the Paradox of Postcolonial Authorship*, Farnham: Ashgate.

Richter, David, ed. (2007), *The Critical Tradition: Classic Texts and Contemporary Trends*, Boston, MA/New York, NY: Bedford/St. Martins.

Rody, Caroline (1994), "The Mad Colonial Daughter's Revolt: J. M. Coetzee's *In the Heart of the Country*," *South Atlantic Quarterly*, 93: 157–180.

Rorty, Richard (2010), "Redemption from Egotism: James and Proust as Spiritual Exercises," in Christopher J. Voparil and Richard J. Bernstein (eds), *The Rorty Reader*, 389–406, Chichester: Blackwell.

Rousseau, Jean-Jacques ([1782] 2004), *Reveries of the Solitary Walker*, trans. Peter France, London: Penguin.

Rushdie, Salman (1992), *Imaginary Homelands*, London: Penguin.

Russell, Bertrand (1946), *A History of Western Philosophy*, London: George Allen & Unwin.

Russell, Bertrand (1992), *In Praise of Idleness*, London/New York, NY: Routledge.

Schweizer, Harold (2008), *On Waiting*, London/New York, NY: Routledge.

Sen, Joseph (2000), "On Slowness in Philosophy," *The Monist*, 83 (4): 607–625.

Sher, Benjamin (1991), "Introduction," in Viktor Shklovsky, *Theory of Prose*, trans. Benjamin Sher, Champaign, IL/London: Dalkey Archive Press.

Shakespeare, William (2008), *King Lear*, ed. Grace Ioppolo, New York, NY/London: W. W. Norton & Company.

Shklovsky, Viktor ([1925] 1991), *Theory of Prose*, trans. Benjamin Sher, Champaign, IL/ London: Dalkey Archive Press.

Singer, Peter (1999), "Reflections," in Amy Gutmann (ed.), J. M. Coetzee, *The Lives of Animals*, 85–91, Princeton, NJ: Princeton University Press.

Sontag, Susan (2009), *Against Interpretation and Other Essays*, London: Penguin.

Sloterdijk, Peter (2015), *Stress and Freedom*, trans. Wieland Hoban, Cambridge: Polity Press.

Spivak, Gayatri Chakravorty (1991), "Theory in the Margin: Coetzee's *Foe* Reading Defoe's *Crusoe/Roxana*," in Jonathan Arac and Barbara Johnson (eds), *The Consequences of Theory*, 154–180, Baltimore, MD: The Johns Hopkins University Press.

Spivak, Gayatri Chakravorty ([1967] 1997), "Translators Preface," in Jacques Derrida, *Of Grammatology*, ix–lxxxvii, Baltimore, MD: The Johns Hopkins University Press.

Steiner, George (1989), *Martin Heidegger*, Chicago, IL: The University of Chicago Press.

Sterne, Laurence ([1767] 1998), *The Life and Opinions of Tristram Shandy, Gentleman*, ed. Ian Campbell Ross, Oxford: Oxford University Press.

Stevens, Wallace (1997), *Collected Poetry and Prose*, New York, NY: The Library of America

Stewart, Garrett (1984), *Death Sentences: Styles of Dying in British Fiction*, Cambridge, MA/London: Harvard University Press.

Strauss, Peter (1984), "Coetzee's Idylls: The Ending of *in the Heart of the Country*," in M. J. Daymond, J. U. Jacobs, and Margaret Lenta (eds), *Momentum: South African Writing, 1976–1983*, 121–128, Scottsville: University of KwaZulu-Natal Press.

Tajiri, Yoshiki (2008), "Beckett's Legacy in the Work of J.M. Coetzee," in Minako Okamuro, et al. (eds), *Borderless Beckett/Beckett Sans Frontières*, 361–370, Amsterdam/New York, NY: Rodopi.

Tajiri, Yoshiki (2013), "Beckett, Coetzee and Animals," in Mary Bryden (ed.), *Beckett and Animals*, 27–39, Cambridge: Cambridge University Press.

Thompson, Leonard (2001), *A History of South Africa*, New Haven, CT: Yale University Press.

Turley, Richard Marggraf (2004), *Keats's Boyish Imagination*, London/New York, NY: Routledge.

Updike, John (2007), *Due Considerations: Essays and Criticism*, New York, NY: Random House.

Van der Vlies, Andrew (2010), *J. M. Coetzee's Disgrace: A Reader's Guide*, London/New York, NY: Continuum.

Veres, Ottilia (2008), "On Mourning: The Trope of Looking Backwards in J. M. Coetzee's 'The Master of Petersburg,'" *Hungarian Journal of English and American Studies (HJEAS)*, 14 (2): 233–244.

Vermeulen, Pieter (2010), "Being True to Fact: Coetzee' Prose of the World," in Anton Leist and Peter Singer (eds), *J. M. Coetzee and Ethics: Philosophical Perspectives on Literature*, 269–289, New York, NY: Columbia University Press.

Vogl, Joseph (2011), *On Tarrying*, trans. Helmut Müller-Sievers, Kolkota/London: Seagull Books.

West, Cornel (2011), "Prophetic Religion and the Future of Capitalist Civilization," in Eduardo Mendieta and Jonathan VanAntwerpen (eds), *The Power of Religion in the Public Sphere*, 92–100, New York, NY: Columbia University Press.

Wicomb, Zoë (2010), "*Slow Man* and the Real: A Lesson in Reading and Writing," in Graham Bradshaw and Michael Neill (eds), *J. M. Coetzee's Austerities*, 215–230, Farnham: Ashgate.

Wilm, Jan (2015), "Postcolonial Dystopia: J. M. Coetzee, *Waiting for the Barbarians* (1980)," in Eckart Voigts and Alessandra Boller (eds), *Dystopia, Science Fiction, Post Apocalypse: Classics—New Tendencies—Model Interpretations*, 18–200, Trier: WVT.

Wittenberg, Hermann (2011), "Towards an archaeology of *Dusklands*," *English in Africa*, 38(3): 71–89.

Wittenberg, Hermann (2014), "Editor's Introduction," in Hermann Wittenberg (ed.), J. M. Coetzee, *Two Screenplays*, Cape Town: UCT Press.

Wittgenstein, Ludwig (1980), *Culture and Value*, trans. Peter Winch, ed. G. H. von Wright and Heikki Nyman, Chicago, IL: The University of Chicago Press.

Woessner, Martin (2010), "Coetzee's Critique of Reason," in Anton Leist and Peter Singer (eds), *J. M. Coetzee and Ethics: Philosophical Perspectives on Literature*, 223–247, New York, NY: Columbia University Press.

Yeoh, Gilbert (2000), "J. M. Coetzee and Samuel Beckett: Nothingness, Minimalism and Indeterminacy," *ARIEL*, 31 (4): 117–137.

Zimbler, Jarad (2014), *J. M. Coetzee and the Politics of Style*, Cambridge: Cambridge University Press.

Index

THE ROLE OF POLITICAL CULTURE IN IRANIAN POLITICAL DEVELOPMENT

The Role of Political Culture in Iranian Political Development

DAL SEUNG YU
Hankuk University of Foreign Studies, Seoul, South Korea

Ashgate

Published by
Ashgate Publishing Limited
Gower House
Croft Road
Aldershot
Hampshire GU11 3HR
England

Ashgate Publishing Company
131 Main Street
Burlington, VT 05401-5600 USA

Ashgate website: http://www.ashgate.com

British Library Cataloguing in Publication Data
Yu, Dal Seung
     The role of political culture in Iranian political
     development
     1. Political culture - Iran 2. Iran - Politics and government
     I. Title
     320.9'55

Library of Congress Control Number: 2001097948

ISBN 0 7546 1775 0

Printed and bound by Athenaeum Press, Ltd.,
Gateshead, Tyne & Wear.

Contents

List of Tables

Introduction

The analysis of the impediments to political development is an important discussion of our time, with major theoretical and political consequences. While this discussion is controversial, and many different possible obstacles have been introduced as responsible for political underdevelopment, one major factor that emerges is the cultural one.

In this study, I will try to explain the major cultural impediments to political development in Iran. I will focus on the historical popular attitudes in Iran towards political management of the society and on the way in which these attitudes tend to slow political development. Iran's political system has been evolving for more than a century, prompted by socio-economic progress, but the traditional viewpoints which could be considered patriarchal regarding government and sovereignty have considerably impeded political development in Iranian society.

Socio-economic development created favorable conditions for the establishment of democratic institutions in Iran. And yet, due to traditional cultural influences, these institutions were not able to reach their potential. For example, elective government, separation of powers, legislative parliament and political parties have not developed the strength they would need to have to promote and support democracy. Instead, these institutions are being employed in a way that is compatible with authoritarian principles. In fact, these institutions, which were created for a democratic purpose, have simply been transformed into new tools for authoritarianism.

The power relation in Iran is still vertical, rather than horizontal, and people stand in a dependent relation to the systems of political sovereignty. The persistence of traditional culture between people and their governors, as I will show later, contributes to this relation. While political institutions are more or less changeable, political culture takes longer to evolve. Thousands of years of Eastern autocratic tradition in Iran have deeply affected the attitudes and beliefs of the people, and although imported Western values have also impressed themselves onto popular beliefs and viewpoints, even penetrating traditional attitudes to some extent, they have not been able to wipe out the old cultural values.

1

The Asiatic mode of production is the foundation of culture in the Iranian society, as it has been for many years. But now this system is no longer the foundation of Iranian politics. The expansion of world capitalism into Iran has caused profound socio-economic transformation, which of course included life-style changes. Generally, there were many factors favorable to political development, factors that exposed the political systems and cultures of this society to change. But these changes could only take place slowly because of the presence and deep roots of traditional culture; any progress in this respect is usually subjective and unstable. When I look at the political processes in Iran, I can see that in practice, a small group is governing and a large group still is obeying; both groups consider old styles more suitable for the management of the state. Although the people are sometimes mobilized in politics, they are prevented from participating in policy-making.

In this study, I want to show that in the traditional political culture of Iran, especially in the governing class's attitude towards the country's management and in the people's attitude towards their role in politics, the expansion of institutional participation and competition are still considered impediments to political development. But institutional participation and competition are necessary to the establishment of Western-style democracy which requires broad public participation in the following:

1. economic development
2. the entry of new social groups and classes into political activity
3. the separation of powers and roles of the branches of government to enable participation and ensure the system's efficiency in solving social, economic and political difficulties.

One of my hypotheses is that the functioning of any political system has a deep relation to traditional values. Traditions and customs are not temporary but stable. Even revolutions cannot easily and rapidly sweep them from the scene.

The behavior of political leaders and the beliefs and tendencies of the masses regarding political authority are greatly affected by the traditional pattern of authority. Therefore, the study of some of the stable aspects of political culture has basic importance for recognizing present political processes.

It is important to understand how the patterns of authority are connected with political leaders' behavior and people's attitudes, which are the major factors in political development. In Iran, the concept of democracy and the methods of democratic government have not been associated with traditional beliefs and thought. Rather, the statesmen have interpreted them in a specific way, according to their interests and perceptions. They have presented their own beliefs, attitudes, and feelings as those of the people, calling autocracy democracy. This is one of the important problems of political development in contemporary Iran.

The major question I am going to address in this study is whether political development, meaning participation and competition, can possibly be anchored in a traditional political culture such as that which exists in Iranian society, in spite of the apparent impediments.

My principal hypothesis is that the traditional political culture, a major impediment to political development, has its roots in the socio-cultural system of Eastern autocracy and its foundation, that is, the Asiatic mode of production. The dependent variable in this system is the weakness of democratic political development in Iran; the independent variable is the political culture.

With respect to my hypothesis, this study consists of four chapters. In the First and Second Chapters, I try to explain the nature of the traditional political culture in Iran. This political culture consists of several elements, including beliefs and attitudes towards political management of the society.

In the Third Chapter, I discuss the favorable aspects of development and the challenge they pose to the traditional system. As well as changes that have happened as a result of the penetration of world capitalism into the Asiatic mode of production, other factors have been introduced, such as commercial expansion, the monetary economy, industry and the growth of the middle class and Western influence, demand for the expansion of popular participation in political management and the establishment of democratic institutions.

But the traditional political culture created an environment that caused some adaptations and deviations in the nature of these institutions as they were developing. Western systems such as elective government, legislative parliament and political parties could not provide the people with participation and competition.

The Fourth Chapter, through field research and discourse analysis, explains the ways in which traditional methods, values, attitudes and beliefs have forced these Western institutions to change in nature as they are established in Iran, so that in their adapted form, they fail to provide popular participation in political processes.

The traditional political culture in Iran grew out of a productive system called the Asiatic mode of production. The political system that evolved in this context is called Eastern autocracy. In such a system, the government with one hand controls the arrangement of all society's affairs and therefore establishes the bureaucracy, and with the other hand, directly exploits great masses of peasants. The king is the main figure of government and has the roles of both a manager and an authoritarian governor. As to social management, the governing classes' political culture is one of absolute authority and the people's culture is one of absolute obedience, servitude, and fear of political campaigns.

Although many studies have been made regarding political culture and its role in the expansion of a political system no considerable research has taken place regarding the impediments of traditional political culture to democratic development.[1] Among the major reasons for this is the fact that studies of political culture have mostly been done within the framework of systems theory, and political culture was mostly considered as an organic part of a political system. Naturally, the optimistic attitude of these modernist scholars prevented them from considering the impediments that traditional political culture places in the way of political development.

In the same way, many investigations have been made in comparative studies of the process of the development of political culture.[2] These studies recognized the role of traditional political cultures in changing the nature of modern institutions (such as elective government, legislative parliaments, and political parties). There have been some discussions regarding the difficulties of political development in third world countries, but they are mostly short and scattered. Still, I have made use of many of these writings, which will be referred to in different parts of this study.

1 Theoretical Basis and Conceptual Framework

Before beginning any substantive discussion, I have to consider the roots and elements of political cultural trends and their present situation in Iran. I would also like to address three important components of the conceptual framework and methodology of this study, namely:

> 1. a discussion of political cultural processes and my concept of them, specifically the relation between political systems and political development
> 2. an overview of some theories of political development
> 3. some remarks on the method of investigation.

I think it is necessary to explain these subjects in order to establish the theoretical basis of this study.

1. Political Culture and Political Development

As I have already explained, I consider the political culture, from the viewpoint of political management of the society, to be an independent variable in my discussion of political development. Therefore, it is necessary to define political culture and the processes of its development.

There have been many discussions of the definition of the concept of political culture and the role of culture in political processes.[3] Political culture was first formulated as the methodological and theoretical framework for studying some political affairs, especially in comparative politics. Those who propounded this concept believed that it could be used for the study of political conditions. They believed that some reasons for political development and underdevelopment might be provided by studies of political culture. At the same time, they hoped to be able to find the roots of the functions of political institutions in political culture.

The concept of political culture is summarized in the following theory:

1. There is a certain political culture in any society, which directs and impresses popular feelings on the political processes.
2. Political behavior, in any society, is rooted in a series of beliefs, feelings and knowledge that make up the political culture.
3. These beliefs, feelings and knowledge transform specific political processes, and that transformation is not accidental.
4. The members of society and of the political system internalize these beliefs, feelings and knowledge, so that they become a part of their character and behavior. As Sidney Verba says, the political culture is a system of beliefs, values and symbols, which are the basis and source of political action.[4]

My discussion here revolves around the meaning of the concept of political culture. First of all, I take a look at political leaders' views regarding political culture, I will address questions such as: What are the components of political culture? From where has it been derived? How can it affect people's behavior? How is it reflected in high political affairs? What relation does it have with other parts of political life? How much does it determine the nature of the political system? Finally I will briefly explain my own conception of political culture and its role in political development.

Formulation of the Concept of Political Culture

Basically, political culture has been propounded as a theoretical framework in comparative politics. There are four trends in comparative politics, namely, systems theory, culture theory, development theory and class theory.[5] The theory of political culture is rooted in the study of culture itself.

It was Karl Marx who recognized the relation between politics and culture for the first time. As is well known, he considers culture a part of the ideological facade and false consciousness. Marx explained culture in relation to its dependence on social, economic and political factors. [6] Max Weber, on the other hand, explained social, economic and political factors in relation to the culture.

In 1871, one scholar, I.B. Taylor, tried to rewrite the concept of culture to make it a complex whole, including beliefs, arts, moralities, laws, customs and rules, bringing elements of sociology into anthropology. Later on, the concept of culture acquired hundreds of meanings in the social sciences. [7]

Some sociologists described culture as including all social habits and behaviors. Each group of scholars emphasized a special aspect of culture, some emphasizing historical aspects, some, moral aspects, and some others, psychological aspects.

Alfred Kroeber and Talcott Parsons believed that we should separate the two concepts of culture and society from each other. Until then, anthropologists explained culture using the same ideas as sociologists utilized for the concept of society. That is to say that sociologists used the concept of culture in order to separate social heredity from biological heredity. Kroeber and Parsons believed that it is better to use the concept of culture for values, ideas and symbols, rather than for forms of human behavior. Parsons paid great attention to culture and in his book *Towards a General Theory of Action* described it as a system. Parsons' ideas were emulated by his students and followers, and accordingly, an important tradition was created in American sociology. Harold Lasswell also studied the systemic relation between culture and personality. [8] His studies were affected by research emphasizing national character and culture. Lucian Pye established a new way of thinking in the theory of national culture. Sidney Verba and Gabriel Almond suggested a wider political cultural concept than national character. They suggested that the concept of political culture gives us the opportunity to use the anthropological, sociological and psychological disciplines to study the individual's political behavior.

In 1956, Gabriel Almond brought the concept of political culture to political science. [9] He employed this concept in order to classify comparative studies of political systems. In 1963, he published a book with Sidney Verba called *The Civil Culture*. Therein, they described political culture as the attitudes of individuals towards their own political system. They have described political culture as meaning, if we talk about political culture of the society, the political system, but something that has been internalized in the feelings and values of people. People make this culture internal, internalizing the social system in the process.[10]

Almond's ideas were emulated by authors and researchers including Lucian Pye and Sidney Verba, whom I have already mentioned. Their studies of political affairs from the viewpoint of political culture have influenced many researchers, and the topics in this chapter are mainly based on their studies of political culture in the second half of the 20th century.

To begin with I take a look at the concept of political culture from the viewpoint of the pioneers' studies. In the following, I discuss this viewpoint, which is sometimes called the orthodox viewpoint.

Description of Political Culture

The concept of political culture has not been given a unique description in the writings of researchers, who only suggest processes in their political studies. There is a group of these concepts, connected to the orthodox viewpoint, which are very close to each other. Sidney Verba explains that political culture is a system of values, symbols and beliefs, which are the basis of political action. Lucian Pye says that political culture is a bridge between micro analysis, meaning individual political behavior in its psychological aspect, and macro analysis, meaning political sociology. Political culture tries to employ behavioral analysis in studying important political concepts such as political ideology, government, legitimacy, nationality and sovereignty. Political culture, according to its adherents, is a basic concept, giving a more accurate and scientific method for understanding other concepts, such as ideology, national character, national mentality and political psychology.[11] By connecting the two, individual and social analyses, I would be able to study both individual behavior and the nature of systems. By finding the roots of political culture, I can study both the historical changes in political systems and the individual's present experiences.

Lucian Pye says that the political behavior is so deeply rooted in the character of a nation that it forms a tradition that offers strong resistance to the political-economic powers of the new life.[12] Government, power, sovereignty, governor and so on are very abstract concepts that vary from time to time and place to place and cannot therefore correctly explain the political nature of the nation.

The Content of Political Culture

The content of political culture is, to a great extent, specific to any society, so studies of different political cultures tend to stress different subjects. The ultimate test of any theory of political culture is its value for comparative analysis and generalization. So far, some progress has been made in comparative studies, where the similarities between political cultures have been attributed to similarities in the types of political system. For instance, Almond and Verba investigated "The Civil Culture" and described it as the foundation of democratic political systems.[13]

It appears that some common dimensions of political culture could possibly be attributed to political institutions and to the evolution of the citizenry's political mindset. It seems that more studies in this respect could explain the growth of a political mindset, common dimensions of historical development, or even both. I can start by propounding some general concepts relevant to all political cultures. In democratic systems, for instance, citizens have an optimistic view of their political system and the effectiveness of political participation, and a clear sense of the separation of government and private interests. Traditional cultures, meanwhile, lack all these things.

Attitude Towards Power and Authority

Political cultures differ in their attitudes towards the nature and specifics of power and authority in the following ways:

1. whether they differentiate power and authority
2. how power and authority are separated
3. the attributes of legal power (such as physical force, safeguards of people's rights, moral legitimacy and social welfare)
4. the degree to which power and legitimacy are concentrated or distributed.[14]

In democratic cultures, legitimacy includes the restriction of political power used by political leaders. In traditional cultures, the restriction of power is weak. This phenomenon, already obvious in traditional countries, was worsened by colonialism.

Basis of Legitimacy

In traditional societies, domination is a sacred matter, connected to religion. In this respect, political leaders claim a higher place and position than the people. In modern cultures, political decision-makers just claim proficiency in their professions. So, in democratic systems, political affairs become ordinary, like many other jobs, and access to high political positions does not belong to any special family or group. In traditional societies, the success of political leaders depends on the fulfillment of special customs. Therefore, the correct performance and proficiency in the fulfillment of these customs would seem to be an important standard for the continued possession of political power. In modern societies, political culture requires the main place to be given to the intellect in solving affairs.

Political Equality and Hierarchy

The preceding discussion leads logically to a key difference between traditional and modern cultures. As mentioned, traditional cultures emphasize hierarchy, meaning that people are not equal in terms of political rights, and that some groups should rule because of their religious positions, while others should obey. But in modern culture, people consider themselves equal to each other.[15]

Authority and Freedom

The question of whether freedom or authority is used in the management of a society is a question that, taken together with other factors, determines the political cultural habits in a system. Modern cultures mostly emphasize freedom, while traditional cultures emphasize authority.

Cooperation and Competition

Democratic policy depends on a multitude of interactions, and these activities require confidence and the sharing of information for cooperation. In various political cultures, balance has been established between cooperation and competition in different ways. One of the important requirements of modern complex institutions is the establishment of confidence. When political culture includes suspicion, there is no alternative for policy except authority. In democratic cultures, the confidence of the people is strongly connected to political function.[16]

Political Culture, A Part of General Culture

There are different definitions for culture. But, still, most anthropologists consider culture to be a general concept including the beliefs, morality, customs, knowledge and art of a society. Culture is a concept that is abstracted from a series of actions but is not a behavior itself. If, like many anthropologists, I take culture to be a human "creative environment", it will include such things as tools and technology.[17] In fact, however, this part of culture, which is called material culture, will not concern us here.

Political culture is not a separate culture connected to the general culture of the society. Rather, it is one part of the general culture. And political values, beliefs and feelings are a part of general values, beliefs, and feelings. We are going to isolate that part of the culture which contains the political feelings from the generality of culture and call it political culture. Of course, political culture does not merely consist of beliefs, values and feelings, but is directly related to the policy of government, authority and sovereignty.

There are some beliefs, values and feelings that exist in general culture that do not apparently relate to policy, but which have political content. For example, individual beliefs on human nature have an important political content. In traditional cultures, there are suspicions regarding human nature which limit political confidence, and so this quality itself affects the political process. In such cultures, the masses' participation in politics brings instability instead of stability.[18] The belief in the goodness of human nature, on the other hand, might be a reason for believing political leaders.[19] There are two main categories of individual belief on the role of human nature, called the active and passive roles. If cultural systems encourage people to take any effort, those people may expect more from government and ask for more participation. The belief in human inability to change the environment, on the other hand, may affect political tendencies in the other direction. Robert Scott's studies on political cultures in Mexico perfectly illustrate this matter.[20] Thus, human political beliefs are more than just attitudes towards the political and party affairs.

However, when discussing political culture, I do not mean the scattered tendencies of these people or that group, but tendencies that form part of the common belief system of a society. But how, then, do we discover these common beliefs?

The answers given by the pioneers in the study of political culture are that, for this subject, I can rely on two criteria:

1. what beliefs are determinative in political systems, meaning what are the "foundational" beliefs?
2. and what general beliefs do most people possess? [21]

Following this method, I reach subjects that are important on the national level. For instance, I can consider political identity to be one of the most important subjects in political culture. It is in the units to which individuals belong family, tribe, nation or region that political culture is defined. This subject is very important for political development. A person would not only physically and legally, but also psychologically, feel himself a citizen of a country and system.[22]

National identity has another aspect: the feeling of brotherhood. The individual foundational tendency of a society is only to trust members of one's family, not other people. In such a culture, people would be suspicious of those who participate in policy-making: this fact itself has consequences. For instance, the suspicion of people towards political leaders makes the political leaders depend on the use of force in governmental management.[23]

Expectations Placed on Government

Another important group of beliefs helps determine what a political society has to perform. Here I deal with the people's expectations in a political society. The question to be asked is: What is the people's opinion about political institutions? In replying to this question I can consider the parochial (restricted civil) culture. In this culture, people do not have any expectation of public institutions or even know anything about the role they may have.

Expectations placed on the government itself depend on the belief that changing the environment is appropriate and possible. Therefore, the kind of expectations placed on government determines another aspect of political culture. Members of the society are at the same time the members of various sub-systems, such as tribe, nation and family. The fact is that these members expect the society to do something for their tribe, nation and family or for the whole country. In some cultures, government duties are measured by local advantages and in some others through national advantages.[24]

Legitimacy

One of the other important aspects of a culturally determined viewpoint regarding the information of government is the legitimacy of decision-makers. The question is how much the government as a decision-maker is accepted by the people and how competent the people are for government. In traditional systems, and especially in the Asiatic mode of production, loyalty and obedience do not depend on social contracts and the ruler claims divine right, causing the prevalence of the belief among the people that sovereignty belongs to a special group of people. In this respect, I can define two poles in political culture. At one pole, there is the overly optimistic view that the government is not only good, but divine, and at the other, the pessimistic view that the government is the enemy of people. Both of these poles represent impediments to political development.[25]

Method of Decision-Making

One of the general beliefs related to political culture relates to the method of decision-making in the political system. To put it in a simplified way, for the sake of discussion: I can consider a two-pole structure that, at one pole, has a culture whose people only consider whether their government is making good decisions for them or not, and at the other pole, a culture whose people give the political decisions themselves first priority. The first culture makes less of a contribution to democratic development and the second culture, more of a contribution to democratic policy.

In a culture where ordinary people do not expect to participate in decision-making, it is said that the status of the people in the political system is that of subject; when they participate in decision-making, their status would be that of citizens.

In such cultures, when the participation in decision-making is connected with belief in the accompanying law, it is said that the political culture is more favorable for creating a democratic system. But if either of these elements (the participation or the belief) is missing, it would be more prepared for populism.[26]

2. The Concept of Political Development

The concept of political development covers a wide range of topics that stretches from the processes of nation-state formation to the establishment of legal governmental institutions and the settlement of political equality. Here I concentrate my discussion on the main aspects of Western democracy, in order to explain the political processes of Iranian society. Generally, political democratization can be considered to take place at two levels. One is the level of political structure and the other has to do with the method of action of the political system. The method of action of the political system depends on the political views of the members of the political system, as does the political structure itself. One of the hypotheses in this study is that there is a difference between the two levels of democratic development.

There have been many discussions of these two aspects of democratic development. Among them, Martin Lipset[27] and Samuel Huntington [28] were focused on the first aspect, and David Held [29] on the second aspect. I will discuss them here only very briefly in order to provide definitions for my development indicators, as follows.

Major indicators in democratic development:

    A Political Structures
1. Popular sovereignty
2. Legal government
3. Popular participation in decision-making
4. Political freedom and tolerance of different groups in the society
5. Freedom of assembly and the press, and to form political parties
6. Tolerance of different thoughts
7. Government response to the desires of the people.

Generally, political development in this viewpoint means attaining a system in the country's affairs in which all people participate in the determination of their fate and society's fate, relying on political institutions to do so:

> B Political Methods and Views
> 1.Encouragement of independent and active participation
> 2.Belief in democratic values and their realization
> 3.Presence of competitive values
> 4.Belief in the importance of the distribution of power instead of its concentration.

As I already explained in this study, democratic structure cannot create democratic development without the presence of democratic attitudes and methods. Democratic institutions and structures will end in autocracy without the prevalence of democratic methods. This is the basic hypothesis of this study. I argue that in the absence of democratic beliefs, democratic institutions in Iran became weak and were changed into instruments of authoritarianism. The basic line of my argument is that the decline of the Asiatic mode of production under the pressure of capitalism led to favorable conditions for political development, but the survival of the old system's political culture limited political development. My conclusion is that political development, meaning the growth of democracy, needs both democratic-minded citizens and democratic institutions.

Under the new authoritarian policies or autocracy, there is mobilized participation instead of independent participation, forced solidarity instead of real competition and belief in the charisma of demagogues and in bureaucracy, instead of democratic institutions. People and political leaders believe in "powerful leadership", meaning the concentration of power in specialized institutions.

3. Some Remarks Regarding the Method of Investigation

Some short explanations seem necessary before going further into my discussion. As I have already explained earlier in this introduction, my main argument is that after the decline of the Asiatic mode of production and Eastern autocracy, the culture that resulted from this system is still an impediment to the processes of democratic development. Since the decline of the Asiatic mode of production, important changes have taken place in the structure of the political system: for one thing, important democratic institutions have been established in the European pattern. But for political views, reform did not work as fast as for institutions. The slowness of the process of development in this respect caused some flaws in democratic institutions. For this reason, the major part of this study concentrates on the subject of how views, values, methods and beliefs left over from the past culture have continued to exist among political leaders and the masses and have been the cause of their political behavior in different areas of political management of the society, including political participation.

I divide the subject of political development into two sections that consist of positive factors and negative factors for development. Positive factors are those related to reform in socio-economic relations and the creation of new institutions. Negative factors are those connected to the survival of the past culture. The first group is related to the structure of political systems and the second group, to culture.

Positive factors include the growth of new productive relations and the decline of the Asiatic mode of production:

1. Growth of foreign trade.
2. Growth of production for export.
3. Growth of monetary relations.
4. Growth of market economy.
5. Growth of the middle class.
6. Growth of the number of intellectuals and increased literacy.

These changes in society and in the economy led to political movements for changing the structure of the political system, and finally, to the creation of new political institutions. Consequently, the structure of political systems allowed for more public participation.

Secondly, the negative factors are related to traditional political culture and the presence of the values favorable for authoritarianism, including:

1. The beliefs, traditions and values of patriarchy.
2. Belief in the value of political concentration.
3. Belief in rigid hierarchy.
4. Belief in the importance of charisma.
5. Distrust towards the role of the individual.
6. Totalitarian religious values.
7. Distrust towards new institutions.
8. Political pessimism, distrust and opportunism.

The combination of these old cultural values with new political institutions, such as elective government, separation of powers, legislative parliament and political parties, gives the political system and processes the following attributes:

1. Passive, controlled and mobilized participation rather than independent and active participation.
2. Domination by the executive instead of real separation of powers.
3. Dependence on leadership in place of voting.
4. Populistic tendencies on the one hand and elitism on the other, instead of commitment to democratic principles.
5. Corruption of elections by political leaders, instead of a reliance on real votes.

These attributes indicate a new type of authoritarianism, as opposed to traditional authoritarianism on the one hand or genuine democracy on the other. I call this "new authoritarianism" to distinguish it from traditional authoritarianism and genuine democracy. Therefore, I can summarize the basic line of argument as follows:

1. Reform of the Asiatic mode of production → Reform in political structures.
2. Reaction of traditional political beliefs to reformed political structures → New authoritarianism.

In order to change the new authoritarianism into genuine democracy, I should rebuild the political culture would have to be rebuilt. If I want to compare the nature of political development in Iran with the European model, I can refer to the following chart:

Table 1.1   Comparison of Western Democracy and the New Authoritarianism

Western democracy	New authoritarianism (Iran)
Emphasis on individual freedom	Emphasis on the public interest
Emphasis on competition	Emphasis on unity and harmony
Active and independent participation	Passive, mobilized and controlled participation
Separation of powers	Concentration of power
Limitation of governmental power	Concentration of power by government
Confidence in public decision-making and the people's vote	Tendency towards strong roles for charisma and personality
Belief in the legal basis of governmental power	Belief in the holy basis of governmental power

The new authoritarianism is created when the methods and views from the right-hand column of the above chart, which came from the political culture of the Asiatic mode of production and Eastern autocracy, are acted upon within political institutions modeled on those of the West. Western-style institutions have been remade according to traditional views.

The positive factors for development (political, social and economic reform) and the negative factors for development (the remaining culture from the Asiatic mode of production) could be described in the following chart:

Table 1.2   Influence of Traditional Culture on the Function of the Political System

Positive factors for development	Negative factors for reform (remnants of traditional political culture)	The function of the political system (new authoritarianism)
Political, social and economic reform	Presence of traditional patriarchal values	Domination of government by executive power
The growth of capitalistic relations	Authoritarian values	Domination by governing party
The growth of the market economy	Belief in the role of charisma and personality	Charismatic leadership
The growth of the middle class	Value on hierarchy	Passive and mobilized participation
The growth of the intellectual's influence	Values of concentration of power	Elitism, populism and political instability

The degree of political development is the outcome of the conflict between two variables, such as political, social and economic reform balanced against the resistance of traditional political culture. The greater the political, social and economic reform and the less the traditional culture, the more extensive political development would be; in the reverse case, political development would be more restricted and authoritarianism more extensive. These proportions can be shown on a graph whose horizontal axis is political, social and economic reform and whose vertical axis is the rate of cultural resistance:

Table 1.3 Cultural Resistance and Reform

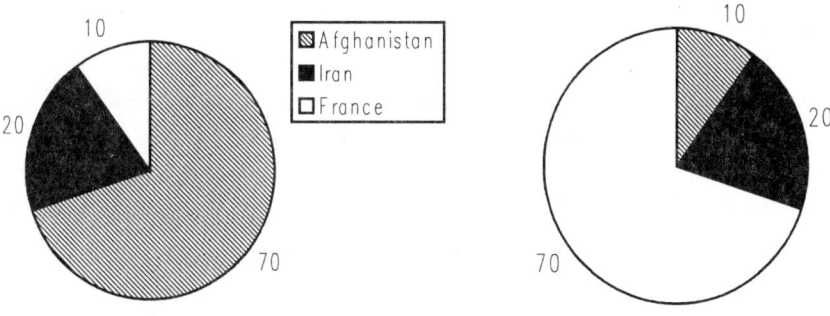

Legend: Afghanistan, Iran, France

Rate of Culture Resistance   Rate of Political, Social and Economic Reform

In this study, I will try to show the connection between the cultural variable and the authoritarian variable in each case, relying on field research and political discourse analysis. For example, it is shown that if the patriarchal values are more powerful in a group, the group defends dictatorship more strongly. Or as the middle class and literates grow more numerous in any society, they vote for the domination of the governing party less. As political elites have more tendencies towards pessimism and opportunism in their views, they will defend authoritarian leaders more. Meanwhile, when they have fewer tendencies towards pessimism and opportunism, they defend democratic methods more. I will show that the number of connections between cultural views and authoritarian values could not be accidental.

Cultural Basis of Development

In this study, I work from a specific viewpoint regarding the relationship between culture and development. In order to clarify the subject of this discussion, I should first refer to the important theories regarding political development in particular. Although the discussion of human evolution and political-economic change is of long standing, theorization of political development only goes back to the years after World War II, when the fate of underdeveloped countries motivated this discussion. But most of these postwar development theories are rooted further in the past: Hobbes, Locke, Rousseau, Hegel, Marx, Durkheim, Spenser and Weber's thoughts are very important in this respect. It would be outside the scope of this study to review the theories of these scholars one by one, so I will explain just a part of the important discussion regarding development.

The main component of political development is restriction of governmental authority. This restriction started with the separation of society and government. The growth of civil society was encouraged by economic development and by thought regarding separation of society and government. In the realm of thought, the theories of the social contract and the demarcation of the roles of government and the individual, which were first presented by Hobbes, Locke and Rousseau, were the theoretical bases of modern democracy. The theory of the social contract separated the origin of government from forces outside the society and presented the government as a human-made institution. Based on this theory, Hobbes advocated a powerful government, but he recognized that government has to protect social rights. Locke conceived this theory in another way, establishing the liberal thought which believed in the restriction of governmental authority. I can consider the theories of the social contract and liberalism as the theoretical bases of politically developed systems, but cannot consider them as constituting a universal discussion of development with relevance to underdeveloped countries. As already mentioned, discussions of Third World development arose after World War II, especially the decolonization period.

There are different theories regarding the factors for development, mainly classified into four categories. Political-economic development theories can of course be classified in different ways, since they actually include different factors that promote development, but one way to classify these development theories is by the factor they emphasize most strongly. Using this system, I can classify the theories of development as follows:

1. Theories that emphasize political factors.
2. Theories that emphasize economic factors.
3. Theories that recognize the separation of political and economic structures of society as the main basis of development.
4. Theories that emphasize cultural factors.

Theories that Emphasize Political Factors

The theory of the social contract, which I have alrealy mentioned, could be considered a political theory of development. According to this theory, government is a result of the social contract. Individuals, who live in a state of nature before the establishment of government, will organize society by making a contract. In Hobbes' theory, this government is powerful. Rights, law, injustice and justice were established along with the government. But Locke believed that human beings have rights naturally, that civil society existed before the establishment of government, and, moreover, that the area of civil society is separate from the area of government. People protect their natural rights, and governmental responsibility is restricted to maintaining the system and protecting civil liberties.

The theories of the social contract and the establishment of government, all-important as they are to the history of theories of political development, face many critiques today and are no longer considered workable theories, though they may possibly have followers. The main problem with the theory of the social contract, aside from the lack of historical evidence, is the logical question of how people could make a contract that binds not only themselves but also later generations.

Theories that Emphasize Economic Factors

Some of Marx's thought emphasizes economic factors for development, as does dependency theory, which has been influenced by Marxist thought. It will be helpful here to consider dependency theory; I would like to discuss various models of this theory and define the distinctions between it and my theory.

In dependency theory, it is said that development and underdevelopment are two aspects of a unique phenomenon, meaning that development in one part of the world has a direct relation to the underdevelopment of another part. This is not to say that all underdeveloped countries possess traditional societies and all developed countries possess modern societies. Both development and underdevelopment can occur in modern societies. Development in dominant countries was made possible by the capital and wealth of underdeveloped countries.[30] According to this theory, the world economy has, since the beginning of the colonial period, grown into a complicated network in which the economic surplus of dominated countries is continually transferred to dominant countries, there to be changed into stores of capital and development. Relations between developed and underdeveloped countries (also classified as centered and surrounding countries) have a full-scale reflection in political structures. The governments of the surrounding countries are the means of exploitation between center and periphery within their own countries. These governments, because of the system of capital-storing, can only govern through authoritarianism. Merchants, big capitalists, bankers and mine owners within these countries have direct connections with the central countries' governors. Release from dependency would be possible only through socialistic revolution.[31]

The main criticism of this theory comes from a group of neo-Marxists who do not believe that the political processes and the fate of dependent countries are chained to centered countries, disconnected from any level of political, social and economic progress. These neo-Marxists believe that they should also consider the growth of domestic productive forces and social classes. Dependency theory in its radical form approaches dogmatism and metaphysics, whereas international reality is more complicated.

Theories Emphasizing Structural Separation and Occupational Specialization: Systems Theory

The theory of structural separation is rooted in the theories of Durkheim and Spenser. Talcott Parsons, the American sociologist, inspired by these theories and by Weber's thought, devised systems theory. Later, other scholars, such as Gabriel Almond, Bingham Powell, Sidney Verba and Lucian Pye, continued his studies and explored new areas. In their theories, society is considered as a system consisting of interrelated structures or a set of elements. Each of these elements within the system has a specific job which contributes towards maintaining the system and its function in the environment. Development is actually the increasing specialization of these elements and the expansion of structures and their separation from each other. A developed society is a society in which jobs have been specialized and the new institutions are compatible with the environment.

The source of these theories is Spenser's thought, which states that society advanced from a simple condition to a complicated structure as a living organism. Durkheim also worked on creating harmony and interrelation. Malinowsky and Radcliffe Brown, in analyzing the primitive society, also went on to study how the social customs in a more dispersed area became employed as elements in a comprehensive system. Parsons used systemic analysis for social systems; David Easton used it for political systems. Gabriel Almond and Bingham Powell explained political reform according to the degree of separation between the specific jobs within given political structures. In their analysis, any specific job within a modern system has its specific structure. In developed systems, policy is an intellectual method that values specialization, public interest and efficiency. These values will conflict with the traditional society's values, in which hereditary roles and tribal relations mix with specific jobs and interests to form the basic for policy.

Almond and Powell have described five attributes of the politically developed system: [32]

1.Extractive capability: the capability of the system to extract material and human resources from the environment.

2.Regulative capability: the capability of the system to control the behavior of individuals and groups.

3.Distributive capability: the capability of the system to distribute goods, services, honors, status and opportunities.

4.Symbolic capability: the capability of the system effectively to employ national symbols, such as names (e.g., Mohammad in Muslim countries), flag and so on.

5.Responsive capability: the capability of the system to maintain a relationship between inputs and outputs.

The capabilities of the system increase through structural separation. Development of these capabilities makes it possible for the system to confront four basic subjects of political development - government-building, nation-building, political participation and fair distribution - in a better way. Participation means the participation of the greatest number of people who want to share in making decisions about their political destiny.

Theories that Emphasize Culture

Sidney Verba and Lucian Pye studied the social structure from a cultural perspective, and made a new conceptual framework. I use their approach in this study, but I believe that the cultural aspects of development are slower than the other aspects, and in this respect, at least, can act as an impediment. Those theories that consider the role of culture as an important factor in development are mostly inspired by Max Weber's thought. Weber, in evaluating the reasons for the development of capitalism (and with it, modernism) gives greatest priority to values, approaches and beliefs. He introduced the intellectualization of Protestant morals and culture in the period of the Reformation as the basic factor in creating the capitalist mentality in the West, which in turn led the West to attain political-economic development.[33]

The "modern man" theory grew out of this approach. According to this theory, reform of the society is accomplished by "modern man." The modern man has a special culture which makes him active, ingenious, extravagantly ambitious and self confident, and a flexible and talented planner. These attributes are exactly the opposite of the traditional man, who generally is a conservative, pessimistic and passive planner.

David McClelland also put forward a theory of development giving priority to the cultural factor. In this theory, he emphasized "the success mentality" as a factor for development and revival.[34] According to McClelland, this success mentality does not exist in all cultures to the same degree. Development happens in those cultures which have a high level of the success mentality. He points, for instance, to a wave of success-mentality adventures in children's books in Europe, which led to political and economic development.

McClelland's theory takes Weber's ideas in a different direction. While Max Weber put more emphasis on institutions, McClelland makes personality, or the social-psychological aspect, more important. According to McClelland, development is influenced by values, approaches and personality. Weber, meanwhile, says that the basic characteristic of a modern society will be the intellectualization of the productive system, bureaucracy and social systems.

Talcott Parsons, using Durkheim's theory on one hand, and Weber's theory on the other hand, made use of the concept of culture in his systems theory. In Parsons' theory, culture is both a system of its own and a part of the greater set of social systems. Culture consists of values and carries values from generation to generation. Values in their own right make political institutions and collective goals and inform individual's actions. Values determine the people's actions, that is, political action. According to Parsons' analysis, values, goals and institutions have been combined in political reality and could possibly be separated through analysis.

As Parsons says, culture connects to policy through different channels. The most important channels are:

1. values
2. institutions
3. philosophy, ideology and religion
4. socialization
5. determination of collective goals
6. actions which cover all of these.

Parsons emphasized culture so much that he called himself a cultural determinist. He believed that culture is the foundation of different parts of social systems. Culture is what connects individuals to social systems. It can be a part of another system, although it is a system itself. Culture is a part of the political system. Parsons made use of a more restricted concept of culture than what sociologists had used before. He defined culture to encompass values, ideas and symbols, which determine human behavior. In this study, I will use Parsons' definition of culture. Culture, therefore, connects to the political system in the following ways:

1. transfer of values
2. shaping of institutions
3. legitimization and justification of values
4. determination of public goals
5. political socialization.

Meanwhile, Parsons gives systems theory cohesion. From Durkheim he takes the concept of the social agreement as a principle, and values as being in the employ of this principle. Culture relates to the political system of the society, which may not harmonize with it in some stages. Therefore, culture causes problems for and slows the political system, which is related to the productive system. This slowing and causing problems is what I consider in this study.

Resources of Political Culture

Political culture takes many forms. In the section of my discussion, which relates to the political culture of Iranian society in the past, I refer to the worldview, ideology and beliefs of the people of this society, in order to extract the approaches and views relating sovereignty, government and legitimacy. As already mentioned, political culture is that part of general culture which includes people's views and feelings towards political institutions. Political culture also includes some of people's views regarding human nature which do not deal directly with political subjects, but are the source of political behavior itself. Optimism and pessimism, for instance, have two special political effects, which will be discussed in detail later.

Religion is a part of society's culture which has much to say regarding political institutions and legitimacy. In researching the views and approaches of the people of a given society towards policy, that society's religion and the different manifestations of that religion are very important. Nowadays, political ideologies are also an important source of political culture. Political ideologies have clearer theories. In underdeveloped countries, such as Iran, religion and its different manifestations determine the form of political action and take political power.

For this reason, and to reveal the elements of the political culture of the Iranian people, especially those elements that relate to political power, authority, legitimacy and cooperation – that is, the political management of the society – I refer to the worldview, religion and fundamental ideologies of this society in past and recent history.

2 Ancient Culture: Absolute Authority

Part One: The Asiatic Mode of Production and Eastern Autocracy

Before any discussion of the effect of the political culture of Iranian society on recent political processes and institutions, I need to recognize the particular nature of this political culture and introduce its bases, sources and character. The traditional political culture of Iranian society originated in the Asiatic mode of production, and through this association acquired the character which affects political processes even today. So, before I discuss the appearance of this political culture, I will first recognize and introduce its basic element, the Asiatic mode of production.

General Character of the Asiatic Mode of Production

Treatment of what I should call the Iranian historical system requires a comprehensive discussion which takes into account the socio-economic evolution of society. In short, I need to ask whether all societies have passed through the same evolutionary stages and whether there has existed any system called the Asiatic mode of production as a distinct productive system. This is a continual discussion among Marxist and non-Marxist scholars. And yet, the purposes of the study of Iranian political culture, in a socio-economic system based on the Asiatic mode of production, I do not need to reference this discussion. Whether or not the Asiatic mode of production is considered a distinct productive system or taken as only the shape of feudalistic evolution in the Asian region, the reality is that the

Asian historical system had special characteristics which differentiated it from European feudalism. I stress that the culture of the Asiatic mode of production was not the culture of European feudalism.

Moreover, the discussion regarding the determination of the evolutionary stages of human societies has not reached any important conclusions, as demonstrated by Stephan Done's book, *The Rise and Fall of the Asiatic Mode of Production*. Even if I consider Marx and Engels' theories, I will not reach any conclusion, because what they have written is too brief and ambiguous to contribute to this discussion. Both supporters and detractors of the Asiatic mode of production have strongly relied on their scattered statements.

Marx used the terminology of the Asiatic mode of production in some of his works; in *Critique of Political Economy*, specifically, he writes: "we can designate the Asiatic, the ancient, the feudal, and the modern bourgeois methods of production so many epochs in the progress of the economic formation of society." [35] Marx devoted himself to his theory of capitalism and spent the last twenty years of his life on that subject; consequently, his ideas about systems prior to capitalism were much less developed. This caused some debate among those of his followers who tried to interpret his statements on the Asiatic mode of production. Russian scholars, who sooner than others engaged in a Marxist survey of history, beginning in 1920, set aside the concept of the Asiatic mode of production, and went to a single line theory of history, in which all societies passed through the same stages of primitive communism, slavery, feudalism, capitalism, etc.

Some Marxist scholars defended the theory of the Asiatic mode of production. Karl Wittfogel was the definitive scholar of the Asiatic mode of production, but his theory was ignored for many years, until finally, in 1960, the Asiatic mode of production was again taken into account and defended by many scholars, including Russian scholars, whose ranks increased day by day.

Meanwhile, whatever name we give to the socio-economic system in Iran, a recognition of its general character and basic principles seems necessary. In my opinion, the study of social phenomena is impossible if considered apart from historical causality and the general structure of the society, acknowledging that there still exists a theoretical debate on the nature of this system, I will for the purposes of this study call it the Asiatic mode of production and will now describe its general character.

The Asiatic Mode of Production: Geographical Area

The term the *Asiatic mode of production* was first used to distinguish the social system of a group of countries from European feudalism. Geographically, feudalism was found in Europe and Japan, where it was the social system for thousands of years, while most countries aside from Europe and Japan had the Asiatic mode of production. The major American civilizations will therefore also be placed under the name of the Asiatic mode of production, although geographically, of course, they are not in Asia. Meanwhile, even though Japan is in Asia, it did not partake in the Asiatic mode of production. Iran is among those countries that exemplify the character of the Asiatic mode of production.

The Asiatic Mode of Production: Basic Character

In 1853, Marx, writing in the "New York Daily Tribune", described three basic aspects of the character of the Asiatic mode of production: 1. the use of artificial irrigation in response to natural conditions, 2. a system of scattered villages, and 3. a mixture of handicrafts and domestic agricultural production.

Wittfogel has made many sweeping studies of the Asiatic mode of production; and he calls the societies that engage in this mode of production hydraulic societies. (Most of the descriptions in this chapter are taken from Wittfogel's book *Eastern Despotism*.) Wittfogel says that the Hydraulic society was created for agriculture in dry areas. According to him, the dry areas of the earth can be utilized only under specific historical conditions and by creating specific social institutions. For a long time, primitive people knew about the dry areas, but had no need to control the water until they discovered the possibility of grain production and increasing nutritious plants, at which time they started to think about damming the water of fertile lands. At the same time, people began to see the possibility of large-scale agriculture through social cooperation, and this development enabled the creation of hydraulic society and of despotic governmental institutions. In this way, those societies that created artificial irrigation developed different social institutions and had different futures than did the societies that could rely on rainwater. Agriculture in the areas of moisture and rain was small-scale and did not require much cooperation for utilization of water. Irrigation could be accomplished by a family or a group of neighbors. But transferring water from faraway places required large-scale efforts from a large group of people. The construction of dams, the digging of canals, the changing of water-flow patterns and the distribution of water among people required too much work to be accomplished by a small group of neighbors or relatives. Tasks such as these necessitated organization, guidance and special cooperation, which were made possible only through the empowerment of leading authorities, in a manner directed by culture. In hydraulic societies, the social system changed to despotic government. Some European observers called this government "Eastern Despotism".

In China, the digging of canals in the northern plains goes back to before the year 221 B.C. At that time, the Chinese government still had not completed its centralization. In fact, there were many regional governments in China, and a kind of dispersion of power, similar to feudal dispersion, had taken place. But in feudal Medieval Europe there was never any sign of similar public works. The construction of irrigation canals occurred alongside the centralization of government and the beginning of empire in China. The Sui kings, ending centuries of political disorder, reunited the country "all-under-heaven", and the gigantic Imperial Canal of China, called "Yun-Ho" (Transport Canal) was dug. This canal was more than 1200 kilometers long, and more than a million men and women worked on it.

Herodotus described how, in the Achaemenian dynasty in Iran, the king himself supervised the main affairs of irrigation. The king first sent the water to the lands that most needed it, and then to other lands, according to their needs. According to Wittfogel, Greek historians were clear that the government in Iran was in charge of water distribution. Some documents describing 10th and 16th century A.D. Iran show that irrigation was an important and intricate matter. Ann Lampton says that, at the time of Abbassid, Merv's water bureau had ten thousand employees and there was a dam in Merv with four hundred watch managers.

The Asiatic Mode of Production: Massive Bureaucracy

One of the characteristics of the Asiatic mode of production is massive bureaucracy. This bureaucracy has been seen throughout Iranian history, and has long been counted as its biggest source of power, wealth and glory. The bureaucracy also formed the big institutions, and science and art grew up under the protection of this big system.

Meanwhile, the lands worked by the peasants were owned by big landowners who, unlike European and Japanese feudals, usually lived in cities and government centers. This was one of the reasons for the failure of agriculture in the Asiatic mode of production.

The bureaucracy sorted groups vertically into the top, middle and low tiers, with each tier occupying a social position related to its political position in the governmental system. At the top of this system in Iran was the king. Some of these administrative positions became inheritable. The members of farming communities were exploited by this system, though they cultivated the land communally.

The administrative system in Iran had a well-developed system of communications, everything in the country was under the control of the central government, whose close supervision of all affairs was aided by good roads and an express postal system. The Achaemenian postal system astonished Herodotus. In the Islamic age, caliphs imitated the ancient Iranian postal system: Under the caliphs, the postmaster was the manager of the communications service, and so supervised the different affairs of the country. Today, the custom of close supervision of communications still exists. (In China, likewise, at the time of the Ching dynasty (1616-1912), there was a wide postal network, which had two thousand express post stations and fifteen thousand stations for foot messengers. The express postal system employed thirty thousand horses and seventy thousand postmen.)

The Asiatic Mode of Production: The Nature of Property Ownership

Property ownership has a complex nature in the Asiatic mode of production. It had two basic faces: on one hand, the government owned all lands; and on the other hand, the lands were in the hands of peasants and the members of communal society. Therefore, property ownership and taking possession were always two different affairs. At the same time, the government gave ownership of the lands as patronage to individuals favored at court, who also served the system in their own way. But this relation cannot be considered similar to the system of feudalism in Europe and Japan. In the Asiatic mode of production, government could take the lands away from landowners whenever it wanted.

I will discuss this matter in detail later, but here I would just like to note that it is my opinion that, in the end, it was government who was the beneficiary of the peasant's product. Peasants used their products for their livelihood, and the government took a portion as tax, which went to support the huge expenses of the court. Moreover, all peasants, whether slave peasants or free peasants, had to do forced labor for the government, building the palaces, temples, tombs and other works of government.

The Asiatic Mode of Production: Universal Slavery

Some writers have said that the Asiatic mode of production was a kind of slavery. Except for the king, who was at the top of the governmental system, and probably some big royal families, all people were considered slaves. In other words, there were no institutions to defend the people's rights against the king and others in high positions. In ancient Iran, those who visited the king had to prostrate themselves before him, and he was generally called "the Lord on the earth" (these customs did not exist in Europe). This tradition, in which the king is the Lord on the earth and thereby related to God, gives the political culture of the Asiatic mode of production its slavish character.

Summary of Distinctions between the Asiatic Mode of Production and European Feudalism.

There are a number of important distinctions between the Asiatic mode of production and feudalism, which are outlined in the chart below.

Table 2.1   Comparison of European Feudalism and the Asiatic Mode of Production

	European feudalism	The Asiatic mode of production
Power	Scattered	Concentrated
Property ownership	Powerful	Weak
The role of the government	Limited	Absolute
Possession of production surplus	Feudal nobles	Bureaucracy

Part Two: The Roots and Character of Traditional Political Culture in Iran

The traditional political culture of Iran determined many aspects of politics and the political management of the society. In describing the character of Iranian political culture, I will need to refer to the Iranian worldview, ideology and also some aspects of the popular culture of Iranians, which have ancient historical sources.

The roots of the Iranian worldview and the Iranian people's attitudes regarding political subjects, as a part of general culture, go back to Islam, and then Avesta, and at last to the period of mythological beliefs. Therefore, though I will not attempt a detailed history, I will try to quickly review the past, mostly concentrating on the attitudes, ideas and beliefs that relate to the important political subjects of authority, legitimacy and government.

The ancient sources of the Iranian worldview can be found in the Rig-Veda. The Rig-Veda is a collection of hymns in praise of the gods, which the Iranian shared with the ancient Indians, along with a common culture, before the two separated.[36] Later, these Iranian peoples developed the Zoroastrian culture, which created some changes in people's political attitudes.

In the Rig-Veda, the universe was divided into three parts: earth, heaven and atmosphere. The earth was like a bowl at the bottom of the universe, and the heaven like an inverted bowl at the top. The heaven and the earth were a couple, the father and mother of the world.

Some researchers have claimed that the oldest ancient Indo-Iranian god, called Diyaos, shares a common lexicographical root with "Zeus Pater" from Greece and "Jupiter" from Rome.[37] Diyaos was originally the presiding god. This position was later given to Varona, who was also called Arte or Arshe, meaning the order of universe. "Arte" was used to mean "true course of morality", and even "right".[38]

In ancient Indo-Iranian mythology, Mitra and Varona were symbols of the two different divine and human aspects of government. Together, they controlled the order of the universe. In the Rig-Veda, the chief god was Asora ("The Great"). After becoming the greatest god, Varona was also called Asora. Eventually, Ahura, a variant of Asora, became the title of the greatest god of the Iranians.

Social Hierarchy

One prominent scholar, Georges Dumezil, claims that the order of the universe in Indo-Iranian thought was a reflection of the social systems of these peoples. In Mesopotamian thought as well, the order of the universe resembled the earthly governmental system.[39]

According to his claim, Aryan society was divided into three castes. These castes consisted of "dinyaran" (priests), "rezemyaran" (soldiers) and "producers" (peasants and artisans). Mithra was the master of human affairs and Varona was the master of the divine world. Kingship belonged to dinyaran and had both divine and human aspects; in other words, the king was both earthly ruler and messenger of the divine.[40]

In Iranian epic literature also, the kings had both political and religious power at the same time. They attributed their power and authority to their connection to the gods: their role as representatives of the gods was the origin of their legitimacy. The kings considered themselves the representative of the Ahura Mazda on the earth. The carvings on Achaemenian tombs show the kings performing the sacrificial ceremony in front of the holy fire on the altar. A wing-spread falcon atop the king's head symbolized Ahura Mazda ruling over heaven and protecting the earth and the king who is his representative on it. "Dariush", the second king of the Achaemenian dynasty, was one of the most famous Iranian kings to expand the theory of the king as representative of Ahura Mazda.[41]

Political Culture of Zoroastrianism

In Zoroastrianism, according to the doctrine which developed in the Sassanid, the world is the battlefield of the forces of good and evil, a battlefield that will exist until the final victory of good over evil.[42] The material world is the creation of Ahura Mazda, who laid it as a trap for Ahriman, the god of evil, who will at the end be defeated in this battle. In this doctrine, humans are holy creatures because their souls exist prior to their bodies, [43] and their help is essential to Ahura Mazda for his success in his fight against Ahriman.

In Iranian mythology, Kayumars was considered to be the first human and the first king as well.[44] In this way, religion and government were connected, with the king, who was the head of both government and religion, as the symbol of their connection. In Zoroastrianism, the king enjoyed complete superiority over the social system. Religion was synonymous with the social system and with justice, which was interpreted as observation of "class function". "Class function" required that each class had to fulfill its duty and not intervene in the work of other classes. Today, some Islamic Republic theorists, as I will show, formulate this same idea as "genuineness of duty."

As Ardasher, the Sassanian king, put it, religion was the basis of kingship, which in turn was the protector of religion. Whatever is without any basis or foundation will collapse and whatever is without a guard or protector will disappear. When religion and kingship are combined in one person, they create a strong foundation that even Ahriman cannot harm.[45]

One of the Sassanid writings states that when Zoroaster takes over the government, Judgement Day will take place. Resemblance between this thought and Shi'a thought regarding the twelfth Imam, who will bring the Imamate and government together, is completely clear. Respecting the relationship between religion and government, there is an opinion written in one of the religious writings of the Sassanid, called "Denkard", as follows:

> The religion of omniscience (is) like a mighty tree with one trunk, two great branches, three branches, four off-branches and five roots. And the one trunk is the Mean, the two great boughs are action and abstention, the three branches are humat, hukht and huvarsht, that is, good thoughts, good words and good deeds. The four off-branches are the four religious castes by which the Religion and secular life are (both) maintained, the priesthood, the warrior caste, the caste of husbandmen, and the caste of artisans. The five roots are the five (degrees of) government whose names in Religion are

manpat (householder), vispat (village headman), zandpat (tribal chieftain), dehpat (provincial governor) and the Zarathrushtotom (the highest religious authority and representative of Zoroaster on earth). (Over and above these) is another, the chief of all chiefs, that is the King of Kings, the governor of the (whole) world. [46]

In spite of all that, the king in the Iranian religious system is different from the king in other religious systems, such as the kings of Egypt and Mesopotamia. In those two religious systems, there is no mention of an evil king.[47] Apparently, the king could not be evil. Pharaoh was God and the Mesopotamian kings were representatives of the gods. But the Iranian king just did God's will and did not have a metaphysical aspect, so he could, in fact, be evil. In Pahlavian literature, in fact, a distinction was made between good and evil kings. Zoroastrian moral dualism was reflected in kingship: as in the universal system, in which there are both Ahura Mazda and Ahriman, in society, also a part of the universal system, there are both good and evil kings. The good king is the supporter of Ahura Mazda and the evil king, the executor of Ahriman. The good king is the best creation of God and the person closest to Him. His position is that of a divine. Moreover, he is the protector of the divine system. But the evil king is the closest associate of Ahriman.[48] This concept is different from that of the ideal king, the innocent Imam, of the Shi'ite. Eventually, however, the Sassanid kings came to declare themselves the family of God.[49]

When the good king rules over the people, the world will flourish and nature and society will be harmonized. However, if any evil king rules over the people, drought and famine will take over everywhere. Therefore, in Zoroastrian thought, not all kings are charismatic. If the king is righteous, he has legitimacy and will help the good force in the battle of good and evil,[50] but if he is not righteous, he will help the evil force. (Note that "righteous" should not be taken in its current meaning. Justice meant the very protection of class function, which meant everyone stays in their place.) The divine light is also not particular to the king. Any man who fulfills class function, meaning that he does his own job well, in his own place, will possess his own particular divine light. The king's divine light, meanwhile, is greatest but not eternal: if a king strays from the correct path, he will lose the divine light.[51] This is demonstrated in the mythological literature; when Jamshid Jam left the correct path, he lost his divine light and Zahak conquered him. However, all Iranian kings, divine light or no, always acted to protect the kingship system, throughout Iran's ancient history.

This idea that if the ruler is good, the country will flourish, and everyone will achieve happiness, still penetrates the Iranian people's view towards governments and creates a part of political culture.

Roots and Elements of Political Culture in the Islamic Period

The Islamic period seems to be more a continuation of the previous period than an interruption. The basic subjects of Islamic political thought, compared with the previous time, have changed a little. The Sunni viewpoint on some important subjects such as political legitimacy is of course different from pre-Islamic thought in Iran. But in the Shi'a viewpoint, these differences are minimal.

The combination of religion and government, which is one of the basic manifestations of the culture of the Asiatic mode of production, is an important principle in the Zoroastrian, Shi'a and Sunni viewpoints. But from the standpoint of political authority and legitimacy, while there are many similarities between the Zoroastrian and Shi'a viewpoints, these two both differ from the Sunni viewpoint. As I will explain later, in the Sunni viewpoint, the caliph, as a ruler, does not have any metaphysical connection with God. He is simply an executor of Islamic law. However, the ideal pre-Islamic Iranian king and Shi'a Imam, in some ways, have a special relationship with God.

I will now briefly discuss these subjects in the context of Iranian political culture in the Islamic period, which started when Arab nations conquered Iran in the seventh century. At first, in lands which previously had been governed by Persian kings, a caliph was installed, but local princes were left in place. Over time, Shi'ism, an Iranian version of Islam, developed.

Khaje Nizam al-Mulk, the great Seljuk vizier, tried to revive ancient

Iranian kingship and change the source of his legitimacy.[52] But he did not have much success in this respect. In the sixteenth century, the Safavid dynasty took the throne in Iran and Shi'ism prevailed with a different culture from the Sunnites. The Safavid kings declared themselves the descendant of the Shi'a Imams and inaugurated charismatic rule.

In Sunni thought, the source of a caliph's authority was considered to be the fulfillment of the orders of God among Umma (Islamic community). The Islamic Umma was founded by the Prophet of Islam, and his successor, the caliph, supervised the execution of Islamic law in his nation. Religion (church) and government (state) were not separated; each was an aspect of a single law.[53] The government took responsibility for the people's morality and happiness. In this respect, there is no difference between the political thought of the Sunnites and the Shi'ites.

Regarding the subjects of power and legal authority, there is an important difference between the Islamic and Christian viewpoints. In Islam, there is no difference between legal authority and power, and Islamic law just recognizes one high position, the Imam. The concept of the two swords, holy and unholy, which existed in the Western world of the Middle Ages and has been an important fact in Western political culture, has never existed in Islamic political culture, where the religious system and the governmental system are the same. The struggle that has existed between Pope and king in Europe could not have happened in the Islamic world, where political and social life are one and inseparable. Religion rules over every aspect of life. In this respect, because policy has not been separate from religion and morality, politics could not develop as an independent field.[54]

After the decline of the caliph and the sultan's rise to power, there were some changes in religious theory, creating separate realms for religious and secular power,[55] and providing doctrinal support for the sultan's power. But in Eastern autocratic government, separation of religion and government seems impossible. Separation of religion and government, on the rare occasions when it occurred in Iranian history, always caused some political crisis (for example, the Qajar and the Pahlavi dynasties). So the relationship between the caliph and the sultanate was ceremonially marked by the sultan receiving "the robe of honor," meaning that he was the appointed sultan, from the caliph. Eventually, this became purely ceremonial, and it was actually the sultan who appointed and dismissed the caliph.

Muslim scholars, tending to believe that tyranny was better than anarchy and that the presence of the sultan was necessary for keeping the Islamic lands, yielded to an agreement with this theory, and extended it still further. At last, Imam Mohammad Ghazali, the great philosopher of Islam, said that the caliph is he whom the sultan appointed.[56]

But according to Islamic law, Ijtihad belongs to the Imam, meaning that he possesses the knowledge to act upon the Quran, the Sunna and the Hadith. This did not describe the sultan. Ghazali theorized that Muslims should follow the great religious leaders in religious matters. Eastern autocracy accepted this great degree of independence of religion from government, but it later caused some difficulties for autocratic rule.

Khaje Nizam al-Mulk, a Sunni Muslim, chose a new theory of government, opposed to caliphate theory, which could be called "the divine law of kings." According to this theory, the king governed because of God's will. Regarding the source of the king's authority, he said, "The supreme God chose a person among creation in every age, and gave him the royal and praiseworthy arts." He did not approve of this theory, and just expressed it as a principle. Instead, he spoke in detail regarding the use of royal government in society. According to him, the king was the instrument of God's will, which brings order and safety to society. The ability of the king himself and God's favor and attention were the sources of the king's power. In Khaje Nizam al-Mulk's view, this fact was not at all inconsistent with royal succession. Therefore, the source of the king's power will be God's favor, the ability of the king himself and heritage. He presented a decree from one of the pre-Islamic kings, who said: "know that, I have this reign given by glorious God and inherited from my father... and won my rule by the sword."[57]

Meanwhile, in Khaje Nizam al-Mulk's theory, governmental law still was rooted in divine law. But the king's power was absolute. As he was selected by God, subjects should follow him. The people had to obey the king without questioning his legitimacy. He never said what to do if the king was cruel, whether they still had to obey him or not.

Basis of the Political Culture of Shi'ism

The attitudes, beliefs, values and political viewpoint of Iranians are rooted mainly in the two traditions of ancient kingship and Shi'ism. These two share some characteristics, but there are differences between them as well. These points will be clarified through a brief description of a few aspects of Shi'ism that relate to government. Meanwhile, in order to consider the positions which Shi'ism has taken on recent political questions, it seems necessary to survey its theories regarding governments and the changes it has undergone.

At first a political group, Shi'ism believed that leadership of the people was the right of Ali, the fourth caliph, and his descendants. This group eventually became a religious movement. Later, many disaffected social movements turned to Shi'ism as an ideological weapon against their rulers. Shi'ites divided into three sects: The Zayd sect, the Ismail sect and the Twelfth Imam sect. Here I discuss the last, which is the dominant religion in Iran.

The Shi'a theory of government has its origins in a few major sources. One of these sources is mysticism, which, in some part, is rooted in ancient thought. According to this thought, after human creation, a divine light (also called the light of Mohammad) penetrates someone who has been selected from each generation, and also is passed from Ali to his descendants. Therefore, they possess Imamate knowledge. Imamate means that one has the right to rule the Muslims. It is a continuation of the prophethood of Mohammad.[58] This conception of the Imam, connecting God and humans, also has similarities with Iranian ideal kingship.

The second source of Shi'a governmental theory forms the basis of the political theory of Shi'ism: the justice doctrine, which has been propounded in scholastic theories since the first Islamic philosophers. According to this doctrine, justice is an inherent attribute of God, which means that God never refuses his permanent guidance to the people. He always sends someone to guide them towards the right path. The Imamate is the continuation of the institution of prophesy.

When a legal government is formed, the Imamate and Velayat (rule) will be united. But while the twelfth Shi'ite Imam is absent on some affairs, the jurists or religious scholars control and arrange Muslims' affairs as "deputies" (or successors). The business of governmental force and compulsion is in the hands of tyrant-governors. As I will explain later, this part of Shi'a thought sparked change and prepared the way for a new movement, which led to Islamic government and the Velayat-e Faqih (rule of the jurist).

The formation of the Safavid dynasty, the first Shi'a government in Iran in 1501, was one of the important turning points of Shi'a governmental thought. The Al-Buyeh kings (945-1055), who ruled long before the Safavid, were, though Shi'ites, officially subordinate to the caliph (although they themselves appointed and dismissed the caliph). But the Safavid government, which actually began as a religious and sectarian movement, was Shi'a in all respects. When the Safavid dynasty took power in Iran, Shi'a jurists faced many difficulties.[59] As already explained, Shi'a jurists believed that Imamate and Velayat (rule) were reserved for the innocent Imam who, by having the Imamate knowledge through God, deserved such a position. But now Shi'a scholars had to adapt themselves and their theories to political realities. Till then, they had been in opposition to the government and could develop theories freely, but with the formation of the Shi'a government, they had to conform their theories to the existing realities.

At last, a new theory was founded among Shi'a ulama. Under this new theory, the basis of government would be the innocent Imam.[60] But during the time of the Imam's absence, jurists, as public deputies of the innocent Imam, should manage the general affairs of Shi'a society. (It is worthwhile to mention that the twelfth Imam had four special deputies.) The relationship between jurists and the people was called Velayat ("rule"). Thus, the Shi'a jurists, theoretically (not practically), granted themselves the right to manage the people's general affairs, independently from government. This principle gave them the position of "deputies of Imam" and the right of "Velayat-e Faqih" (rule of the jurist). These concepts still exist among Shi'a jurists and have become a basic principle of the Islamic Republic system. They are expressed as followed by one of the greatest Shi'a ulama during the Safavid dynasty, Seyyed Mohammad ben Ghoreiysh Hosseini Sabzdari, who wrote in his book, "Zein al-Arefin": "And at this time…that the Twelfth Imam…is covered and hidden from sight…the possessors of this glorious position are the divine ulama who are the same as jurists and Mujtahdiin (s, Mujtahid) …responsible for other people, who cannot attain such a position and are to follow them…"[61]

A New Development in the Shi'a Political Culture

The establishment of the first Shi'a dynasty in Iran and the changes that followed had important consequences for the political culture of Iran. After the establishment of the Shi'a dynasty, Iran went through extensive social, political and religious changes. Before 1501, when the dynasty began, Shi'ites were an opposition religion and ideologically rejected any state that was not led by Imam Mahdi, who was the Hidden Imam. So there had to be a new theory to justify and legitimize a Shi'a state. Hence there appeared the theory of Niabat (vice-gerency) according to which the Safavid Shahs would rule the Shi'ite country with Islamic justice until the appearance of the Hidden Imam.

The Safavid dynasty laid the foundation for a new identity: the Iranian Shi'a identity. The first Shah of the Safavid dynasty, Ismail I (1501-1524), announced the Shi'ite Twelve Imami to be the official religion of Iran. The radical followers of this charismatic leader made the Sunni ulama leave Iran for the Ottoman Empire, while Shi'a ulama from all over the Ottoman Empire settled in the new Shi'a country. The Safavid Shahs needed religious leaders to legitimize their political power, and the Shi'a ulama, who accepted Ismail as the vice-gerent of the Hidden Imam, gradually gained considerable authority, social power and prestige. They gained the right to act as religious jurists and to collect religious taxes. This gave them an economic independence which was very important in itself. Sunni ulama were deprived of such independence.

Some of the most important Shi'a institutions, practices and rituals appeared at the time of the establishment of the Safavid dynasty. One of these was Marja-e Taqlid (sources of emulation), an important position in Shi'ism that represented clerical hierarchy and power.[62] From that time until the Islamic Revolution, Iranian history was an arena of dual authority divided between the state and the Shi'a clerics, who developed important social ties with the whole community and, especially, established functional and even personal connections with the bazaaris, which were to play an important part in succeeding Iranian historical events.

The bazaar was traditionally the major center of socio-economic life in the cities of Iran. During the reign of the Safavid dynasty, many clerical centers, mosques and religious schools were constructed within bazaars. Bazaaris paid their religious taxes to the ulama. This economic support helped the ulama to grow in number and power. Rich bazaaris even built mosques as the combined power of the bazaaris and ulama increased while the religious, social and economic connections between the state and the bazaaris decreased.

The Theological Basis of Clerical Authority

The political order in pre-Islamic and Islamic Iran was an axial order, outside of the society. The social order was legitimized as divine order. The notion of the Shah as a shadow of God on earth and the notion of the vice-gerency of the Hidden Imam were adopted by all political leaders. The Safavid dynasty combined these two sources of legitimacy, but the Qajar dynasty mainly adopted only the notion of the shadow of God as its legitimizing source of power.[63] This externality of the political order to society meant that the Iranian ruling dynasty was dependent on religion, and on religious authority, which had a monopoly over religious matters in the Muslim community. The clergy had extensive social, educational and judicial responsibility. The state and the clergy needed each other while, at the same time, competing with each other. The Shi'a ideas of state resulted in a weakening of state power:[64] one can say that the state was not a full sovereign organ. According to the most accepted theory of society, the state was only legitimized as the defender of Umma against the threat of non-Muslims. Most important twentieth-century movements in Iran bear the marks of this alliance between the state and the Shi'a clergy. The traditional bazaar of Iran was an important economic, as well as social, center. It was a commercial hub, and a center for workshops, guilds, banks, educational and religious institutions. The bazaaris also had links with peasants and tribal groups.

The Foundation of a Powerful Clerical Power

Contrary to Max Weber's claim,[65] there is no duality of centers of distinct authority in Islam. There is no theological legitimization for such dualism, as there is in the European Catholic Church. In Islam, there is no such thing as two realms of power, one belonging to the state as the realm of secular affairs and the other belonging to the church as the realm of power of God on earth.[66] Meanwhile, the Shi'a theory of state denies the divine legitimacy of political power. The Safavid dynasty, which was surrounded by Sunni Ottomans, who did not recognize any political power in the Muslim community other than the sultanate, established the powerful body of Shi'a clerics. Paradoxically, while, the Safavid dynasty tried through an office namde sadr to incorporate the Shi'a clerics into the state machinery, as a result of their economic independence the power of the clergy increased considerably, so that soon the power of some major ulama surpassed that of governors and even of the Shah.[67] The main source of the Shi'a ulama's theoretical power was the doctrine of gheybat (absence), which was incompatible with the existence of any sovereign political power other than the reign of the Hidden Imam. Even the claim of the Safavid dynasty to be the vicegerent of the Hidden Imam did not give the dynasty full sovereignty over the Umma. According to Shi'a theology, the Shi'a Muslim community was supposed to await its Hidden Imam, who would establish the just reign of the Imam.

After the fall of the Safavid dynasty, the Shi'a ulama attempted to create regular education centers and a well-defined hierarchical discipline for the ranking of the Shi'a ulama. The so-called Marja-e Taqlid and Ijtihad were examples of this attempt. However, the ulama did not construct an independent institution of power.[68] Instead of this, they pursued the alliance with the bazaaris, which gained them prominent sources of influence.

As already mentioned, the interconnection between the clergy and the bazaaris had far reaching consequences for the later development of Iranian history. Shi'a ulama compensated for their lack of a central organization by reinforcing their position in the civil sphere of society.[69] The ulama connection to the bazaaris was institutionalized through several systems, such as the collecting of religious taxes, and the holding of several religious rites and ceremonies. Bazaaris in their turn enjoyed ulama support in relation to the state.

The state needed a clerical state-wide networks as a means of control over the whole country because of several social and political considerations. One of these was the tribal base of the Iranian state before the Pahlavi dynasty. Jihad (holy war) was another factor: ulama had the power to declare holy war against an enemy and mobilize the country.

The Qajar Dynasty and the Clergy

The Qajar dynasty in its turn attempted to create a religiously legitimized state. Agha Mohammad Khan, the founder of the Qajar dynasty, began to use Shi'a symbols abundantly, though he resisted ulama intervention in state affairs. His successor, Fath Ali Shah (1797-1863), developed a closer relation with the ulama.

He ordered the building of new religious places, mosques and madrasah, and he repaired shrines. He exempted inhabitants of the holy city of Qom from taxation. He encouraged major ulama to settle in Tehran, the capital of the Qajar dynasty.[70] In his reign, the Auqaf (endowments) property of the ulama increased drastically. The ulama reciprocated by recognizing the legitimacy of the temporal rule of the Qajar Shahs. Mirza Abul-Qasim Qomi, the chief Mujtahid of the time, announced, as a new theological legitimization of the Shah's power, that God had made the Shah his lieutenant on the earth for the preservation of order and the clergy for the protection of religion.[71] Later, other prominent theologians such as Kashif al-Ghita created a division between the political and religious leadership of the Hidden Imam, so that political leadership should belong to the Shah and religious leadership to the ulama. The ulama reached such a prominent place that their fatvas (verdicts) were more important than the Shah's decrees, and in conflicts between ulama and local governors, the Shah took the side of the ulama. In many cases, ulama supporting oppressed people succeeded in deposing local governors. The ulama used their privileges to reinforce their position in the social, educational and political life of Iran.

One of the theological developments that reinforced the ulama's power was the victory of the Usulis over the Akhbaris. The Akhbaris did not believe in the interpretation of religious sources. Instead of this, they believed in Hadith and Khabar. However, the task of interpretation of religious sources reinforced the mujtahids' position and the institutionalization of ijtihad.

The growth of foreign influences was another factor that in its turn increased the social prestige of the clergy as the defenders of native values. The Qajar concessions to foreign companies created an opposition to the government in the people and the ulama, and set the stage for political unrest and several movements. One of the most typical examples of the ulama's reaction to concession was the tobacco movement.[72] In this movement, the clergy, working through an organized network for the first time, gained leadership of the resistance against an English company which had a monopoly over the sale and trade of tobacco in Iran. Major ulama used fatva as an important means of mobilizing people against the company and the government. Finally, Mirza Hasan Shirazi, the most important Mujtahid, declared a fatva forbidding people from using tobacco, which was obeyed by everyone, everywhere in Iran. Even Naser al-Din Shah's wives observed this religious verdict. This movement showed the great influence of the ulama in Iran. Playing their part as guardians of religion most skillfully,[73] they constructed a political network and institutionalized their political leadership. The clergy led a victorious movement and showed that they were the civil counterparts of the state.

The Clergy and Modern Ideas and Institutions

The twentieth century held many challenges for the Shi'a clergy in Iran. Various movements and extensive programs of modernization called for clerical reaction and response. The Constitutional Movement was one crucial event that deeply involved the ulama. The Qajar dynasty's connections with foreign powers had caused the Qajars to lose credibility as the protectors of the Islamic community. The ulama were at first unacquainted with constitutionalism, but as they were against the absolute power of the state, and they were leaders of the community, they were pushed into participation in the movement and soon became the leaders of the Constitutional Revolution. Gradually, they developed significant theological and theoretical justification for the Constitutional Movement, in spite of crucial opposition from one of the main Mujtahids of Tehran, named Sheikh Fazl Allah Nuri, who believed that Constitutionalism was opposed to Islam. Nuri and some of the other ulama believed in shariat (law of God) as the fundamental law,[74] that the Quran is the fundamental law for Muslims. The Constitutionalist ulama argued against them that whereas the Quran is the foundation of religion, fundamental law determines the principles of the state, the limits of the government and the rights of a nation.[75]

Mirza Mohammad Hussein Naini was one of the major pro-Constitutionalism Mujtahids. In a famous book, he provided the most prominent arguments in defense of Constitutionalism. Using Quranic verses and the sayings of the Prophet and of Shi'ite Imams to condemn tyranny, he argued that the best way to avoid tyranny in a time of gheibat (the absence of the Imam) is a Constitutional form of government.[76] Naini considered tyrannical power to be sherk (a usurpation of God); his Constitutionalism was not intended to justify a separation between the political and the religious powers of the ulama, but the core of his theory was rather the necessity to limit government. Nuri, on the other hand, opposing the idea of parliament, argued that dealing with the affairs of people is the responsibility only of qualified Mujtahids, not of any grocer or shopkeeper.

Monism not Dualism

In the twentieth century, the relationship between the clergy and government became increasingly full of conflict. The Pahlavi dynasty's modernization pushed the clergy to the margins of society. The Pahlavis tried to limit the clergy to mosques, secular courts everywhere deprived clerical groups of judicial activity, the graduates of religious schools were forbidden from becoming judges, and the secular schools and colleges began to dominate the religious schools.[77]

The Pahlavi dynasty even laid a hand on Vaqf (religious endowments) and challenged the traditional financial independence of the clergy. The ulama's condition had improved due to state Auqaf,[78] but the Pahlavi dynasty planned to bring the Auqaf under state adminstration and get it out of the ulama's control. The ulama were also opposed to government land reform due to be carried out on the Auqaf.[79]

In the 1940s and 1950s, a series of new religious intellectuals, such as Mujahadin and the followers of Ali Shariati, became interested in the Iranian political scene and contributed to a revolutionary Shi'ism among the religious younger generation, Ali Shariati attacked conservative ulama for their passive waiting for the Hidden Imam. This development, in turn, motivated the clergy to enter the political scene with some new engagement and a new theory of state.

This was the context in which Ayatollah Khomeini published a book, called *Islamic Government*, which came to have a crucial effect on the political history of Iran. In this book, which consisted of a series of lectures to theological students, Ayatollah Khomeini postulated a government in the Muslim community and rejected the traditional ideas about the control of jurisprudence as the only legitimate way to hold authority during great occultation.[80] He tried to justify the necessity for an Islamic government in Iran. Shi'ite political theory, so far, had stated the necessity of protecting the community against foreign invasion and the need for order in the community as the main justification for a state in the Muslim community. Ayatollah Khomeini added another reason, namely protection against moral corruption, which made the existence of a secular government virtually impossible. He emphasized that the only way to prevent the emergence of anarchy and disorder and to protect society from corruption was to form an Islamic government.[81] He also rejected the de facto acceptance of political rulers and argued for the application of the law of God (Shariat).

According to Khomeini, religion was not independent from the state. He claimed the clergy to be heirs of the mantle of the Prophet and to be leaders of the community. This theory was accepted by the radical clergy as an ideological and theoretical vehicle for the movement and establishment of the Islamic Republic of Iran.

The Growth of the Influence of Shi'a Clerics in Iranian Society

I hope to have made clear that the explosion of the Iranian Islamic Revolution in 1979 did not happen without any premise or background. It was the climax of a political movement within Shi'a doctrine which had had a long evolution.[82] The events and concepts I have discussed so far are related to the important historical transformations, and especially doctrinal changes, through which Shi'ism passed before arriving at this point.

Shi'ism, in its beginnings, seemed opposed to government, though not actively so. At the time of the Abbasid dynasty, Shi'ites believed that a just government would be established when the hidden Imam appeared on Judgement Day, which was a justification for withdrawal from public life in the meantime. Shi'ites even had a principle of "dissimulation", which justified hiding their religion and pretending approval of the official religion and government. In the sixteenth century, a group of extremist Shi'ites managed to take over the government through a factional movement and founded the Safavid dynasty. The Safavid kings, who claimed divinity and charisma, considered themselves sons of the Seventh Imam, and when they ascended the throne, suppressed all other factions of Shi'ism, appointing religious leaders at will. But, at that time, Shi'a clerics possessed economic independence. They could establish a basis for separation from government through religious taxes.

The shape of Shi'a authority, unlike authority in the Catholic Church and among Sunnites, was scattered. In the Ottoman Empire and in Egypt, the religious authority was located in the capital and under the control of the political ruler. But in later periods, after the Safavid dynasty, Shi'a authority became both scattered and free from the direct supervision of government. Dispersion of government after the decline of the Safavid also had an important role in this process.

In the Qajar period, after almost two decades of political dispersion, political centralization was again strengthened in Iran. But the Qajar kings did not resume ancient custom and did not make religion subordinate to government. They took the neutral position and did not create any impediment to clerical independence. They did not even try to subject the religious authority to royal authority. Then competition between the two basic schools of Shi'ism at that time the Akhbari and the Usuli, ended in the victory of the second school, which was important to doctrinal change in Shi'ism because the system of Velayat-e Faqih, which had been discussed in recent decades, actually would be expressed within the framework of the Usuli school. Whereas the Akhbari school believed that believers could make decisions as to religious affairs, themselves, by interpreting the Quran and the Traditions of the Prophet and the Imams correctly, but the Usuli school was opposed to this opinion and believed that all pious men had to follow a Mujtahid. In the mid-Qajar dynasty, the Usuli opinion prevailed over the Akhbari school. Later, another institution developed, the Marja-e Taqlid, which was followed by everyone, in case of general consensus. But this kind of consensus has less often been realized in practice. Although there was no obligation to have a Marja-e Taqlid, it was considered ideal. This kind of tradition has given a great deal of power to clerics.

At the end of the Qajar period and the beginning of the Pahlavi period, some new elements emerged, some of which challenged clerical influence and some of which strengthened it. Among these new elements were colonialism, Westernism and reform, which threatened the foundation of the clergy, although, but on the other hand, the influence of colonialism and the beginnings of a fight against it led people towards the clergy. In 1891, Shi'a clerics joined the anti-tobacco monopoly movement, strengthening their connection with the people and the bazaaris.[83] But in the Constitutional Revolution, as has already been explained, clerics agreed to the establishment of a constitutional monarchy, while standing against Reza Shah creating a republic, because that seemed akin to secularization. Reza Shah's reforms of the judicial and educational systems, traditionally which had been in the hands of clerics, seriously injured the economic and cultural basis of the clergy. Relations between the regime of Mohammad Reza Shah, the last king of Iran, and the United States also ended in the domination by foreigners and unbelievers of Muslims, which was intolerable for clerics. All of these led Shi'a clerics to a new doctrine, Velayat-e Faqih.

The theory of Velayat-e Faqih, although considered an innovation in Shi'ism, has roots in ancient culture. Political and social changes and the change in Shi'a doctrines prepared the way for the new theory, which laid the foundation for the Islamic Revolution and the new Islamic government. Despite its long development and its inspiration in ancient thought, the new theory as formulated by Ayatollah Khomeini and formed by the religious movements of the previous three to four decades was an innovation. As already said, the great Shi'a clerics traditionally refrained from intruding in governmental affairs. This custom continued until the period of Ayatollah Boroujerdi, who was the Marja-e Taqlid after the Constitutional Revolution, and who only pronounced upon and interfered in governmental affairs when regulations contrary to Islamic law were approved (before him, Ayatollah Kazem Yazdi and Haeri had done the same). In 1949, when various political forces became very active in Iran, Ayatollah Boroudjerdi held a meeting in order to discuss the urgent affairs of the time. In that meeting, in which participated the great ulama, it was decided that clerics should not interfere in politics. When Ayatollah Kashani was elected member of parliament and then speaker of the Majles (parliament), Boroudjerdi tried to distance himself from him. The madrasa (theological school), at that time, was not interested in interfering in political affairs. The Islamic radical groups, such as Fedaiyan-e Eslam (the Devotees of Islam), could not exercise influence even in Qom. Ayatollah Boroudjerdi went so far as to express opposition to politicizing the Palestine question.[84]

Notwithstanding this preference for non-interference in politics, the clerics did oppose some governmental moves towards reform. They proclaimed the new educational system a depraved institution and even prohibited listening to the radio. The Madrasa isolated itself from the new generation who were trained in new schools.

After Ayatollah Boroudjerdi, Ayatollah Shariatmadari became the Marja-e Taqlid, continuing on Boroudjerdi's path. At the same time, Ayatollah Khomeini, who had been an unknown cleric, rose to fame. Ayatollah Khomeini, who preached in a small mosque, gradually found many followers among reformists and the youth. Those opposed to the outmoded madrasa gathered around him.[85]

In 1963, a referendum put forward by the Shah to approve the "Revolution of the Shah and People" prompted the great clerics to enter politics united for the first time. They arranged a statement in opposition to the referendum and sent it to the Shah via telegram. The Shah got angry, calling them "black reactionaries". The bazaaris supported the clergy and the Tehran and Qom bazaars were closed for three days.

After this move, Ayatollah Shariatmadari returned to non-interference. But Ayatollah Khomeini continued his opposition and found some followers among lower-ranking clerics, such as Rabbani Shirazi, Mohammad Gilani, Hashemi Rafsanjani and Khameni. This group, who had radical beliefs, gradually increased their influence in Qom. From then on, all religious ceremonies, such as Ashura and mourning processions, became politicized. In the provinces also, the radical clerical influence increased. At that time, "capitulation" (as it was called by the Iranians) was signed between the Shah's regime and the United States. Under this agreement, the Americans won extraterritoriality in Iran, to which Ayatollah Khomeini intensely objected, causing him to be sent into exile in Iraq, which increased the opposition of the clergy to the Shah's regime.

Before 1969, Ayatollah Khomeini believed in the constitutional government, and his objection to the Shah's regime was due to its violations of constitutional law.[86] But gradually he came to believe that the colonial influence had so increased in Iran that it was impossible to stem it by defending constitutional law. The "Velayat-e Faqih" may have been derived in part from these considerations. Meanwhile, national affairs were one of the most important issues in the contemporaneous clerical opposition to the government.[87]

Velayat (rule) is a controversial and deeply rooted subject in Shi'a jurisprudence. This concept has been given different expressions within historical discussions. As I have already explained, Shi'a jurists expressed the doctrine that Velayat or government of the people belonged exclusively to the innocent Imams. Respecting government during the Imam's absence, and even Shi'a duties, many changes have been made in Shi'a jurisprudence throughout history. Until the Safavid dynasty, Sunni kings were the rulers. Of course, the Al-Buyeh kings (945-1055) were themselves Shi'ite, but they accepted the caliphate and left the Shi'ites free as to proselytization and religious customs. Therefore, before the Safavid, Shi'ites considered all governments usurpers, but believing in the twelfth Imam, and according to the concept of taqiya (dissimulation of belief in the time of danger), they did not get involved with government and tried to hide their opposition.[88]

In the Safavid period (starting in 1501), the Shi'ites' circumstances changed. The Safavid government was Shi'a and this presented the Shi'a ulama with a great dilemma. On one hand, the clerics could not consider the government tyrannical (because it was Shi'ite); on the other hand, they, the clerics, did not themselves rule. Some resolved this dilemma by saying that the kings ruled on behalf of the jurists, who were the deputies of the hidden Imam. Meanwhile, some religious affairs, such as reclaiming the Imam's property, Auqaf and "charitable affairs", were managed directly by the ulama.

For a long time after the decline of the Safavid dynasty, Iran experienced riots and disunity. During this period, government remained oblivious of religion and the clerics, which meanwhile obtained economic independence, increasing their power and influence. The Qajar kings did not have any religious authority.[89] Nor did they have anything to do with religion as an institution. During their time, therefore, the scope of clerical influence was broadened. Government no longer interfered in determining the Friday prayer leaders and chief of the clergy. The clergy in other Islamic countries did not have such independence. On the other hand, clerics remained aloof from governmental affairs. However, some clerics believed that Velayat meant management of all of Muslims' affairs. Moreover, they believed that the authority of the qualified jurist, during the time of the Imam's absence, was equal to the absent Imam's authority. This theory was described in "Tahrir al-Vasile", another book written by Ayatollah Khomeini.

Ayatollah Khomeini asked why, if the Imam's property and charitable affairs are under the authority of the Imam's deputies, should not other common affairs of Muslims be under the authority of the Imam's deputies as well?[90] Ayatollah Khomeini explained that during the Imam's absence it was necessary for the Imam's deputies to take on the Velayat of Muslims. This necessity meant that any qualified jurist was obliged to take on the Velayat of Muslims, and further, that this obligation would be taken away from others, and thereafter, Muslims should obey only the Imam's deputies.[91]

According to this view, the Velayat was divided into two types: Velayat-e Takvini (genealogical rule) and Velayat-e Tashriei (canonical rule). Velayat-e Takvini belongs to the Imams and Velayat-e Tashriei, the spiritual one, belongs to the Imam's deputies, who are jurists. Deputies also have general authority over all of Muslims' affairs. In Ayatollah Khomeini's opinion, there is no reason to consider some affairs of Muslims as belonging to the deputies, and some others, not.

Part Three: Political Culture of Eastern Autocracy

In the previous part, I surveyed the foundations and general elements of political culture in Iran in order to uncover the character of this political culture. Building on this more general survey, I would now like to introduce some of the specific elements of this political culture. These include the foundations of legitimacy, power, authority and sovereignty, and the incidental aspects of Eastern autocratic government.

Based on what I have described, the following elements can be recognized as part of Iranian culture.

Table 2.2 Elements of Culture of Authoritarianism

Basic Attitudes	Resultant Tendencies
1. Authoritarian attitudes	Distrust of progress
2. Patriarchal attitudes in all political relations	Emphasis on the role of personality in the management of political affairs
3. Hierarchical approach to politics and government	Tendency towards isolation and avoidance of politics
4. Combination of religion and government	Tendency towards elitism and charisma
5. Confusion of morality and politics	Collectivism
6. Centralist attitudes in all political and social domains	Opportunism
7. View of government as a great master	Lack of any mass participation or minimal, controlled, participation
8. Widespread pessimism towards politics	Vertical control instead of horizontal control

In the following, I will briefly explain some important attitudes and traditions.

Authoritarian Attitudes and Patriarchal Tendencies

All nations have had a period of authoritarianism in their history, but under the Asiatic mode of production, authoritarianism was of a special intensity and duration. Eastern autocrats had so much authority that they were close to absolute despots, with complete domination over their people, in both soul and property. They issued laws as commands. They could punish anyone at will, and even confiscate anyone's property as they liked, without any pretext. Although the kings consulted with big royal councils, no institutions could limit their power. Although remnants of primitive (tribal) democracy continued to exist for a long time, the tribal democratic institutions had lost their real power from the very beginning of kingship. People became subjects who just had to obey. The kings fulfilled all legislative, administrative and judicial roles. They apparently participated in trials. The ministers of justice treated government opponents brutally.

Khaje Nizam al-Mulk, in his book called "*Siyastnameh*" (the Book of Government), said that people and country both belong to the king: "The reality is that all lands and peasants belong to the king."[92] Nizam al-Mulk also said, in a speech written for Bozorgmehr, the prime minister of Anushirvan, the Sassanid king, that: "Authority belongs to the king, and the king has given it to the army, not the people. And the army is not compassionate or favorable towards the people, and when the army uses prison, fetters and oppression, then what would be the difference between them doing so, and the king?"[93] So, people and country were subordinate to the king, and only the king had a right to possession and deciding punishment.

Centralism and Hierarchy

Expecting the government as a system to be responsible for all public works is an attitude current in Asian society, including in Iran. Under the Asiatic mode of production, government had an important managerial role. The government had an extensive organization and accomplished big construction projects, such as roads, dams, canals and many other small and big works. This context allowed the attitude, that all works should be done by the central government to become an important aspect of political culture.

Governmental organization, besides being extensive, had a special system. In the Sassanid government, officials were known by their dress and horses. The state security service was considered one of the most important departments of this government. The absence of feudalism in Iran led to the centralization of government, and prevented the local landowners from getting any important authority. In Europe, feudalism ended in the dispersion of power; under the Asiatic mode of production, instead of geographical dispersion, there was factionalism in the central governmental system, which sometimes ended in violent royal conspiracies. For this reason, political distrust became an important cultural attitude in Eastern autocratic governments. This attitude still exists in the Iranian government.

Attitudes of Opportunism and Servility among the Elite and the Masses

Authoritarianism, political centralism and the ultimate concentration of all property rights (that is, land rights) in the king's hands, made all people subjects. This reality spawned a specific cultural attitude and was, in turn, protected by the same attitude. The concentration of power and court conspiracy made the king suspicious of all who showed special ability and personality in court. Under these circumstances, capable people would not be promoted in court. They owed their professional positions to humbleness. Prostrating themselves before the king was the least of their expressions of servility. Obedience to the king was the most fundamental attitude of the people.

Fear, Distrust and Suspicion

One of the important motivating attitudes among ruler and masses in the

Eastern autocratic systems was suspicion and distrust. Since there was no legal way to change the government, the only way to change seemed to be through deposing the king. The history of court intrigues showed that the king always had competitors who tried to take his place, and in order to do that, usually made plans to kill him. For this reason, the king was suspicious of all courtiers.[94] Courtiers also, as already explained, were always suspicious of each other.

Parricide, fratricide and filicide happened often in the history of the Asiatic mode of production, including Iran. One of the Egyptian Pharaohs, Papyrus, advised his son not to trust anyone, not even to explain his problems to his brother, and to be careful when he slept.[95]

Serving in high positions in court was like playing with fire. Those who did knew that their lives and those of their families were constantly in danger. In Iran, a large group of great ministers, from Bozorgmehr to Barmakian, Khaje Nizam al-Mulk, Amir Kabir and Ghaem Magham Farahani were sacrificed to court suspicions. Fear, distrust and suspicion were the basic elements of the political culture of the political elites.

The same fear and distrust existed among the masses. The Eastern autocratic system was controlled through public fear. The government could not tolerate any competing political force. The culture of the Asiatic mode of production was full of talk about torture and punishment. A dictionary could have been written about the different kinds of tortures in Iranian society.[96] Wittfogel said that maybe the Asiatic mode of production, which was based on a system of canals which traversed mountains, valleys, deserts and everything else, could not be established without the establishment of an atmosphere of fear of government. Without such an atmosphere, the many dams and canals might have been exposed to danger, and together with them the culture itself.

Fear has often been reflected in the literature and stories of countries under the Asiatic mode of production. Enlil, the god of Mesopotamia, reflecting the fearful appearance of an Eastern autocratic ruler, was the symbol of governmental power and, at the same time, a symbol of fear. Pictures remaining from ancient Egypt depict Pharaoh with a snake wrapped around his forehead. The symbol of ancient Egyptian kingship was a falcon with spread wings, covering everything under creation.

Torture was everywhere in the ancient East, the tools and methods of torture being openly discussed. These multitudinous tortures were commonly continued in Iran until the Qajar period.[97]

Suspicion

Under the conditions of government by fear, no one believes anyone. People see the shadows of spies everywhere. Everyone fears that confidence in another will expose himself or herself to dangers and unexpected misfortunes. This historical distrust and suspicion has probably caused people in modern times to be less inclined towards participation in political parties. On the other hand, this disinclination towards participation only creates more fear and insecurity. This kind of attitude is one of the impediments to political participation and political development. As I will show later, in Iran, people's political participation in voting is greater than their participation otherwise, including their activities in assemblies and political organizations. A political elite that has been trained within the same culture will not help in the elimination of such suspicion.

Attitudes Towards Obedience and Total Submission

In patriarchal culture, the attitudes of hierarchy and total obedience complete each other. Obedience to one's elder brother, father and government as considered a value. Everyone must obey their superiors.[98] In Western societies, obedience to authority has also been espoused, but total submission was never considered a principle or priority. In ancient Greece, a good citizen had to have four virtues: military valor, religious sacrifice, civic responsibility and moderation. But from the time of Homer through the classical period, total submission to governmental authority was never considered a virtue for a freeman. Total obedience was the domain of the slaves. In medieval times, the knights did not believe faithfulness to the kings required total submission. There were limits on the obligations to masters.

Under the Asiatic mode of production, if someone wanted to remain alive, he should not awaken the almighty state. Total submission was the only way to survive. As I will explain later, religion and ideology suggested the same thing. In Mesopotamian mythology, the "good life" meant "life in submission". Mesopotamian soldiers were told that soldiers without a king were like sheep without a shepherd.

This attitude is clearly reflected in the history of the countries under the Asiatic mode of production, including Iran. The great army of Darius III, the Achaemenian king, was terribly defeated by the small army of Alexander, who had discovered this Eastern mindset and therefore attacked the king's camp first in his battles with Iran. After the destruction of the king's camp, the army of Darius indeed became like sheep without a shepherd and was defeated. Likewise, when the Arabs invaded Iran to conquer the rich lands, without any armaments but faith, they could still defeat the Sassanid army. Total submission to superiors, which existed hierarchically from the lower classes through the ministers, has not often been the source of governmental power, but sometimes it becomes a governmental weakness. A Greek citizen learned a sense of duty to the government and city, but Eastern subjects learned how to be faithful to the king.[99]

Meanwhile, total submission was at once a result of the insecurity in autocratic society and itself the reason for the continuation of this condition. It was the penalty which people paid for living in a society with such a productive system and social system. Even today, with conditions continually changing the people are paying the penalty for this culture.

Political Alienation and Indifference

As long as humans create vast power without eliminating the elements of power that create political and economic domination, people will be alienated. Alienation has of course never been particular to the Asiatic mode of production. But alienation in Eastern autocratic government had its special depth and intensity. In this society, subjects did not have any say in government. Eastern autocratic monopolized power took everyone to the highest level of alienation. In ancient Greece, this alienation might have taken only the shape of loneliness, because at least people felt they shared in their political fate. A citizen could cure the pain of his loneliness. But the subjects of Eastern autocratic government did not have any cure for their illness. Alienation and suspicion affected even rulers. There were many cases in which rulers were obliged to kill all of their children and relatives, in order to keep and strengthen their power.[100]

As I will explain later in detail, the above-mentioned attitude itself led to another characteristic in popular political culture: political indifference. Fear, total obedience and lack of any trust in the government will make people indifferent to their political fate. In Eastern autocratic societies, most people not only have been deprived of the right of participation in their fate, but also consider their alienation a good. Many times, people utter the phrase, "I am not a statesman," with pride, seemingly unaware of the self-effacement of the statement. The growth of mysticism in Iran has not only a social and religious basis but is also related to this concept of political life. Belief in withdrawal and resignation are still continually seen, the effects of culture among the people of Eastern society.[101] Proverbs such as "Make silence your motto", "Go easy, Come easy, Don't get hurt", "Let the wind carry you", "Tranquility is in seclusion"[102] and hundreds of other such sayings illustrate this basic attitude.

Opportunism and Hypocrisy

Opportunism and hypocrisy are two other expressions of the political culture of the Asiatic mode of production. In these societies, because of the weakness of civil society and of the middle class, it was common to mimic the fashions of the ruler. People were playthings of powerful rulers who kept them busy with different things every day. Rulers have toyed with their people since the distant past; this practice does not just belong to our era of mass media. The following description could almost apply to the shifting fashions of our time: "At the time of the Valid government, people thought and discussed only architecture, and at the time of Suleyman Abd al-Malek, the thought and discussion of the people were of food and marriage, because the king took delight in these two. At the time of 'Umar bin Abd al-Aziz, anyone who ran into someone else said, 'last night I read the whole Quran,' because they were greedy in worship and obedience, and most of the people's talk was of religious duties and supererogatory prayers."[103]

Opportunism and hypocrisy are impediments to the development of genuine popular opinion. One day, the people follow one opinion, and another day, another which may be the exact opposite of the previous one. There are many proverbs recorded in Dehkhoda's *Amsal va Hekam* which reflect these attitudes, including these: "Water is in the hand of Yazid,"[104] "The door which is closed by God will not be opened,"[105] "Easy will live he who takes it easy."[106] People in the collectivist societies which were created in Western Europe, post-World War II, behaved the same as people in Eastern autocratic society. But there, different parties and the institution of civil society balanced these behaviors.

The Attitude of Charisma and the Personality Cult

All of these relations and attitudes lead to charismatic tendencies. In chapter four of this study, I will explain this tendency and its effect with the help of the results of field research. Here it is sufficient to mention that the people of Eastern autocratic societies, when seeking any public improvement, look to some powerful person or metaphysical force. Historically, those who were not able to solve problems and organize affairs looked to a leader with metaphysical powers to solve things for them.

The same tendency sometimes led to worship of those dictators who could finish an important job through force. Individuals such as Reza Shah of Iran emerged under such conditions. In democratic culture, the means seem important, but in Eastern culture, the ends seem much more important than the means. If a cruel leader could point to any visible accomplishments, people would not complain about his style.

3 Positive Factors for Political Development

In this chapter, I want to discuss the factors favorable for development. In the following chapter, I want to show how cultural elements reacted against these favorable factors and transformed the political system into something I call "New authoritarianism". The argument of this study is that traditional culture did not progress at the same rate as other factors favorable for development, such as the growth of new social groups and productive relations, along with support for new political institutions. (It is, in fact, the nature of culture to move more slowly.) Consequently, the functioning of these democratic institutions has been affected, and they have been emptied of their original content and been given an orientation which is closer to authoritarianism than democracy.

First, I will need to deal with the reform of the Asiatic mode of production and the establishment of new institutions. The expansion of the world capitalist market during the rush of European colonialism into the East forced the Asiatic mode of production to change. New economic relations started to grow within the Asiatic mode of production; new social classes and groups sprouted up, and demanded and won political participation. Because of new conditions, including the new relations with the developed European countries, millions among the masses looked to affect national and political affairs, for the first time. The governing class was weakened and the new much larger middle class, motivated by its economic and social life, demanded a part in managing the country. The old governmental institutions had not been responsive to new demands, so the creation of new institutions seemed necessary. Meanwhile, the European countries which had entered these societies changed both the economic and the political structure of the society. In those countries in which there was direct interference and colonialism, such as India, the effects, including the changes towards democracy, were naturally greater.

While many changes regarding the establishment of new political institutions, and even democratic principles, were accomplished through the influence of the European model and by Europe's direct interference, however, the traditional political culture could not be changed quickly or easily. As a result, in spite of the changes in some political structures, the system's political function still seems far from democratic in the ordinary sense. Traditional attitudes in government were resistant to change, and the masses could not find their suitable place in the political management of the society. Although traditional authoritarianism was ended, a new authoritarianism had taken its place. I believe that I should look for the major reasons for this in political culture, which had not changed along with the structures of political management. As I have pointed out, culture changes slowly. The regulations of legal constitutions and political institutions could be changed quickly, but the society's culture, whether among political elites or the people, could not be changed by the same processes and at the same speed.

In examining the factors favorable for development, I will start with the previous socio-economic system in Iran, asking what new forces influenced it, and how. What changes were made and what new demands were created in the area of political management of the society? In this chapter and the next I will be looking at how cultural factors interact with these demands and changes. What I will discuss here relates to the effect of cultural factors on structures and institutions. I will leave the effect of cultural factors on political functions and processes to Section Three.

Part One: Positive Factors for Iranian Development

Decline of the Asiatic Mode of Production in Iran and the Creation of Factors Favorable for Development

In this chapter, I want to discuss the evolution of political, social and economic change in Iran, and to show how Iran faced the challenge of political and economic development, with the result being the creation of a new authoritarianism.

Extensive relations between Iran and Europe began in the mid-nineteenth century. Europeans had entered into political and economic relations with Iran before, during the time of the Safavid dynasty, but these relations had not achieved any great importance by the time of the collapse of the Safavid regime and the extensive internal battles that followed its collapse. When the Zand dynasty took power and Karim Khan Zand had consolidated Iranian affairs, Europeans again proposed extensive political and commercial relations, but Karim Khan Zand was suspicious of foreigners and did not reply favorably. But when Iran again achieved political consolidation at the time of Fath Ali Shah of the Qajar dynasty and Europe once again moved to establish relations with Iran, Fath Ali Shah could not resist. He had failed in war against Russia and been required to sign some conventions opening Iran's doors to European trade. Under the Golestan and Turkaman Chay treaties, Iran had granted many privileges to Russia, agreeing, for instance, that only 5% customs would be charged on goods imported from Russia. Later, other European countries took advantage of this convention.

The expansion of economic relations with Western countries caused transformations in all areas of political and economic life in Iran. Among the important ones, I can cite the growth of new social groups and classes, the creation of new governmental institutions, the demand for the political participation of new groups, the creation of nationalism, the politicization of Islam and the creation of class, social and cultural gaps. All of them, in a way, reacted with traditional political culture, affected it, and were in turn, affected by it. Contemporary Iranian history has been full of changes and great events.

From the mid-nineteenth century, then, Europe entered into extensive political and economic relations with Iran, influencing the traditional system both politically and economically and leading it down a new route. The Constitutional Revolution, the beginning of modern Iranian history, in which a liberal government took power in Iran, was a result of these developments. But the internal and international situations did not let this new liberal government manage Iran as it wanted. Internal turmoil and the West's demand for the establishment of a powerful government in Iran paved the way for the authoritarian regime of Reza Shah. In World War II, because of his tendency to cooperate with Germany, Reza Shah was removed by the Allies and succeeded by his son Mohammad Reza, and a new period of democratic political development began before Mohammad Reza Shah could establish another authoritarian government. But cultural and class divisions and international conditions did not allow the situation to be continued, and authoritarianism again ruled in Iran. Even after Mohammad Reza Shah was deposed, authoritarianism continued in a new form.

I can divide the political development of Iranian history into six periods:

1. from the mid-nineteenth century through the Constitutional Revolution
2. from the Constitutional Revolution to the beginning of Reza Shah's government
3. the government of Reza Shah
4. from the government of Mohammad Reza Shah through the 1953 coup
5. from the 1953 coup through the collapse of the Pahlavi dynasty
6. the Islamic Revolution and Islamic Republic.

In this chapter, I will discuss the major changes in the contemporary history of Iran and the above-mentioned periods. But it is worth mentioning that I am not going to give a full treatment of contemporary Iranian history.

I will only be emphasizing those subjects related to political development and cultural impediments to that development.

Imperialism and Development in Iran

It is widely agreed that imperialism changed the future of Iran in the same way as it did that of many other Eastern countries. The major economic transformations that accompanied imperialistic relations consisted of development of the export economy, development of the merchandise economy, disintegration of the Asiatic mode of production and the integration of Iran's internal economy into that of Europe. The Eastern autocracy had fallen and new authoritarianism was established. Modern European culture entered Iran, influencing the formation of groups and classes and changing traditional culture. Under the influence of colonialism, Iranian history moved in a different direction, and yet the power structure in Iran after these transformations was not too much different from before.

In Iran, the king had high position and political power, but under the Qajars, at the time of the first extensive relations between Iran and Europe, the top political positions were not the top religious positions. The Qajar kings, unlike the Safavid kings, did not claim an Imamate position. This separation of power was a big problem for Eastern autocratic government, weakening kingship and strengthening clerical power.

One of the characteristics of Iranian government in the last two centuries was its patrimonial aspect. Because of the country's internal instability and the continual changes of dynasties, the government was very dependent on the tribes. This meant that Iranian governments were basically tribal governments. Moreover, the decentralizing forces were stronger than the centralizing ones. A king's power depended not only on the power of his own tribe, but also on his skill in balancing the power of one tribe with that of the other tribes. Meanwhile, as we have seen before, the Asiatic mode of production meant that Iran had a basic difference from European feudalism: the king's relations with local authority were not based on a contract. In this respect, trading and class groups did not take power and status for themselves (the process that resulted in independent cities in Europe).

The Qajar kings appointed the local and national authorities of their government from among members of their own tribe. The king's authority was a patriarchal relation. The army also was patriarchal. The top military officers were appointed from among the king's relatives. The Qajar bureaucracy was the same. In Iran, exchanging bribes for governmental positions was commonplace. Iranian bureaucracy was totally different from the Weberian concept, which was based on rationality.

The Growth of the Middle Class in Iran

In the nineteenth century, the Iranian-European relations that had begun in the seventeenth century underwent a great transformational process. One of the Europeans who traveled to Iran in the seventeenth century, Olearius, wrote that there were 12,000 merchants, including Tartars, Turks, Jews, Armenians, Georgians, English, Dutch, French, Italians and Spaniards, engaged in trade in Esfahan, the Safavid capital.[107] At that time, Iran's most important export item was silk, and the value of exported silk was more than 20,000 pounds. During the Qajar period, manufactured European goods entered Iran; cotton exports from Iran decreased. Industrial raw materials increased, growing from 19% to 60% of total exports. The export of grains and rice increased rapidly; rice export, for instance, increased by a factor of 58. This expansion of business relations with Europe developed Iranian trade and the Iranian market rapidly, allowing many merchants to become wealthy and famous. Trade was so brisk and so profitable that even some groups of courtiers and clerics entered business. Foreign trade was the driving force of middle class economic activity, and from 1800 to 1812, within 12 years, foreign transactions increased twelve-fold.

The merchant class, empowered by the growth it had created, demanded a share in the political management of the society. The Qajar kings, because of their dependence on foreigners, were not to their liking. Iranian merchants, who had to pay more custom duty than foreigners (who paid only 5% custom under their contract with the Qajar government), demanded that the government prevent the intrusion of foreign capital.

The Growth of Private Landownership

The growth of foreign trade affected landownership as well. As already explained, landownership under the Asiatic mode of production belonged only to the king, who gave the lands to his tribal leaders and courtiers. At the beginning of the Qajar government, the four important categories of landownership were:

1. khaliseh lands (crown lands)
2. tuyuls (lands belonging to governmental officers)
3. vaqfi property (lands given as gifts by the government)
4. private property.

In the beginning, most of the lands were royal domain and were distributed among the tribal leaders and courtiers' relatives. As business and the cash economy developed, the Qajar kings first made the tuyuls into khaliseh lands and then sold them. During the growth of the merchandise economy, they needed cash to buy European luxury goods and travel to Europe for entertainment. Many tuyuldars also took advantage of royal corruption to convert tuyuls, the governmental lands, into private lands, as production of exportable goods made land cultivation very profitable.

During this process, for the first time, the amount of private land in Iran exceeded the combined tuyuls and khaliseh lands. It seems an important change in the Asiatic mode of production. Ann Lambton, who wrote a book called, *Landlord and Peasant in Persia*, said that "the main source of wealth of the country at this period, as earlier, was the land and its produce, just as the possession of land was also the main source of power and influence. In spite of this, or perhaps because of it, the method of assessment and the effectiveness of the collection of revenue varied in different parts of the country. Some areas were over-assessed while some were underassessed. To introduce some order and system into this state of affairs was a prerequisite to financial reform, upon which the success of any wide system of reform would in turn depend. The various types of land-holding which had existed at earlier times are found, though their relative extent varied. Khaliseh land at this period still occupied a considerable area of the country; it was for the most part in a state of decay and made little contribution to the revenue. In view of this, and because of the constant need of the ruler for money, the general tendency of the period was for khaliseh to be converted into private property by sale."[108]

In other words, the proportion of private lands to khaliseh lands so increased that in 1924, just four percent of cultivated lands were in the hands of the government. Private landowners became such an important and influential class that, during the time between the Constitutional Revolution and the White Revolution, they were the most important political force in Iranian politics. Along with the commercial bourgeoisie, they had had an active role in the Constitutional Revolution, in which they tried to create new institutions and political arrangements in order to take the reins of government from a group of corrupted courtiers. Now these two classes demanded the restriction of the absolute power of kings and insisted on participation in the political fate of the society.

The Iranian commercial bourgeoisie, with a central role in the trading institutions of traditional bazaars, gained much socio-economic influence and demanded political influence as well. The decline of the Asiatic mode of production had reduced the influence of the central government in the market. Before this, the guild's chief was determined by the central government; merchants and tradesmen did not have any political power. Through the Constitutional Revolution, which I will explain below briefly, merchants, tradesmen and landowners, finally took power, and from the Constitutional Revolution through the White Revolution, the landowners and bazaaris had a majority in the Iranian Majles. Then, the White Revolution, the new wave of reform and new international conditions replaced the landowners and bazaaris with a new middle class consisting of governmental officers and intellectuals, who got a major share in power.

The Constitutional Revolution and the Creation of New Political Institutions

The Constitutional Revolution, which took place in 1906, was among Iran's biggest revolutions and most important recent historical events. It had two basic aspects: a nationalistic aspect and an anti-autocratic aspect. (The Islamic Revolution, as I will explain, was the continuation of these same attitudes.) The Constitutionalists wanted to overthrow the autocratic power of the king and make it possible for some new groups and classes to achieve political participation. One of the main reasons for this uprising against the Qajar government was the influence of foreigners, especially Russians, on the kings of this dynasty.

The merchant and landowner classes, along with the middle and low-level clerics, were the driving force in the Constitutional Revolution. There are many writings regarding the role of the bazaaris and bourgeoisie in the Constitutional Revolution, we need not go into them here, but I would just like to quote from Ahmad Kasravi, the famous historian of Iran, who himself witnessed many events. He wrote about the role of Azerbaijani bazaaris as follows. "In this history, we remembered the Azerbaijani bazaaris many times. They tried more than anyone else for constitutional progress. They gave support either through their money or through their efforts. In those days, some of them demonstrated many abilities themselves. They participated in all meetings and contributed to public thought, and if it was necessary, did not hesitate to spend money. And in case of difficulty, they took the lead in closing the *bazaars* and going to meetings."[109]

The bazaaris, because of their activities in the Constitutional Revolution, took a majority in the first Majles. Maybe for this reason, the first Majles was one of the most liberal and undertook many basic reforms. Among them were the expropriation of the tuyuldars, the institution of a national bank, and the establishment of secular courts. The first Majles also approved the first Iranian constitution. But the nationalistic actions of the Majles at last provoked both Russia and Britain, who finally gave an ultimatum to the Majles and stopped its activities.

The Participation of Clerics in the Constitutional Revolution and Their Influence in New Political Institutions

Iranian clerics established a hierarchy among themselves. Some belonged to the upper class, some to the middle class, and some to the lower class. In the tobacco concession movement, which was like the constitutional movement on a small scale, even high clerics also had participated. In this movement, clerics and merchants came together to struggle against the British company which had monopolized tobacco in Iran, and won. In the Constitutional Revolution, some middle-level clerics and the clerical lower class participated very actively, and Naini, the highest-level clerical jurist, participated as well. However, when the Constitutional Revolution became more radical and the press issued some attacks on religious beliefs, high-level clerics withdrew from the constitutional movement and some of them started active opposition to it. Ahmad Kasravi wrote about Tabriz as follows: "As we explained, in this city…the great clerics eschewed the constitution more than others…the fact is that here the groups of small clerics cooperated more with liberalization."

Some of the great clerics had completely different concepts of what kind of reform was needed. One of the high-level clerics, Sheikh Fazl allah Nouri, in Tehran, for instance, demanded legitimate government, meaning religious government, instead of constitutional government (meaning the liberal secular government). Because of this quarrel with constitutionalism, he cooperated with Mohammad Ali Mirza, the despotic Qajar prince, and managed to rally all the great clerics against the constitution. On the other hand, twenty middle-level clerics of Tabriz sent a letter to the Russian tsar, asking him to send back Mohammad Ali Mirza, who had run away to Russia, so that they could force him to acknowledge and respond to the Constitutional movement. Ahmad Kasravi reports that, of these twenty, one was a prayer leader, one a preacher, and eighteen others all religious jurists. In the Islamic Revolution also, as I will show, except for Ayatollah Khomeini, it was the middle-level clerics, never the high-level clerics, who were involved.

In the nineteenth century, at the time of Iran's boom in trading, some of the great clerics were doing business and owning land, for instance, one of the three mujtahid of Esfahan in Naser al-Din Shah's time, Seyyed

Mohammad Bagher, had four hundred caravansaries and two thousand shops. He was also a jurist. The power of Esfahan's governor was nothing compared with his. It was the governors who came to him, even sometimes waiting hours to be permitted to enter. The wealth of Mirza Javad, the Friday prayer leader of Tabriz likewise reached 16,000 toman, a huge sum at that time. Moreover, he was the owner of 200 villages. In 1886, he sent Amir Nezam, the governor of Tabriz, out of the city because he had encouraged people to wear European clothes. In this respect, his authority was greater than the governor's.

Clerics such as these first thought that under a constitutional government, their power would be even greater. But when they saw that the middle class and intellectuals were getting power, they rejected constitutionalism. This division helped weaken the government and prepare the ground for Reza Shah's government.

The Constitutional Revolution, the 1906 constitution and constitutional institutions were the achievements of powerful forces. The demands of the middle class had little in common with those of the big landowners and clerics. After the French Revolution, the bourgeoisie had tolerated the feudal nobility everywhere. Thus, instead of revolution from the roots, the "revolution from the top" became the order of the day. Germany and Japan followed the same path, as did Iran's Pahlavi regime, which instituted the "structure of modern absolute government". Notwithstanding these forces, the direct role of the imperialist countries in influencing the course of political development in Iran still should not be neglected.

Imperialist Governments and Reform in Iran

The imperialist governments played important roles in the political development of Iran. During the constitutional movement, Britain, one of the main imperialist powers with influence in Iran, first cooperated with the constitutionalists. Because the Qajar kings and princes were under the influence of the Russians, due to the Turkomanchay convention, by means of which the Russian government had undertaken to help the Qajar princes ascend the throne, it seemed compatible with British interests for a liberal government to come to power, and for the king's power to decrease.

But in spite of Britain's cooperation, to a certain degree, with the constitutionalists, the basic element of the Constitutional Revolution, namely nationalism, was unacceptable to the British imperialist government. When the first Majles wanted to stop taking foreign loans, establishing a national bank and national loans, instead, Britain interfered and stopped this process, thereby, obliging the Majles to take loans from Russia and Britain.

The second Majles was also opposed to taking loans and considered it harmful to the country's credit. At that time, however, the government had an urgent need for money, and so in spite of its misgivings, the Majles wanted to pledge the royal jewels as collateral for a loan from a Frenchman. But, Russia and Britain interfered once again. The Russians put troops on the Northern frontiers of Iran to pressure the Majles, and the Majles was finally obliged to take loans from Russian and British banks.[110]

New Authoritarianism: Interaction between Reform and Traditional Culture

The government that came into power with the Constitutional Revolution was a liberal one. The Majles basically consisted of representatives of the bazaaris, the new landowners and the clerics. But this government was not able to assume the powerful desired by the constitutionalists. It could not quiet internal agitations, manage the insurgent tribal chiefs or hold its own on the international front. International conditions were also completely changed for Iran by the October Revolution in Russia, when Russia abandoned Iranian policy and Britain became the dominant foreign influence. In addition, with the Bolsheviks' ascendancy in Russia, Britain had to revise its policy towards Iran. So far, Britain had preferred a liberal, weak government. But with the appearance of the Bolsheviks, a strong government had to be established to make Iran a barrier to communism. Internal and international conditions came together to make a stronger and more effective government necesary.

It was under these circumstances that the authoritarian government of Reza Shah came into existence, a result of the weakness of the constitutional liberal government and the bourgeoisie in establishing stability and central authority in Iran. Coming to power, Reza Shah did not take any action against the bourgeoisie and landowners, and tried to stabilize conditions for the benefit of Britain.

Reza Shah's government was the first modern absolute government in Iran. The Shah accomplished this by centralizing power and policy-making in the hands of the new middle class, creating national unity, establishing a modern army, suppressing opposing tribes, instituting legal, educational, financial and administrative reforms, and creating a modern bureaucracy (not an Asian bureaucracy). Reza Shah's authoritarianism was similar to Eastern autocracy in certain cultural aspects but fundamentally different, on the whole, in its nature and content.

The government of Reza Shah kept the institution of the Majles, along with other constitutional institutions, but interfered extensively in the election to the Majles, packing it, by various means, with deputies from among the court followers. This practice was continued from the fifth Majles to the fourteenth. It is one of the characteristics of new authoritarianism.

Reza Shah appointed middle-level military officers, instead of old politicians and members of the old royal families, to manage the country. With some of his measures, such as the establishment of modern education and the creation of secular courts instead of religious courts, Reza Shah achieved a reduction in the influence of clerics in these institutions, traditionally under the clerics' control. During his reign, the proportion of clerics in the Majles was reduced from 13% to 1%.

The delay of economic development in Iran and the weakness of the Iranian bourgeoisie were precisely the results of the creation of absolute government and the system of reform from the top. This form of development, though profitable for national development, hurt democratic development. This reform did not involve cultural reform.

New Efforts at Democratic Development

At the beginning of World War II, the Allies entered Iranian territories and defeated the Iranian army with no significant resistance, deposing Reza Shah (who had intended to cooperate with Germany) and sending him into exile. With Reza Shah's departure, his extremely young son, Mohammad Reza, became the king of Iran. In the first period of Mohammad Reza Shah's government, the liberalist forces emerged once again in Iran, taking power in the Majles. Various political parties and groups also became active and took an important role on the political stage of Iran. In 1944, a coalition of parties that had arisen among the middle class established the "National Front" and gained a great deal of influence. In 1951, in the fourteenth Majles, they managed to gain a majority, and Dr. Mohammad Mossadeq, the head of the front, became the prime minister of Iran. The front had as its aim to increase the power of the Majles, emphasizing the execution of constitutional law and undertaking the nationalization of Iranian oil, which was in the hands of a British company.

In the beginning, the National Front had many important successes, and managed to pass the bill to nationalize the Iranian oil industry through the Majles. This was Iranian nationalism at the climax of its power, and nationalizing the oil industry was the achievement of the greatest nationalist goal. It was the first time that an oil-producing country ever canceled this, one of the worst imperialist arrangements. But the National Front and Dr. Mohammad Mossadeq were not able to see this great work through to its completion. Their failure was related both to the weakness of the National Front and to the diplomacy of Mossadeq's government.

At the time of the struggle with Britain, the National Front was badly divided due to disputes between religious and secular forces, which opened the way for the royal court to move against the front. Dr. Mossadeq's diplomacy, which insisted on "Negative balance policy", meaning equal independence from both the Eastern and Western blocks, isolated Iran in the international arena. When Mossadeq nationalized the British oil company, Britain began an economic siege on Iran and managed to put the Iranians under hard pressure.

For all the reasons I have just mentioned, the court was able to stage a coup in 1953, with the help of the United States, removing Dr. Mossadeq from government. The Shah, using the political parties he had set up, then tried to reinforce his social base, and through apparently legal means, concentrate power in his hands. Thus, he established the "New Iran Party", which tried to bring different classes, trades and associations under its influence and build an extensive front in support of the court's authority. At the same time, the United States now influenced Iran's policy more than ever. Relations between Mohammad Reza Shah's government and the United States became so close that in 1959, a mutual military convention was signed between them, in which the United States guaranteed to defend Iran against foreign attack.

But Mohammad Reza Shah could not completely dominate the landowners, who had influence on the social structure of villages, and were in the majority in the Majles. In the nineteenth Majles, sixty-one percent of the deputies were big landowners. But the Shah wanted to promote a new policy for the new international and internal situations, including Land Reform and support for the great bourgeoisie, in order to re-insert Iran into the world market, and to do this, he had to find a way to remove the substantial impediment posed by the great landowners' power.

Finally, in 1962, the Shah managed to get the Land Reform law approved, by dissolving the Majles and with other political maneuvers. With the execution of Land Reform, the influence of landowners in the Majles and in the villages decreased greatly. This decline in the landowners' influence, resulting from peasant migration into the towns, was an important factor in the later Islamic Revolution.

At the start of Mohammad Reza Shah's move towards authoritarianism, the bazaaris stood firmly opposed, while the clerics also maintained their support for constitutional law and opposed the laws for women's liberation. Meanwhile, Ayatollah Khomeini rose against "capitulation". But the Shah's regime, with the help of the military and security forces, could break through all opposition and assert its power. Thus, he continued his father's government and "new authoritarianism" until the 1978-79 revolution.

Nationalism and the Fate of Authoritarianism

The Shah's regime, after its victory over those forces which had constrained its power, and after reaching the peak of authoritarianism, soon fell into crisis and was overthrown by the Islamic Revolution in 1978-79. Many books have been written regarding the problems which brought the authoritarian government of the Shah to crisis and fall, and I will not go into them in this study. Let me only briefly point out the clear role of cultural factors in the Islamic Revolution, even in its outward appearance and ideology. One of the remarkable characteristics of this revolution is its ideology, which is unique among contemporary revolutions and movements. The Islamic Revolution of 1978-79 was one of the most important revolutions in the world, laying the foundation for a new political, ideological and social system.

As a political milestone, the Islamic Revolution, seemed a staggering event to many people of the world. But for those who have studied contemporary Iranian history, it is not so difficult to understand. The Islamic Revolution was the continuation of the movement which began in the mid-nineteenth century as a reaction against imperialism and a struggle for the establishment of a national identity. Some of the most important manifestations of this movement were the Tobacco Concession Movement (1891), the Constitutional Revolution (1906) and Oil Nationalism (1950). Here I discuss the nationalist movement in Iran.

Iranian nationalism, in terms of its psychological and ideological aspects, can be divided into two branches: secular nationalism and religious nationalism. In Iranian history, these two branches have sometimes allied themselves and sometimes confronted each other. In the Constitutional Revolution, secular, liberal nationalism managed to win, and when liberalism could not fulfill the role of national government, the authoritarianism of Reza Shah took over in Iran. Under the leadership of Dr. Mossadeq, the two forces of religious and secular nationalism united to restrict the power of government, revive the Majles and nationalize the oil industry, and in the beginning had important successes. But the gap between the two branches of nationalism made it difficult for Dr. Mossadeq and led him to weakness and failure.

After the failure of Dr. Mossadeq and his removal in the United

States-court coup, Mohammad Reza Shah gradually strengthened the foundation of his government, moving towards authoritarianism. Once again, the nationalist, democratic movement was unsuccessful. One of the important effects of these events was that religious leaders and nationalists judged the coalition government and secular nationalism ineffective, and decided they would be more effective and decisive for national independence and identity on their own. In this way, the banner of the struggle against imperialism fell into the hands of the religious movement. This cycle had an important effect on later stages of political development.

Ayatollah Khomeini, instead of supporting constitutional law, propounded the thought of Velayat-e Faqih (rule of the jurist). Jalal al-Ahmad and Dr. Ali Shariati, who will be discussed in detail later, spoke to the religious feelings of the people in order to mobilize them against a government dependent on imperialism and the superficial aspects of Western culture.

On the other side, Mohammad Reza Shah appealed totally to the United States. He had signed a mutual military agreement and the capitulation treaty, provoking a sharp reaction from the people and the clerical leaders. Now it was the religious branch of the nationalist movement that won the leadership of Iranians in the movement.[111] The Pahlavi regime placed an intense emphasis on reform, secularization and the concentration of power, but this reform was not accompanied by reform in political culture. Socio-economic reform, meanwhile, brought with it other changes that had their own political consequences. For instance, rural groups rushed to the cities, where, while maintaining their own traditional culture, they became a potential political force. This was a force that could easily join up with extremist movements, and with its cultural background, lead the anti-imperialist and anti-autocratic movement onto a new route.[112] And indeed, after the political, economic and social crisis that Mohammad Reza Shah's regime experienced in the mid-1970s, these new forces entered the battlefield. Those who had constituted the reserve corps of radicals became the active soldiers of the anti-regime religious leaders. The failure of secular nationalism in the struggle against foreign domination of Iran led to Islamic fundamentalism.

Islamic fundamentalism considers cultural domination to be the basis of foreign dominance, and therefore puts the struggle against cultural invasion ahead of any other struggle. The previous secular styles of nationalism, such as liberal nationalism, democratic nationalism and the minor leftist movements, had assumed that it would be possible to important Western political institutions, with their roots in Western thought, while at the same time struggling against political and economic domination by the West. But Islamic fundamentalism emphasizes that, to effectively struggle against foreigners and Western domination, it is also necessary to return to native institutions. Only by means of genuine ideologies and native institutions can the struggle against Western domination succeed. In other words, the struggle against foreigners means primarily the struggle against foreign culture. A return to native culture is absolutely essential.[113]

After the Islamic Revolution, this became the official attitude of the Islamic Republic of Iran. The return to native culture is one of the important tenets of the Republic and the presence of traditional institutions, thought and ideology in the constitutional law of the Islamic Republic is a reflection of this attitude. The presence of traditional culture in new political processes and institutions is the subject of my chapter four.

Part Two: Traditional Culture and New Political Institutions

In the previous part, I discussed the decline of the Asiatic mode of production in Iran and the creation of elements of democratic development. Among these elements I singled out the new political institutions and principles that had been established and I discussed liberal movements, especially the creation of new demands for expansion of political participation and even new political institutions and principles. Now, before I discuss the different elements of traditional culture affecting political behavior and political processes, it is necessary to sum up the discussion of the previous chapter, and also to speak about the effect of traditional culture on new political institutions.

As I already explained, with the expansion of the world capitalist system and the growth of new socio-political forces, native political institutions, such as the institutions of traditional despotic government, waned. Another reason for the weakening of native institutions lay in their complicated relations with Western governments. Native institutions could not resist powerful foreign governments, and with their failure, resistance and anti-alien movements became more cultural in nature. Furthermore, nationalist intellectuals (such as Jamal al-Din al-Afghani), unable to inspire their country's government against imperialism started to pay attention to the masses of people and organize them instead, thereby pushing the masses, who had previously had nothing to do with politics, into the political field.

The former despotic governments, having lost their power bases because of their dependence on foreigners, could not resist popular movements and soon failed. Liberal intellectuals who entered the political field wrote new constitutional laws according to the Western patterns and established new political institutions and new principles on that basis. But after the overthrow of Eastern autocratic government, the liberal intellectuals found themselves surrounded by a traditional, underdeveloped society. In such a society, the constitutional laws that these intellectuals had written after the Western pattern were quickly put to the test. The result was that, soon after the approval of laws and creation of democratic institutions, new authoritarian governments arose. The liberal intellectuals who had been unable to bring order to the society, creating chaos instead, had to relinquish their positions to military officers, who were also from the middle class but did not have the same democratic views or even consider democratic methods an effective way to govern the society. The government of Reza Shah in Iran exemplified this process.

Authoritarian generals, though they spent so much effort on national development and economic reform, did not abide by democratic principles, and therefore damaged the democratic system. They would not return to the former forms of legitimacy, but nor did they rely on democratic legitimacy. Meanwhile, in spite of various reforms, these authoritarian governments, which depended on bureaucracy (an inheritance from the Asiatic mode of production), have been basically the shapers of the political scene of Iran in current history. Even those governments which took power through elections are no better than their predecessors, the military governments. For them, elections are just a means to give legitimacy to their authoritarianism. They try using any means to win elections through various maneuvers, not through the real support of the people.

The Institutionalization of the Political Management of the Society and the Methods of Authoritarianism

The institutionalization of political management means the establishment of governmental authority in the society, using different political structures and institutions. It means the systematization of the activities in which rulers, organizations and social groups relate with each other. Among rulers and subjects a system of cooperation will be organized,[114] with the effect that political decisions then depend less on individuals. This aspect of the modern system was a great development in the democratic countries, and due to the demands of modern society, and it also made some progress in Iran.

Various modern institutions, especially democratic institutions, were of course established in Iran, as discussed in the previous part. But in general, the authoritarian system in Iran tries to reorganize every new institution according to authoritarian principles. As a result, politics is still to a great extent the domain of individuals and personalities. The institutionalization of political management in this society will mean the deeper penetration of government into society, but true democratic institutionalization would actually mean the expansion of reciprocal links between government and the people to achieve the greatest overall effectiveness of the system.

The most recent method of institutionalization of political management of the society is the establishment of parliament. This transformation, to which I referred in the previous discussion, ended in the creation of the Majles in Iran. Iranian intellectuals and reformers hoped that approval of the constitutional law and establishment of the Majles would both provide popular political participation and guarantee political liberties. But the experience of later events showed that the establishment of the Majles by itself could not achieve democratic objectives. Furthermore, democratic institutions could even be used for non-democratic purposes. Authoritarian leaders such as Reza Shah, after taking power through coups and dominating the country, sometimes resorted to reforming the constitutional law, in order to gain legitimacy and legalize their authoritarian governments.

Constitutional law and the Majles could not enjoy complete success in the institutionalization of politics, although they played an important role in the expansion of the influence of the government in society. In other words, on the one hand, they successfully promoted one aspect of political development, the "nation-building" and "government-building". But they were not successful with the other aspect, democratic development. The inefficacy of the Majles and its laws in this part of political development was the result of their incompatibility with the culture of the society. These institutions, which actually had been imported, in no way agreed with traditional beliefs. As already mentioned, the reform of cultural attitudes, beliefs and traditions is nothing to be accomplished quickly and within a short time. The governing elite of Iran had another concept of the imported institutions and put them to authoritarian ends, and this way reduced the credibility of these institutions among the people. The continuing strength of traditional culture gave some of the authoritarian governors the opportunity to control these democratic institutions and empty them of their contents. Reza Shah and Mohammad Reza Shah's regimes exemplified this process. They used certain elements of traditional culture, such as patriarchal attitudes, for their own purposes.

Bureaucracy Instead of Representative Institutions

One of the reasons for the dispersion of power in Iran is the low level of institutionalization in politics and of popular participation. This dispersion of power is different from the concept of distribution of power that was discussed before. The dispersion of power means the distribution of power among influential, but non-public institutions that can endanger the normal functioning of the system. For instance, Shi'a clerics in Iran are the most important power center, and the influence of this power center sometimes causes the institutionalization of political affairs to change course and align with the demands of the powerful. The weak level of political institutionalization, on the other hand, brought more power to the executive and the bureaucracy. The Majles in Iran, having almost a hundred years of experience in political management, was able to take Iranian society towards institutionalization, but could not take it far enough, nor impart to it democratic methods, as is normal in democratic countries. For the same reason, the executive still has the basic role in the management of the society, and is still the basic and central institution of the government. This executive or bureaucratic organization works through a traditional bureaucracy, which is its only means of contact with the people. The weak level of political institutionalization caused the gap between civil society and government usually to be filled by executive force. In developed democracies, the various democratic institutions connect civil society to government.

In Iran, different factors increase the extent and importance of bureaucratic organization, among which culture is important. Not only is the culture itself a factor in bureaucratic centralization in Iranian society, but it also plays a role in other factors. For instance, the role in economic development which governments have undertaken in recent decades gives them the chance to use the favorable aspects of culture to increase executive power. Also, in Iran, governmental positions traditionally are a source of social prestige. Therefore, government is still the source of wealth and power for many people. This is the result of a cultural attitude that each person in the government has a share in authority and considers himself an owner of public property. In other words, governmental positions are considered a kind of "tuyul". Government officers consider themselves entitled to divide governmental positions as an income source among their relatives, and personal relationships, instead of knowledge, are the criteria for attaining governmental positions. Attitudes left over from the times when tribes and dynasties governed the country, and treated it as their private territory, are still a part of Iranian culture. In the modern, developed democracies, such attitudes have almost completely disappeared. The country as a legal entity is separate from powerful landowners. Ideally, attaining political positions relates to the individual's knowledge, not to tribal, political, family or religious connections, and political office, before being a way to benefit from the country, is seen as a kind of service.

Charismatic Leadership Instead of Democratic Legitimacy

According to Lucian Pye, building popular legitimacy is a part of the process of political development. In modern Iranian history, the search for political legitimacy has been essential. Even when legitimacy has been achieved through fraud, the fact remains that governments have recognized that they need this legitimacy as much as they need, for example, force. In modern times, there is rational bureaucracy, but it is not sufficient to guarantee the unity of the system. In the same way, the institutionalization of the principles of political management in society, although a sine qua non for political stability, is still not enough to guarantee the unity of the system. Political legitimacy is another important political provision. The institutions of a functional political system not only extend the influence of government all over the society, but also make this influence appear reliable and legal to the people. Political systems have to justify their sovereignty to the main players in the political scene, and to their supporters. This sovereignty should have moral authority. Without it, the political effectiveness of the government will be decreased. Socio-political institutions make the structural links between society and government and give legitimacy its psychic and emotional aspects. In countries such as Iran, in which these political institutions are not too strong, these issues have even more importance.

Legitimacy is created in many different ways. In Iran, traditional patriarchal legitimacy gradually gave way to ideological legitimacy. Charismatic legitimacy is also important in Iran. Charismatic leadership at its best is the leadership of someone who, according to his or her followers, is unmistakable and has metaphysical characteristics. Under these circumstances, the leader's successors will undoubtedly try to maintain charismatic authority. The relationship between the charismatic leader and his successors is the relationship between the professor and the student. But the examples of charismatic leadership in its pure form are few. Charismatic leadership is weak and eventually gives way to the normal process of leadership; therefore, it will likely move towards legal legitimacy. In the meantime, considering the restrictions of legal legitimacy and the power of traditional culture and bureaucracy, client-like relations fill some of the deficiency legal legitimacy. Client-like relations, in a way, were created by the former patriarchal culture.[115] In patriarchal relations, the relationship between government and the elite becomes like the relationship between patron and client. Patron-client relations exist between two persons of different political, social and economic ranks. The high-ranking person (patron) uses his influence for providing the low-ranking individual benefits, and in return the low-ranking person (client) helps his patron in different ways.[116] In this system, political stability depends mostly on agreement between the ruling regime and the influential elite, who are in turn dependent on government for keeping their position.

Reliance on Personality Instead of Legitimacy

One weakness in the political institutionalization of a society (and in the accompanying) is the establishment of regimes based on the individuality of leaders. These regimes depend mostly on a leader's personal qualities. The regime of Reza Shah and the other regimes of Iran, to a large extent, have these characteristics. In the modern period, unlike in traditional systems, even the personality-based regimes became dependent for day-to-day efficacy on institutional methods, bureaucratic means and military force, more than before. But the lack of efficient political institutions gives ambitious persons the chance to obtain authority through non-institutional methods. Under such conditions, factors such as political decision-making, rhetorical gifts, personal connections and personal prestige gain importance.

Although modern autocrats try to hide themselves under the cover of free elections and multiple parties, it is tradition and ancient culture that let them control the functioning of modern institutions and make their personal leadership permanent.[117] Individuals dependent on the regimes were controlled sometimes by charismatic leaders and sometimes by non-charismatic leaders. The messianic attitudes rooted in traditional culture create a favorable basis for charismatic leaders and make them into mythic figures, and the myth in turn takes root in the culture, feeding the power even of the charismatic leader's successor. The charismatic leadership of Ayatollah Khomeini was rooted in the customs of the Iranian nation. Even the authoritarian rulers who do not possess charisma, such as Reza Shah, try to make themselves appear charismatic.

I have explained that in modern societies, one sees less of the personalization of politics, or the dependence of politics on individuals purely. What exists in practice is a mixture of personality politics, bureaucracy and military force. For this reason, leaders attempt to transform political parties and bureaucratic and military organizations into their own personal bodies of defenders.[118] Individual faithfulness to the leader is considered the basic standard of political management and rewards, and military forces are faithful to the leader himself, not to their people or country. The ruler is always careful that no individual within the military or bureaucracy becomes powerful enough to threaten his authority. These rulers are very sensitive to their competitors' power and act cruelly in this regard. A prime example is the relationship between Reza Shah and Razmaram.

With the transformations that have been wrought in traditional systems, and with the creation of new authoritarianism, authoritarian regimes generally hide behind elective governments and parties, pretending that the bureaucracy, security forces and political police do not interfere in politics. The reality is that the armed forces and bureaucracy are faithful to the ruler individually and only interfere in politics and elections in his interest. The preservation of these authoritarian rulers depends on their skill in political maneuvers, secret deals and deceptions. The political parties, as well as groups which are not outwardly parties but act as such, have an important role in authoritarian and bureaucratic governments. Authoritarian rulers sometimes, because of the expansion of their influence and their reliance on populist politics and popular mobilization, resort to one-party rule.[119] The Hezb-e Rastakhiz ("Resurgence Party") in Iran at the time of Mohammad Reza Shah was such a party. In this regime, political power was completely under the control of the party and all political activities fell under its supervision. The government program was the same as the party program, and all governmental institutions, at least apparently, shared the ideology of the ruling party. Although there is no one-party monopoly in the Islamic Republic, the one official ideology almost has such a role. Considering the lack of political institutionalization in the society, the single party or ideology acts as the cement of the system. The single party or ideology also can be substituted for tribal and ethnic relations and other patriarchal relations. In other words, the fragmented aspects of identity are united into a single identity and become the cement of social relations.

Populism versus Institutional Participation

If traditional authoritarian systems do not show any interest in popular participation in politics, and the modern authoritarian systems pay attention to restricting and controlling participation, populist regimes make political mobilization of the masses top priority. In spite of all this, the controlled participation under these regimes is not competitive participation (in the style of genuine democracies). These regimes pay attention to mobilized participation, making mass mobilization the basis of their policy. They rely on the collective action of the people and try to involve them in demonstrations and rallies every day, to create solidarity with the regime. Although this policy is an easy and cheap means of charming the masses, it is also an effective object for the pride of the people, and gives them a feeling of identity.[120] The masses, who had been excluded from politics in the traditional systems and new authoritarian systems, rejoice to feel themselves a part of the political scene.[121]

Populist regimes do not, in terms of democratic criteria, have any qualitative differences from the bureaucratic authoritarian regimes, but what gives them a dimension of populistic democracy is the involvement of the people in politics. The Islamic Republic regime has some of these characteristics. Its ability to mobilize gives it great power and enables it to spur people to great sacrifices. This regime is the result of the alliance between the masses and their leaders in the course of a great revolution. It cracks down on all opponents. Successful competitors do not have any compassion for past comrades and present rivals. Mass mobilization gives self-confidence to this regime in its difficult confrontation, allowing the regime to be more cruel than the previous one, which was overthrown by the revolution. Samuel Huntington called this new regime radical praetorianism.[122]

In populist or radical praetorian regimes, political processes are not sufficiently institutionalized. In this regime, popular participation at the institutional level is restricted. The masses now entering politics have no previous experience in political action, and the political institutions lack the necessary mechanisms for properly entering them into the political play. The necessary culture has not been created for institutional participation, and this lack of effective political institutions causes power in the society to be dispersed among elites. Consequently, political actions and loyalties among individuals become unstable. The political players, instead of considering the entire society's interests, look after powerful social groups. Both people and politicians become more apolitical. Various social and economic classes intrude into politics, bringing anarchy to the political field. If the expansion of political participation does not occur along with institutionalization, the participation causes political instability instead of stability, and threatens socio-political security instead of increasing it.

Nativism Instead of Political Reform

When Western culture entered Iran, it provoked an intense reaction against it in different parts of the society. Given the intense infatuation of other parts of the society with Western culture, this intense reaction created a big gap between traditional and modern culture. The reaction of traditional culture against modern Western culture took the form of an attitude of nativism among some classes of the society. I will discuss nativism in detail later, but here it will suffice to say that nativism is an extreme movement for return to traditional culture, whose effect in the contemporary political process sometimes takes unusual forms.

Nativism means one-sided rejection of Western culture and the embrace of anything native. Within the Iranian Constitutional Movement, a superficial acceptance of Western culture on one side, and nativist attitudes towards culture on the other, confronted each other. Although one group of clerics accepted the principles of liberal constitutional government, another group deeply opposed it; this important gap was always a source of weakness for progressive movements in Iran. Where such cultural gaps were present, new political institutions did not gain necessary stability and legitimacy. Consequently, political development, meaning the expansion of participation and competition, faced many difficulties. Fundamentalism was a part of the attitudes against Western culture, and against constitutionalism itself. The deep cultural gap decreased the effectiveness of the political systems and constitutions that arose from the Constitutional Movement. Meanwhile, the political gap itself is a fact of the centralization of power and an impediment to democratic development.

In short, political institutions which had grown out of popular anti-autocratic movements, within the beginning of the modern period in Iran, had lost their effectiveness, power and prestige. Traditional culture sometimes changed and sometimes directly held out against change. As a result, democratic institutions not only could not gain the stability they needed, but they also became either pawns in the hands of authoritarians or targets of the attacks by traditionalists. In the next section, I will discuss the functioning of these institutions in reaction to traditional culture.

4 Negative Factors for Political Development: Traditional Culture and Democratic Development in Iran

In the First Chapter of this study, I began by trying to introduce and identify the basic elements and sources of traditional political culture in Iran. Then, in the Second Chapter, I studied the creation of new demands for political development and the concurrent establishment of new democratic institutions. I went on to explain how the new democratic institutions, which were mostly derived from Western democratic models, lost part of their nature and effectiveness among the masses and the political elite due to the influence of the dominant traditional culture. In the political management of society, democratic methods were replaced by a type of authoritarianism that I call new authoritarianism, which is totally different from traditional authoritarianism and Eastern autocracy in its practical methods, principles and sources of legitimacy, although ancient Eastern autocracy certainly affected the cultural basis of new authoritarianism. In other words, new authoritarianism is the result of the reaction between new democratic principles and institutions on the one hand and traditional attitudes, beliefs and cultural values on the other.

New authoritarianism utilized democratic institutions in a specific way that was not in agreement with their real nature. For instance, the Majles and elections became the source of authoritarian rulers' legitimacy; political parties became the means of domination for these rulers; and popular participation became controlled mobilizations in which the element of competition was removed. In this Chapter, I would now like to demonstrate how traditional attitudes, beliefs and cultural values, relate to the functioning of the system based on field research and discourse analysis. In order to do this, I will first explain the authoritarian functioning of the system, and then show its relationship with cultural variables.

Part One: Authoritarian Functioning of the System

If I want to summarize the result of the interaction of European political institutions and culture with the traditional culture of Iran, I can call it "new authoritarianism": a form of government in which democratic institutions and rights exist, unlike in past authoritarianism, but in which neither are these rights conceived of properly, nor are these institutions used as the real means of governing. The actual system of management is an oligarchy, undertaking its rule in the name of the people through the exploitation of some democratic customs and institutions. This authoritarianism is allied with traditional culture in different ways. I will first refer to some of the important characteristics of authoritarianism, and later discuss its connection with traditional culture.

In this part, I will use political discourse analysis to demonstrate the presence of traditional views. One of the reasons for this is that in Iran, the political discourse plainly reflects the presence of traditional values and views in current political movements and approaches, and exposes it more clearly and with greater emphasis than can be achieved with field research alone The Pahlavi regime, while struggling for reform in different areas, at the same time followed and preserved the oldest Iranian imperial traditions in the political management of society. The Pahlavi shahs tried to exploit these traditions for the legitimacy of their system. The Islamic Republic government, however, follows the Shi'a tradition, which has an important basis in Iranian culture, and gets its legitimacy from this tradition. The Islamic Republic of Iran was not only established by a special tradition, but also officially protects this tradition.

In addition to studying political movements, thought and discourse to show the connection of the nature of the political system to cultural views and values, I also use field research. Particularly, in the Second Chapter of this study, I have referred to some important aspects of systemic authoritarianism post-constitutionalism. There is no need for further detailed discussion regarding the authoritarian functioning of political systems in Iran here. Rather, my discussion here will be concentrated on the presence of traditional views in the political process.

Traditional Culture versus Western Culture

One of the main premises of modernism is that humans can establish their social environments through conscious activities. Modernism in Europe, in its first stage, recognized two important aims: economic development and progress towards democracy. The first aim was considered to be obtainable through technological processes and the second, through people's freedom and equality. Modernism in Europe was home-grown, having gradually evolved from traditional values and attitudes based on religious tradition. Modernism in Europe was, to a great extent, the secularization of religious values. As traditional values gradually changed, they opened the way to new attitudes towards reform and towards the future.

In modern times, European values, thought and ideals extended all over the world, including Iran, and were suddenly face to face with the traditional values and ideals of Iran, which were connected with religion. Many thought that, in order to expedite modernism (economic progress and political development), they had to eradicate tradition as soon as possible. A gap was created between tradition and modernism, especially insofar as modernism meant a set of Western concepts. Modernism was, among other things, an imposition by Western countries on underdeveloped countries, and this aspect of modernism, along with the industrialization it brought with it, had its own negative results. So when modernism, seen as an imposed culture, or at any rate Western culture, was accepted by the political elite, it brought cultural alienation and provoked disputes in Iranian society, especially among Iranian intellectuals. Some intellectuals found themselves looking at the relationship between tradition and modernism in a new way. Under these circumstances, tradition drew new attention to itself, as the cultural identity of a society and nation. The viewpoints of Jalal Al-e Ahmad in his book, *Westoxication*, and Dr. Ali Shariati's attack on cultural alienation and the creation of discourses, which have been accepted as a basis of Islamic Republic ideology, belong to this category of reflection on the clash between tradition and modernism. Some called these movements "cultural nationalism". I would like to explain more about these movements, which led to the growth of a new political culture in Iran, a culture which has shaped itself on the basis of traditional values by confronting modernism.

Three main attitudes have been found among Iranian intellectuals, faced with Western culture and its power and conflict:

1. Complete acceptance of all elements of Western culture. Seyyed Hasan Taqizadeh, one of the leaders of the Constitutional Movement, was the representative of a thought.
2. Accepting that a part of Western culture which related to economic and social reform and its association with "Eastern ideality", including the pre-Islamic culture. Ahmad Kasravi, a historian and consititutionalist, was the outstanding supporter of this attitude.
3. Selection only Western technology and Western economic principles, while rejecting other attitudes and values of Western culture on the basis of Islamic values. Seyyed Jamal al-Din Afghani was a representative of this attitude.

Among these three, it was the first that held sway at the time of the Constitutional Movement and the third that has had the most influence on the political culture of Iran most recently. The thought of Seyyed Jamal al-Din Afghani and his followers including their reaction against Western culture, gradually became the paradigm and prevailed in political discourse. This attitude took hard anti-Western aspects, supporting the reaction against Western culture and making the return to traditional culture the main focus of its work. This means that among the important tendencies of political culture, which include imperial, liberal, leftist and Shi'a tendencies, it is Shi'a culture that has now risen to dominate the others.

Imperial political culture took its legitimacy base from the two thousand five hundred years of Iranian Imperial history. In the modern period of the Pahlavi kingship, however, this culture could not support important elements of political development such as political participation, competition, tolerance and basic freedoms, and for this reason dissatisfied groups moved towards cultural alternative ideologies.

One of the alternative tendencies was the national-liberal tendency, which was rooted in the Constitutional Revolution and reacted against the tendency supporting imperial culture. This tendency reached its highest point in the movement of Oil Nationalism; thereafter it lost influence in the face of Shi'a culture.

When talking about the various tendencies of Iranian political culture, it is worth mentioning that dogmatism and the worship of violence and personality, are important characteristics. Children are brought up in homes and schools in an atmosphere that celebrates, holy war, retaliation and stoning.

In the Second Chapter of this book, I referred to some of the discussions about the reasons for the decline of imperial culture and the strength and prevalence of Shi'a culture. I mentioned that the Pahlavi shahs' adherence to foreign imperialism and the prevalence of foreign culture in Iran provoked a tendency towards traditional culture. Keeping the balance between the imperial and Shi'a traditions had been a source of political authority and stability; demolishing this balance caused the crisis. The Pahlavi shahs, through their connection to the foreigners and some superficial modernism, provoked a strong reaction towards the Shi'a tradition. One Western researcher who has studied the historical balancing of imperial and Shi'a customs and the importance of the continuity of custom in Iranian history says that what has kept Iran unified as a country, despite its tribal and geographical dispersion, is the way it leans on custom. In his opinion, leaning on authority is one trend that provides permanence, within the history of Iran.[123] The threat of Western political and economic domination over Iranian identity provoked the people's reaction against Western culture and the return to traditional culture. It was a way to keep their identity.

"Westoxication" versus Westernism

Jalal Al-e Ahmad, one of the university intellectuals, issued a book in 1962 called "Westoxication", which quickly became famous,[124] and in which he criticizes the intellectuals who had gotten caught up in Western culture, calling Western culture the basic principle of Iranians' misfortune. He calls the intellectuals after the Iranian Constitutional Revolution "Westernists" and "rootless," and he appeals to the clerics (who were, in his opinion, the only group resisting Western culture) to confront Westernism.

Although Jalal Al-e Ahmad was attacking Western culture, he was actually inspired by Western thought, and the "Westoxication" book presented a confused concept based on dependence theory.[125] Still, it was

Al-e Ahmad who was most influenced on Iranian intellectual thinking after World War II. His theory had a great impact and became an important political theory. Dr. Ali Shariati formulated another aspect of the same attitude, and spread it among Iranian students. His thinking regarding "return to oneself" became an important cultural movement. These theories and writings turned some existing tendencies of Islamic culture into political discourse, shaping the ideology of the Islamic Revolution. Nationalism, populism and social justice were some of the subjects which found a place for themselves in this discourse. After the Islamic Revolution, Iranian intellectuals tried to unite these concepts into an organized political culture.[126]

The Pahlavi government's push towards development and modernism happened at such great speed that it created a reaction in the traditional classes. Although Reza Shah and Mohammad Reza Shah considered cultural reform in their strategy for development, the culture, by its very nature, was unable to change as fast as they would have liked. Therefore, the economic and political reforms that did get carried out caused cultural division,[127] which promoted political crisis and a new style of traditional culture. Reza Shah and Mohammad Reza Shah did not want to move the structure of the political system towards democracy; instead, they wanted to create as many cultural changes as they could. This inclination was obvious in various fields, such as education and entertainment. The effort to displace tribal culture as quickly as possible and to promote the supposedly sublime aspects of Western culture ended in alienation and the beginnings of disillusionment and rebellion among the traditional classes and the deprived urban people.[128]

Even some leftist intellectuals showed a slightly different manifestation of the same tendency, labeling the West a disorder in the natural change of the production system in Iran. They theorized that if imperialism had not penetrated Iran, Iran could have taken its own natural path towards development. Even among the most modernist Iranian intellectuals, such as Ahmad Shamlu, the contemporary poet, and Samad Behrangi and Reza Baraheni, both writers, a kind of nostalgia for the past was created for traditional culture developed.[129] These intellectuals also complained about Western political and cultural penetration in various ways, and may even have unconsciously aggravated the movement of "turn to the past".

All Iranian intellectuals religious and non-religious, reacted intensely to dependence on the West. The only difference was that the religious intellectuals considered the basic intolerable element of dependence to be cultural dependence, while many of the non-religious intellectuals considered economic dependence to be the worst aspect, and cultural dependence to be a side issue.

In my opinion, it would be wrong to underestimate the importance of culture. One writer on third world politics has said that it is not possible to explain political movements in developing countries, through economic development and political reform alone. These movements also cover complicated cultural disputes, which must not be neglected. In order to better understand these movements, it will be necessary to leave the framework of current paradigms and look at things with a broader view, in such a way as to take the cultural facts into account.[130]

The Islamic Revolution surprised many Western scholars and intellectuals, who had assumed that the secularization process that the Pahlavi regime was continuing to pursue in Iranian society, would be impossible to turn back. But in a country such as Iran, where power has not been completely institutionalized, culture plays a very important role. People still look at politics with distrust. For this reason, people have more confidence in traditions which have ancient roots.

Many cultural values, attitudes and beliefs in Iran go far beyond the limits of the Pahlavi regime or the government of the Islamic Republic. Among these are the attitude towards authority structure. Authoritarianism is an attitude that has been seen equally in both the Pahlavi and Islamic governments. Mohammad Reza Shah considered himself to be above the law and most of the time, in the Islamic government, the leadership makes it clear in its speeches that it considers itself to be above the law, as well. There is no difference between the government and the regime. The Islamic Republic government has also tried to put the trade unions under the supervision of the government.[131]

Dependency and Liberation

The discussion of dependency that was started in 1962 by Jalal Al-e Ahmad's book "Westoxication" reached a climax at the beginning of 1970, with the concepts of "dependent capitalism" and "dependent government," which appeared in leftist writings. In 1971, Marvin Zonis said that the most important political affair in contemporary Iran might be foreign encroachment on Iranian sovereignty and the relation of foreigners with internal policy.[132]

Peter Avery said that when European invaders in Iran resisted being integrated or assimilated into Iranian culture, Iranians tried to keep their independence by balancing one European power against another power. This was the major job of Iranian diplomacy in the nineteenth century. But in the twentieth century, Mohammad Reza Shah did not continue this method, and gradually the United States came to dominate Iran. In the middle of the twentieth century, foreign influence threatened not only the bases of Iranian custom, but also Iranian identity and pride. Foreign powers' strong support of Reza Shah and Mohammad Reza Shah caused the shahs to rule over people with haughtiness, provoking Iranian reaction.[133] The development strategy of the Pahlavi government, aiming leave the authoritarian structure untouched in the political area while changing the culture as soon as possible, created crisis. Dependency discussion was actually a discussion of the governmental, social, economic and cultural diseases of Iran. The discussion of dependency and how to defeat it very soon prevailed among all intellectuals, religious and non-religious.

Mohammad Reza Shah could not develop an organized political culture for reform in his country. The shah's resistance against democratization weakened the bases of reform and secularization among the new middle class, intellectuals, workers and groups whose participation seemed necessary to support reform. Therefore, the dissatisfied groups, including the Islamic group led by the clergy, went towards alternative ideologies.

As already mentioned, the concept of "westoxication" by Al-e Ahmad expressed became an important subject among Iranian intellectuals. "Westoxication" presented an anti-modern, populistic and traditionalistic theory. Pessimism towards the achievements of the West and modernism were important aspects of "Westoxication," persuading many Iranian intellectuals to review their blind acceptance of Western culture.[134] Al-e Ahmad impeached the hegemony of Western modern culture in Iran. He attacked the intellectuals for being elements in the expansion of "Westoxication" in Iran, and his inspiration was Sheikh Fazlollah Nouri, who criticized the foundation of the Constitutional Revolution. Al-e Ahmad introduced the clergy as the only group which could defend Iran's cultural identity.

"Westoxication" and the Opposition to Technology

Jalal Al-e Ahmad pushed his opposition to Western culture even further, into opposition to technology, following Daryoush Shayegan, another Iranian anti-Western intellectual, who said that Western thought has always moved towards rejecting all aspects of faith, which are the idealistic heritage of Asian civilization, and that this characteristic of Western culture has resulted from the technical thought of the West. Shayegan defended Eastern idealism against technical intellect and Western science. In his opinion, Eastern thought was the only remaining human thought. He did not accept the theory of intellectuals at the beginning of the twentieth century, who said, that Iran could take on Western technology, without accepting its culture. He said that Western technology and thought make a unique total. It is impossible to take the technology while staying safe from its demolishing results.[135] Shayegan also considered Islam and Shi'ism as a shaping source for a tribal commemoration of Iranian society and introduced the clergy as the main protectors of tradition.

Shayegan labeled the West "extra existentialistic." He considered the West a unique generality, not a combination of different things. When the 1979 Revolution took place, amended his theories somewhat, writing that these civilizations are not two separate geographical worlds and two opposite cultural poles; they are instead two constellations, whose stars enters each other's world.[136]

Reza Davari, another Iranian intellectual, went even further than Shayegan, rejecting not only technology but also Western humanism, which he considered the Western thought axis. He described humanism as Westernism. Reza Davari said that modernism has its roots in the West, and the West has spread it everywhere and we have lived many years under its dejected and dried branches. These dried branches, even now that we are seeking shelter in Islam, are still hanging above us.[137] He believed that in order to get rid of these branches, we have to annihilate modernism. But how would it be possible? Through expanding a new mentality, separate from the Western mentality and even superior to it, whose basis is in sacred revelation, rather than belief in humanism and the separation of religion from politics. This would imply a kind of Islamic Renaissance that rejects the achievement of intellectuality. Rejecting "Westoxication" was not sufficient; we have to criticize the very nature of Western civilization and history.

Hereafter, the matter of returning to Islam became a dominant discourse for the Iranian revolutionary elite. This discourse, which is still the prevailing discourse, is expressed in various ways but it is based on the thinking that there is an Iranian, Islamic and Eastern culture on one side and a Western culture on the other side, that will use the political and economic domination of the West to destroy the Iranian, Islamic or Eastern culture. Jalal Al-e Ahmad, Dr. Ali Shariati and others were all asking for a return to a culture which had remained hidden and which, because of the rush of the West, was facing destruction.[138] They were looking for identity and "cultural genuineness".

I have to consider the concept of "Westoxication" to have begun as a political reaction, rather than an organized mental and cultural movement. But then Al-e Ahmad took it further, seriously criticizing the path that Iranian intellectuals had chosen, with their slogans such as "we should take the positive aspects of Western civilization" and "it would be possible to accept Western civilization, considering Iranian religion and tradition"; he was explicit in his judgment that these visions were superficial and credulous.[139]

Return to Moral Priority

As I have explained, paying attention to moral and religious salvation is one of the important functions of traditional culture. This moral approach has determined the current movement in Iranian political culture. From the second half of the nineteenth century until the 1970s, the main emphasis for Iranian governments and intellectuals had been overcoming the retardation they felt in comparison with the West. As a result, the reform tendency in various areas was the basic priority of all political movements. The liberal nationalism of the constitutional movement under the Reza Shah dictatorship and the authoritarian government of Mohammad Reza Shah were all pursuing the same goals.[140] But in 1970, due to changes in the political discourse and the creation of new discourses, the desire to address and remedy perceived retardation gave way to distrust and corruption. The West, which had been seen as a blueprint for prevailing over retardation by liberal nationalist intellectuals, gradually started to be attacked as a pattern for corruption. Western culture was targeted as a symbol of corruption preparing the grounds for the 1979 Revolution.

Some new anxieties and concerns were propounded in the 1979 Revolution. Ayatollah Khomeini said that the West can conquer all spheres, but will not be able to gain salvation and prosperity, because it is morally corrupt, a prosperous society could only be established through correct behavior and morals. Nationalism, he pointed out, although opposed to the West and desiring Iranian freedom from imperialism, was nevertheless influenced by the West. Islam was worried about morals, not renovation.[141] This was a complete paradigm shift in the political discussion, because while the liberal constitutionalists, Islamic reformists and small groups of social democrats in Iran had had some disagreements during the 1960s and 1970s regarding how to overcome the country's perceived retardation, there was no important disagreement about the necessity of development itself and catching up to the West. With the Islamic Revolution, however, the matter of the establishment of a morally just system and a politics based on tribal (civil) religion took the primary place in the attitude towards politics. This thought was not just expressed in the religious city of Qom, but also propounded among intellectuals who had gone to Europe and even among University professors and people such as Jalal Al-e Ahmad and Ali Shariati.

Constitutionalists and reformists considered the military power and political structure of the West to be the important issue; these were the features of Westernism they wanted to emulate. Islamists, on the other hand, viewed the cultural sovereignty of the West as a domination over Muslims, which could not be tolerated. Therefore, in order to confront this domination, Muslims had to revive the Islamic culture against Western culture. This change was also to be seen in the political paradigms and discourses occurring in other Islamic countries at that time, but the Shi'a tradition in Iran gave more power to it. The independence of the Shi'a clerics in Iran, which has been discussed before, played an important role in this development.[142] The matter of confrontation with the cultural "invasion" of the West was expressed in terms of domination over Islam, and became a current concept, introduced in textbooks as well, as I will explain later.

Part Two: Relation of Traditional Culture to the Authoritarian Functioning of the System

The basic elements of Iranian political culture can be seen both in the Pahlavi authoritarian government and in the opposition to the Pahlavi regime and the return to traditional and tribal (civil) culture: both systems display authoritarian attitudes and tendencies that can be clearly seen in the functioning of the system. So we need to step back and study the very attitudes, beliefs and approaches which create the foundation for this authoritarian tendency. To this end, I will study both the attitudes and beliefs among the governing elite and the current beliefs and values among the masses.

The Culture of the Governing Elite and Authoritarianism

The attitude of governing groups, wherever it is derived from, has crucial effect on political development. This attitude is the origin of a series of political behaviors which, in total, make up the government function. In Iran, this attitude is basically determined by authoritarian and hierarchical characteristics, due to historical reasons that I have already explained. The attitude of the governing political elite towards the management of the society, whether in religion or tribal customs, conforms to authoritarian and pyramidal characteristics. Nizam al-Mulk, the great vizier of Seljuk, said that above any position, no matter how high, God has set an even higher one, and he advised the king to respect these hierarchies.[143]

Iranian society was always a pyramidal society, in which the authorities were as stairs, one on top of another. The highest worldly position was king, who was above everyone else. The following hierarchy held true in most historical periods of Iran, before and since Islam:

1. kings and princes
2. military officers
3. clerics (who of course had their own internal hierarchies as well)

4. scholars and secretaries
5. subjects.

As I have already explained, this hierarchy was observed in Avesta, as well as in Sassanid times. Any breach of this pyramidal system was considered a danger for the empire.[144] The Quran also says to obey God, the prophet and the governors.

The Safavid shahs revived the custom of great Iranian kings, leaning on Shi'ite ideology, after a long period in which the kings were completely outside the Shi'ite hierarchy. The Safavids kept this structure, in which the dynasty was part of the entire structure of society, and it remained the same until the time of the Qajars. (Of course, in the Qajar period, the patrimonial aspect of government increased and the tribal chiefs got more powerful positions in the authority pyramid.) This structure remained the same, with few changes, from the time of the great ancient kings until the constitutional movement, when the first stages of political development started.

In Iran, although there was a rigid class and authority structure, social movement at the individual level was possible. This fact was related to the nature of Eastern autocracy, in which the concentration of authority required the weakness of other power bases. The flourishing of people such as Haji Baba Isfahani, Sadrat, Amir Kabir and Gham Magham Farahani, more than it related to classical inspiration, related to the nature of authority in Eastern autocracy.

At the time of the Qajar dynasty a new factor entered the society which intensified the division into classes. This fact was the expansion of the monetary economy. The Qajar shahs, in order to get more money, sold not only the lands, but also positions. This custom went so far that Lord Curzon said that there was no position lower than the kingship which could not be sold.[145] Naturally, the traders were the only class who benefited from such a situation.

In the modern period, certain institutions, such as constitutional law, legislative parliament and elective government, have brought changes, but, as I have explained, these institutions were not able to change the authoritarian and patriarchal nature of the political system all at once, nor change the manor system into a system of citizenship. I look for the reasons, on one hand, in the establishment of an absolute government, and on the other hand, in the presence of a traditional culture and the reviving of it.

Here I am not trying to explain anything about the establishment of a despotic government; my point is simply that a despotic government produces traditional values in conformity with its own needs. Meanwhile, many of the beliefs, approaches and cultural values in Iran go beyond the limits of the Pahlavi regime or Islamic Republic government, and are seen in both systems. Among them is the attitude towards the subject of authority and power. Mohammad Reza shah considered himself higher than any law and did not differentiate between the regime and the government. In the Islamic Republic also there is no difference between these two. The Islamic Republic has tried to put trade cooperatives under the supervision of the government.[146]

Attitudes, Approaches and Beliefs of the Governing Political Elite

The attitudes of the Iranian governing elite towards participation and competition could be considered the axis around which its political culture rotates. The governing elite in Iran, both before and after the Constitutional Movement, has considered its power relations with the people to be the domestic equivalent of imperialism versus dependency, reckoning the following of the masses as part of its power. Even in the modern period, in spite of the prevalence of Western democratic thought, the governing elite still considers itself superior to the people, and believes that the people do not deserve to participate independently and actively in their fate. Authoritarian culture creates a special character of spirituality and personality in those who govern that makes the authority system, as I will explain later, deeply rooted and slow to change. Fear, lack of security, distrust of others, opportunism, the inclination to misuse others, avoidance of responsibility and the leaving of responsibilities to higher authorities are some tendencies and approaches of the governing elite; they are in fact the basic characteristics of the Iranian ruling culture. A prominent Western researcher, Marvin Zonis, did an extensive investigation regarding the tendencies of the Iranian elite during the time of Mohammad Reza Shah.[147] It is impossible for me to continue his investigations among the governing elite of the Islamic Republic of Iran, either generally or specifically, at the present time. But considering all indications, including the presence of many ancient cultural elements in recent times and the continuation of the structure of despotic power, I can say confidently that the same tendencies exist among the Islamic Republic governing elite. Let me just briefly address some of these basic tendencies, namely insecurity, pessimism, distrust, and opportunism and the abuse of power.

1. Insecurity

In Iran, lack of security is an important aspect of political life. Security has traditionally been in short supply in Iranian life,[148] for both the political elite and the masses. For one thing, Iranian cities and cultural centers have always been exposed to the danger of attack by nomadic tribes. Overall insecurity increased to the point that, especially from the time of Naser al-Din Shah (the Qajar shah) until the time of Reza Shah, hunger and annihilation were threatening the life of the people.[149]

The feeling of insecurity can be broken down into its component feelings, such as loneliness, anxiety and insolvency. Among the political elite, insecurity was chiefly related to the anxiety arising from a lack of political justice. According to Zonis, 72% of the political elite in Mohammad Reza Shah's time themselves admitted a lack of justice, regulations and principles. The Iranian people and political elite do not consider the surrounding world a secure world, but see it as an enemy, as threatening. The political elite, specifically, think the masses are illogical, greedy and ignorant, and tend to discourage active political participation by the masses; under the Pahlavis, even their passive participation was discouraged. This has changed somewhat in the Islamic Republic, which encourages controlled popular participation, although people are also encouraged to consider the views of Mujtahid in political affairs in order to avoid any fault.

A researcher who has done some investigations among the middle class concluded that this feeling of insecurity also existed among these classes. He says that the Iranian middle class teaches its children not to trust anyone, because others are always out to deceive simple people.[150] The child-rearing customs in Iran tend to reinforce this attitude of distrust. Child-rearing in Iran is authoritative, and children are not permitted to make any comment or have self-dependence. The Western concept of children's rights is not recognized by Iranian parents, and this commonly holds true among the political elite, as well.

Some serious shortcomings in the Iranian bureaucracy result from this distrust. There is a great fear of losing one's position and job, which are the basic sources of power, income, respect and, of course, security in Iran. Terms of office are usually short. Mohammad Reza Shah, in order to stabilize his authoritarian government, changed cabinets 27 times within ten years (1940-1950). Between 1941 and 1952, about 400 changes took place in ministerial positions.[151] (It is interesting that these transformations were accomplished among only 142 persons.) Such waves of change have come continuously in the Islamic Republic as well, even reaching down to the lower levels of organizations. I myself, in four years of study at the Faculty of Law and Political Science at Tehran University, saw four different chancellors.

2. Pessimism

Pessimism is another approach and attitude which has a negative effect on the process of political development. Lucian Pye said that, without a feeling of trust, the political promise of development will probably cause pessimism. In a pervasive distrustful atmosphere, the people consider any promises by political leaders as just one more conspiracy to take everything into their own hands.[152]

Not only public pessimism but even pessimism in private spheres, will extend to the political domain. (By pessimism, of course, I do not mean a critical view of governmental affairs, which, far from harming political development, would be good for it.[153]) Researchers believe that the more pessimistic the political elite is, the greater the grudge they will hold against the political system, although they themselves are a part of it. According to the investigations of Marvin Zonis, the Iranian political elite is pessimistic about the Iranian political system and considers it full of injustice and partiality. The following chart shows the opinion of the political elite at the time of Mohammad Reza Shah regarding injustice in the system.

Table 4.1 **Existence of Injustice from the Viewpoint of Respondents (Political Elite)** [154]

Injustice rate	Percentage of Respondents
Too much injustice	46.7
Much injustice	25.2
Not too much	18.6
Little injustice	1.2
Did not answer	8.3

This chart shows that more than 70% of the political elite in Iran at that time believed that there was a great deal of injustice in the Iranian political system (almost half said too much injustice), while less than 2% believed that there was little injustice in the political system of Iran.

3. Distrust

Most Western researchers who have studied Iran and its culture have discussed the great prevalence of distrust among the people and the political elite. The reality is that the prevalence of distrust is a cultural characteristic of all underdeveloped countries. These societies cannot achieve conditions of cooperation and association in the direction of development and reform. In order to create a developing system, however, people have to understand the necessity of common effort.[155] In order to establish a national political system, the existence of confidence in relations between people is an important factor. Sidney Verba, one of the founders of the political culture process in development, has written that an increase in political participation level causes interruption and political conflicts if it comes before people have learned how to trust each other.[156] Another researcher suggests that the conflicting messages of modern and traditional value systems made to associate with each other for the first time, put the political players in confusion, lead them astray and cause an expansion of the feeling of distrust.[157] Most researchers, however, believe that distrust has deep roots and has an essential relation with the conditions of agricultural society.

Marvin Zonis, in order to determine the distrust rate among the political elite in Iran, proposed some comments and asked respondents to agree or disagree with them. The first comment was: "The universe is a place full of risks, wherein people are basically dangerous and wicked." Only 10% agreed, while a little over 80% disagreed. This result would tend to indicate that there is not too much distrust among the Iranian political elite, but it does not end here. The next comment was: "Most people, in order to further their interests and get benefits, use inequitable means." Around 60% agreed with this statement and 30%.

The third comment was: "I do not trust those who show too much friendly behavior." Almost 60% disagreed with this; about 35% agreed. It seems as though the political elite of Iran reproach distrust when it is presented in the abstract. In reality, however, they display great distrust and their answers to the fourth comment were another example of this. The comment was: "I believe that most of my companians stab me in the back if they think that this will advance them faster." Almost 55% agreed; 40% disagreed.

This research shows that a member of the political elite of Iran sees his working area as full of enmity and feels the need to be extra cautious. Such attitudes have a clear relation with the Eastern autocratic system. The more active the political elite are, the higher their rate of distrust. Experience in the political area confirms the attitude of distrust.

4. Opportunism and the Abuse of Power

Marvin Zonis says that the Iranian political elite is the incarnation of Machiavelli's words regarding the acquisition of authority in any possible way. This elite changes color every day, depending on the situation, chameleonlike. Social mobility up the stairs of power is accomplished not through personal abilities, but by juggling and flattery. When a member of the government declares a policy, other people in power neither believe him nor take him seriously, sure that this policy is only a tactic for some other, hidden, strategy. About 80% of the Iranian political elite believe that their compatriots will generally undertake any specific act for their own benefit.[158]

Such distrust and pessimism towards everyone, such distrust of the honesty of other politicians and officials and the lack of independence in decision-making are big impediments to political development. The attitudes of the political elite, the dominant culture of authoritarianism and the weakness of the bureaucracy prevent the mobilization of human potential, which is a necessity for development. The Iranian political elite generally serves the bureaucracy for its own benefit, and, for this reason, the bureaucracy will also be in the employ of a "wise leader."

Authoritarianism, seen in this way, solidifies itself from every aspect. Everything is subject to the personal power of the person in the highest political position. Everything is scrutinized from the viewpoint of the system and of security. Alexis de Tocqueville says that a nation that asks for nothing except to keep the security and system is heartily a winner.[159] The attitudes and tendencies that I have looked at here, which determine the Iranian political elite, are suitable for stability keeping, not for changes and reforms.

The masses, meanwhile, show the same attitudes as the governing political elite. Some Western authorities have said that pessimism is an Iranian characteristic, just as the Iranian habit of breaking promises is also a part of the Iranian personality.[160]

Insecurity, meanwhile, is the other very characteristic attitude of the Iranian people and political elite. One Western researcher says that the feeling of insecurity whether at the personal or the national level, is one of the most particular characteristics of Iranians in recent history.[161] Marvin Zonis shows that the more active the members of the Iranian political elite become, the less insecure they feel, similarly, the more powerful they are, the less obedient they will be.

Curiously, though, Zonis shows that the increasing rate of these advantages in the political elite is subordinate to a different order which itself is interesting. His investigations show that the longer members of the political elite are in the employ of the system, the more insecurity, pessimism and distrust they will show. The presence of these tendencies in the most powerful, active and veteran members of the political elite is greater than in the less active members of the same group.[162]

Going back to the advantages discussed above (greater political activity means greater security, greater power means less obedience): We can observe that they serve the authoritarian system in various ways, and are reproduced by the system. Such attitudes naturally prevent effective participation in politics and give the initiative to whoever occupies the superior political position, meaning the king or the highest leader. This is an impediment to political development. What happens under such circumstances is that everyone is exchanging favors and benefits, all the time. The members of the political elite, different authorities, political parties and concordant groups all carry on transactions for small benefits. In developing systems, trading takes place only in elections and parliamentary activities, but in the traditional system, such as in Iran, such business takes over all procedures of political life. One researcher says that in Iran, everyone is a businessman, from the head of the family to the government employee, including teachers, policemen, officers, professors, people in high political positions, party leaders, labor cooperative members and leaders and journalists. Where there is no regular, established basis or principle for the control of political leaders and of scattered units of authority , such a situation is inevitable.[163]

The Relationship Between Political Authoritarianism and Religious Authoritarianism

Researchers have seen a meaningful relationship between religious authority and authoritarian attitudes towards politics, and have also found some connection between religious doctrines and political movements. According to the evaluations of these researchers, Islam is a religion with a very high level of authoritarianism. (Shi'ism, with its millennial beliefs, has ever more fertile ground for political movements and charismatic views, which could help explain the recent political movements in Iran and the differences between Iran and other Muslim countries in the Middle East. However, this is not the focus of my discussion; I mention it only in passing.

One researcher, Donald Smith, has done some studies regarding the structural effects of Islam, Hinduism, Buddhism and Catholicism on political attitudes.[164] He was able to determine three levels of authority that have a direct connection with political attitudes and the political management of the society. These three levels are:

1. dogmatic authority, or belief in absolute realities
2. guiding authority, or the comprehensiveness of religious orders
3. institutional authority, or the structures necessary for enforcing rules.

According to Donald Smith's analysis, the interplay of these levels of authority determines the degree to which a religion is authoritarian. He also established that the more authoritarian the religion is, the more authoritarian the accompanying political culture will be, while the less authoritarian the religion is, the more it will be compatible with the political culture of democratic political constitutions. Finally, Smith established that the higher the degree of dogmatic authority in a religious system, the greater its tendency will be to lean towards ideological political culture.

If one calls the lowest authority zero and the highest three, the following chart shows how high a level of authoritarianism each of these religions has.

Table 4.2 Breakdown of Levels of Religions' Authority and Total Degree of Authoritarianism by Religion

Religion	Catholicism	Islam	Hinduism	Buddhism
Dogmatic authority	3	3	0	1
Guiding authority	3	3	3	0
Institutional authority	3	1	1	0
Total grade of authoritarianism	9	7	4	1

Donald Smith has completely studied Islam, but if I evaluate the level of authoritarianism in Shi'ism, using his standards, I find a total grade higher than 7, especially after the success of the Usuli school and the Akhbari school and the institution of Ijtihad (which is a powerful institution for enforcing the rules).

We can see, therefore, that there is a relationship between the authority structure of a religious system and the forming of the people's attitude towards political authoritarianism. But another important aspect of this subject is that the more authoritarian a religion is, the greater capacity the religion will have to confront any other authoritarian system. Such a religion has a greater potential to mobilize people for political struggle, as well, as revealed in the 1979 Iranian Revolution.

Another fact that emerges from this chart is the low degree of authoritarianism in Hinduism. Perhaps this characteristic, along with the direct presence of Britain in India, was among the elements which made the political development rate in India so different from that of Iran. Although India was also among the Asian societies, it has made more progress with respect to democratic development than have societies such as Iran. Wittfogel concluded that the main reason for this was the direct presence of the British people in India, and the growth of political organizations and the middle class, supported by the British government.

Donald Smith's studies have been built on by other researchers, some of whom consider his analysis inadequate because of the emphasis he places on religious structure. They point out that we also have to pay attention to the content of the religion, from the viewpoint of whether it encourages surrender or movement. If the authoritarian teachings of a religion go into the direction of adaptability, its role will naturally change as time goes on. In Hinduism, for instance, there is the caste system; therefore political surrender and adaptability are accepted more easily. Another important variable is the commentary aspect of religious teachings. Some religious principles and teachings have ambiguities in them which can be interpreted in various ways. In Iranian ancient thought, for instance, the king enjoying favors from God was conditional. The political opponents of the king could claim that the king had lost the "divine light." In ancient Egyptian and Mesopotamian myths and customs, on the other hand, there were no conditions for the kings' enjoyment of God's attention. Religions that have interpretable aspects can get new interpretations when the political, economic and social conditions change, which means that they allow change to happen more easily.

Some have said that Donald Smith's studies can explain how much influence religion has on politics, but not in what direction that influence will go. In order to fill this gap, other people have investigated the direction of the religious effect on politics. One of these people is Guenter Lewy, who did an extensive survey of the relation between religion and revolution.[165] He studied millennial movements in various countries and among religions with various doctrines. One of the most important of these doctrines is the ideal association of happiness in this world with salvation in the other world; another one is the struggle with corruption and social disease. Shi'ism not only has a high degree of authoritarianism, but its viewpoint also changes according to the demands of the society, especially during revolutionary movements.

In Guenter Lewy's analysis, the connection between happiness in this world and salvation in the other one gives certain characteristics to the political culture. One of these characteristics, which relates to my discussion here, is paving the way for a charismatic leadership. A leader with charisma gives legitimacy and holiness to the revolutionary movement and to fundamentalism. Due to Guenter Lewy's findings, we know that, given all the differences among millennial movements, the charismatic aspect is the determining element of any millennial movement. The element of charisma is what changes the followers of a religion or faction into a political group.

The charismatic movement flourished in the conditions of socio-political crisis in the society and created many reforms. But the fact is that the religion's capacity to legitimize the changes and to generalize the policy is an important factor. This is what makes the difference between a millennial religion, such as Shi'ism, and other religions.

Political Participation and Attitudes Relating to Political Culture

As I have mentioned many times now, attitudes towards participation and competition are important principles of Western democracy, which I have chosen as a standard for Iran. Now I would like to analyze the Iranian people's attitude towards the subjects of participation and competition. As I already mentioned, democracy needs democratic citizens, and democratic institutions (a favorable factor) alone are not enough for the democratization of a system. The attitude towards participation in Iran is one of the unfavorable principles for development. A survey of public opinion shows that Iranians do not have any correct imagination of political participation and its necessity.

In a public opinion survey of a group consisting of students (including religious students, university students), governmental employees, doctors, engineers, lawyers (a group in which more than 60% had some higher educations), the question "What is your definition of political participation?" was asked. Around 35% replied that participation means cooperation between the people and government. Another 16% said that participation means being present at elections. Ten percent described political participation as "being informed of society affairs" and 9% described it as "having the right to vote and having impact on one's political fate."

In this group, about 25% gave a correct definition of political participation. More interesting was that 35% considered political participation to be the cooperation between government and the people,[166] a viewpoint related to the communal aspect of traditional culture in the society. Among this particular statistical group, the higher the educational level of the responders, the stronger their belief in the idea that political participation consists of a mutual relation between the government and citizens.

When asked about the existence of political participation in Iranian society, just 35% gave a positive reply, and 45%, meaning less than half of the respondents, expressed the opinion that there is no political participation in Iranian society. But do the 35% giving a positive reply even have the correct image of political participation? The next question allowed them to give an idea of their image of political participation, and it is quite limited. Those who stated that political participation does exist in Iran were asked what makes this political participation possible. Among them, 19% replied "through the promotion of the political culture of the society," 9% replied "through an active presence in the political scene," 12% replied "through free activities of political parties," 7% "through progress in the country development program." The fact that only 12% considered the free activity of political parties as the basis for political participation in the society derived from their limited imagination of what constitutes political participation. In today's complicated society, how can political participation be assured without the full-scale operation of political parties?

In another question, the respondents were asked: "In your opinion, what is indicated by the establishment of political parties and their activities?" Just 15% replied that this is a sign of "political participation in the society." There was a response to the question of "whether there is freedom of party activity in the constitution." Only 52% knew that such an article exists in the constitution.[167]

This research was performed among 344 people of whom 150 (43.6%) were students, 150 were religious scholars, and the remaining were doctors, lawyers and so on. The following chart summarizes their definition of political participation.

Table 4.3 Definitions of Political Participation

The meaning of political participation	Percentage
1. Cooperation between people and government	35
2. Active presence in state affairs including elections	16
3. Having information regarding society affairs	10
4. Having the right to vote and have an impact on one's political fate	9
5. No answer	30

Attitudes Towards Competition

I consider the way in which competition is perceived to be one of the standards of the democratic attitude. As I have already mentioned often, participation and competition are the first indicators of democracy, according to Robert Dal's research. Here I present a method of research whereby Iranian ideas regarding competition can be evaluated. It has been carried out among university students, religious students and employees, who are the most active and aware groups of Iranian people in the current political situation. The following chart presents the results of this research carried out in 1996. The questions are given here in brief.

Table 4.4 Attitudes Towards Political Competition

	Yes	No	No Answer
People who make political decisions mostly have differences of opinion; would it be better if they had a consensus of opinion?	73%	16%	11%
Would it be better if we had only one party in the country, so as to maximize the consensus of opinions?	61.2	22.8	16
Should parties always have agreement (that is, is it a problem if they sometimes have differences of opinion)?	51.6	30.4	18

The results of this research show that the Iranian respondents are very sensitive to agreement and correlation. This sensitivity may have risen from political conditions or the anxiety over destabilizing or intensifying democracy, but it probably also have deeper roots in the traditional culture, which has always put an emphasis on shared values and correlation in ideas and tastes.

Other researchers have asked the same statistical group about the necessity of free activities among the political parties. It is interesting that 41% of the respondents were opposed to the establishment of political parties and their free activities. Asked to explain the reason for their opposition to the free operation of political parties, 35% gave "former activities of parties," 22% said "rubber-stamped parties" and 43% gave "dependence on foreign powers and lack of human ideology."[168] Asked what they would do if parties began being allowed to operate freely, just 9% answered: "I would actively take part in the party." Of those 9% giving this particular answer 32% were university students, while only 18% were religious students, which would tend to indicate that religious students, who are closer to traditional attitudes, adhere less to political party freedom.

Regarding the reason for the failure of activity among Iranian parties, 26% of religious students marked the "lack of a suitable political structure for democracy," while 80% of the university students selected this item. On the other hand, the answer "the dependence of political parties on foreigners" was chosen by 65% of the religious students and only 14% of the university students as the reason for the failure of the party campaign.

The respondents' attitude regarding the influence of a liberal elite party campaign shows that they are afraid that political competition creates turbulence in the society. When the respondents were asked about the influence of party activities on society, 21% of them indicated that such activities would "make disorder in the society," 4% said that party activities would "increase dependence on foreign powers," and a total of 66% agreed that they would create pride for the system.

The position that university students, religious students and employees granted to the free activities of political parties as a condition of political participation shows their low attention to political competition as one of the elements of the democratic management of society. When the respondents were asked which of the following four ideas they considered necessary for providing political participation, only 7% marked the free campaign of political parties (if you do not count those who chose "all of the above"), as you can see in the following chart.

Table 4.5 Conditions Considered Necessary for Political Participation

	Percentage
1. Growth of political culture	19
2. The active presence of people in the political scene	19
3. Free activity of political parties	7
4. All of the above	35

This attitude was tested by another question. Respondents were asked to give their level of agreement to the following statement, using a number between 1 and 100:

"People with strange and bad ideas should not have permission to act freely in Iran and to explain their opinions to the public." The following chart shows the level of agreement with this statement for the different groups:

Table 4.6   "People with strange ideas should not be allowed to act freely."

Respondents	Agreement Level
1. University students	55.5
2. Religious students	70
3. Employees	50.5
4. Other respondents	45.5

As the above chart shows, most of the respondents believe that freedom of speech and freedom of organization have to be restricted for groups they consider to have strange or bad ideas.

Association of Authoritarian Tendencies with Democratic Values in People's Beliefs

While discussing the Iranian people's views regarding democracy, I have shown how there are many authoritarian values, even within the beliefs of those who consider themselves democratic. I would like to point out as well that many of those who support democracy do not believe that democracy can solve society's problems. Most supporter of democracy believe that a dictatorship can solve serious social problems better than a democracy.

Careful research in Iran makes clear that this can be seen in the Iranian people's beliefs. In a group consisting of university students (30%), religious students (30%), governmental employees (20%) and other educated individuals (20%), the participants were asked to choose one of the following ideas:

1. Democracy is the best method for solving all the affairs of a society.
2. In order to solve some serious affairs of the society, the powerful hands of a dictator are needed.

More than 65% of the respondents chose the second idea. Comparing the replies of university students and government employees with those of religious students shows that the latter group believes more in the powerful hands of a dictator for problem solving than do the former groups. In other words, the group that seems closest to tradition, due to its social and religious origins, supports authoritarianism more than do groups that are closer to modernism.

This great variation in people's beliefs when defending democratic principles is one of the weak points of Iranian democratic development. People can be divided into three groups based on their political tendencies with respect to democratic and authoritarian tendencies:

1. The stable democrats who reject every aspect of authoritarianism and defend democratic development. This group makes up a small percentage of the population. In this statistical population, it comprises less than 30% of the respondents.
2. Authoritarians who are opposed to democratic development and clearly defend the autocratic government. This group also comprises a small percentage of the population.
3. Groups whose tendencies and values include a combination of authoritarian principles and democratic styles. A great number of people fall into this group. They are neither stable democrats nor strict authoritarians. The large size of this ill-defined group makes the development of democracy difficult.

I have mentioned the idea, upheld by various researchers, that in order to develop democracy, people have to keep aloof from authoritarian deeds.[169] In Iran, many of those who verbally support democracy do not actually apply democratic principles. A great portion are actually semi-authoritarian, authoritarian, of two minds or in some other way only semidemocratic. Of course, with progress on the industrialization path, and with socio-economic growth, the number of those who have stable democratic attitudes increases every day.

In the 1997 presidential election, Iranians supported democratic orientation. More than 20 million out of 30 million voters voted for a candidate who has put democratic development at the top of his agenda. Therefore, I can say that the people have seriously decided to live in a democratic society. But I cannot say that this decision and this orientation will continue in Iran. Iranians still pay more attention to the results achieved by the government than to its working style. (As already explained, in Western democracy, the facts are the opposite, meaning that people in a Western democracy put more emphasis on the democratic style than on the actual results achieved by government.) The Iranian emphasis on results means that the failure of Mohammad Khatami's government in difficult economic areas (unemployment and inflation) may discourage people from their democratic feelings and people may change their opinion regarding their support of democracy and look in other directions. Among real democratic citizens such a probability would be low.

This vacillation in people's democratic attitudes comes from habits and attitudes left over from traditional culture. Many have accepted democratic values, but opposing internal beliefs affect their attitudes unconsciously. Moreover, most authoritarian values have actually kept a conscious place in people's minds. Field research has also confirmed the relationship between the attitudes and values of traditional culture and authoritarian tendencies. This research, which was done among 400 students from three distinct geographical areas of Tehran, shows that the more traditional the students are, the more attention they pay to authority. The downtown students were from poor families on the outskirts of the city, an area where traditionalism still has strong power. The midtown students were from the new middle class families, which have kept aloof from traditionalism, and the uptown students were from wealthy families, attending schools where they were only with the children of other wealthy families. All three groups of students were requested to answer the following questions, giving one or two answers for each:

1. For studying in your free time, who would be the best person to

choose the book for you?

    1.my teacher 2. my parents 3. myself 4. my friends.

2. When you have any problem with your classmates in school who can you ask for help?

    1. the superintendent 2. my teachers 3. my parents 4. my friends.

3. When you want to choose a book for study from the library, who would be better the best person to introduce a suitable book to you?

    1.the librarians 2. my teachers 3. myself 4. my friends.

In reply to the first question, the downtown and midtown students mostly marked the first and second alternatives, while the uptown students chose the third and fourth alternatives. This fact shows that the downtown students, who are closer to traditionalism, like their teachers and parents to make decisions for them; what is surprising is that the midtown students, from families who have kept aloof from traditionalism, also like their teachers and parents to make decisions for them. The wealthy uptown students have more confidence in their own decisions and in those of their friends, who are at the same level as them.

In the second question the same result was seen. For downtown students, the superintendent was seen as a better resource for authority. A small percentage of these students chose the fourth alternative (friends) as their resort in solving their problems. In the uptown areas, however, a high percentage of the children think their parents and friends are suitable for helping them solve their problems.

In the same way, in the third question, the number of people who chose teachers and librarians as a suitable resource for choosing their books was highest among downtown children, lowest among uptown children. The following chart is a summary of this research.

Table 4.7 Relationship between Traditional Tendencies and Authoritarian Views

Question	Downtown (%)	Midtown (%)	Uptown (%)
For studying in your free time, who would be the best person to choose the book for you?			
Teachers /parents.	65.6	51.8	42.5
Myself /friends.	34.4	20.5	65.6
When you have any problems with your classmates in school, who can you ask for help?			
Superintendent/teachers.	71.2	62.2	40
Parents/friends.	28.2	37.8	60
When you want to choose a book for study from the library, who would be the best person to introduce a suitable book to you?			
Librarians/teachers.	73.1	64	32.5
Myself/friends.	26.9	46	77.5

This research shows that as one's thinking gets closer to traditionalism, the tendency to depend on a higher position increases. This tendency, in a way, can be considered to be a tendency to authoritarian approaches.

The Combination of Religion and Politics

In addition to the creation of discourse about turning to the past, turning to

Islam and turning to the clergy, which was mentioned in the previous part, there are many other symptoms that show the presence of a powerful tendency among Iranians to be willing to allow religion and politics, and religion and government, to mix. One of the most important such symptoms was the people's vote for the Islamic government on April 1, 1980. In this vote, more than 89% of the people voted for the combination of religion with politics and government. Later, when liberalism and Islamic fundamentalism came into some conflict, people still mostly took the part of Islamic fundamentalism, and liberalism was not effectively supported. For this reason, in the early years of the Islamic Revolution, when electing the deputies of the Assembly of Experts, people voted for those clergy who demanded Islam in every aspect of the government. Therefore, as I will show, the Islamic Republic Constitution was approved on the basis of a combination of religion and government.

Meanwhile, research shows that the intellectual classes of the society still believe in 'this combination to a great extent. Polls of university students, government employees and other professionals confirm this idea. In a survey, 64% of the respondents evaluated the combination of religion and politics positively and just 19% did not support this combination, while 17% did not respond.[170]

Considering the pattern I have chosen for democratic development, such an attitude seems to be a great impediment to democratic development. In the political management of society, according to the pattern which I have considered as an indicator, the government cannot have anything to do with the religious and moral affairs of the people. A religious and moral government will by its nature be drawn to authoritarian tendencies.

Education and its Alliance with Tradition

Regarding the role of tradition in politics, Clifford Geertz has said that past rules, customs, beliefs and practices or, as he puts it, policy in the past, have a strong influence on underdeveloping policy.[171] This fact has even more importance when, after a radical transition, a new government comes to power. The new Islamic government in Iran, in order to reply to the many questions which it faced, used past culture as a guide We can gain insight into this by surveying the educational system and textbooks, which is one of the ways to understand the elements of political culture and its relation with tradition in a political system. Louis Althusser considers the educational system to be an ideological organization of modern societies that has taken the place of the church.[172] Education has great importance in the legitimation and justification of a political system.

In Iran, the Qajar government had based its power on tribal origin, while the Pahlavi regime, which had come to power through military authority, used education and the manipulation of the educational system in order to justify its legitimacy. Ayatollah Khomeini, before coming to power, criticized modern education, after the Islamic Revolution, modern education was still used as a tool for legitimacy; he tried to adapt the content of textbooks, using Islamic values and attitudes and coordinating them with traditional values. I can use the content of these books as an example of the influence of traditional culture on new political culture, and we can also compare the content of the books under the Pahlavis and in the Islamic Republic. Concentrating on education should give us very useful information since it is the most important means of socialization in Iran (in the West, family and press have more important roles in this respect). I will briefly review some of the research that has been done regarding the textbooks of elementary courses before and after the Islamic Revolution. This research was carried out on Persian textbooks for various elementary courses, the reasoning for the choice of books in Persian being that these books have the greatest political impact in Iran.

One of the most important subjects which can be seen in the textbooks of the Pahlavi time is the emphasis on the shah (king) as the central figure of the nation and the country, along with worship of him for his efforts in renovating Iran. The following chart shows the most important political subjects of Persian textbooks during the Pahlavi regime.

Table 4.8 Political Subjects of Pahlavi Textbooks[173]

Subject	Second Grade	Third Grade	Fourth Grade	Fifth Grade	Total	%
Iranian custom and myth (pre-Islam)	7	9	4	5	25	39
Worshipping the shah	0	8	3	0	11	18
Government propaganda (modernization efforts)	0	6	3	0	9	14
Patriotism	1	2	4	2	9	14

This chart shows that in the Pahlavi regime the myths and customs of ancient Iran (before Islam) have a primary place in the textbooks, making up 39% of all the subjects in the books. The king's praise comes in second place.

In the textbooks of the Islamic Republic of Iran, there is less emphasis on any individual; they mostly pay attention to religious affairs. Heritage before Islam has been omitted, and the stress is placed on Islamic traditions. People are pictured in long Arabian outfits. The Islamic Republic justifies its legitimacy through the efforts it has made to restore the purity of Islam, placing great emphasis on pure religious traditions. (In the Islamic Republic, religious customs take up the major part of political culture.) In the following chart, the subjects of Islamic Republic elementary course books have been classified.

Table 4.9 Political Subjects of Textbooks in the Islamic Republic of Iran[174]

Subject	Second Grade	Third Grade	Fourth Grade	Fifth Grade	Total	%
Islamic customs and faith	4	6	9	13	32	40
God	7	6	4	12	19	24
Anti-authority messages	2	1	4	12	19	24
The importance and worth of martyrdom	0	2	0	6	8	10
Ayatollah Khomeini's characteristics	0	0	0	2	2	2
Total	12	15	17	35	80	100

Traditional Principles as the Basis of the Islamic Republic of Iran

The traditional principles of Shi'ism are seen most prominently in the constitution, and are the basis of the Islamic Republic of Iran. A considerable part, though not all, of the principles of the Islamic government since the 1979 Revolution have been based on the viewpoints of Shi'a jurisprudence concerning government and morals, and these viewpoints have been included in the constitution and enacted as laws.[175] If I compare this with the pattern in Western democracy, I encounter some important discrepancies between these two. Here I address two areas in which the Islamic Republic differs markedly from two Western pattern: the basis of government and individual freedom.

1. The basis of government: the Islamic Republic of Iran is officially a theocratic government and has established the settlement of divine rule in society as its major aim. The unity of this thought with traditional thought is completely clear, stretching recognizably from ancient Iranian thought to

Shi'ism, and from there to the Islamic Republic constitution. The Islamic government was at first based on belief in the unity of the Umma (Islamic community). The ancient Iranian tradition of theocracy is obviously seen in this principle. The disputes that took place between the Shi'ites and Sunnites at the time of the Umayyad and Abbasid collided with this principle, of course. The Shi'ites, as already mentioned, established their kalam (theology) on a different basis than previous jurists, basing it on the Imamate principle, the government of the innocent Imam, the absence of the twelfth Imam and the mandate of the jurist (Velayat-e Faqih) during the absence of the twelfth Imam.

2. The individual and individual freedom in the Islamic government: Iranian regulations and the speeches of Islamic Republic leaders still contain many ambiguities regarding the socio-political role of the people.[176] Without going into a detailed discussion, I can say that the jurists make clear that a fatalist school is not currently dominant in the Islamic kalam.[177] Shi'a thinkers, especially, are under the influence of schematics who accept a limited freedom in interpreting the religious law's application But this freedom belongs to jurists, not normal individuals. In the Islamic Republic, ordinary juridical and political governing are left to the Velayat (guardianship) position, which is the final judge for struggles and affairs. This position is occupied by a person elected by jurists and by the Assembly of Experts. Therefore, contrary to what happens in the Western democracies, Iranian people do not have full authority to determine their own government nor established the basis of sovereignty. However, within specified limits, people do enjoy freedom, individual security and the right to participate in political affairs.

Iranian people have traditionally granted great respect to the clergy, and the root of this tradition reaches back to the pre-Islamic period.[178] This great respect has allowed the influence of clerics to grow and the religious viewpoint and culture to enter into the political area. The 1979 Revolution provided a new possibility for Shi'a clerics to expand the attitudes and approaches of Islamic culture, taking Shi'a culture to a new dimension in the society of Iran. These advances were most successful among the deprived, largely illiterate, masses of the rural areas and the city outskirts. This becomes obvious at rallies and mourning ceremonies, such as Ayatollah Khomeini's funeral, where one can see that Islamic culture hegemony prevailed more among these classes.[179]

The constitution of 1979, like the constitution of 1906-1907, is a mixture of traditional elements (divine rule) and elements of Western democracy (popular rule). In the constitutions of the West created since the Reformation, which incorporate the separation of religion and government, there is no ambiguity in the popular sovereignty. But in Iran, the presence of traditional elements in the constitution has created some complications and ambiguities. The constitution of 1906-1907 referred to the principle that authority resulted from the people (article 26), on the one hand, but, on the other, gave some groups of clerics the power to prevent the approval of any rules against Islam. Moreover, the constitution also stated that the monarchy was a divine present which had been given to the king by the people (article 35). There are many differences of opinion regarding articles 26 and 35 of the first Iranian constitution, which I cannot go into here,[180] but what is obvious is the role of Iranian traditional attitudes and values in that constitution.

After the success of the 1979 Revolution and the establishment of the Assembly of Experts for approving the constitution (instead of a constitutional assembly), Ayatollah Khomeini sent a message to the Assembly of Experts explaining that the new Iranian constitution should be one hundred percent Islamic.[181] This message encouraged the supporters of the theory of the Velayat-e Faqih to establish a theocratic government. The principles of the Velayat-e Faqih were at the center of many discussions in the parliament as it was considered as a plan for the constitution. Its opponents considered it incompatible with popular sovereignty, while its supporters argued that Velayat-e Faqih did not deny the people's participation or vote, because people had to choose and recognize the jurist as a leader, and the jurist's activities were being limited by laws and traditions.

The right to popular sovereignty appears in article 56 of the constitution of the Islamic Republic of Iran. Considered on its own, this article upholds the right of popular sovereignty, with the following wording: "Absolute sovereignty over the world belongs to God, and it is He who has placed man in charge of his social destiny. No one can deprive man of this God-given right."[182] Stated this way, this principle is not congruous with the theory of the Velayat-e Faqih. But the constitution, considered as a whole, weakens the right to popular sovereignty, while leaving it some authority.[183]

It is right that absolute sovereignty belongs to God, and it is right that God never directly intrudes in sovereignty, but has sent some regulations for human beings, according to the constitutions, which the clergy can interpret. They are the guardians of religion. (In ancient Iran, it was the jurists who had this responsibility.) This right of interpretation restricts popular sovereignty, so one can properly say that in the Iranian constitution, the right of sovereignty has been divided between the people and the jurists. In this respect, in the second constitution of Iran more than in the first one, tradition found a place for itself.

Elitism, meanwhile, is also an element of Shi'a culture and has come into the Islamic Republic constitution, Shi'ism was born as a minor and secret movement, and one of its tendencies has been to hold that the majority government is not necessarily a correct governorship. Shi'a history is full of accidents, wherein a small group turns against the majority.

Shi'ites accepted the majority opinion during the events of the Abu Bakr election to caliphate. One of the basic values of Shi'ism is that religious affairs should not be left to those who do not know the real meaning of Quran and Hadith. Elitism is at the forefront in Quranic verses. People have to follow the jurist in religious affairs. Therefore, the constitution is actually bringing this old Islamic culture into a new political era. The Council of Guardians has to confirm the competence of presidential and deputy candidates, which means that there is no confidence in the people's decision-making capabilities. Compare this with the fact that no mechanism has been invented to prevent jurists from misusing their power. This reality arises from the theory that one who becomes a jurist is far above the temptation of misuse.[184]

The new values of Western culture regarding popular sovereignty were unable to drive out Shi'ism's cultural values, which have been mingled with the Iranian mentality. In Europe, if there were not an explicit line dividing government from religion, the principle of popular sovereignty could not have kept its place as the governing principle either.[185]

Tradition and the Element of Populism in Islamic Political Culture

The culture of the Islamic Republic of Iran contains many important elements of populism and corporatism which were created, on the one hand, by a combination of traditional culture with internal conditions and, on the other hand, by the international conditions prevailing after World War II. Before I would like to discuss this move, but first let me define populism and corporatism as the terms will be used here.

Populism, in its simplest and most extensive meaning, consists of a viewpoint which worships ordinary people. In Iran, populism is inspired by tribal (civil) values and traditions, often objecting to foreign power over economy and culture. Corporatism, arising from the same sources, emphasizes the compatibility of various groups and class interests within the society, and keeping peace among them.[186] These two tendencies appeared in Iran along with the theoretical opposition to capitalism, with the motto of "No East, No West," and with socialism. Foreign domination of Iran and the creation of radical tendencies in the world (in Algeria, China, Cuba, Palestine) had an important influence on the views of religious and secular intellectuals, aggravating the kind of "Third World" ideology that I have already referred to. This ideology penetrated many parts of society, even traditional sections and Shi'a clerics.[187]

There was a transformation at the time of Mohammad Reza Shah, as I discussed before, creating some new comments on Shi'a values among the Shi'a clerics. Ayatollah Khomeini, Ayatollah Taleqani and Ayatollah Beheshti were among those clerics who imported these new justifications and movements into Shi'a theory. Ayatollah Khomeini, by mingling the old traditions and new ideas, started a movement which gradually changed him into a charismatic leader, and he introduced populistic tendencies into his programs. The motto of "put the dispossessed into power" became the main motto of the 1979 Revolution. The charismatic authority of Ayatollah Khomeini itself became the source of legitimacy for the political system after the revolution. The domination of religious customs in Iran was the basis for the 1979 Revolution.[188]

Coordination between populistic tendencies and Shi'a traditions in supporting the dispossessed has shaped the programs of the Islamic Republic of Iran. Shi'a customs have a large capacity to take care of the masses.[189] The mourning ceremony in Moharam and the Fetr feast are among the ceremonies which always gather the people together on an extensive scale. The customs which usually join people together are the customs of Shi'ism, not the customs of imperial culture and these customs have had an important role in mobilizing people for revolutionary movements. The first big gathering against the shah's regime, which led to the 1979 Revolution, started from the Fetr prayer ceremony. Mosques were the important gathering places of the masses who opposed the shah's regime.

Conclusion

The main subject of this study has been the cultural impediments to democratic development in Iran. First, I have searched for the roots of the political culture of Iranian society in the Asiatic mode of production and Eastern autocracy, and then I have shown the presence of this culture in the contemporary period and its relation with the authoritarian functioning of the system. My major question has been the relation of political underdevelopment to the cultural element, from the viewpoint of the political management of society. My basic hypothesis has been the connection of the recent political culture in Iran with the traditional culture of the Asiatic mode of production and its resistance against the needs of democratic development. Therefore, I first recognized and introduced the positive aspects and necessities of democratic development in order to show the resistance of unfavorable cultural aspects against it.

Since the middle of the nineteenth century, with the expansion of world capitalism into Iran, the Asiatic mode of production has declined in this society and gradually broken up; as a result, some new relations and social classes have formed, asking for political participation. The international situation demanded various changes in the ancient style of governorship. The Eastern autocratic system and old authoritarianism confronted the necessity of transformation. When at last the transformation happened, however, instead of a democratic system in the European style, new authoritarian systems were established, resulting from a combination of democratic institutions and principles with traditional culture.

I have explained the characteristics of the new authoritarian system as follows:

1. mobilized and passive participation
2. the domination of executives and bureaucracy in government
3. the domination of the governing party
4. dependence on the role of personality and individual leadership

5. a combination of religion and government.

As already explained, in the noble democratic style, instead of mobilized and passive participation, active and independent participation exists; instead of domination by administrative workers, there is a separation of powers; instead of domination by the governing party, there is competition; and instead of a combination of religion and politics, the impartiality of government in conscientious affairs prevails. The main part of my analysis is that this authoritarian functioning of the system or, generally, authoritarianism in Iran, has a direct connection with the attitudes, approaches and values of traditional culture and with the elements of traditional political culture. Among these attitudes and values I can count the following:

1. the traditional tendency to lean towards the authority hierarchy based on differences in individual position
2. the presence of patriarchal values
3. a traditional approach in leaving all affairs to the central government and governmental organizations
4. a feeling of distrust and suspicion in the political elite and the masses
5. belief in the roles of personality and leadership and charismatic ideals, and disbelief in the roles of individuals and mass groups
6. attitudes towards the government as a religious and moral institution.

The characteristics and functions of authoritarianism have the elements of traditional culture, on one hand, which I counted above, while on the other hand exhibiting basic variables to which I have allocated a major part of my study so as to survey their relation. This investigation, which has been done by using field research and political discourse analysis, was a trial for my main hypothesis regarding the positive relation between authoritarian variables and political culture variables.

My discussion dealt with the area of political culture. In order to prevent a generalization of the discussion, I restricted my field activity to the category of political culture. The scope I chose consisted of the attitudes, values, beliefs and approaches of political rulers and the people towards their role in society management. The state's management style has been considered to be defined by the role of political rulers and the masses in political decision-making. In the same way, I divided the requirements of political development into two major parts:

1. the expansion of political participation to respond to the necessities of economic development and the entrance of new social groups and classes into political activities
2. the separation of political roles and institutions to provide ground for this participation and increase the efficiency of the system for solving the socio-economic and political difficulties of the modern period.

I stressed that the values and functions of the political elite, as well as the beliefs of people about political power, political legitimacy, and authority, were to a great extent, affected by the traditional authority pattern. This is why I needed to recognize some basic and stable characteristics of the traditional political culture.

The concept of democracy and the kind of democratic government that was introduced into Iran along with social and economic change was not compatible with the traditional views and values of this society, so that from the very first, democracy was expressed in a way that was a long distance from democracy's primary principles and the European pattern. The political rulers have exploited people's traditional attitudes in order to mix autocratic content in with democracy.

In viewing political development from the point of view of political culture, I have used some of the theories and concepts of scholars such as Gabriel Almond, Sidney Verba and Lucian Pye. Using the viewpoint of political culture is one of the procedures which has increased my understanding of what happens in the political area.

Study of the political culture has been done in two major ways:

1. field research on the attitudes, tendencies and approaches of the political elite and the masses
2. the surveying of political accidents, movements and discourse.

I have used both methods, in order to compensate for any shortcomings in the field research and any untruthful answers. The field research on the political elite and the masses in Iran, who react very strongly to measurement means like a questionnaire, cannot be given a high level of credit.

I prepared my study in three main sections. The first section tracked and recognized traditional political culture in the history of thought, religion and political functions, and explained the important elements of political culture in the political management of society. The second section described the development challenge in the modern period and the reaction of traditional political culture to it. The economic and political influence of the West in the colonial period, along with the transformations caused by world capitalism in the society of Iran, forced the Asiatic mode of production to change. My third section, which depended on detailed studies, field research and discourse analysis, tried to investigate the influence of traditional culture on the operation of new political institutions, along with changes in the real role of institutions and the reality of political activities.

Within these three sections, I arranged the contents and analysis as follows:

1. First, I allocated a chapter to a discussion of conceptual frameworks. In this chapter, I explained the theoretical basis of my research and some of the most important concepts, including the fact that, regarding the historical evolution pattern of Iran, I am using the theory of the Asiatic mode of production. I expressed the characteristics of this system without entering into detailed and controversial discussions, but I did include some theoretical justifications and some public specifications of the Asiatic mode of production and the Eastern autocratic style of government. The object of this discussion was to determine some of the most important characteristics of political culture arising from the Eastern autocratic system. During this discussion, I talked about the qualities of property ownership, massive bureaucracy, absolute authority, the influence of religion on all parts of the society and the role of governors and the masses in the political management of the society. As already explained, recognition of how the culture has risen from Eastern autocracy and the Asiatic mode of

production had great importance, and I have dealt with it throughout the study.

A section of the theoretical framework chapter was allocated to a discussion of the concept and meaning of political culture and the way it functions in this research. In this context, I discussed the proponents of this concept and how it has been used in macro political theories. As I have said, the analysis of political culture stresses the hypothesis that: 1. each society has a specific political culture which gives meaning and direction to the political process; 2. political behavior in a society is determined by a series of beliefs, attitudes and norms which make up the political culture; and 3. these beliefs, attitudes and values are internalized by the person and appear in the person's behavior. The political culture of the society also partakes of the general culture. The levels of confidence versus distrust, pessimism versus optimism, and security versus insecurity are among the attitudes relating to the general culture of the society which have important political meaning as well. Belief in political hierarchy and equality, and tendencies towards tribal and national fidelity are some of the attitudes that have an even more direct relation with the political culture.

In order to advance the research on political culture, I have used both field studies and the analysis of political accidents, movements and discourses, explaining along the way that religion and ideology are very informative in finding the attitudes and approaches and feelings of people regarding political realities. Because religion and ideology (which itself can be a part of religion) are among the belief systems used to promote political legitimacy, I have not neglected the relation between religion and political content.

2. In my second chapter, I discussed the relation of Eastern autocratic political culture with the productive system of this society, and some of the public characteristics of this culture. Bureaucratic centralization and political hierarchy, the authority of a governmental religion, the lateral struggles within a big bureaucratic organization, the presence of the tendency towards distrust and insecurity, opportunism among the political elite and among the masses are some of the most important specifications of political culture in Eastern autocratic governments. Authoritarianism has been the clearest characteristic of political commanders of Iranian

governments throughout history. Cruelty has always been a characteristic of authoritarian political systems, which still exist in recent times, only with new methods.

In Iranian history, centralized governments and powerful imperials took away the people's liberty and rights, imposing a system of public slavery. In Iran, there was no civil royalty and no feudalistic separation based on other principles. Instead, a massive bureaucracy was formed that dominated everything, was completely authorized by the king.

The political culture of the masses in such a system was determined by characteristics such as absolute obedience, absolute surrender, fear of the government, suspicion, political indifference, servility and alienation to politics. These characteristics, which are reflected in all customs, slang stories, proverbs, literature and the people's behavior, are still familiar characteristics for observers.

The Eastern autocratic government governed people by creating fear among there. It did not tolerate any political forces outside the government. The ancient literature of the middle ages in Iran was full of the worship of fear and punishment. A list of the kinds of tortures used by the government in order to collect taxes and maintain political control would be interminable. Indisputable obedience to the government was the first principle in Eastern autocratic governments. Everyone had to obey someone else, except for the king who just ordered. In European and Greek culture, indisputable obedience would not have been considered a superior good.

Indisputable obedience carried insecurity and political suspicion and indifference with it, yet it still kept its effect. In Iran today some people still express proudly that "I am not a statesman." Of course, this attitude among the people does not mean that they deny the mobilization requests of the government. But it does mean that they claim no right to oppose the government.

Hypocrisy, flattery and servitude are the other manifestations of the current culture in Eastern autocratic governments. Such a culture ensures that rough leaders have more success. The other face of this culture is the creation of charismatic tendencies. The infirm feeling of the people makes them always look for a savior who shows metaphysical force against the bullies' power. This charismatic leadership, as Weber said, at last reverts to traditional leadership.

3. In Eastern autocratic governments, religion fulfills the role of political control along with its other roles. In such governments, religions are openly political. The full-scale union of religion with politics required that I allocate some chapters to a survey of religion in the history and thought of Iranians. In this society, religion has three major roles: legitimizing political power, expanding the ideology of political sovereignty among the masses, and establishing the rules and regulations of social and moral life.

In surveying religion and government in Iran, I tried to introduce subjects such as political legitimacy, political authority and the principles of the political management of society. As already explained in detail, the universal system, as presented in this religion, is the reflection of the political system in Iran. The quality of government authoritarianism, the class system and the king's place in the centralized government are exactly reflected in the universal system. In the religious beliefs of ancient Iranians, the king was the one who coordinated the system of the society with the system of the universe. The king was the divine executor on earth.

Religion also stresses justice and class function. Justice meant maintaining the system of the society in accordance with the system of Iranian imperialism. Society was divided into three major classes, and class function meant that any class or trade had to pay attention to its specific job. The king's class function was sovereignty and the class function of the peasants and tradesmen, who made up 99% of society, was working. The king had the divine light which did not belong to the others.

In Islam, among the Sunnites, the caliph is the watchman of religion and divine law. But he did not have a divinely determined position. Among the Shi'ites, however, the Imam has a divine position. In this respect, Shi'a thought is close to ancient Iranian thought. Khaje Nizam al-Mulk, the great vizier of Seljuk, although he was a Sunnite, tried to revive the imperial thought of Iran in his book called "Siyasatname," propounding the divine right of the king instead of the caliph theory, and trying to follow the ancient Iranian style in state management.

According to Shi'ite theory, the Imamate is the continuation of prophethood and divine guidance. The divine judgment never leaves the people without guidance, and always appoints some Imams in order to direct them. The government belongs to those who have divine light. The twelfth Imam, the epochal Imam whose name is Mahdi and who one day will appear to spread justice all over the society, is currently absent, but in his absence, the jurists are entrusted with the management of Muslim affairs.

When the Safavid dynasty took power in the fifteenth century, they named themselves the seventh Imam. The Shi'a jurists, who until then had considered any government to be a usurper in the absence of the twelfth Imam, made some changes in their doctrine, introducing the Safavid kings as representatives of the qualified jurists of the time. But reality was exactly the opposite, and it was the king who appointed the clergy positions.

Under the Qajars, Shi'a clerics received political independence in addition to the economic independence they had attained under the Safavids. Furthermore, in reaction to imperial power, people turned to the clerics, causing the clergy in turn to gain too much power. The independence of religion and government made the clergy powerful and the government weak. After repeated governmental crises, the clergy finally pushed the secular government aside and took over the government itself. Paving the way for this required many changes in Shi'a doctrine, which I explained in detail.

4. After introducing the basic elements of traditional political culture in Iran, I then paid attention to its reaction to the values and patterns coming from Europe. The expansion of world capitalism and of imperialism were the greatest accidents to challenge the Asiatic mode of production and Eastern autocracy. Due to their expansion, Iranian society, like many other societies, faced unprecedented changes. New socio-economic relations progressed and new social groups and classes entered the scene of socio-political life. Consequently, new values and figures of the new culture of the West entered the society. As a result, some new institutions and methods of managing the state were established, challenging the ancient institutions and methods that depended on traditional culture. In the second section of this study, I discussed the forces which challenged the Asiatic mode of production.

Iran did not easily yield to the attack of imperialism, but it was finally defeated in the military and political fields. Due to the failure of these two, the only field that continued to resist was the cultural field. Finally with the successes of a new civilization heavily influenced by Western civilization, the resistance against imperialism went sow, leading to concepts such as "westoxication" in Iran. This may have been because the new Western civilization challenged all aspects of Eastern civilization.

Many Iranian intellectuals who considered their country's military defeat by imperialistic governments to have resulted from military weakness and the inefficiency of the political system, at first decided to use Western industry, technology and political institutions to reform their society, while rejecting Western culture and defending the cultural identity of their own society. This vision was the basis for many political movements and events and the Iranian ideological reformations. In order to reform the administrative system, which showed its weakness in the face of the rush of imperialism, some transformations took place and new institutions were created according to the Western pattern, such as an elective government and a legislative parliament.

I have tried to explain how the presence of traditional culture, indeed, the insistence on a return to traditional culture in order to keep the identity of a society, can condition new democratic principles and institutions. These were the circumstances that caused government in Iran to become a mixture of authority and selection, not the same as the old authoritarianism nor Western democracy. The governments of Reza Shah and Mohammad Reza Shah in Iran were managed in this style. Various doctrines were founded to legitimize this combination; "Velayat-e Faqih" is an example. In my second section, I discussed this doctrine in detail.

Meanwhile, the civil political institutions in Iran were weakened or destroyed, at the same time as new political institutions were unable to grow. The constitutions soon changed to nothing more than pieces of paper, leading soon after to the creation of an authoritarian and then a populistic government. Instead of organizing the legislative institutions, the administrative organs and bureaucracy often took over the basic role in state management themselves. This regime depended on individual leadership or charisma to fill the empty place of constitutionalism. This failure of democracy shows that democratic institutions also need democratic citizens to sustain them.

5. In my third section, I detailed the quality of traditional culture's reaction against political development, relying on field research and discourse analysis. I surveyed the effect of the beliefs, tendencies and attitudes of the political elite and the people on political functions and procedures, on the basis of the above-mentioned research and analysis. The main purpose of this chapter was to discuss the place of culture in shaping the democratic experience. I did not consider the political culture to be the only reason for the defeat of democracy, but only tried to recognize and introduce some cultural variables which had a negative relation to the growth and enhancement of democracy and show the alliance of these variables with traditional culture.

I divided this section into two parts, in the first of which I paid attention to the cultural impediments to development in Iran, and, in the second of which I paid attention to the situation between Iran and Western countries. Generally, the reaction, propelled by traditional culture, to political institutions taken from the European pattern, created a method in the political management of Iran which could be described as "new authoritarianism," a manner of governorship wherein, contrary to traditional authoritarianism, the institutions and democratic rights as well as popular participation rights in state management have been recognized, but these rights and institutions are not used as the means of real sovereignty for the people, but mostly as a means of legitimizing the sovereignty of the group that really governs.

In the modern period, the political elite need the participation of the masses, because of either internal or international pressure. But it can employ this participation in aid of its own authoritarianism, which is possible because central authority has deep roots in the consciousness of the people, as does the government bureaucratic system. Elections are also, to a large extent, free from real content or meaning.

The beliefs, tendencies and attitudes employed by authoritarianism for its own legitimation and power are not related directly to its policy. As explained in my chapter covering the conceptual framework, some of the tendencies and beliefs which generally exist in a culture can have political consequences and be considered a part of the political culture, including feelings such as trust versus distrust, pessimism or optimism, and security or insecurity. These feelings and beliefs, both among the political elite and the masses, have a direct relation with political development.

6. The presence of traditional political culture and its effect on the political process and political system in Iran is very evident. The Pahlavi government, while propagating the most modern aspects of Western culture, in some areas, was defending the most ancient traditions in the political management of the society. These ancient traditions strengthened the authoritarian system and legitimized it. On the other hand, the movements opposed to this regime were also defending ancient Iranian traditions, including the Shi'a customs.

Political and economic reform in Iran began with Western political, economic and cultural penetration, and these reforms clearly had a double effect. On the one hand, there was an effort made for political reforms in democratic development, but on the other hand, the reaction to foreign penetration took the form of a turning to traditional culture as a way to keep the national identity. Therefore, the political transformations in Iran took on an equivocal shape, with democratic reforms and the culture of nationalism all mixed together. But democratic culture was unable to ally itself with traditional culture to create a new cooperative culture. Instead, these two cultures entered a coexistence of conflict, and Iranian political life of the contemporary period has resulted from that. Political reform was perceived as connected with imperialistic penetration, which provoked the reaction of traditional groups and their followers. For this reason, "returning to the tradition" became a big political and mental event in Iran, leading to the Islamic Revolution.

Three main attitudes were found among Iranian intellectuals faced with Western culture and colonialism: 1. undisputed acceptance of all Western culture and civilization; 2. the alliance of Western material culture with Eastern intellectuality; 3. the acceptance of Western technology and economy depending on Islamic values. These three tendencies struggled with each other for a century. The Pahlavi shahs, with the exception of some values which were confirmed by the legitimacy of kingship and authoritarianism, were pursuing a full-scale reform in accordance with Western culture. Their dependence on foreign power and their political autocracy caused the growth of a reaction against Western cultural appearances.

As already explained in detail, Jalal Al-e Ahmad, an intellectual and academic writer, published a book in 1962 called "Westoxication," which was the beginning of a new paradigm, attacking the intellectual movement that had entered Iran along with the Constitutional Revolution as a kind of social disease. Al-e Ahmad said that in order to confront this disease, we have to return to the traditional culture, protected by the clergy. Dr. Shariati was another intellectual who wrote many books and made many speeches in that direction requesting a "return to ourselves." Shariati's theories and writings turned some of the existing tendencies in the Islamic culture into political discourses. Nationalism and populism were the basic content of these movements, and these movements and thoughts in turn became the basis of the Islamic Republic Revolution.

7. I have studied all the various political movements and discourses involving a return to the traditional culture. These movements and discourses explicitly ask for a return to a previous culture, but their support for the traditions is not just for appearance. Some of the most important principles of the constitution and the foundations of the Islamic Republic of Iran were established on the basis of tradition. In addition to political discourses, I have also paid attention to the relation of the functioning of the system with the attitudes, values and approaches of the political culture. As I have explained in detail, in an Eastern autocratic situation, attitudes such as pessimism, suspicion, insecurity and distrust prevail among the political elite in their relation with the people and the people with the government. I have discussed the existence of such attitudes among the Iranian elite and the people and studied related views, which make up a major part of the political culture.

In this context, I discussed the important research of Marvin Zonis. In Zonis' research on Iran it becomes clear that insecurity is the most important aspect of political life there. This shortcoming brings with it other feelings such as anxiety, loneliness and distress. In a Zonis survey, 72% of the political elite at the time of Mohammad Reza Shah complained about the absence of political justice and security. According to another study on the Iran middle class, this class also suffers from such feelings.

Such attitudes, which have their roots in political autocratic culture, serve to produce more political autocracy. Another important tendency of the Iranian political elite is opportunism. As already mentioned, Zonis considers the Iranian political elite to be a personification of Machiavelli's words regarding the acquisition of power in any possible way. This elite changes its colors daily, like a chameleon, using hypocrisy, flattery and opportunism to climb the stairs of authority. Around 80% of the Iranian political elite believe that whatever their colleagues do is for their own benefit, not for the nation's interests. In such an atmosphere, the political elite is released from taking responsibility, thus pushing all responsibilities towards an authoritarian person at the top of the government. Democracy, on the other hand, requires confidence between the government and the people, and government needs to be responsible towards the people.

8. The research and field studies I have used to survey the relation of attitudes, tendencies and cultural beliefs with the different elements of the authoritarian system show in various ways how the most important authoritarian characteristics of the system relate to the attitudes and tendencies of traditional culture. Some of this research predicts in theory exactly what is being seen in practice in Iran: how people are looking for a powerful person or "the powerful hands of a dictator" to solve society's problems. The field studies also show how people pay attention to bureaucracy and obey the central government, how the more traditional students expect more from authority to solve their affairs, how people grant a moral role to the government. Generally speaking, the very strong correlation between authoritarian function and cultural attitudes in various areas of political life is very important, and explains the solidarity between them.

Political culture is undoubtedly not a stable and everlasting fact, and it is undergoes transformations. These transformations, however, happen very slowly. Even so, the political culture in Iran may be on the brink of changes and transformations. Two historical events, namely the 1997 presidential election and the 2000 parliamentary election in Iran, indicate progress in the attitudes of Iranian people towards politics. In these two elections, Iranians for the first time had an independent election; in other words, their election was not guided. The government and dominant wing moved away from rigging the election. In 1997, people voted for a candidate who explicitly defended democratic development. I hope that this movement will continue towards a stable democratic culture. However, experience shows that Iranian transformations are contradictory, and for a more reliable judgment we will have to wait longer still.

Notes

1. See: Gabriel Almond and Bingham Powell, *Comparative Politics: A Developmental Approach* (Boston: Little Brown and Co., 1966). Sidney Verba, "Comparative Political Culture" in Lucian Pye and Sidney Verba (ed) *Political Culture and Political Development* (Princeton: Princeton University Press, 1985), pp. 512-560. Robert Ward, "Culture and Comparative Study of Politics" *American Political Science Review XVIII* (March 1972), pp. 190-201.

2. See: Mehran Kamrava, *Politics and Society in the Third World* (London: New York Routledge, 1993). Manwoo Lee (ed), *Culture and Development in a New Era and in a Transforming World* (Seoul: Kyungnam University Press, 1994).

3. See: Stephen Chilton, "Defining Political Development," *Western Political Quarterly Vol 41, No 3* (September 1988), pp. 419-445.

4. Sidney Verba, "Comparative Political Culture" in Lucian Pye and Sidney Verba (ed), *Political Culture and Political Development* (Princeton, Princeton University Press, 1985), p. 513.

5. Ronald Chilcote, *Theories of Comparative Politics* (Boulder, Westview Press, 1981), pp. 7-11.

6. *Ibid*, p. 217.

7. *Ibid*, p. 218.

8. Harold Lasswell, "Person, Personality, Culture", *Psychiatry II*, pp. 533-561.

9. Ronald Chilcote, *op. cit*, p. 220.

10. Gabriel Almond and Sidney Verba (ed), *The Civil Culture* (Princeton, Princeton University Press, 1963), p. 14.

11. Lucian Pye, Introduction: Political culture and Political development in Lucian Pye and Sidney Verba (ed), *op. cit*, p. 8.

12. Gabriel Almond and Lucian Pye (ed), *op. cit*, p. 3.

13. *International Encyclopedia of Social Sciences, Vol II* (New York: The Macmillan Company and The Tree Press, 1968), pp. 212-217.

14. Lucian Pye, *op. cit*.

15. Lucian Pye, *op. cit*, p. 22.

16. *International Encyclopedia of Social Sciences, op. cit*.

17. *The New Encyclopedia Britannica Vol 5 Fifteenth Edition* (1993), pp. 874-883.

18. Carole Pateman, "Political Culture, Political Structure and Political System", *British Journal of Political Science Vol.1 Part 3* (July 1971), pp. 291-305.

19. Peter Blau, "A Theory of Social Integration", *American Journal of Sociology LXV* (May 1960), pp. 545-556.

20. Robert Scott, "Mexico: The Established Revolution" in Lucian Pye and Sidney Verba (ed), *op. cit.*

21. Sidney Verba, *op. cit*, p. 523.

22. Peter Blau, *op. cit.*

23. Sidney Verba, "Comparative Political Culture" in Lucian Pye and Sidney Verba, *op. cit*, p. 538.

24. See: Richard Fagen, "Relation of Communication Growth to National Political Systems in the Less Developed Countries", *Journalism Quarterly XLI* (Winter 1964), pp. 87-94.

25. Sidney Verba, *op. cit*, p. 542.

26. *Ibid.*

27. Martin Lipset, "Social Requisites of Democracy Revisited", *American Sociological Review No 59*, pp. 1-22.

28. Samuel Huntington, "The Third Wave: Democratization" in Benjamin Barber, *Strong Democracy* (Berkeley: University of California Press, 1984).

29. David Held, *Models of Democracy* (Cambridge: Polity Press, 1987).

30. Paul Baran, *Political Economy of Growth* (New York: Pelican, 1957), p. 432.

31. Paul Baran and Paul Sweezy, *Monopoly Capital* (New York: Monthly Review Press, 1966), p.205.

32. Gabriel Almond and Bingham Powel, *Comparative Politics* (Boston: Little, Brown and Company, 1966), pp. 195-202.

33. Alan Swingwood, *A Short History of Sociological Thought* (London: Macmillan, 1991), p. 153.

34. David McClelland, *The Achieving Society* (Princeton: D. Van Nostrand Company, 1961), p. 134.

35. Howard Selsam and Harry Martel, *Reader in Marxist Philosophy* (New York: International Publishers, 1963), p. 187.

36. The Indo-Iranian tribes emigrated towards the Flat of Iran beginning from about 2000 B.C. See: Reza Jalali, *Rig-Veda* (Tehran: NashereNogre, 1349/1970), p. 2.

37. Dariush Shayegan, *Adyan va Maktabha-ye Falsafi-ye Hend* (Tehran: Amir Kabir, 1356/1977), p. 56.

38. Mohammad Reza Jalali Naini, *Rig-Veda* (Tehran: Nashr Noqre, 1372/1993), p. 35.

39. Herni Frankfort, *Kingship and the Gods* (Chicago: The University of Chicago Press, 1971), p. 215.

40. Fatholla Mojtabaii, one of the interpreters of Avesta, the oldest religious scripture, claims that the Aryan community was formed of three castes or classes corresponding to the ones mentioned above: Fatholla Mojtabaii, *Shahr-e ziba-ye Aflaton va Shahr-e bastan* (Tehran: Anjoman Farhang Iran Bastan), p. 43. On social order of Iran also see: George Dumezil, *Les dieut des Indo-Europeens*, Paris, 1952. Macdonell and Keth, *Vedic Index of names and subjects*, pp. 247-710.

41. Abdolhosein Zarrin Kub, *Tarikh-e Mardom-e Iran qabl az Eslam* (Tehran: Amir Kabir, 1364/1985), p. 41.

42. Kameran Fani, *Zartosht, Syasastmadar ya Joduger* (Tehran: Nachre Parwaz, 1369/1990), p. 18.

43. R.C. Zaehner, *The teaching of the Magi* (London: The Macmillan Company, 1956), p. 18.

44. Farhang Rayaii, *Tahavol andishe syasy dar shahr-e bastan* (Tehran: Nashr-e Qumes, 1372/1993), p. 67.

45. *Ibid*, p. 44.

46. R. C. Zaehner, *op. cit*, pp. 86-87.

47. See: Henri Frankfort, *op. cit.*

48. Fathallah Mojtabayi, *Shahr-e Ziba-ye Aflatun va Shahi-ye Armani-ye Iran-e Bastan* (Tehran: Anjoman-e Farhang-e Iran-e Bastan, 1352/1973), p. 120.

49. Hassan Pirnia, *Eskandar* (Tehran: Ofset Roshdiye, 1342/1963), p. 146.

50. Fathallah Mojtabayi, *op. cit.*, p. 109.

51. Duchesne Gudleman, *Symbols and Values in Zoroastrianism* (New York: 1966), p. 147.

52. Javad Tabatabaii, *Dramadi Falsafi bar Tarikh-e andisha-ye syasi dar Iran* (Tehran: Entesharat Kavir, 1377/1998), p. 43.

53. Hatem Qaderi, *Andishaha-ye Syasi dar Islam va Iran* (Tehran: S.M.T, 1378/1998), p. 21.

54. Erwin Rosenthal, *Political Thought in Medieval Islam* (New York: Cambridge University Press, 1958), pp. 8-9.

55. Muhsen Kadwer, *Nazeryay doult dar faqh-e Shi'a* (Tehran: Nashr-e Nay, 1376/1997), p. 14.

56. Erwin Rosenthal, *op. cit*, p. 43.

57. Javad Tabatabaii, *Khaje Nizam al-Mulk Tousi* (Tehran: Tah Nou, 1375/1996), p. 72.

58. Ann Lambton, *State and Government in Medieval Islam* (New York: Oxford

University Press, 1991), p. 220.

59. Seyyed Hassan Amin, "Hamiyat dar Feqh-e Shi'I va Sonni", *Kiyan No.24*, pp. 24-32.

60. Masoud Kamali, *Revolutionary Iran* (New York: Ashgate, 1998), p. 42.

61. *Ibid.*

62. See: Abbas Amanat, In between the madrasah and the marketplace, S. Arjomand (ed), *Authority and political culture in Shiism* (New York: State University of New York Press, 1988).

63. Said A. Arjomand, *The Shadow of God and the Hidden Imam* (Chicago: University of Chicago Press, 1984), p. 47.

64. Hamid Algar, *Religion and State in Iran 1785-1900* (Berkeley: University of Califonia Press, 1969), p. 29.

65. Max Weber, *Economy and Society* (New York: Bedminster Press, 1968), p. 1174.

66. Abbas Ali Amidzanyani, *Mabani-e Andish-e Syasi dar Islam* (Tehran: Padzphegahe Farhang-e Andish-e Eslam, 1375/1996), p. 57.

67. R. M. Savory, *Iran under the Safavids* (New York: Press Syndicate of the University of Cambridge, 1980), p. 28.

68. See: Abbas Amanat, *op. cit.*

69. Masoud Kamali, *op. cit.*, p. 61.

70. Hamid Algar, *op. cit.*, p. 44.

71. Said A. Arjomand, op. cit., p. 223.

72. Mehdi Malekzadeh, *Tarikh-e Enqelab-e Mashrotiyyat-e Iran* Vol.1 (Tehran: Ketabkhane-e Soqrat publishing, 1328/1949), p. 128.

73. Nikki Keddie, *Religion, and Rebellion in Iran* (London: Frank Cass and Co. Ltd) p. 66.

74. Fereydun Adamyyat, *Ideologi-ye Nehzat-e Mashruitiyyat-e Iran* (Tehran: Payman, 1355/1976), p. 413.

75. *Ibid.*

76. Abud Hadi Hairi, *Shi'ism and Constitutionalism in Iran* (Leiden E. J. Brili, 1977), p. 191.

77. Shaul Bakhash, *The reign of the Ayatollahs* (New York: Basic Books, 1990), p. 22.

78. Sharough Akhavi, *Religion and Politics in Contemporary Iran* (New York: State University of New York Press, 1980), p. 57.

79. *Ibid.*, p. 19.

80. Ayatollah Ruhollah Khomeini, *Velayat-e Faqih* (Tehran: Muasese-ye Nashre Athar-e Imam, 1373/1997), p. 17.

81. *Ibid.*, p. 19.

82. See: Nikki Keddie and Eric Hooland, *The Iranian Revolution and The Islamic Republic* (Washington, D.C: Middle East Institute, 1982).

83. See: Nikki Keddie, *Religion and Rebellion in Iran: The Tobacco Protest of 1891-1892* (London: Frank Cass, 1966) and Nikki Keddie (ed), *Religion and Politics in Iran: Shi'ism from Quietism to Revolution* (New Haven: Yale University Press, 1983).

84. Mohammad Borghei, "Iran's Religious Establishment", in Samih Farsoun and Mehrdad Mashayekhi (ed), *Political Culture in the Islamic Republic* (London: Routledge, 1992), p. 59.

85. *Ibid.*, p. 72.

86. Hossein Bashiriyeh, *State and Revolution in Iran 1962-1982* (New York: St. Martin's Press, 1984), Ch. 3.

87. *Ibid*, p. 54.

88. Hamid Algar, *Religion and State in Iran 1785-1906* (Berkeley: University of California Press, 1969), p. 3.

89. Hossein Bashiriyeh, *op. cit*, p. 55.

90. See: Ayatollah Ruhollah Khomeini, *Islamic Government* (New York: Manor Books, 1979).

91. Seyyed Hassan Amin, *op. cit.*

92. Nezam al-Din, *op. cit*, p. 236.

93. *Ibid.*

94. Shahpour, the Sassanid king, appointed his son Hormuz to the governorship of Khorasan. After a while, Hormuz felt that his father had become suspicious of him. So he cut off his hand and sent it in a tray to his father. Mohammad Javad Mashkur, *Iran-e Bastan dar Tarikh-e Aqvam va Padeshahan pish az Eslam* (Tehran: Amir Kabir, 1347/1969), p. 396.

95. Karl Wittfogel, *op. cit*, p. 155.

96. See: Mahili Khalili, *op. cit.*

97. Henri Frankfort, *The Birth of Civilization in the Near East* (New York: Doubleday Anchor Books, 1956), p. 92.

98. Karl Wittfogel, *op. cit*, p. 153.

99. Karl Wittfogel, *op. cit*, p. 154.

100. Hassan Pirnia wrote that when Ardasher, the Achaemenian king, took the throne, he decided to kill all of his children. He gathered many of his princes and princesses and killed more than 100 people at one time. See: Mahili Khalili, *op. cit*, p. 61.

101. Jamlile Kadivar, "Eqtedargeraii az Manzar-e Farhang-e 'amme", *Rahbard No. 8*, pp. 11-20.

102. *Ibid*, pp. 28-30.

103. *Ibid.*, p. 39.

104. Ali Akhbar Dehkhoda, *Amsal va Hekam* (Tehran: Chapkhane-ye Sepehr, 1374/1995), p. 3.

105. *Ibid*, p. 20.

106. *Ibid*, p. 32.

107. Charles Issawi, *The Economic History of Iran 1800-1914* (Chicago: The University of Chicago Press, 1971), p. 11.

108. Ann Lambton, *Landlord and Peasant in Persia* (London: Oxford University Press, 1953), pp. 151-152.

109. Many books have been written regarding the role of the Iranian bourgeoisie and *bazaaris* in the Constitutional Revolution in Iran. The following are specifically about the efforts, sacrifices and financial assistance of the Iranian *bazaaris* for revolution:1. Ahmad Kasravi, *op. cit.*, 2. Nikki Keddie, *op. cit.*, 3. Ebrahim Teymouri, *op. cit.*, 4. Coutit Robino, *Gilan Constitutionalism* (Rasht: Taeei, 1352/1976).

110. Peter Avery, *Modern Iran* (New York: Praeger, 1965), p. 141.

111. See: Michael Bonine and Nikki Keddie (ed), *Modern Iran: The Dialectics of Continuity and Change* (New York: State University of New York Press, 1981).

112. Nikki Keddie, *Iran and the Muslim World* (London: Macmillan, 1995), p. 103.

113. As I will explain in Section Three, the theories and remarks of Jalal al-Ahmad and Ali Shariati are reflected in this attitude.

114. Lucian Pye, "The Concept of Political Development", *Politics in Transitional Societies*, Harvey Kebschull (ed) (New York: Appleton-Century-Crofts, 1973), p. 51.

115. James Scott, "Patron-Client Politics and Political Change in Southeast Asia", *The American Political Science Review Vol. LXVI* (March 1972), pp. 91-113.

116. Eric Wolf, "Kinship, Friendship, and Patron-Client Relations in Complex Societies", in Michael Banton (ed), *The Social Anthropology of Complex Societies* (London: Tavistock Publications, 1966), pp. 1-22.

117. Jacqueline Braveboy-Wagner, *Interpreting the Third World: Politics, Economics, and Social Issues* (New York: Praeer, 1986), p. 37.

118. Samuel Huntington, "Social and Institutional Dynamics of One-Party Systems" in Samuel Huntington and Clement Moore (ed), *Authoritarian Politics in Modern Society* (London: Basic Books, 1970), p. 7.

119. *Ibid.*, p. 14.

120. Theda Skocpol, "Social Revolutions and Mass Military Mobilization", *World Politics Vol. XL No. 2* (January 1988), p. 149.

121. *Ibid.*, p. 150.
122. Samuel Huntington, *Political Order in Changing Societies* (London: Yale University Press, 1968), chapter 4.
123. Peter Avery, "Balancing Factors in Irano-Islamic Politics and Society", *Middle East Journal Vol. 50 No. 2* (Spring 1996), pp. 177-189.
124. Jalal Al-e Ahmad, *Gharbzadegi* (Tehran: Forudos, 1372).
125. Mehrzad Boroujerdi, "Gharbzadegi", in Samih K. Farsoun and Mehrdad Mashayekhi (ed), *op. cit.*, p. 39.
126. Samih K. Farsoun and Mehrdad Mashayekhi, "Iran's Political Culture", *op. cit.*, p. 4.
127. Hossein Azimi, "Din, Farhang va Touse'e", *Ketab-e Touse'e No. 4* (Winter 1371), pp. 25-61.
128. Mehrdad Mashayekhi, "The Politics of Nationalism and Political Culture", in Samih K. Farsoun and Mehrdad Mashayekhi (ed), *op. cit.*, p. 95.
129. *Ibid.*, p. 96.
130. James Manor, *Rethinking Third World Politics* (New York: Longman, 1991), p. 4.
131. *Ibid.*, p. 1.
132. Marvin Zonis, *op. cit.*, p. 304.
133. Peter Avery, *op. cit.*
134. Mehrzad Boroujerdi, "Gharbzadegi", *op. cit.*, p. 37.
135. Mehrzad Boroujerdi, op. cit., p. 42.
136. Daryush Shayegan, "Ideology shodan-e sonnat", *Zaman-e Nou* No. 12, p. 45.
137. Reza Davari, Engelab-e Eslami va Vaz'e Konuni (Tehran: Markaze Farhang-e Alame Tabataba'e, 1360), p. 59.
138. Daryush Ashuri, Ma va Moderniyat (Tehran: Mosasse-ye Farhangi, 1376), p. 136.
139. *Ibid.*
140. Afsaneh Najmabadi, "Iran's Turn to Islam: From Modernism to a Moral Order", *The Middle East Journal Vol. 41 No. 2* (Spring 1987), pp. 202-217.
141. *Ibid.*
142. *Ibid.*
143. Marvin Zonis, *The Political Elite of Iran* (Princeton: Princeton University Press, 1971), p. 118.
144. Richard Nelson Frye, *The Heritage of Persia* (London: Weidenfield and Nicolson, 1962), p. 54.
145. George Nathaniel Curzon, *Persia and The Persian Question Vol. I* (New York: Longman, 1892), p. 438.
146. James Manor, *Rethinking Third World Politics* (New York: Longman, 1991), p. 1.

147. Marvin Zonis, *op. cit.*

148. See: Leonard Binder, *Iran; Political Development in a Changing Society* (Berkeley: University of California Press, 1962).

149. Sir Percy Sykes, *A History of Persia Vol. 1* (London: Macmillan Co., 1921), pp. 80-82.

150. Raymond Gastil, "Middle Class Impediment to Iranian Modernization", *Public Opinion Quarterly Vol. 22 No. 3* (Fall 1958), p. 328.

151. Marvin Zonis, *op. cit.*, p. 144.

152. Lucian Pye, *Political Personality and Nation Building* (New Haven: Yale University Press, 1962), p. 55.

153. Lucian Pye, "Political Culture and Political Development", in Lucian Pye and Sidney Verba (ed), *op. cit.*, p. 22.

154. Marvin Zonis, *op. cit.*, p. 260.

155. Lucian Pye, *Aspect of Political Development* (Boston: Little Brown and Co., 1966), p. 10.

156. Sidney Verba, "Comparative Political Culture", in Lucian Pye and Sidney Verba (ed), *op. cit.*, p. 500.

157. Leonard Binder, *op. cit.*, pp. 306-307.

158. Leonard Binder, *op. cit.*

159. Alexis de Tocqueville, *Democracy in America Vol. 1* (New York: Vintage Books, 1945), p. 150.

160. Peter Avery, "Balancing Factor in Irano-Islamic Politics and Society", *Middle East Journal Vol. 50 No. 2* (Spring 1996), pp. 177-189.

161. Joseph M. Upton, *The History of Modern Iran: An Interpretation* (Cambridge: Harvard University Press, 1960), p. 3.

162. Marvin Zonis, *op. cit.*, p. 15.

163. Leonard Binder, *op. cit.*, p. 228.

164. See: Donald Eugene Smith, *Religion and Political Development an Analytic Study* (Boston: Little, Brown, 1970).

165. See: Guenter Lewy, *Religion and Revolution* (New York: Oxford University Press, 1974).

166. Ali Darai, Jame' Ruhaniyat-e Tehran va Naqsh-e An dar Tahavolat-e Nezam-e siyasi-ye Jomhuri-ye Eslami-ye Iran (Payannameh-ye Karshanasi-ye arshad, Tehran University, 1375), p. 237.

167. Ali Darai, *op. cit.*, p. 238.

168. Ali Darai, *op. cit.*, p. 239.

169. See: Larry Diamond (ed), *op. cit.*

170. Ali Darai, *op. cit.*, p. 142.

171. See: Clifford Geertz, *The Interpretation of Culture* (New York: Basic Books, 1973).

172. Louis Althusser, "Ideology and Ideological Apparatuses", in B. Cosin (ed), *Education, Structure and Society* (London: Penguin, 1972), pp. 37-49.

173. Rasool Nafisi, "Education and the Culture of Politics in the Islamic Republic of Iran", in Samih K. Farsoun and Mehrdad Mashayekhi, *op. cit.*, p. 167.

174. Rasool Nafisi, *op. cit.*, p. 168.

175. Manoucher Parvin and Mostafa Vaziri, "Islamic Man and Society in the Islamic Republic of Iran", in Samih K. Farsoun and Mehrdad Mashayekhi, *op. cit.*, p. 117.

176. *Ibid.*

177. H. Kung and Josef Van Ess, *Christianity and the World Religions* (New York: Doubleday and Co., 1986), p. 76.

178. Bertold Spuler, "Iran: The Persistent Heritage", in G. E. Von Grunebaum (ed), *Unity and Variety in Muslim Civilization* (Chicago: University of Chicago Press, 1992), p. 172.

179. Manoucher Parvin and Mostafa Vaziri, *op. cit.*, p. 129.

180. See: Mastafa Rahimi, Qanun-e Asasi-ye Iran va Osul-e Demokrasi (Tehran: Ibn Sina, 1336).

181. Mohsen Milani, "Shi'ism and the State in the Constitution of the Islamic Republic of Iran", in Samih K. Farsoun and Mehrdad Mashayekhi, *op. cit.*, p. 144.

182. Qanun-e Asasi-ye Jomhuriye Eslami-ye Iran (Tehran: Majma' elmi va Farhang Majad, 1374), p. 51.

183. Mohsen Milani, *op. cit.*, p. 154.

184. Abbasali Ranjani, Mabani-ye Feqhi-ye Qanoun-e Asasi-ye Jomhuriye Eslami-ye Iran (Tehran: Daftar-e Markaz-e Jahad-e Daneshgahi, 1362), p. 79.

185. Mohsen Milani, *op. cit.*, p. 155.

186. See: James Malloy (ed), *Authoritarianism and Corporatism in Latin America* (Pittsburgh: University of Pittsburgh Press, 1977).

187. Manochehr Dorraj, "Populism and Corporatism in Post-Revolutionary Iranian Political Culture", in Samih K. Farsoun and Mehrdad Mashayekhi, *op. cit.*, p. 214.

188. Ali Reza Sheikholeslami, "From Religious Accommodation to Religious Revolution: The Transformation of Shiism in Iran", in Ali Banuazizi and Myron Weiner (ed), *The Religion and Ethnic Politics* (New York: Syracuse University Press, 1986), pp. 227-255.

189. *Ibid.*, p. 230.

Bibliography

Abrahamian, Ervand (1983) *Iran Between Two Revolutions*, Princeton: Princeton University Press.

Adamiyyat, Fereydun (1323/1944) *Amir Kabir va Iran*, Tehran: Kharazmi.

Afghani, Ali Mohammad (1364/1985) *Doktor Baktash*, Tehran: Entesharat-e Negah.

Al-e Ahmad, Jalal (1356/1977) *Gharbzadegi*, Tehran: Entesharat-e Ravaq.

Algar, Hamid (1960) *Modern Iran*, London: Frank Cass.

Algar, Hamid (1970) *Religion and State in Iran: 1785-1906: Clergy-State Relations in Qajar Period*, Berkeley: University of California Press.

Almond, Gabriel and Verba, Sidney (ed) (1963) *The Civic Culture*, Princeton: Princeton University Press.

Arjomand, Said A. (1984) *The Shadow of God and the Hidden Imam*, Chicago: University of Chicago Press.

Arjomand, Said A. (1988) *The Turban for the Crown*, New York: Oxford University Press.

Avery, Peter (1965) *Modern Iran*, New York: Praeger.

Banuazizi, Ali (ed) (1986) *The Religion and Ethnic Politics*, New York: Syracuse University Press.

Baran, Paul (1957) *Political Economy of Growth*, New York: Pelican.

Bashiriyeh, Hossein (1984) *State and Revolution in Iran, 1962-1982*, New York: St. Martin's Press.

Binder, Leonard (1962) *Iran: Political Development in a Changing Society*, Berkeley: University of California Press.

Bonine, Michael and Keddie, Nikki (eds) (1981) *Modern Iran*, New York: State University of New York Press.

Braveboy-Wagner, Jacqueline (1986) *Interpreting the Third World: Politics, Economics and Social Issues*, New York: Praeger.

Chehabi, Houchang E. (1990) *Iranian Politics and Religious Modernism*, London: I.B. Tauris & Co.

Chilcote, Ronald (1981) *Theories of Comparative Politics*, Boulder: Westview Press.

Curzon, Lord (1892) *Persia and The Persian Question*, London: Longman, Green and Co.

Dahl, Robert (1971) *Polyarchy: Participation and Opposition*, New Haven: Yale University Press.

163

Daneshvar, Simin (1357/1978) *Savushun*, Tehran: Kharazmi.

Darton, Russel (1988) *Citizen Politics in Western Democracies*, Chatham: Chatham House.

Diamond, Larry (ed) (1993) *Political Culture and Democracy in Developing Countries*, Boulder: Lynne Rienner Publisher.

Diamond, Selarry (ed) (1988) *Democracy in Developing Countries*, Boulder: Lynne Rienner Publisher.

Entner, Marvin (1965) *Russo-Persian Commercial Relation 1914-1928*, Gainsville: University of Florida Press.

Esposito, John (1980) *Islam and Development*, New York: Syracuse University Press.

Farsoun Samih and Mashayekhi, Mehdad (eds) (1992) *Political Culture in the Islamic Republic*, London: Routledge.

Frankfort, Henri (1956) *The Birth of Civilization in the Near East*, New York: Doubleday Anchor Books.

Frankfort, Henri (1969) *Kingship and the God*, Chicago: University of Chicago Press.

Frye, Richard (1962) *The Heritage of Persia*, London: Wiedenfeld and Nicolson.

Geertz, Cliford (1973) *The Interpretation of Culture*, New York: Basic Books.

Giddense, Antony (1989) *Sociology*, Cambridge: Polity Press.

Hejazi, Mohammad (1344/1965) *Sereshk*, Tehran: Entesharat-e Ebn-e Sina.

Held, David (1987) *Models of Democracy*, Cambridge: Polity Press.

Hoveyda, Fereydoun (1980) *The Fall of the Shah*, New York: Oxford University Press.

Huntington, Samuel (1967) *Military Order in Changing Societies*, New Haven: Yale University Press.

Huntington, Samuel (1981) "Social and Institutional Dynamics of One-Party Systems", in Huntington, Samuel (1991) *The Third Wave: Democratization in the Late Twentieth*, London: University of Oklahoma Press.

Huntington, Samuel and Moore, C. (eds) *Authoritarian Politics and Modern Society*, London: Basic Books.

Issawi, Charles (1971) *Economic History of Iran*, Chicago: University of Chicago Press.

Kamravd, Mehran (1993) *Politics and Society in the Third World*, London: Routledge.

Keddie Nikki (1966) *Religion and Rebellion in Iran: The Tobacco Protest of 1891-1892*, London: Frank Cass.

Keddie Nikki (ed) (1983) *Religion and Politics in Iran: Shi'ism from Quietism to Revolution*, New Haven: Yale University Press.

Keddie, Nikki (1995) *Iran and The Muslim World*, London: Macmillan.

Kung, H. and Ess, Josef Van (1986) *Christianity and The World Religions*, New York: Doubleday and Co.

Lambton, Ann (1981) *State and Government in Medieval Islam*, London: Oxford University Press.

Legge, James (1993) *The Chinese Classics Vol. I*, London: Oxford University Press.

Lerner, Daniel (1958) *The Passing of Traditional Society*, Glencoe: Free Press.

Malloy, James (ed) (1977) *Authoritarianism and Corporatism in Latin America*, Pittsburgh: University of Pittsburgh Press.

Manor, James (1991) *Rethinking Third World Politics*, New York: Longman.

McClelland, David (1961) *The Achieving Society*, Princeton: Van Nostrand.

Milani, Mohsen M. (1994) *The Making of Iran's Islamic Revolution*, Colorado: Westview Press.

O'Donnell, Gullerm (1973) *Modernization and Bureaucratic Authoritarianship*, Berkeley: Institute of International Studies University of California.

Parsons, Talcott (1951) *The Social System*, London: Routledge and Kegan Paul Ltd.

Pye, Lucian (1962) *Political Personality and Nation Building*, New Haven: Yale University Press.

Pye, Lucian (1965) *Asian Power and Politics*, Cambridge: Harvard University Press.

Pye, Lucian (1966) *Aspect of Political Development*, Boston: Little Brown and Co.

Pye, Lucian and Verba, Sidney (eds) (1965) *Political Culture and Political Development*, Princeton: Princeton University Press.

Randal, Vicky and Thebald, Robin (eds) (1985) *Political Change and Underdevelopment*, London: Macmillan.

Rosenthal, Erwin (1958) *Political Thought in Islam*, Cambridge: Cambridge University Press.

Sartori, Giovani (1962) *Democratic Theory*, Detroit: Wayne University Press.

Selsam, Howald (ed) (1963) *Reader in Marxist Philosophy*, New York: International Publisher.

Skocpol Theda (1979) *State and Social Revolutions*, New York: Cambridge University Press.

Soruton, Roger (1982) *A Dictionary of Political Thought*, London: Macmillan.

Spuler, Bertold (1992) "Iran: The Persistent Heritage", in Grunebaum, E. (ed) *Unity and Variety in Muslim Civilization*, Chicago: University of Chicago Press.

Swingwood, Alan (1991) *A Short History of Sociological Thought*, Macmillan

Tocqueville, Alexi de (1945) *Democracy in America Vol. 1*, New York: Vintage Books.

Upton, Joseph (1960) *The History of Modern Iran: An Interpretation*, Cambridge: Harvard University Press.

Weber, Max (1968) *On Charisma and Institution Building*, Chicago: University of Chicago Press.

Wittfogel, Karl (1981) *Oriental Despotism*, New York: Vintage.

Zaehner, R. C. (1956) *The Teaching of the Magi*, London: Allen and Unwin Ltd.

Zonis, Marvin (1971) *The Political Elite of Iran*, Princeton: Princeton University Press.

Index